Secondary Education
Focus on Curriculum

JUDY REINHARTZ
The University of Texas at Arlington

DON M. BEACH
Tarleton State University

HarperCollins*Publishers*

DEDICATION

As always to Den.

JR

This book is dedicated to those educators who have had a profound impact on my understanding of curriculum and the curriculum development process, especially Weldon Beckner, Joe Cornett, Norm and Gilda Greenberg, and Don Rush. This book would not have been possible without their mentoring.

DMB

Executive Editor: Christopher Jennison
Full-Service Manager: Michael Weinstein
Production Coordinator: Cindy Funkhouser
Project Coordinator, Text and Cover Design: Caliber/Phoenix Color Corp.
Production Manager: Priscilla Taguer
Compositor: Caliber/Phoenix Color Corp.
Printer and Binder: R. R. Donnelley & Sons Company
Cover Printer: The Lehigh Press, Inc.

SECONDARY EDUCATION: Focus on Curriculum

Library of Congress Cataloging-in-Publication Data

Reinhartz, Judy.
    Secondary education : focus on curriculum / Judy Reinhartz, Don M. Beach.
        p.   cm.
    Includes bibliographical references and index.

    ISBN 0-06-045361-3

    1. Education, Secondary—United States—Curricula.   2. Curriculum planning—United States.   I. Beach, Don M.   II. Title.
LB1628.5.R45   1992
373.19′0973—dc20   91-40293
                                                                          CIP

95 94 93 92   9 8 7 6 5 4 3 2 1

Contents

CHAPTER 2
Historical Development and Definitions of Secondary Curriculum   22

PART TWO

Foundations of Secondary Curriculum   43

CHAPTER 3
Philosophical Perspectives: Foundations of Curriculum   45

CHAPTER 4
Social Foundations of Curriculum Development   67

CHAPTER 5
Foundations of Human Development and Psychology   86

CHAPTER 6
Characteristics of Secondary Students   109

PART THREE

Curriculum Development Process 127

PART FOUR

Curriculum Development for the Secondary Classroom 165

PART FIVE

Content Areas of the Secondary School Curriculum 223

CHAPTER 14
Science in the Secondary School Curriculum   301

CHAPTER 15
Other Subjects of the Secondary Curriculum   329

Preface

Following a decade of national reports and reforms, which have often been in response to political pressures and perceived crises, it is time for educators to carefully and realistically examine the complex nature of curriculum development. The purpose of *Secondary Education: Focus on Curriculum* is to provide educators and curriculum specialists with a comprehensive and in-depth discussion of important areas in secondary education, focusing particularly on curriculum planning and development. The main objective of the text is to help educators make more effective instructional decisions and implement them in secondary classrooms.

This book introduces and explains the various foundations and components of secondary education within the curricular programs of grades 7–12 and presents current information gathered from studies and research to provide contemporary and realistic examples. We recognize that curriculum development is often perceived as "hard work," but the benefits of developing a good curriculum far outweigh the time and effort expended in the planning and development process. The product of the curriculum development process should result in improved teaching and learning.

Secondary Education: Focus on Curriculum provides not only a theoretical and historical perspective of secondary education, but practical applications as well. The early sections of the book draw upon our years of experience working with teachers and school districts in various settings and are based on current research as it relates to the design and implementation of curriculum for secondary students. As the title of the book indicates, secondary education is the context and the focus is on curriculum with the principles of planning and development serving as the conceptual framework.

This book differs from other curriculum texts in a number of ways. First, it is written specifically for secondary educators. Many curriculum textbooks are concerned with curriculum development at all levels of the educational spectrum, from kindergarten through grade 12. This wide brush stroke approach provides a general orientation to the curriculum development process, but is too general in its look at schooling in America. With such a generic approach to curriculum these texts are vague regarding the specific needs and characteristics of adolescents and lack the specificity and in-depth analysis of the content, structure, issues, and programs that are critical to understanding adequately the curriculum development process for secondary education.

Other curriculum texts do not deal with any specific grade level or model, but rather discuss curriculum development from a theoretical, abstract perspective. This text is designed to provide practical, concrete examples that will have direct applications for secondary educators. Other texts, which study curriculum in theory almost exclusively, seem more appropriate for highly advanced and specialized courses.

For us, curriculum planning and development provide the cornerstone for what happens instructionally in secondary schools. It is important then, for educators to view curriculum development in a positive light because it is critical for improved instructional effectiveness. With an emphasis on the practical aspects of curriculum development, this book seeks to cultivate a positive attitude toward curriculum development. As you read this book, we hope the following aspects prove helpful:

1. Theory and research are translated into a pragmatic language that educators can use and understand.
2. Issues presented in the recent reform documents are addressed.
3. No single approach is advocated regarding the "best" type of secondary curriculum or program; rather, several models are presented, which allow secondary educators to choose the appropriate format.
4. The text has a "Your Turn" section at the end of each chapter, which is designed to involve the reader in a practical way in the use of the information presented.

In Part One of the book, an overview of secondary education is presented, with particular attention given to the recent reform reports and the structure of secondary education. The first chapter sets the stage and uses the various reports of the last five years as a starting point for discussion. Chapter 2 presents the historical development of secondary education, beginning with colonial times and ending with the contemporary nature of secondary education.

In the foundations section, Part Two, the philosophical, social, and psychological forces that impact curriculum development are discussed. Part Three provides the big picture of the curriculum planning and development process, including a description of the various models of curriculum development. Part Four provides the basics by focusing on curriculum development at the classroom level. Procedures associated with writing goals and objectives, selecting resources, and developing unit and lesson plans are covered. These specifics are designed to help educators be more effective in developing curriculum. In this part, models for evaluating the curriculum are also discussed.

In the next section, Part Five, each of the major content or subject areas of the secondary school curriculum is discussed. This section examines current data relative to teaching the subject and provides a list of the various units and topics that are traditionally a part of each curriculum area. The text concludes with a look at future issues confronting the secondary curriculum and describes the change process that is a part of curriculum development as new curricular programs are implemented.

It is our hope that *Secondary Education: Focus on Curriculum* will provide the reader with a comprehensive framework to use in developing and modifying curriculum for the secondary schools as they work to improve the curriculum in their district.

PART
ONE

The Status, Nature, and Historical Development of Secondary Education

*P*art One is a general introduction to the book. Chapter 1 provides an overview of the organizational structure of the secondary school (middle school, junior high school, and high school) in light of the reform movements of the 1980s. The chapter ends on an optimistic note by focusing on the mission of American secondary education.

Chapter 2 provides a historical chronicle of the past and how it has

1

influenced contemporary practices. Starting with colonial America, the chapter traces the development of content and programs in secondary education to the present.

Part One concludes with several definitions of the term *curriculum*, and the authors add their definition to the list that exists. The conceptual framework discussed throughout the book provides a general orientation to curriculum planning and development of secondary programs. Part One sets the stage for what comes later in the book by providing a glimpse of where we have traveled and where we want to go in secondary curriculum.

Chapter
1

The Status and Nature of Secondary Education

*I*n recent years the scrutiny of educational programs and the demand for change in the secondary schools have escalated. Not since the Sputnik era have educators and noneducators alike attempted so vigorously to explain the decline in scholastic achievement scores (SAT, ACT), the poor performance of American students on the National Assessment of Educational Progress (NAEP), and the increase in dropouts among adolescents (Brown, 1984). During the 1980s, these three indices—low scores on college entrance exams, low achievement scores on the NAEP, and a high dropout rate—have helped fuel and push the reform movements of secondary schools forward. In times of reform, it is not unusual to place the blame on someone or something. In this situation, the blame has been placed on the curriculum and programs of the secondary schools. In Figure 1.1 six areas of the curriculum, mathematics, science, reading, writing, geography, and history, are featured. In each of these curriculum areas, the question "What do our 17-year-olds know?" is answered. It is evident from the figure that high school students have acquired only rudimentary knowledge in each of these curriculum areas. With students' lack of higher order thinking or problem solving skills evident, the fundamental question that has been raised by the critics is, Why have the public schools failed?

3

Mathematics

- **6 percent** can solve multi-step problems and use basic algebra.
- **51 percent** can compute with decimals, fractions, and percents; recognize geometric figures; and solve simple equations.
- **100 percent** know some basic addition and subtraction facts, can add and subtract two-digit numbers, and recognize relationships among coins.

Science

- **7 percent** can infer relationships and draw conclusions using detailed scientific knowledge.
- **41 percent** have some detailed scientific knowledge and can evaluate the appropriateness of scientific procedures.
- **97 percent** understand some basic principles—for example, simple knowledge about plants and animals—and **100 percent** know everyday science facts.

Reading

- **5 percent** can synthesize and learn from specialized reading materials.
- **39 percent** can find, understand, summarize, and explain relatively complicated information.
- **99 percent** can comprehend specific or sequentially-related information, and **100 percent** can carry out simple, discrete reading tasks.

Figure 1.1 What Do Our 17-Year-Olds Know?

In all of the fault-finding rhetoric, Tanner (1984) is concerned that the misguided attacks on public education may lead to misguided remedies. In the article "The American High School at the Crossroads," he says,

> . . . midcentury American public education has been buffeted incessantly by conflicting clamors for reform [and with] each clamor for reform [there] is eventually . . . a clamor for counterreform to undo the excesses of the previous one. The schools have become so inured to attacks from every conceivable and inconceivable source that they have come to regard these attacks as part of the ceremony (p. 5).

As this statement suggests, innovations have come and gone depending on the sociopolitical events at the time. Shifts from the use of instructional television and modular scheduling in the 1960s to mastery learning, computer technology, and academic excellence in the 1980s have contributed to ". . . waves of conflicting and contradictory criticism and reinvented demands for reform" (Tanner, 1984, p. 5).

The concern for academic excellence at the secondary level is not new and has not diminished with time. On the contrary, the call for excellence has intensified, and the momentum for analyzing and reforming secondary schools has increased. The following list provides a sample of the numerous studies conducted during the last decade which have scrutinized some aspect of secondary education:

The Paideia Proposal: An Educational Manifesto (1982)

High School: A Report on Secondary Education in America (1983)

A Nation At Risk (1983)

Horace's Compromise: The Dilemma of the American High School (1984)

What Do Our 17-Year-Olds Know (1987)

Everybody Counts (1989)

Science for All Americans (1990)

Writing

• **27 percent** can perform a persuasive writing task earning a rating of "adequate or better"; **3 percent** earn the highest rating of "elaborated."

• **44 percent** perform "adequate or better" on a piece of informative writing; **11 percent** are capable of "elaborated" writing.

• **57 percent** can complete a narrative writing task rated "adequate or better"; **7 percent** earn the rating of "elaborated."

Geography

• **27 percent** could identify likely areas of soil erosion using maps of elevation and rainfall.

• **53 percent** of students are able to identify a cause of the "greenhouse effect."

• **85 percent** can locate the Soviet Union on a world map, and **84 percent** can identify countries in the Middle East from a series of lists.

History

• **5 percent** are able to interpret historical information and ideas.

• **46 percent** understand basic historical terms and relationships.

• **99 percent** know simple historical facts.

The reading, mathematics, and science figures refer to the performance of 17-year-olds; the geography, history, and writing assessments tested high school seniors.

Source: Reprinted from O'Neil, J. (September 1990). What do our 17-year-olds know. *ASCD Curriculum Update, 32,* 7, 4–5. Used with permission.

Figure 1.1 *Continued*

Crossroads in American Education (1989)

The Geography Learning of High School Seniors (1990)

The U.S. History Report Card (1990)

Learning to Read in Our Nation's Schools (1990)

Learning to Write in Our Nation's Schools (1990)

As a result of this national attention given to the mission and curriculum of secondary schools, the study of educational programs in those schools seems timely and appropriate. Within the present social milieu, critics are venting their frustrations by pointing their fingers at everyone and everything associated with secondary education. In response to this clamor, an examination of secondary curriculum is not only appropriate but necessary.

This chapter examines secondary education by providing an overview of the nature, organizational patterns, mission, and aims of grades 7–12. The chapter ends with the question: What is the mission of the secondary school to prepare adolescents for the twenty-first century?

SECONDARY EDUCATION AND THE REFORM MOVEMENTS

With each succeeding decade following the launching of Sputnik, reform movements have been initiated, commissions formed, and reports written concerning the nature of secondary education, namely grades 7–12. A descriptive study by Conant (1959) provided the blueprint of what has come to be known as the American comprehensive high school. As a part of the introduction to his report, Conant described the general characteristics of American education and identified the unique features of what he called the "comprehensive high school." In developing his concept of the modern high school, he divided all high schools into two general categories regardless of whether students were there for three or four years. One category included all specialized high schools that had a strict academic focus. These were located most often in urban centers. Examples in this category included the Bronx High School of Science in New York City, the Boston Latin School, and the Central High School in Philadelphia. The other general category included schools whose programs corresponded to the educational needs of all students in a community by concentrating on vocational education programs as well as academics. Since some communities opted for separate vocational schools, Conant emphasized the need for using the phrase "degree of comprehensiveness" of a high school (p. 13).

The Conant report was significant for several reasons. First, it raised a key question about the mission of the high school. Secondly, it asked: Can a high school satisfactorily fulfill three separate functions? Conant asked,

> Can a [high] school at one and the same time provide a good general education for all of the pupils as future good citizens of a democracy, provide elective programs for the majority to develop useful skills, and educate adequately those with a talent for handling academic subjects—particularly foreign languages and advanced mathematics? (p. 15)

To help educators answer this question and evaluate the comprehensiveness of high schools, Conant prepared a checklist. He sounded a word of caution, however, by suggesting that valid judgments about secondary education should be made on a school-by-school basis. The checklist as presented in Box 1-1 is a modified version which reflects the contemporary secondary school and includes the major questions concerning the general and elective high school programs in addition to the arrangements for academically talented students. Also listed are the criteria for making a judgment about these questions.

Although the Conant report identified several weaknesses in the secondary schools, the report indicated that these weaknesses could be corrected with minimal effort. Based on the information included in the study, the following conclusions were generated:

1. The academically talented students were not being challenged
2. The range of academic subjects was limited and should be increased
3. Girls and boys should be encouraged to take courses in mathematics, science, foreign language, English, and social studies

The report ended with 21 recommendations for improving secondary education, including many different areas that ranged from counseling to special programs for slow learners. A modified list of these recommendations is provided in Box 1-2. It contains several themes that continue to appear in later studies and more recent reports. Although the list is lengthy, Conant did not feel radical change was needed to significantly improve secondary schools, provided communities and school boards followed his recommendations.

Box 1-1 **Checklist for Evaluating a Comprehensive High School**

 I. Are offerings adequate to support the general education component? Criteria used to evaluate:
   a. Courses in English and American literature and composition
   b. Courses in social studies, including American history
   c. Use of ability grouping as needed
 II. Are offerings adequate to support the nonacademic elective program? Criteria used to evaluate:
   a. Vocational and commercial programs for all interested students
   b. Supervised work experience opportunities
   c. Special provisions for very slow readers
 III. Are there special programs and opportunities for academically talented students? Criteria to evaluate include:
   a. Courses to challenge the highly gifted
   b. Special instruction to develop advanced reading skills
   c. Summer sessions offered for able students
   d. Individualized programs (absence of tracks or rigid programs)
   e. School day organized to maximize instruction
 IV. Are other program components present?
   a. Adequacy of the guidance service
   b. Student attitude toward school and learning

Modified from Conant, J.B. (1959). *The American high school today.* New York: McGraw-Hill, pp. 19–20.

A more recent Carnegie report (1983), a sequel to the Conant report (Brown, 1984), had a less optimistic view about the American high school. Unlike other reports, the Carnegie study is based on actual classroom situations in specific high schools across the United States. Boyer, working with members of an advisory board, wrote the report, which subsequently led to the publication of the book *High School: A Report on Secondary Education in America* (1983). The purpose of this report was to identify ways to improve secondary education, and 12 themes were identified that established an "agenda for action." Four goals and functions of the high school were identified. These include:

1. Developing critical thinking and communication skills through a mastery of language
2. Learning about the human heritage through a curriculum that includes the human experiences common to all
3. Preparing for work and continuing education by taking elective courses that help increase potential and aptitudes

Box 1-2   # Recommendations for Improving Public Secondary Education

1. Establish a counseling system

2. Develop individualized programs

3. Establish programs required for all in the areas of general education and electives

4. Establish standards for passing and failing

5. Consider ability grouping

6. Diversify programs for the development of marketable skills

7. Develop programs for academically talented and highly gifted students

8. Create an academic inventory

9. Organize the school day to include homerooms

10. Establish prerequisites for advanced and academic courses

11. Do not rank students in class according to grades in all subjects, but in identified courses

12. Publish an academic honors list

13. Offer summer school opportunities

14. Develop a curriculum that includes
    a. English composition
    b. developmental reading for students with special needs
    c. foreign languages
    d. multiple science courses
    e. multiple social studies courses

Modified from Conant, J.B. (1959). *The American high school today*. New York: McGraw-Hill, pp. 44–46.

4. Fulfilling civil and social responsibilities by serving school and community

The book *High School* established the framework for the reform agenda, especially for grades 9–12. There was no simple solution to the transformation of high schools across the United States, but it was clear that something needed to be done. For Boyer (1983), high school subjects need to relate to "our independent, interconnected, complex world" (p. xiii), and if the promise to revitalize the high schools is to be fulfilled, Americans need to be prepared to meet this challenge and take action.

Another document, *A Nation at Risk*, was drafted by the National Commission on Excellence in Education (1983) and has received the widest coverage and generated some of the most intense debate. This report examined the "quality of education in America" (p. iii) and the opening line, "Our nation is at risk," (p. 5), set the tone. The report continued by saying that ". . . the average graduate of our schools . . . today is not as well educated as the average graduate of 25 or 35 years ago . . ." (p. 11). Next, the report proceeds to list several risk indicators that have contributed to the current state of affairs. These indicators are presented in Box 1-3. Unlike the previous studies, *A Nation at Risk* discusses education in the context of its contribution to our national security, economic survival, and world leadership. It "sounds a warning that there is a rising tide of mediocrity in our schools . . . [that] threatens our very future as a nation and a people" (p. 5). It recommends that graduation requirements be increased from 21 to 23 credits. In 1982 only 2 percent of the students met this recommendation but by 1987 the percentage had increased to 12 (ASCD, 1990).

Taken together, the reform movements and documents that have been generated have presented some contradictory prescriptions. But, according to Tanner (1984), they share many similar elements, including the need for a common core of studies comprised of English, mathematics, science, social studies, and computer science. These subject areas, labeled by *A Nation at Risk* as the "Five New Basics," form the foundation of the common core. The issue of standards relative to the core curriculum has also been raised by Vanderslice (1982), president of GTE Corporation, when he notes that ". . . twenty states do not require a single math or science course as a prerequisite for a high school diploma" (p. 31).

Another common element of these reports is the call for more testing of students and in some cases the testing of teachers. The reports also tend to overgeneralize, use exaggerated language (such as risk, critical, urgency), make reckless accusations, and often skew or distort data (Tanner, 1984). Lastly, in their attempt to overcome mediocrity or reorder the educational program, these reform documents reaffirm and build a case for general education with a greater emphasis on mathematics and science. As Sizer (1984a) notes, education in the twenty-first century will require ". . . older remedies, or to put it . . . humbly, different compromises" (p. 37). This fundamental deviation from the current state of affairs will require not simply ". . . knowing what is to be done and why," but having someone to carry it out (Monasmith, 1984, p. 39).

Field work conducted by Hall, Hord, Rutherford, and Huling (1984) is encouraging in that they have ". . . found widespread interest in change" and the ". . . high school staffs are ready and willing" (pp. 52, 62). These researchers note that even though the stereotypical programs are being questioned, the data on high schools are limited and there is a need for more descriptive studies on how secondary schools work with more attention given

Box 1-3   # A Nation at Risk: The Imperative for Educational Reform Indicators

1. International comparisons of student achievement, completed a decade ago, reveal that on 19 academic tests American students were never first or second and, in comparison with other industrialized nations, were last seven times.

2. Some 23 million American adults are functionally illiterate by the simplest tests of everyday reading, writing, and comprehension.

3. About 13 percent of all 17-year-olds in the United States can be considered functionally illiterate. Functional illiteracy among minority youth may run as high as 40 percent.

4. Average achievement of high school students on most standardized tests is now lower than 26 years ago when Sputnik was launched.

5. Over half the population of gifted students do not match their tested ability with comparable achievement in school.

6. The College Board's Scholastic Aptitude Tests (SAT) demonstrate a virtually unbroken decline from 1963 to 1980. Average verbal scores fell over 50 points and average mathematics scores dropped nearly 40 points.

7. College Board achievement tests also reveal consistent declines in recent years in such subjects as physics and English.

8. Both the number and proportion of students demonstrating superior achievement on the SATs (i.e., those with scores of 650 or higher) have also dramatically declined.

9. Many 17-year-olds do not possess the higher-order intellectual skills we should expect of them. Nearly 40 percent cannot draw inferences from written material; only one-fifth can write a persuasive essay; and only one-third can solve a mathematics problem requiring several steps.

10. There was a steady decline in science achievement scores of U.S. 17-year-olds as measured by national assessments of science in 1969, 1973, and 1977.

11. Between 1975 and 1980, remedial mathematics courses in public 4-year colleges increased by 72 percent and now constitute one-quarter of all mathematics courses taught in those institutions.

12. Average tested achievement of students graduating from college is also lower.

13. Business and military leaders complain that they are required to spend millions of dollars on costly remedial education and training programs in such basic skills as reading, writing, spelling, and computation. The Department of the Navy, for example, reported to the Commission that one-quarter of its recent recruits cannot read at the ninth-grade level, the minimum needed simply to understand written safety instructions. Without remedial work they cannot even begin, much less complete, the sophisticated training essential in much of the modern military.

Box 1-3 **A Nation at Risk: The Imperative for Educational Reform Indicators — Continued**

14. Computers and computer-controlled equipment are penetrating every aspect of our lives — homes, factories, and offices.

15. One estimate indicates that by the turn of the century millions of jobs will involve laser technology and robotics.

16. Technology is radically transforming a host of other occupations. They include health care, medical science, energy production, food processing, construction, and the building, repair, and maintenance of sophisticated scientific, educational, military, and industrial equipment.

Source: Reprinted from National Commission on Excellence in Education. (1983). *A nation at risk: The imperative for educational reform.* Washington, D.C.: U.S. Department of Education, pp. 8–10.

to the ". . . real processes and characteristics of high schools" (p. 62). Perhaps the interest in secondary education fostered by the reform reports can produce studies that more accurately assess the curriculum and programs of secondary schools.

More recently, subject matter specialists have offered recommendations in their respective areas (social studies, English language arts, mathematics, and science). These recommendations will be presented in greater detail in Part Four of the text.

ORGANIZATIONAL PATTERNS OF SECONDARY SCHOOLS

When speaking of *secondary schools*, it is important to note that secondary education in the United States takes a variety of forms. The form is often dependent upon several factors which may include: (1) the history of the educational system, (2) the educational philosophy of the school district, (3) the degree of participation of citizens in decisions, and (4) the financial resources of the community. Generally, the term *secondary education* is used to refer to grades 6 or 7 through grade 12. These five or six years of education comprise the secondary schools. The term *high school* usually refers to the last four years of schooling, grades 9–12. The specific curriculum of secondary education and the grouping of grades to form specific organizational patterns varies from state to state and school district to school district. However, we accept the general premise that secondary schools encompass grades 7–12.

The common organizational patterns, or grouping of grade levels, in schools are the 6-2-4 or 6-3-3 and the 8-4 pattern. In the 6-2-4 or 6-3-3 patterns (6 years of elementary school, 2 or 3 years of junior high, 3 or 4 years of high school), the junior high school plays an intermediary role between the elementary years and high school. In this arrangement, the junior high school begins in the seventh grade and ends in either the eighth or ninth grade, and it is during these years that the students make a transition to high school.

The other popular, yet older, arrangement is the 8-4 pattern. Eight years are spent in what would be considered the elementary school and four years in the high school. In the 1900s the 8-4 pattern was the most common arrangement for school organization, but it has given way to organizational patterns that have programs and activities more appropriate for the developmental characteristics of the preadolescent, who is classified as neither an elementary student nor a high school student. The preadolescent is considered to be somewhere in-between and is often referred to as a transescent.

Middle School

One such school organizational pattern is the middle school, which has evolved in recent years out of a concern to meet the special developmental needs of the preadolescent. While not universally accepted, the middle school is important enough to merit discussion here before focusing on the organizational patterns of the junior high school and the high school.

During the 1960s, critics were extremely vocal about the shortcomings of the junior high school, which was viewed as a miniature high school with an emphasis on academic and athletic competitions (McEwin and Alexander, 1982; Wells, 1989). The junior high school was criticized because "it failed to serve as a bridge between childhood and adolescence" (Reinhartz and Beach, 1983, p. 5), and was not effective in providing a transition from elementary school to high school.

To help in this transition, the middle school begins with grade 6 and continues through grades 8 or 9, depending on the local school system (Editorial, *Middle School Journal*, 1988). Tickle (1988) notes that the middle school as an organizational pattern had initial appeal, and has ". . . brought into consciousness . . . many major professional issues" (p. 3). Nevertheless, it has been slow in achieving the goals of meeting the needs of the preadolescent. One of the problems has been that the curriculum and instructional program did not always reflect the uniqueness of the student population. According to McEwin and Alexander (1982), in 1977, 15 states had 100 or more middle schools (over 1500) but by 1982 there were 5000 operating. Currently, there are over 30 different middle school configurations that have been identified (Center for Research on Elementary and Middle Schools, 1987, 1988). An editorial in the *Middle School Journal* (1988) suggests that one of the reasons that middle schools have been slow to catch on is that they lack ". . . identity in the media and elsewhere" and moreover, Americans ". . . fail to recognize the existence . . . of a middle level of education [and] . . . assume that the two-level organization, elementary and secondary, still prevails" (p. 27). Although the two-level organizational arrangement has been declining for several years, the stereotype of the two levels has persisted in the media, colleges and universities, state educational agencies, and educational publications.

The original blueprints for the middle school called for a special philosophy, curriculum, and methodology that truly reflected the needs of this age group by (1) involving them in cooperative group work, (2) allowing them to make choices and explore career opportunities (Natriello et al, 1988), (3) encouraging them to participate in interschool activities and sporting events, and (4) providing them with challenging academic programs with a wide variety of course offerings. In *Turning Points* (1989), the Carnegie Council task force recommended that middle schools improve their programs by:

1. Creating small communities for learning such as schools within schools and student and teacher teams
2. Teaching a core academic program which stresses literacy, critical thinking, health, ethics, and citizenship
3. Fostering success for all students by eliminating tracking by achievement level and providing for cooperative learning, flexible instructional time, and instructional resources
4. Empowering teachers and administrators to make decisions about experiences of middle grade students by giving them greater control over the instructional program
5. Hiring teachers who are experts at (and have a desire for) teaching young adolescents

The greatest concern has been that these students, who at age 11 or 12 are expected to sit through lectures, take notes, read chapters, and take tests, are not ready physiologically and developmentally to fully assume these student roles.

Staffing the middle school with teachers trained to work with preadolescents has also been difficult. More often than not, the scenario follows the sequence of the elementary teacher moving up or the secondary teacher moving down (Reinhartz and Beach, 1983). According to the Carnegie Council on Adolescent Development (1989), many middle school teachers are not adequately prepared to teach in the middle school. Valentine and colleagues (1981) document this lack of qualified personnel by noting that only 44 percent of middle school teachers had taken university courses to help them teach at this level and 72 percent of the teachers indicated that their information and training came from inservice and staff development sessions.

Another reason the middle school has yet to fulfill its objectives is that the curriculum has not changed. If an elementary or junior high school curriculum is in place, it has remained without substantive changes. According to Bennett (1976), Boydell (1981), and Tickle (1988), the fixed curriculum, which has specific subjects and a set format that dictates classroom instruction, has not changed. Therefore, the hopes of educators for improving curriculum and instruction at this early secondary level have not materialized.

Junior High School

With a focus on adolescence in the early decades of the twentieth century, significant changes were made in the structure of secondary schools. According to Tanner (1972) these changes resulted in the emergence of ". . . a new school unit which came to be known as the junior high school" (p. 50). From 1930 to 1959 junior high schools grew at a phenomenal rate, increasing from 1,842 to over 5,000 (Gutek, 1988).

The 8-4 plan was reorganized to a 6-2-4 plan to permit more educational opportunities and help students prepare for high school. As discussed in the next chapter, the junior high school was originally designed to allow for experimentation with programs and curricula to meet the needs of the early adolescent. For Gutek (1988), some of the main reasons that led to the growth of the junior high include:

1. Heavy immigration from Europe
2. Industrialization and technological developments
3. Emergence of the United States as a world power
4. Impact of progressive education and pragmatic philosophy on the schools

In addition to these factors, the work of Hall (1904), which described the developmental nature of adolescence and its educational implications, provided educators with a pedagogical rationale for separating early adolescents from elementary students and high school students.

Economic considerations also contributed to the growth of the junior high school and the 6-2-4 or 6-3-3 pattern. As enrollment increased and more schools were needed, constructing junior high schools was a more appealing choice than building additional elementary or high schools. This alternative school unit helped relieve enrollment burdens and proved to be an economically feasible choice. The junior high school also offered numerous advantages —libraries, gymnasiums, and auditoriums—over the elementary school while providing a transition to high school.

There are many forms of the contemporary junior high school, and their goals are diverse. According to Gutek (1988), goals that are typical of the junior high school include:

1. Providing a transition from elementary to secondary education
2. Introducing learners to separate subjects and disciplines
3. Recognizing and providing for physical, physiological, emotional, and social changes that take place in adolescents
4. Introducing students to a range of careers and occupations
5. Providing opportunities for social and physical as well as educational development
6. Providing articulation with programs in the senior high school

To complement these goals, the junior high school has a curriculum similar to that of the high school, with specific subjects or courses. These courses generally fall into one of two categories—required and elective. The required courses include English language arts, mathematics, social studies (history, geography), science, health, and physical education. The elective courses often include fine arts (art, music, band, choir), vocational subjects (home economics, typing, shop), and foreign languages (Gutek, 1988).

The junior high school years are considered the ". . . bridge builders between the educational skills and subjects of the elementary school and the more complex and differentiated subjects of high school" (Gutek, 1988, p. 207). Junior high schools represent traditional institutions for the youth of today. Like middle schools, junior high schools were created to serve a specific population and form a safe passage through which elementary students moved into high school.

High School

The public high school first appeared in the latter part of the nineteenth century and it ". . . established the basic institutional framework of the American public school system" (Gutek, 1988, p. 213). The high school generally includes grades 9–12 and, more recently, a senior high school of grades 10–12. As this later arrangement would suggest, in some communities the high school grades are coupled with three years of junior high.

Most high schools in the United States have between 1,000 and 2,000 students, with others having under 750 students (Hall, Hord, Rutherford, and Huling, 1984). The "average" or "typical" school has an academic comprehensive curriculum with such courses as band, athletics, and drama perceived as extra- or co-curricular experiences that play a major role in the school day. The typical American high school serves a diverse student population. According to Gutek (1988), no other educational institution tries to accomplish so much, namely to:

1. Provide an education for the vast majority of adolescents
2. Provide programs of academic excellence for talented American youth
3. Provide the practical training needed for useful and productive vocations and occupations
4. Provide an atmosphere that will encourage worthwhile personal and social development (p. 234)

The recent wave of reform reports have closely examined these objectives and others. The evolution of the American high school is discussed in greater detail in the next chapter. Before determining the direction for change and improvement in secondary education, the process should begin with an examination of the mission, purposes, and goals of the secondary schools.

MISSION OF AMERICAN SECONDARY EDUCATION

Identifying the mission of secondary schools is a difficult task. The task is complicated by variations that exist at the state and district levels. For Boyer (1984),

> . . . to be effective, [secondary schools] must have a sense of purpose, with teachers, students, administrators, and parents sharing a vision of what they are trying to accomplish. The vision must be larger than a single class in a single day. It

must go beyond keeping students in schools and out of trouble, and be more significant than adding up the Carnegie units (p. 20).

Sizer (1984a), Monasmith (1984), and Boyer (1984) believe that secondary schools should emphasize language usage—critical thinking and writing skills—have a curriculum of common knowledge that helps students learn about their past and about themselves, and have school leaders, especially principals, who have a clear vision for rebuilding excellence. In more recent years, there has been a call for linking high schools with businesses; such partnerships, according to an article in *ASCD Update* (1989), are growing.

Since 1918, *The Cardinal Principles of Secondary Education* have been the accepted set of assumptions and educational objectives that have guided the mission of the high school. While other studies (Brown, 1973) have attempted to update and improve upon the original principles used in 1918, the results have been remarkably similar. Table 1.1 compares the goals embodied in the Cardinal Principles with the national goals stated in 1973; the words may be different but the outcomes are essentially the same. Chapter 2 provides additional discussion on the impact of these principles on the historical development of secondary education.

Table 1.1   A COMPARISON OF NATIONAL GOALS AS ESTABLISHED IN 1918 AND 1973

Cardinal Principles of 1918	National Goals of 1973
Health (Physical Fitness)	Adjustment to Change (Mental Health)
Command of Fundamental Processes	Communication Skills Computation Skills
Vocation	Occupational Competence
Civic Education	Responsibility for Citizenship Respect of Law and Authority Appreciation of Others
Worthy Home Membership Worthy Use of Leisure Ethical Character	Knowledge of Self Critical Thinking Clarification of Values Economic Understanding The Achievements of Man Nature and Environment

- - - - - (Broken Line) Separates interrelated goals

———— (Solid Line) Separates unrelated goals

Source: Reprinted from Brown, B. F. (1973). *The reform of secondary education: A report to the public and the profession.* New York: McGraw-Hill, p. 188. Used with permission.

Because of the similarity between the 1918 goals and the more recent ones, Hass (1984) suggests a need for a more contemporary set of guiding principles that would more adequately address the questions: What type of curriculum is needed for all students who will function as adults in the twenty-first century? and What lifelong learning skills might best serve them for the future? Offermann (1984) comments that "American educators must establish priorities for all students that express a vision of quality education for all" (p. 54).

For Boyer (1985), the first order of business is to establish the mastery of language as the preeminent goal of education, not as just another subject but as the means by which students can pursue all subjects. In addition, Boyer (1985) calls for a common core of learning which he defines as

> . . . a study of those experiences and traditions and ways of living common to all people . . . the way we share and use symbols in our connections with each other, the way we have a sense of history . . . the way we participate in groups and institutions . . . [and] the way we have a relationship with nature . . . (p. 1).

Boyer (1988) also believes it is crucial that disciplines go beyond facts to develop an understanding of human commonalities, for "if we focus on the trivial—if we measure that which matters least—testing will suffocate school reform" (p. 7).

Clearly, the recent scrutiny of American secondary education has not only called attention to the current status of educational programs but has also raised questions about the nature of secondary education itself. Because some of the questions posed and the issues raised by the critics of secondary education are valid, it is essential to examine the whole concept of secondary education relative to curriculum and instruction.

In this chapter, we have set the stage by describing the issues, organizational patterns, and mission of secondary education. In the parts and chapters that follow we will trace the historical evolution of secondary education; discuss the philosophical, sociological, and psychological foundations of curriculum development; examine the various models of curriculum development and evaluation; describe the role of secondary educators in the curriculum development process—especially at the building and classroom levels; analyze the current state of the art for each of the major subjects or content areas in the secondary curriculum; identify curricular issues; and discuss the process of curriculum change.

SUMMARY

Chapter One set the stage for the study of secondary education by focusing on the current state of affairs. It began with an introduction that examined the earlier efforts, begun in 1959 with the Conant report, to reform secondary schools. This report identified the unique features of what Conant called the comprehensive high school. This model of a high school became the forerunner of the modern high school.

The Conant report was significant because for the first time it raised the key question concerning the mission of the high school. Although Conant did not feel radical change was needed, he made several recommendations for improving secondary schools. More recently, a number of reform reports, such as *Crossroads in American Education, What Do Our 17-Year-Olds Know, Science for All Americans*, and *Everybody Counts*, have focused on secondary education. These studies of the secondary school have several elements in common, namely an emphasis on a core curriculum and the issue of standards in curriculum, a call for testing students and teachers, and a tendency to overgeneralize and use exaggerated language. However, in the last analysis, these and subject-specific documents build a case for examining educational programs and for improving all areas of the high school curriculum, especially mathematics and science.

The second part of the chapter discussed the various organizational patterns of secondary schools. Each level of secondary education was presented, with specific attention focused on the middle school, the junior high school, and the high school. The junior high school was popular at the turn of the century and has continued to be a dominant force in the education of early adolescents. However, about 1960, critics became extremely dissatisfied with the junior high level of schooling and proposed the creation of the middle school. The middle school was designed to be a more appropriate intermediary between the elementary grades and high school. Finally, the high school was described as the major component of secondary education and the focus of much of the recent attention.

The chapter concluded with a discussion of the mission of secondary education in America. The last section posed questions concerning the kind of secondary curriculum that will be needed to prepare students to function as adults in the twenty-first century.

YOUR TURN

1.1 You have been asked to make a recommendation about what changes should be made in the next five years to help prepare students to meet the challenges of the next century. Before you can make any recommendations you will need to conduct a study of a local high school—looking specifically at the student population, the curriculum, the facilities, the faculty and staff, and the test scores over the past five years. Once this study has been completed, make recommendations based on the data you have collected.

With your list of recommendations prepared, read *A Nation at Risk* and compare your recommendations with those presented in this document. Feel free to revise your list at any time and then compile a final list of recommendations that you believe would help this school become a model for the state and the nation.

1.2 A school district is considering going to a 6-3-3 arrangement, with a middle school replacing the junior high school (currently grades 7–8). Many of the teachers and administrators believe that everything is fine as it is and that it is not necessary to change, even if in name only.

You feel that the change to a middle school is not only desirable, but absolutely necessary. The dropout rate during grades 7–9 is the highest it has ever been, and the school program at this level is not working for many students; there are many students at risk. You have to convince these educators that the middle school is the way to go.

(a) Before you begin, visit a junior high school and a middle school and record your impressions. Then read at least one article from the *Middle School Journal* and review the material in this chapter.

(b) Make a list of the advantages and disadvantages of the program to share with the faculty and staff.

(c) What are the advantages and disadvantages for the students? Interview several students to get their opinions about the school format, the program (curriculum), the teachers, and the administration. What transitional problems have they encountered as they moved from the elementary school to the middle/junior high school?

(d) Consider the changes that would need to be made. It is essential that you make this an intellectual and not an emotional argument. You must have facts and figures to support your position.

1.3 You have been asked to summarize at least two of the reform documents for the members of a local school board. Using the Carnegie report as a guide, consider the following questions as you review the reports:
(a) What should secondary schools teach?
(b) What constitutes a common core of learning?
(c) How does the report deal with the issue of educating minority students?

1.4 In Chicago, at the 1988 annual meeting of the Association for Supervision and Curriculum Development, Ernest Boyer ended his presentation by describing a "Firing Line" exchange between Bill Buckley and Mortimer Adler (the author of *The Paideia Proposal*):

Buckley asked Adler what made him so sure all children can learn. Adler shot back, "Well, Bill, I don't know that all children can learn, but on the other hand, you're not absolutely confident they can't, so I'd rather live by my hope than your doubt."

What were Mr. Buckley and Mr. Adler really saying about education and the ability of children to learn?

REFERENCES

Adler, M.J. (1982). *The paideia proposal: An educational manifesto.* New York: Macmillan.

Allen, R., et al. (1990). *Geography learning of high school seniors.* Washington, D.C.: Office of Educational Research and Improvement, U.S. Department of Education.

Applebee, A.N., et al. (1990). *Learning to write in our nation's schools.* Princeton, N.J.: Educational Testing Service.

Applebee, A.N., Langer, J.A., & Mullis, I.V.S. (1989). *Crossroads in American education.* Princeton, N.J.: Educational Testing Service.

Association for Supervision and Curriculum Development. (September 1989). Face of school-business links changing, *ASCD Update, 31,* 6, 1–6.

Association for Supervision and Curriculum Development. (February 1990). Students increase course load in reform era, *ASCD Update, 32,* 2, 4.

Bennett, N. (1976). *Teaching styles and pupil progress.* Cambridge, Mass.: Open Books.

Boydell, D. (1981). Classroom Organization 1970–71. In B. Simon and J. Willocks (Eds.) *Research and practice in the primary classroom.* London, and Boston, Mass.: Routledge and Kegan Paul.

Boyer, E.L. (1985). Boyer sees symbol system mastery as top priority. *ASCD Update, 27,* 3, 1–2.

Boyer, E.L. (1984). Clarifying the mission of the American high school. *Educational Leadership, 41,* 6, 20–22.

Boyer, E.L. (1983). *High school: A report on secondary education in America.* Washington, D.C.: Carnegie Foundation for the Advancement of Teaching.

Brandt, Ron (1988). On the high school curriculum: A conversation with Ernest Boyer. *Educational Leadership, 46,* 1, 4–9.

Brown, B.F. (1984). *Crisis in secondary education: Rebuilding America's high schools.* Englewood Cliffs, N.J.: Prentice Hall.

Brown, B.F. (1973). *The reform of secondary education*: A report to the public and the profession. New York: McGraw-Hill.

Carnegie Council on Adolescent Development. (June 1989). *Turning points: Preparing American youth for the 21st century.* New York: Carnegie Corporation.

Center for Research on Elementary and Middle Schools. (June 1987). *Special report on middle schools: A description of organizational structures in middle schools and their effects on student-teacher relations and instruction.* Baltimore: Author.

Center for Research on Elementary and Middle Schools. (June 1988). *Grades 6–8 schools move slightly toward organizational structures for balanced student growth.* Baltimore: Author.

Conant, J.B. (1959). *The American high school today.* New York: McGraw-Hill.

Gutek, G.L. (1988). *Education and schooling in America* (2nd ed.). Englewood Cliffs, N.J.: Prentice Hall.

Hall, G.E., Hord, S.M., Rutherford, W.L., & Huling, L.L. (1984). Change in high schools: Rolling stones or asleep at the wheel? *Educational Leadership, 41,* 6, 58–62.

Hall, G.S. (1904). *Adolescence.* New York: D. Appleton & Co.

Hammack, D.C. et al. (1990). *The U.S. history report card.* Princeton, N.J.: Educational Testing Service

Hass, J. (1984). Displacing the cardinal principles. *Educational Leadership, 41,* 6, 39–40.

Langer, J.A. et al. (1990). *Learning to read in our nation's schools.* Princeton, N.J.: Educational Testing Service.

McEwin, C.K. & Alexander, W.M. (1982). *The status of middle/junior high school teacher education programs: A research report.* Boone, N.C.: Appalachian State University.

Monasmith, J. (1984). Rising expectations. *Educational Leadership, 41,* 6, 39.

National Commission on Excellence in Education (1983). *A nation at risk: The imperative for educational reform.* Washington, D.C.: U.S. Department of Education.

National Middle School Association. (May 1988). Recognition of the middle level of schooling. *Middle School Journal, 19,* 3, 27.

National Research Council. (1989). *Everybody counts: A report to the nation on the future of mathematics education.* Washington, D.C.: National Academy Press.

Natriello, G. et al. (July 1988). *An examination of the assumptions and evidence for alternative dropout prevention programs in high school.* Baltimore: John Hopkins University, Center for Social Organization of Schools, ED 299394.

Offermann, D.A. (1984). Designing a general education curriculum for today's high school student. *Educational Leadership, 41,* 6, 50–54.

O'Neil, J. (September 1990). What do our 17-year-olds know. *ASCD Curriculum Update, 32,* 7, 4–5.

Ravitch, D., & Finn, C.E. (1987). *What do our 17-year-olds know?* New York: Harper & Row.

Reinhartz, J., & Beach, D.M. (1983). *Improving middle school instruction: A research-based self-assessment system.* Washington, D.C.: National Education Association.

Rutherford, J.F., & Ahlgren, A. (1990). *Science for all Americans.* New York: Oxford University Press.

Sizer, T.R. (1984a). Compromises. *Educational Leadership, 41,* 6, 34–37.

Sizer, T.R. (1984b). *Horace's compromise: The dilemma of the American high school.* Boston: Houghton Mifflin.

Tanner, D. (1984). The American high school at the crossroads. *Educational Leadership, 41,* 6, 4–13.

Tanner, D. (1972). *Secondary education: Perspectives and prospects* (2nd ed.). New York: Macmillan.

Tickle, L. (1988). In search of quality in middle school curriculum. *Middle School Journal, 19,* 2, 33–35.

Valentine, J., Clark, D.C., Nickerson, N., & Keefe, J. (1981). *The middle level principalship: A survey of principals and programs.* Reston, Va.: National Association of Secondary School Principals.

Vanderslice, T.A. (December 1982). American technology: A dazzling past, a troubled future. *Newsweek, 100,* 23, 31.

Wells, A.S. (1989). Middle school education—The critical link in dropout prevention. *ERIC Clearinghouse on Urban Education Digest,* 56.

Chapter
2

Historical Development and Definitions of Secondary Curriculum

*A*s indicated in Chapter 1, secondary education has undergone extensive study and scrutiny in the last decade. The reform and counterreform issues generally have been curricular in nature and focused on the general purposes of secondary education. Scrutiny and change are not new to secondary education. In fact, the secondary curriculum of today is the result of many changes due to historical factors over the last several hundred years.

While there are many different patterns for organizing the curriculum in the school, as a rule the secondary school curriculum consists of a certain number of specified courses taken in different content areas during different years (ninth grade subjects, tenth grade subjects, etc.). As a result, many of the recommendations concerning the improvement of secondary education revolve around predictable issues such as the common core of learning, required versus elective courses, literary skills, and the role of grades 7–12 ". . . in completing the American educational ladder" (Gutek, 1988, p. 213). For Gutek, "the concept of the 'educational ladder' refers to the single, articulated, and sequential school system that characterizes public education in the United States" (p. 213). And recently, there has been a call for a national curriculum which is centralized and features a strong assessment component (O'Neil, 1989).

At the secondary level of the educational ladder, the common practice has been for each student to select a particular program of study, or track — vocational, college-preparatory, or business education — and then take specific courses to meet requirements within a particular program (Blount and Klaus-meier, 1968). Variations on this process have involved establishing a core of courses required of all students before selecting the specific track courses.

To better understand the current practices and curricular programs in secondary schools, it is necessary to review the major historical periods of American secondary education. The secondary schools of today — middle school, junior high school, and high school — are quite different from the organizational structures and arrangements of the past. The idea of free public education, which is compulsory in most states, to at least the age of 15, is also unique to the American public education system. Many other countries and cultures have a traditional dual system in contrast to the educational ladder, which offers all students a secondary education. A publicly supported educational system that extends from kindergarten through adolescence has become the cornerstone of American educational ideals and values.

HISTORICAL PERIODS

Historically, secondary schools have evolved in response to the social, political, and economic pressures that exist within the society as well as the needs of students, which at given moments ". . . may limit the genuine equality of educational opportunity" (Gutek, 1988, p. 213). Depending on the particular moment in history, the general purposes of secondary education have changed over time. To illustrate how schools respond to given social conditions, Table 2.1 provides a summary of major historical periods and the type of school, the aims or purposes of education, and the social background for the period.

As each historical period in the development of secondary curriculum is discussed, the following list of educational aims which have guided the schools at various times may serve as a useful frame of reference:

1. Preparation for additional learning at college or university levels
2. Preparation for life as adults with the necessary social, academic, and vocational skills to be good citizens
3. Preservation of the present society with its structures and conditions and/or transmission of the culture to the next generation
4. Preparation of individuals who will define and construct a new social order

This chapter will present a historical overview of the development of secondary schools, the evolution of the curriculum within the schools, and the cultural and historical forces within the society at the time that helped shape the educational program. The chapter begins with a review of the Latin grammar school, the dominant form of secondary education during colonial times (1600–1800). The academy, which developed during the new nation period

Table 2.1   SUMMARY OF HISTORICAL PERIODS

Period	School type	Objectives	Background information
Colonial 1600–1800	Latin grammar	To prepare students for college and the ministry	Education primarily for wealthy boys and emphasized the classics, primarily in New England
New Nation 1800–1875	Academy	To provide a practical as well as college preparatory curriculum and varied from school to school	Greater access to education for middle class to provide for life activity and ability to earn a living
Early Twentieth Century 1875–1950	High School	To prepare students for living, entering a profession, or going to college	Growth of the high school with large numbers of immigrant groups and a diversified curriculum
Contemporary Period 1950–1990	Comprehensive High School	To prepare students for life, with more generalized objectives and variety in purpose	Growth of secondary schools continues with the majority of students enrolled in high school; increased demands on the school to provide quality education
Twenty-first Century	Flexible and Specialized	To meet a variety of student needs and learning backgrounds	Growth of special programs for youth, with alternative and social programs provided through schools; choice of programs provided

(1800–1875), will then be discussed. Next, the period of the early twentieth century (1875–1950), with the development of the high school and junior high school, will be described. Finally, the contemporary period (1950–1990) and the development of the comprehensive high school will be examined. The chapter concludes with a presentation of various definitions of curriculum in light of the historical perspectives previously discussed.

Secondary Education in Colonial America (1600 – 1800)

In order to understand the present nature of the secondary school program and the curriculum, it is helpful to review our colonial heritage and our early educational roots. The focus of curriculum for much of our early history centered on content or subject matter and followed a prescribed sequence of study. Secondary schools as we know them today were quite different from those in colonial times, in terms of students, community support, and curricular offerings. In fact, the curriculum of the Latin grammar school in colonial America emphasized, to the exclusion of almost everything else, the fundamental areas of reading and writing in classical languages with some instruction in arithmetic.

The emphasis on education and schools was different in the various regions of the colonies. For example, in the New England colonies,

> The first settlers of America conceived of education primarily as a means of spiritual salvation. The Puritans in New England soon established an educational program patterned after the English system — private tutoring at home and Latin grammar schools for boys who would be entering college for training as ministers (Tanner, 1972, p. 21).

The Puritans viewed the minister as a learned man because of his ability to read and study the scriptures in their original languages of Latin, Greek, and Hebrew. As a result, classical languages dominated the curriculum in the early secondary schools.

While education was important in the New England colonies, it was less important in the other colonies. For example, in the southern colonies, the economic and political system, with wealthy plantation owners, slaves, and poor whites, hampered the development of schools on a large scale. When schools did emerge in the South, they too were influenced by the structure of the Latin grammar schools and by religion, especially the Church of England.

Even though education was viewed as important, the failure of the New England colonies to support education on a voluntary basis led to the passage of laws requiring education for children. The Massachusetts Law of 1647, generally known as the Old Deluder Satan Act, is considered the first law which supported compulsory education. According to Ikenberry (1974) the opening statement gave the law its name because it noted that the object of that old deluder Satan was to keep people ignorant of the scriptures. Therefore it required that every town of 100 households establish a grammar school to instruct youth for the university. This marked the beginning of compulsory secondary schools in this country. This education, however, was not tax supported, and parents had to pay for the tutors in the school.

Founded in 1635, the Boston Latin School was the first secondary school to be established in the colonies. The Latin grammar school became the prototype school of the colonial period with a curriculum that emphasized "mastery of grammatical and stylistic mechanics" (Gutek, 1988, p. 214). The kinds of courses offered varied from one Latin grammar school to another, but the curriculum was typically very limited, extremely rigorous, and exclusively for boys (Zais, 1976). Girls received some early training in the dame schools, but generally did not receive a secondary education.

Although the Latin grammar school was considered a secondary school, the student who attended the school was much younger and would be more like today's elementary school student. Students usually entered at about age seven or eight and normally followed a seven-year curriculum. During the first few years, the young boys learned Latin grammar and translated classical works. By the fourth year, they also learned Greek and wrote Latin compositions. In their seventh and final year, the curriculum for the scholars (as they were then called) consisted of reading the New Testament and a variety of classical authors (Horace, Juvenal, Persius, Isocrates, and Hesiod). They also were required to write compositions and verses in Latin, translate Greek into Latin, study rhetoric and Roman history, and for some, begin the study of Hebrew (Miller and Johnson, 1963; Zais, 1976). Boys who completed this rigorous and demanding seven-year secondary curriculum were considered well qualified for entering the colonial colleges.

Throughout the colonies, the secondary school curriculum was influenced by college entrance requirements, especially those of Harvard and Yale. This college preparatory curriculum "consisted entirely of classical languages, religion, and sometimes a little arithmetic" (Zais, 1976, p. 27). As Ornstein and Hunkins (1988) note,

> . . . the Latin grammar school was one of colonial America's closest links to European schools, and its curriculum resembled the classical humanist curriculum of the Renaissance when schools were primarily intended for children of the upper classes and their role was to support the religious and social institutions of that era (p. 54).

Indeed, the Latin grammar school of colonial America was primarily for the sons of the wealthy and had a narrowly defined curriculum which did not meet the needs of all youth. This narrow focus coupled with "the political impact of the American Revolution and the economic impact of the Industrial Revolution contributed to the decline of the Latin Grammar school" (Gutek, 1988, p. 214). Toward the end of the eighteenth century, a few transitional English grammar and private venture schools were established by businessmen to meet the needs of young apprentices in industry and trades. These schools were the forerunners of what was to become the academy and they offered a more practical and contemporary curriculum, which included the reading and writing of English, ciphering, higher mathematics, some limited courses in bookkeeping, surveying, geography, and more modern history (Beckner and Cornett, 1972).

From colonial beginnings to the birth of the new nation, American secondary education evolved from an almost exclusive focus on the Latin grammar school, with its classical studies for the wealthy, to the emergence of the English grammar school, which became the academy. Our secondary curriculum of today has its roots in this early period, and there have been many elaborations and modifications on this theme over the last 200 years.

Secondary Education in the New Nation (1800–1875)

Because American society continued to change during the colonial years and the scope of the Latin grammar school was limited, a second type of secondary school, which was known as the academy, began in the mid-eighteenth century and spread quickly throughout the nation. Benjamin Franklin is generally regarded as the one who formulated the curriculum for the first academy, which was established in 1751. Although its beginnings were in the mid-eighteenth century, it was not until the early 1800s that the academy was "the dominant form of secondary education" (Beckner and Cornett, 1972, p. 37). One reason for its popularity was that it gave the rapidly expanding middle class access to secondary education and provided a practical as well as college preparatory curriculum.

Academies varied greatly, with no standard or typical format (Ornstein and Hunkins, 1988). Each school was developed to meet the needs of the particular group supporting it. Some academies were developed for religious purposes, others had a business focus, while still others served as college preparatory schools. One distinctive characteristic of the academy, however, was the curriculum. The curriculum was considered to be more practical than that of the Latin grammar school and included the study of the English language (English grammar), history, rhetoric, natural science, arithmetic, geometry, health, and accounting.

In the academies, Latin and classical studies were no longer the dominant subjects, and students could even take a foreign (modern) language based on their vocational needs. In addition to the expansion of language studies to include modern languages, there was a proliferation of other courses, or subjects, within the curriculum of the academies, with some states reporting as many as 50–60 different subjects. Ornstein and Hunkins (1988) note that in the period of 1800–1825 typical subjects included classical languages and literature; basic arithmetic as well as geometry and trigonometry; English grammar, rhetoric, and oratory; geography, surveying, navigation, and astronomy; bookkeeping; foreign languages including French, Spanish, and German; and philosophy. By the turn of the century, this list of courses had been expanded to include the following additional subjects: English literature and composition; advanced mathematics including algebra; science courses including meteorology, chemistry, physiology, health, botany, zoology, biology, physics; social studies courses including world history, ancient history, U.S. history, civil government, political economy; practical courses in home economics and agriculture; fine arts courses in art and music; and physical education or manual training.

Another reason the academy became so popular was the growth of the *common school* at the elementary level. The common school, first established in Massachusetts in 1826, led to the creation of a school board that was responsible for all of the schools in a local area. The academy built upon the student population created by these common schools. As Ornstein and Hunkins (1988) note, these schools were also common, "in the sense that they housed youngsters of all socioeconomic and religious backgrounds . . . and were jointly owned, cared for and used by the local community" (p. 63). Horace Mann, a Massachusetts legislator and the first Massachusetts Commissioner of Education, popularized the concept of the common school by appealing to all segments of the population for support. Mann espoused the ideas that an education gained from common schools had market value, that it would create a stable society and a sense of nationalism, and that it would be democratic in nature and a great equalizer of economic differences. In recognizing the popular appeal of the common school, Spring (1986) notes,

> In the nineteenth century, common school reformers placed their hope for a better tomorrow on the growth of the common school. The rhetoric of the nineteenth century reformer was full of promises to end poverty, save democracy, solve social problems, end crime, increase prosperity, and provide for equality of opportunity (p. 336).

Zais (1976) comments on the impact that the common school movement had on the developing high school when he says,

> The forces of democracy, industrial development, and nationalism . . . contributed to the establishment of the nonsectarian, publicly controlled and supported common (elementary) school and public high school—a unitary ladder of opportunity specifically adapted to the needs and desires of the American people (p. 40).

Thus, the concept of the public high school as a form of secondary education was a step beyond the academy and built upon the ideas and principles of the common schools that had earlier shaped elementary education.

During the nineteenth century, the high school was viewed as an institution where students could prepare to enter college or complete their formal education.

> The idea of high school attendance for all youth, based on the notion of equality of educational opportunity, was a major educational reform . . . [and] was evidence that the American people had rejected the European dual system of secondary education (Ornstein and Hunkins, 1988, p. 66).

The first high school, which was established in Boston in 1821, formed an early model for this new form of secondary education. The high school, however, was not as quick to catch on and did not become a major part of the educational process until near the end of the nineteenth century when the Michigan Supreme Court in 1874 ruled in the Kalamazoo case that high schools could be established and supported with public taxes. The high school was to emerge as the dominant form of secondary education in the early twentieth century and Ikenberry (1974) notes the importance of the Kalamazoo decision by saying, "This landmark decision legalized the future of public secondary education in the United States [and] by 1900 there were over 6,000 public high schools enrolling over 500,000 boys and girls" (p. 133). Thus, while the number of high schools had soared, the number of academies, which had dominated secondary education in the early 1800s, declined to just over 1,200 and the public high school took its place as the new secondary institution (Krug, 1964; Ornstein and Hunkins, 1988).

Secondary Education in the Early Twentieth Century (1875–1950)

Even with the growth of the public high school, only a small percentage of the total youth population attended school. It was not until after World War I and later after World War II that secondary schools, particularly the high school, showed marked gains in enrollment. In fact, it was not until 1940 that over 50 percent of all eligible youth were enrolled in secondary schools. Ornstein and Hunkins (1988) note that in 1900 approximately 12 percent of 14–17-year-olds were enrolled in secondary schools with about 7 percent graduating; in 1980, approximately 94 percent of 14–17-year-olds were enrolled in secondary schools with about 75 percent of the 17-year-olds graduating.

The programs of secondary schools in the United States diversified after 1900, and even though both traditional academic and practical vocational courses were offered, the emphasis remained on the college preparatory curriculum. In fact, during the last decade of the 1800s and the early part of the 1900s, the confusion over curriculum and standards and the arguments between modernists and traditionalists led to the creation of several national committees (Pulliam, 1976). These committees issued reports that helped shape the future direction of secondary schools and the kind of curriculum offered. Two committees, the Committee of Ten on Secondary School Studies and the Committee on College Entrance Requirements, were organized by the National Education Association (NEA) to review the curriculum of the secondary schools.

It was the Committee of Ten that first issued its report in 1893. That committee was very influential. Its recommendations illustrate the emphasis on college preparatory programs and the mental discipline approach to instruction (Ornstein and Hunkins, 1988). The Committee of Ten recommended four types of college preparatory programs. These were (1) classical, which required Latin and Greek languages; (2) Latin-scientific, which required Latin; (3) modern language, which required two modern languages; and (4) English, which required only one foreign language.

Of the four programs of study two programs still emphasized Greek and/or Latin, which is no surprise, for according to Beckner and Cornett (1972), the modern language program did not require Latin or Greek and the English program required only one foreign language. The report of the Committee pointed out that "these two programs [modern languages and English] were considered distinctly inferior to the other two" (p. 38).

The Committee on College Entrance Requirements issued its first report in 1899 and "approved the inclusion of Latin, Greek, French, German, English, history, civics, economics, geography, biology, chemistry, and mathematics in high school curricula" (Blount and Klausmeier, 1968, p. 159). In addition to approving these subjects, the Committee also recommended that the college preparatory function of the high school curriculum should be strengthened. It also made recommendations about the number of credits required for college admission—and indirectly for high school graduation (Ornstein and Hunkins, 1988). The committee recommended that each student should complete at least:

4 units of a foreign language

2 units of English

2 units of mathematics

1 unit of history

1 unit of science

These ten units became the core of the curriculum for high school.

According to Blount and Klausmeier (1968), "The committee also recommended that four hours [periods] of class attendance per week throughout the school year constitute a unit" (p. 160). This recommendation served as a model for the Carnegie Foundation for the Advancement of Teaching, which proposed in 1906 that "five periods of class work per week throughout the school year constitute a unit. This stipulation became known as a *Carnegie unit*, a unit of measurement for college admission" (Blount and Klausmeier, 1968, p. 160).

In 1911, the Committee of Nine on the Articulation of High School and College recommended that the high school program include 15 units. These 15 units were to include 3 units from each of two of the five areas identified as majors (Latin, modern languages, mathematics, social science, or natural science), 2 units in a minor area, 3 units of English, plus 4 units that could be selected from industrial (mechanical) arts, home economics (household science), commercial or business courses, or a field that met the interest of the student.

The recommendations of these committees were widely implemented in the high schools during the early 1900s and continue to exert an influence on secondary schools today. The reform reports of the last decade, as described in Chapter 1, certainly have made similar recommendations. Blount and Klausmeier (1968) have provided a sample of a typical program of studies from 1931 which includes: 4 units of English, 3 units of Latin, 1 unit of European history, 1 unit of American history, ½ unit of economics, ½ unit of civics, 1 unit of commercial arithmetic, 1½ units of algebra, 1 unit of plane geometry, 1½ units of geography, 1 unit of biology, ½ unit of physical education, ½ unit of health, ½ unit of art, and ½ unit of music. This list can be compared with the program of studies required in Texas for graduation (Texas Education Agency, 1984).

All students shall complete a minimum of 21 units of credit to receive a high school diploma. The required units shall include the following:

1. English language arts—4 units
   A. English I, II, III, or correlated language arts I, II, III
   B. The fourth unit of English may be satisfied by English IV, English IV

(academic), correlated language arts IV, introduction to speech communication, research/technical writing, creative/imaginative writing, practical writing skills, literary genres, business communication, debate, journalism, or concurrent enrollment in a college English course.
2. Mathematics — 3 units (if algebra I has been satisfactorily completed in grade seven or eight, the student shall complete 3 additional units of mathematics in grades 9–12).
3. Science — 2 units to be selected from the State Board of Education approved science courses, grades 9–12, subchapter D of this chapter
4. Social studies — 2½ units
   A. World history studies or world geography studies — 1 unit
   B. United States history — 1 unit
   C. United States government — ½ unit
5. Economics, with emphasis on the free enterprise system and its benefits — ½ unit
6. Physical education — 1½ units (pp. 234–235)

Note that the courses in each program are remarkably similar and generally match the recommendations of the various committees.

Another significant group of the early twentieth century that influenced secondary curriculum was the Commission on the Reorganization of Secondary Education. In 1918, this group issued *The Cardinal Principles of Secondary Education* referred to in the previous chapter. These principles helped

> to focus educators' attention on the problem of designing curriculum that would achieve the objectives of health, command of fundamental processes, good home relations, vocation, citizenship, profitable use of leisure time, and good character (Blount and Klausmeier, 1968, p. 162).

To help meet the objectives and encourage experimentation with curriculum design and practice, the Eight Year Study was conducted, beginning in 1933, by the Progressive Education Association. Graduates of 30 private and public secondary schools were allowed to attend one of 300 colleges and universities without meeting the usual entrance requirements. As a result, the 30 participating schools worked with curriculum consultants to reorganize the curriculum into "broad fields, correlated, integrated, and problem type approaches" (Blount and Klausmeier, 1968, p. 162). It is important to note that Ralph Tyler directed the evaluation of the results of the study. The first graduates from the 30 experimental schools entered college in 1936, and they were tracked throughout their college careers to assess their success in college. In the study, 1475 graduates from the experimental schools were paired with an equal number from conventional high schools, and they were matched by age, sex, socioeconomic level, scholastic aptitude, and IQ scores. The significant conclusions reported by the researchers relative to the graduates of the experimental schools are listed as follows:

1. Earned a slightly higher total grade average
2. Earned higher grade averages in all subject fields except foreign language
3. Specialized in the same academic fields as did the comparison students
4. Did not differ from the comparison group in the number of times they were placed on probation

5. Received slightly more academic honors in each year
6. Were more often judged to possess a high degree of intellectual curiosity and drive
7. Were more often judged to be precise, systematic, and objective in their thinking
8. Were more often judged to have developed clear or well-formulated ideas concerning the meaning of education—especially in the first two years of college
9. More often demonstrated a high degree of resourcefulness in meeting new situations
10. Did not differ from the comparison group in ability to plan their time effectively
11. Had about the same problems of adjustment as the comparison group, but approached their solution with greater effectiveness
12. Participated somewhat more frequently, and more often enjoyed appreciative experiences, in the arts
13. Participated more in all organized student groups except religious and "service" activities
14. Earned in each college year a higher percentage of nonacademic honors (officership in organizations, election to managerial societies, athletic insignia, leading roles in dramatic and musical presentations)
15. Did not differ from the comparison group in the quality of adjustment to their contemporaries
16. Differed only slightly from the comparison group in all kinds of judgments about their schooling
17. Had a somewhat better orientation toward the choice of a vocation
18. Demonstrated a more active concern for what was going on in the world (Aikin, 1942, pp. 111–112)

The results from this Eight Year Study indicated that the typical high school curriculum could be modified without handicapping students preparing to go to college. As a result, this study has frequently been cited as the basis for proposing curriculum reform or change in the secondary schools, particularly change that would be atypical of the college preparatory curriculum.

The other significant development in secondary education that occurred in the early twentieth century was the development and evolution of the junior high school. In spite of the recommendations at the turn of the century from the various committees that the schools should maintain the 8-4 elementary-secondary division, the critics of such organization indicated the need for a school that would meet the unique needs of this age group and grade level. As discussed in the previous chapter, the junior high school has become an integral part of secondary education and normally includes grades 7 and 8, and sometimes grade 9.

After about 1920, the junior high school developed rapidly and became a hotbed of experimentation (Zais, 1976). This experimentation of course offerings and instructional delivery systems was spawned to meet the generally accepted purposes or functions of the junior high school. According to Gruhn and Douglas (1956), the functions of the junior high school included:

Integration: learning experiences acquired in such a way that they are coordinated and integrated

Exploration: discovery and exploration of specialized interests, aptitudes and abilities

Guidance: assistance in making satisfying and intelligent decisions

Differentiation: provision of differentiated learning opportunities suited to students' varying backgrounds

Socialization: preparation for effective and satisfying participation in a complex social order

Articulation: gradual transition from the elementary to the high school program (pp. 31–32)

The prototype for today's junior high school is generally credited to Frank Bunker, Superintendent of the Berkeley, California, schools, who in 1910 initiated an "introductory high school" which comprised grades 7, 8, and 9. The concept for this new school was based on (1) the characteristics of the students (early adolescents); (2) the need for a better transition from elementary school to high school; (3) the need to reduce overcrowding in some schools in the district; and (4) the need for a more practical curriculum to match the future occupational needs of the students (Bunker, 1916; Gutek, 1988). Although some school systems still operated with the 8-4 organizational pattern, by the mid-twentieth century "the majority of schools had been reorganized to incorporate the junior high school" (Gutek, 1988, p. 202).

If there is a single characteristic associated with the development of secondary education during the early twentieth century, it is the impact of the various committees on the programs and curricula of the secondary schools. While some flexibility was allowed for the practical or contemporary courses of study, the college preparatory curriculum exerted a tremendous influence on the high schools.

Contemporary Secondary Education (1950–1990)

Following World War II, high school enrollment grew significantly, and the development of the secondary school was influenced by the work of Conant (1959) and his concept of the comprehensive high school. Conant's work was partially in response to a single event that almost immediately produced a profound impact on the secondary curriculum. The launching of the Russian satellite Sputnik in 1957 created a reform movement overnight. Because the Soviets had beaten the United States in the race into space, "the criticisms and voices of alarm turned with renewed vigor to blaming the schools for most if not all of our nation's problems. The schools were accused of incompetence and malpractice" (Beckner and Cornett, 1972, p. 42).

Critics of the educational system blamed the Progressive Education Movement for failing to emphasize science and mathematics and thereby cultivate intellectual skills and knowledge. The federal government responded to the situation by passing the National Defense Education Act of 1958, which began a massive intervention program in public education to "improve the nation's social, economic, and military condition" (Beckner and Cornett, 1972, p. 43).

Funds were provided for teachers to update their skills or retrain in the areas of mathematics and science.

Bruner (1960), using the ideas produced by the various academicians at the Woods Hole Conference, established the concept of the spiral curriculum. It was Bruner's belief that any concept of any subject could be taught at any level if presented in the proper developmental form. This view of curriculum helped to produce what has been called the "alphabet soup" curriculum, because nearly every subject area in the public school curriculum was revised and nearly all of the new materials had names represented by letters. Some of the examples include MACOS — Man a Course of Study for social studies; BSCS — Biological Sciences Curriculum Study for biology; PSCS — Physical Science Curriculum Study for the physical sciences; and ENG 2000, a programmed textbook for English grammar. The impact on the curriculum in both junior and senior high schools was significant, and teachers spent many hours developing curriculum guides and emphasizing the importance of mathematics and science in the world.

Another significant event that had an impact on contemporary secondary education was the Supreme Court ruling in 1954 in *Brown* v. *Board of Education of Topeka*, which declared racial segregation in public schools unconstitutional. This decision "marked the beginning of a concerted movement for civil rights and racial integration" (Gutek, 1988, p. 31). The schools have achieved mixed results from this ruling. Some districts delayed or stalled in implementation and many urban communities that did implement integration procedures experienced "white flight" as white students moved to the suburbs or private schools. The result produced many urban and inner-city schools in which the majority of the students were black.

All of the different arrangements that were constructed to either meet the intent of the ruling or circumvent the ruling put new pressures on the secondary school. With the advent of busing and the decline of the concept of the neighborhood school, the range of student abilities in any one school seemed to increase markedly. Coleman (1966) conducted a research study which examined several issues related to educational inequality. Jencks (1972) interpreted the data from the Coleman report and suggested that regardless of the diversity, "there is no evidence that school reform can substantially reduce the extent of cognitive inequality" (p. 8).

Contemporary secondary education has also been subject to a number of trends and innovations. Beckner and Cornett (1972) provide a sample list of the more common types of experimentation conducted in the secondary schools in recent decades. These include:

1. Modular and flexible scheduling
2. Subject matter reorganization for instructional purposes such as the "new" math, . . . structural linguistics, . . . and aural-oral foreign language techniques
3. Nongrading, or continual progress, organizational practices
4. Team teaching
5. The "Middle School"

6. The addition of courses such as psychology and sociology
7. Increased availability of vocational and technical training
8. Independent study provisions in curricular organization
9. Other approaches aimed at individualizing instruction (pp. 43–44)

More recent curricular strategies include cooperative learning, alternative placement programs, and accelerated programs. In addition to these practices, the magnet high school, with a single focus (e.g., performing arts), and honors or advanced placement programs have also been included in secondary schools in recent years.

This brings our review back to where we started in Chapter 1 with a review of the reform reports generated during the 1980s. By now, many of the concerns and themes expressed in these latest reports should strike a familiar cord with the recommendations issued by earlier committees. Clearly the nature of secondary curriculum development is tied to historical moments or periods that produce different perspectives and emphases.

DEFINITIONS OF CURRICULUM

The brief review of the various historical periods shows how the aims of secondary schools, including their curricular programs, have undergone change over the last 200 or more years. The social, political, and economic conditions at any particular time influence how educators and noneducators alike perceive curriculum. These perceptions help shape a definition of curriculum based on the goals and objectives of the secondary education program. For example, one of the earliest uses of the term *curriculum* comes from the Latin origin, which means to follow a course. Early uses of the term *curriculum* suggest that it meant a prescribed series of courses or subjects a student takes to complete a particular program of study.

While the historical context and aims of education help to shape the definition of curriculum, Wiles and Bondi (1984) note that the first modern use of the term *curriculum* in the United States did not appear until about the 1920s. This modern view saw curriculum as more of a process than a product. One of the earliest to propose such a definition was Bobbitt (1924), who saw curriculum as all of the experiences, both organized and unorganized, that had an educational impact upon learners. Other curricularists elaborate on this view and consider curriculum to be all the experiences children have in school under the guidance of teachers.

These early definitions of curriculum that have process as the central focus have given way to the following definitions:

1. A plan for learning (Taba, 1962)
2. All planned learning outcomes for which the school is responsible (Popham and Baker, 1970)
3. Providing sets of learning opportunities (Saylor, Alexander, and Lewis, 1981)

4. Planned and guided learning experiences with intended learning outcomes produced through knowledge and experience (Tanner and Tanner, 1980)
5. All of the learning of students that is planned and directed by the school to attain educational goals (Tyler, 1957)

Perhaps Tanner and Tanner (1980), who have conducted a historical study of the definitions of curriculum, have provided the most comprehensive list of ways to view curriculum. These various definitions include:

1. The cumulative tradition of organized knowledge
2. Modes of thought
3. Race experience
4. Guided experience
5. A planned learning environment
6. Cognitive/affective content and process
7. An instructional plan
8. Instructional ends or outcomes
9. A technological system of production (p. 36)

An examination of these different definitions yields several general categories that can be helpful in looking at the curriculum development process. Curriculum can be seen as (1) subjects or content, (2) learner experiences, (3) objectives or outcomes, and (4) planned activities for learning. For us, the curriculum is the cornerstone of the instructional process and involves content coupled with planned activities and instructional materials which are directed toward the accomplishment of the aims and objectives related to specific subjects or areas of study.

CONCEPTUAL FRAMEWORK FOR CURRICULUM DEVELOPMENT

The curriculum development process as described in this book has been presented in general terms based on recent reform reports and studies described in Chapter 1. It has also been presented within the context of the "historical roots" described in this chapter. However, curriculum development is a complex, multifaceted process that is shaped by philosophical, social, and psychological foundations, as well as past and recent events. Figure 2.1 illustrates the conceptual framework for the curriculum development process as presented in this book and includes not only the historical context and the foundation areas, but the design and implementation dimensions that are part of the curriculum planning process.

As seen in the figure, the historical developments and the foundations areas explain how belief systems become a part of a school program, how societal forces influence the content of the curriculum, and how the developmental nature of preadolescents and adolescents influences the kinds and types of learning experiences and teaching strategies that can be employed.

The curriculum development process becomes much more specific as it

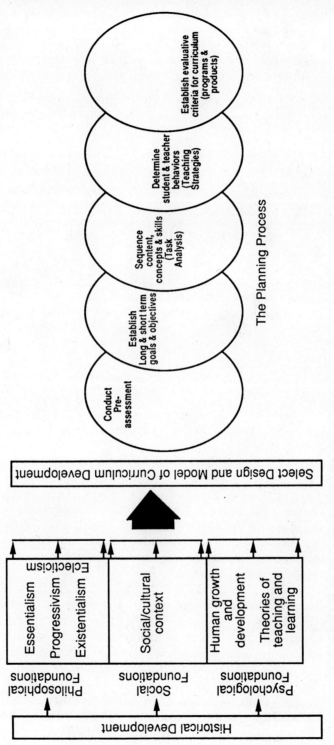

Figure 2.1 Conceptual framework for curriculum development

gets closer to the classroom level. In Chapter 9 various models and designs of the planning process are discussed in detail. At the classroom level curriculum planners and classroom teachers consider resources, scope and sequence, and specific content and concepts as they plan and monitor curriculum development. It is at this level that the curriculum development process becomes most specific.

In the 1990s the curriculum will be interpreted in a broader context, one that is nationally oriented (O'Neil, 1989), connected to the world of business (ASCD, September 1989) as well as to the growing multicultural population (Willis, 1990). The end product is a curriculum that is functional and related to real-life issues. These elements will be woven into the curriculum of the 1990s. According to O'Neil (1990), "the past decade of education reform was marked primarily by efforts to reshape the broad outlines of the school curriculum . . . the '90s may well shape up to be the decade when educators define much more clearly what all students should know and be able to do within and across the various fields of study" (p. 1).

Studying our historical roots provides valuable information regarding the nature of the secondary school programs of yesteryear. It also serves as a starting point for the definition of curriculum and the study of secondary curriculum development.

SUMMARY

This chapter has provided an overview of the major historical periods in the development of secondary education and has discussed the impact of these periods on curriculum development. The evolution of secondary schools in the United States has departed significantly from European models and has produced a truly unique form of free compulsory education for all adolescents.

The Latin grammar school was the dominant form of secondary education during the colonial period (1600–1800). This school was characterized by a limited focus on subject matter, was extremely rigorous, and was almost exclusively for the sons of the wealthy. The purpose of the school was to prepare students in the classical languages (Latin and Greek) so they could enter college. The secondary student in colonial America was much younger than the secondary student today.

Secondary education in the period of the new nation (1800–1875) was characterized by the emergence of the English grammar school and the academy. Although no typical academy can be described, generally these schools incorporated the study of English and modern languages with the classical languages. In addition to the more traditional college preparatory courses, the academies also offered practical subjects to meet the future vocational needs of the students.

Education in the early twentieth century (1875–1950) was greatly influenced by the various committees and commissions that were formed specifically to study the secondary curriculum. This period produced the Carnegie unit—a basis for standardizing courses; the junior high school—a school organization pattern for the early adolescent; and the Cardinal Principles—the dominant guiding principles for secondary education.

Contemporary secondary education (1950–1990) has been influenced by events that have taken place outside of the school. The desegregation order in 1954 and the launching of Sputnik in 1957 have had a major impact on secondary school curriculum and the delivery of instruction. As a result, many innovations have been attempted in the last 30 years to meet the changes in society.

The chapter concluded with a look at various definitions of curriculum and a description of the conceptual framework for the curriculum development process. In reviewing the definitions, it becomes clear that historical events shape our view of curriculum at any given moment in time. Generally, curriculum can be viewed as subject matter or content, the experiences the learners have, the educational objectives and outcomes, and the planned activities for learning.

The curriculum development process is complex and multifaceted and involves not only the historical context, but the foundation areas of philosophy, sociology, and psychology as they impact the models and design of curriculum and the planning process. The historical overview, the various definitions of curriculum, and the conceptual framework provide a starting point for the study of secondary education and the curriculum development process.

YOUR TURN

2.1 You have been asked to defend the Cardinal Principles of Secondary Education against critics who say that they are obsolete and should be replaced. You have been selected as the representative from the local high school to present its view to the school board. To get started, examine the stated goals for high school students in the school district. Do they match the Cardinal Principles? Do the Cardinal Principles meet the needs of all the students in this school? How might you expand or edit the principles to more accurately meet the needs of the students in this high school? Write your own set of Cardinal Principles.

2.2 What issues have shaped secondary education in the 1980s? How will these issues be different in the 1990s? What forces can you project that will impact the secondary curriculum for the year 2000?

2.3 You are an exchange teacher visiting another country and have been asked to provide an overview of the secondary school system in the United States. Your audience has heard that the secondary schools in the United States are not as rigorous as the schools in the country you are visiting. The questions you have been asked to address and respond to include:
(a) Is free secondary education really available to all students?
(b) What factors have made this possible?
(c) By being open to all, aren't your expectations of students somewhat lowered?

2.4 How did the Committee of Ten view the high school and was their view similar or different from the Carnegie Commission discussed in Chapter 1?

2.5 Take a moment and reflect on the time you spent in high school. What do you remember most? What do you remember and wish you could forget? Do you feel that your high school education was comprehensive? What did or did not make it so?

2.6 Obtain a junior high science textbook and a high school science, textbook (life science, for example). Examine the contents closely. How are they similar? How are they different? What conclusions could you make about learning expectations at the junior high level and at the high school level?

REFERENCES

Aikin, W.M. (1942). *The story of the eight-year study: Vol 1 of adventure in American education.* New York: McGraw-Hill.

Association for Supervision and Curriculum Development. (September 1989). Face of school-business links changing, *ASCD Update, 31,* 6, 1–6.

Beckner, W., & Cornett, J.D. (1972). *The secondary school curriculum: Content and structure.* Scranton, Pa.: Intext Educational Publishers.

Blount, N.S., & Klausmeier, H.J. (1968). *Teaching in the secondary school* (2nd ed.). New York: Harper & Row.

Bobbitt, F. (1924). *How to make a curriculum.* Boston: Houghton Mifflin.

Bruner, J. (1960). *The process of education.* Cambridge, Mass.: Harvard University Press.

Bunker, F.P. (1916). *Reorganization of the public school system.* Washington, D.C.: Government Printing Office.

Coleman, J.S. (1966). *Equality of educational opportunity.* Washington, D.C.: Government Printing Office.

Conant, J.B. (1959). *The American high school today.* New York: McGraw-Hill.

Gruhn, W.T., & Douglas, H.R. (1956). *The modern junior high school.* New York: Ronald Press.

Gutek, G.L. (1988). *Education and schooling in America* (2nd ed.). Englewood Cliffs, N.J.: Prentice Hall.

Ikenberry, O.S. (1974). *American education foundations: An introduction.* Columbus, Ohio: Charles E. Merrill.

Jencks, C.S. (1972). *Inequality: A reassessment of the effect of family and schooling in America.* New York: Basic Books.

Krug, E.A. (1964). *The shaping of the American high school: 1880–1920.* New York: Harper & Row.

Miller, P., & Johnson, T.H. (1963). *The puritans: A sourcebook of their writings* 2 vols. New York: Harper & Row.

O'Neil, J. (November 1989). National setting of curriculum standards debated, *ASCD Update, 31,* 8, 1 & 7.

O'Neil, J. (September 1990). New curriculum agenda emerges for '90s, *ASCD Curriculum Update,* 1 & 8.

Ornstein, A.C., & Hunkins, F.P. (1988). *Curriculum: Foundations, principles and issues.* Englewood Cliffs, N.J.: Prentice Hall.

Popham, W.J., & Baker, E.I. (1970). *Systematic instruction.* Englewood Cliffs, N.J.: Prentice Hall.

Pulliam, J.D. (1976). *History of education in America* (2nd ed.). Columbus, Ohio: Charles E. Merrill.

Saylor, J.G., Alexander, W.M., & Lewis, J.A. (1981). *Curriculum planning for better teaching and learning* (4th ed.). New York: Holt, Rinehart and Winston.

Spring, J. (1986). *The American school: 1642–1985.* New York: Longman.

Taba, H. (1962). *Curriculum development: Theory and practice.* New York: Harcourt Brace Jovanovich.

Tanner, D. (1972). *Secondary education: Perspectives and prospects.* New York: Macmillan.

Tanner, D., & Tanner, L. (1980). *Curriculum development: Theory into practice* (2nd ed.). New York: Macmillan.

Texas Education Agency. (1984). *State board of education rules for curriculum.* Austin, Tx.: Texas Education Agency.

Tyler, R.W. (1957). The curriculum then and now. In *Proceedings of the 1956 Conference of Testing Problems.* Princeton, N.J.: Educational Testing Service.

Wiles, J., & Bondi, J.C. (1984). *Curriculum development: A guide to practice* (2nd ed.). Columbus, Ohio: Charles E. Merrill.

Willis, S. (February 1990). The inclusive curriculum, *ASCD Update,* 32, 2, 1, 6, & 8.

Zais, R.S. (1976). *Curriculum principles and foundations.* New York: Thomas Y. Crowell.

PART
TWO

Foundations of Secondary Curriculum

*P*art Two describes the conceptual framework that provides a visual design of the curriculum development process and focuses on the three foundations of curriculum development—philosophical, social, and psychological. These foundation areas play an important role in planning and developing the curriculum for secondary schools. This framework becomes the conceptual cornerstone, and it will be referred to throughout the text.

Part Two contains four chapters, each focusing on one of the foundations of curriculum development. Chapter 3 presents the philosophical foundations, complete with profiles of teachers and a checklist for determining one's philosophical orientation. Chapter 4 focuses on the social issues and forces that impact secondary schools, and it concludes with a discussion of the social trends and problems that secondary students and teachers will face in the decades ahead.

Part Two concludes with an analysis of the psychological foundations. Chapter 5, Foundations of Human Development and Psychology, includes an overview of the principles of growth and development. Four major developmental theories are presented along with a discussion of moral development. A description of the characteristics of adolescent cognitive, physical, and social development is included in Chapter 6. The information in these chapters is critical to understanding and meeting the individual needs of students in the secondary school.

Part Two provides the necessary information concerning the philosophical, social, and psychological forces at work in the educational process. Part Two also presents information about students in secondary schools—who they are and how they learn.

Chapter

3

Philosophical Perspectives: Foundations of Curriculum

As discussed in the previous chapter, secondary curriculum did not develop in a particular decade, but rather, it developed over time in response to a wide range of beliefs about the total educational experience. Throughout history, these beliefs have helped educators and community members in the development of educational programs and practices that are consistent and comprehensive. It is, in fact, these "we believe" ideas or statements that guide the overall functioning of the school. The "we believe" statements influence the aims, goals, content, and organization of the curriculum and are based on a philosophical orientation that has roots in the major educational philosophies. According to Beckner and Cornett (1972), "It may be that teachers and school administrators cannot be classified as philosophers, but they have been guided by the ideas and proposals of philosophers" (p. 47). These philosophical assumptions guide—either directly or indirectly—the decisions made about virtually all aspects of curriculum development (Zais, 1976).

It therefore should not be a surprise that philosophy is crucial to curriculum development. In light of the many reform documents published and state legislative mandates passed during the 1980s (as discussed in Chapter 1), there has often been no clear direction for the changes that have taken place in the secondary schools. Decisions about changes in programs, instruction, and evaluation often were made without well-defined goals and a common public consensus. If curriculum development is to be successful, curriculum specialists should ". . . clearly articulate their positions on controversial issues, . . . [or they will] slip into the all-too-common pattern of reactive thinking and action" (Wiles and Bondi, 1989, p. 40). Without clear direction, the curriculum development process becomes a patchwork of decisions resulting in educational programs that are disconnected, irrelevant, and obsolete. Since philosophy guides the educational decisions, it is one of the foundations for educational practices.

Curriculum development is a very complex process compounded by the difficulty of using various definitions for curriculum. As evidenced by the definitions of curriculum presented in Chapter 2, each definition has a set of underlying beliefs and values about people—their nature and capacity to learn. These beliefs and values are derived from a philosophy that helps provide answers to such educational questions as:

1. What subjects should be taught in secondary schools?
2. How should the subjects be taught?
3. Who should teach them?
4. Should each student take a common core of subjects? Which courses are elective and which are required?

To answer these questions, educators must think carefully and deeply about their responsibilities. Philosophy then, although literally defined as a "love of wisdom," is far more directly related to the way we live our lives. According to Zais (1976),

> . . . all of us engage in philosophizing (in an informal way) as we make decisions. . . . A philosophical disposition to place a higher value on material welfare than on spiritual renewal has caused us to spend more time in productive work activities than in reflective meditation (p. 103).

For most of us, our philosophy of life comes indirectly or informally from family, relatives, teachers, and friends as we grow up and participate in various organizations. As a result, our personal philosophy is often inconsistent and incomplete, which causes our actions to be sometimes contradictory; yet philosophy as a belief system guides our actions.

This chapter focuses on philosophy as one of the foundations of secondary curriculum development. The purpose of this chapter is to encourage secondary educators ". . . to think about what they are doing and why they are doing it" (Silberman, 1970, p. 11). As educators reflect on these questions it enables them to "develop a clear vision regarding the purpose of education and its relation to the meaning of life" (Knight, 1989, p. 3).

This chapter includes a section on the search for a philosophy. In addition, it presents an argument for the role of philosophy in education and describes how it impacts secondary programs. Three widely accepted educational philosophies—essentialism, progressivism, and existentialism—are presented. Sprinkled throughout are profiles of teachers with specific philosophical orientations to show how these philosophies are represented in the school setting.

These major philosophies are at the heart of the curriculum building process, and they give direction and focus to various components of the educational program. Included in the chapter is a conceptual framework for curriculum development. Its significance lies in the fact that philosophical assumptions drive the curriculum development and planning process.

The chapter concludes with a Philosophical Preference Checklist to assist you in determining your philosophical orientation. When you complete this chapter you should have a better understanding of the importance of philosophy in making educational decisions and, hopefully, a better understanding of what you believe about education and how you view the instructional process.

A CONCEPTUAL FRAMEWORK FOR CURRICULUM DEVELOPMENT

Educational philosophy causes us to question and make decisions about the desired ends and means of education; it brings educators "face-to-face with the large questions underlying the meaning and purpose of life and education" (Knight, 1989, p. 3). The conceptual framework of curriculum development shown in Figure 3.1 depicts how the philosophical assumptions guide all other decisions related to the curriculum development process. According to this framework, philosophical assumptions shape beliefs about the nature of knowledge, the societal/cultural context, individual growth and development, and the theories of teaching and learning. Beliefs influence the educational decisions that are made.

A philosophical value system shapes these decisions relative to the ends and means of education and helps to establish a vision, for as Zais (1976) notes,

> Every society is held together by a common faith or "philosophy" which serves its members as a guide for living the good life. It is natural, then, for the adults . . . to want to pass this philosophy—or "knowledge of the good"—on to their children . . . [and so] schools are established to induct the young into the ways of living that adults consider good. Thus, the curriculum . . . whatever else . . . is first and foremost designed to win the hearts and minds of the young to those principles and ideals (p. 105).

Philosophy provides the basis for making decisions regarding the secondary instructional program relative to how it is organized, what subjects will be included, how students will be evaluated, and perhaps most importantly, what the overall purpose of secondary education will be. Philosophy, then, prompts educators working in secondary schools to consider and respond to questions that are value-laden. Responses to particular questions establish educational boundaries that give direction and focus to secondary education and specific programs in schools. As goals are shaped by a basic belief system, so too are the goals shaped by the complexities of the current social milieu.

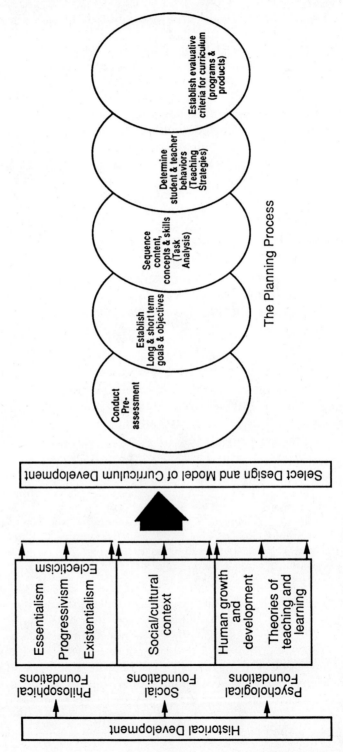

Figure 3.1 The conceptual framework of curriculum development

THREE AREAS OF PHILOSOPHY

Philosophy embodies two aspects: attitudes and a body of knowledge. According to Knight (1989) the set of attitudes may include flexibility, comprehensiveness, and self-awareness. These attitudes help educators evaluate their thinking about school relative to means (strategies and procedures) and ends (goals and objectives). As a body of knowledge, philosophy has been organized into three major areas. These areas seek answers to the questions associated with each of them.

1. *Epistemology:* What is true? What is the nature of truth and how is it achieved? How do we come to know? What are the sources of knowledge?
2. *Ontology:* What is real? What is the nature of reality?
3. *Axiology:* What is good? What is good in ethics as well as aesthetics? What is moral and what is beautiful?

The first area of philosophy, *epistemology*, is the study of truth and deals with educational questions related to ". . . how we know the sources of knowledge" (Beckner and Cornett, 1972, p. 49). In fact, the importance of epistemology in curriculum development can be seen in the continuing debate over whether it is the biblical or the Darwinian version of the origin of man that should be taught (Zais, 1976). In trying to determine which version is authentic or "the truth" and to define knowledge, Zais says, "it is the epistemological question — of all philosophical questions — that is of most concern to curriculum specialists since . . . knowledge is what the curriculum is all about" (p. 111).

Philosophers, in arriving at or determining the "truth," have considered several sources of knowledge, which include:

1. *Received* or *Revealed:* knowledge received from a supernatural source, divine revelation, or domain such as a supreme deity or the human soul, which is accepted by faith and supported by reason and experience.
2. *Authoritative:* knowledge from experts certified as authentic and accepted as true.
3. *Intuitive:* knowledge from the subliminal level involving emotions and a source of creativity.
4. *Rational:* knowledge obtained from valid judgments that have proven consistent with one another and have been based on the organization and interpretation of facts.
5. *Empirical* or *Discovered:* knowledge obtained through the senses which involves testing theories through observation and experimentation.
6. *Constructed:* knowledge constructed from experience in the world and conceptions about the world and universe.

Although one could consider all sources of truth and knowledge in the curriculum development process, Bruner (1960) considered intuition very important because it is the "intellectual technique of arriving at plausible but tentative formulations without going through the analytical steps. . . . [Intuition is] an essential feature of productive thinking, not only in formal academic disciplines but also in everyday life" (p. 13).

Ontology, often called *metaphysics*, is the area of philosophy that seeks to answer the questions: What is reality? What is real? In answering these questions, the individual "tries to distinguish between 'What is real' and 'What only appears to be real' . . . to determine the ultimate reality" (Ikenberry, 1974, p. 199). With the physical universe constantly changing, nothing physical can be considered absolute or ultimate. For Ikenberry, this dilemma has prompted the posing of the ultimate philosophical question, "Is reality mind or matter?" (p. 199).

In order to foster a more complete understanding of what is real, the following fields have often been cited as support for information and insight:

1. *Anthropology* explores the nature of individuals and the relationship between mind and body.
2. *Cosmology* explores the origin, nature, and development of the universe.
3. *Theology* describes the nature of God through beliefs, creeds, and rituals.
4. *Teleology* examines the question of purpose in the universe.
5. *Evolution* establishes the process of change in the universe based on the theory of evolution.

According to Zais (1976), throughout history individuals have used these areas of study to support or explain three major views of reality: (1) reality that exists in a supernatural realm; (2) reality that exists in the natural world—the matter of the universe; and (3) reality that exists in human experience, the individual. Each of these three views of reality impact the educational programs of secondary schools as educators, parents, and others in the community define reality for students.

The final area of philosophical study is *axiology*. This field of study is concerned with the nature of values and seeks to answer the questions: What is good? What is desirable? According to Beckner and Cornett (1972), the study of values usually focuses on three main questions:

1. *Are values objective or subjective?* Are they impersonal or personal? Objective or impersonal values possess intrinsic value and exist regardless of . . . personal feelings or desires—truth, goodness, and beauty for example. Conversely, subjective or personal values are relative to personal desire; truth and goodness depend on the particular circumstances and situations that apply to them.
2. *Are values changing or constant?* Absolute values are constant and unchanging, while changing values respond to . . . immediate needs—they are relative, and always subject to revision.

3. *Are there hierarchies of value?* A person's general philosophy determines whether or not he [or she] believes in a hierarchy of values (p. 51).

Axiological concerns are further divided into two subcategories: *ethics* and *aesthetics*. *Ethics* is the study of moral values and conduct and examines rightness and wrongness of actions. For Ikenberry (1974), "Ethics is concerned with the nature of what is 'good' and what is 'bad' for the individual and society" (p. 202). This field of philosophy serves to provide guidelines for individuals to use in making important decisions in life and seeks to provide guidance for the improvement of society. The importance of this area of philosophy has been attested to recently with concern for ethical behavior in government, business, and, especially, the ministry. Blanchard and Peale (1988) in their book *The Power of Ethical Management* provide three questions to guide ethical behavior. These questions are:

1. *It is legal?* Will I be violating either civil law or . . . [school] policy?
2. *Is it balanced?* Is it fair to all concerned in the short term as well as the long term? Does it promote win-win relationships?
3. *How will it make me feel about myself?* Will it make me proud? Would I feel good if my decision were published in the newspaper? Would I feel good if my family knew about it? (p. 27).

Aesthetics is the study of values related to the nature of beauty, especially in the areas of the fine arts. Questions to be answered in this area of study include: What is art? What is beautiful? What is the purpose and value of aesthetic (artistic) experience and/or expression? For Zais (1976), the questions are more personal and involve, "What should I like? What are those sensations of sight, hearing, smell, touch, and taste that yield the highest level of enjoyment?" (p. 120).

For curriculum developers, the inclusion of aesthetic experiences in the educational program is designed to promote "good taste" and a sense of the quality of life reflected in music, art, theatre, and dance. The focus is often to cultivate in students those "dispositions to like and appreciate what *ought* to be appreciated" (Zais, 1976, p. 121). Aesthetic experiences in schools are designed to provide opportunities for pleasure, creativity, communication, and recreation.

The axiological concerns and questions presented here are of extreme importance to educators in the curriculum development process because the goals of education and the subsequent content and learning experiences "constitute a declaration of what is considered to be of value for the individual and society" (Ikenberry, 1974, p. 202). Beckner and Cornett (1972) provide a list of some value-laden questions that educators should confront in the development of curriculum.

1. Do we teach subject matter or do we teach students? Which should be emphasized?
2. Should a teacher yield to the values and beliefs of the community, or should the teacher teach his or her own convictions about right and wrong?
3. Which character traits and how many should be taught?

Curriculum development, with the resulting content, documents, and strategies, is built on values associated with a "good education."

THE SEARCH FOR A PHILOSOPHY

What is a philosophy? How does a personal philosophy develop? What is the role of philosophy in directing secondary programs toward goals and productive ends? The answers to these questions require more information to formulate philosophical positions that translate into successful school programs. At the beginning of this chapter, it was emphasized that "schooling is a moral venture, one that necessitates choosing values among innumerable possibilities. These choices constitute the starting point in curriculum planning" (Saylor and Alexander, 1974, pp. 144–145).

Determining the purpose and means of education normally generates a series of different opinions. As secondary teachers make decisions relative to instruction, the decisions are based on one or more philosophies. If, for example, educators favor the development of a student's mind, then their beliefs and values reflect an essentialist point of view. If, on the other hand, educators support a school program that encourages students to "be themselves," to engage in self-discovery and self-generated learning, then an existentialist view is held.

Making choices about special programs and students can be traced to a philosophy of education. The answers to critical questions regarding planning for secondary programs are arrived at through the philosophy by examining (1) the means and ends of education in the light of past knowledge, present social concerns, and future needs of society and (2) the needs of the learners (Wiles and Bondi, 1989).

McNeil (1976) has developed eight questions that are helpful in reviewing the assumptions about a philosophy used to screen educational objectives. These questions include:

1. Is the purpose of school to change, adapt to, or accept the social order?
2. What can a school do better than any other agency or institution?
3. What objectives should be common to all?
4. Should objectives stress cooperation or competition?
5. Should objectives deal with controversial issues, or only those things for which there is established knowledge?
6. Should attitudes be taught? Fundamental skills? Problem solving strategies?
7. Should teachers emphasize subject matter or try to create behavior outside of school?
8. Should objectives be based on the needs of the local community? Society in general? Expressed needs of students? (pp. 91–92).

Responses to these eight questions provide reasons or a rationale that help secondary teachers and others involved in the curriculum development process to articulate their attitudes and feelings about each issue. In discussing the importance of educational philosophy, Tanner and Tanner (1987) note that how ". . . sources and influences [on the curriculum] are seen and acted on is determined by the philosophy of the professional staff" (p. 342). Philosophy is also important because it provides a screen through which the general goals of education pass and gives ". . . meaning and direction to actions taken by [secondary] teachers regarding the curriculum" (Beach and Reinhartz, 1989, p. 102).

By examining one's attitudes and beliefs, a value structure begins to emerge. This self-examination process is essential if secondary teachers are to identify their values — their philosophy. A philosophy, according to Bigge (1982), ". . . is a comprehensive . . . theory consisting of a broad pattern of ideas [for] which there is considerable . . . supporting evidence" (p. 1). It should also be noted, however, that few educators adhere to a pure view of any single philosophy, but ". . . whatever the educator's philosophy or beliefs about schools, . . . it is critical that these values be clarified and understood in terms of their implications" (Wiles and Bondi, 1984, p. 79). Later in this chapter you will have the opportunity to assess your own values or ideas — your philosophy of education.

PHILOSOPHIES OF EDUCATION

A philosophy of education includes the guiding principles which influence our thinking about educational content, purpose, and methodology. For Beckner and Cornett (1972), "All educational questions are rooted in philosophy and all philosophy has implications for education" (p. 47). As implemented in schools, educational philosophy statements are clusters of ideas that reflect the general intentions of the program of instruction and emphasize what is good and important. Even though philosophy statements often lack specificity, they ". . . attempt to bring together many perspectives regarding purposes of in-structional programs" (Armstrong, 1989, p. 98). Philosophy, then, is the cor-nerstone when building the curricular program in the secondary school.

The role of philosophy in curriculum development is important because the philosophy governs the way in which we (1) view the student (who), (2) determine the scope or content (what), and (3) establish the sequence (when) of the curriculum, as well as (4) the methodology used to teach it (Reinhartz, 1980). If educators are not aware of the impact of educational philosophy on curriculum and instruction, the educational process becomes vulnerable to externally imposed or societal pressures, which may be fashionable at a given time but are not necessarily educationally sound (Beach and Reinhartz, 1989).

Although entire books and courses have been developed to examine the components, characteristics, beliefs, and implications of educational philoso-phies in great detail, our purpose here is to describe briefly three major philosophies that have had a significant impact on American secondary education — essentialism, progressivism, and existentialism. Each educational philosophy has its roots in one of the traditional or contemporary philosophical systems as seen below:

Educational Philosophy	Root Philosophy
Essentialism	Idealism and Realism
Progressivism	Experimentalism and Pragmatism
Existentialism	Existentialism

Essentialism: The essentialist philosophy cannot be linked directly to a single traditional philosophy but is generally considered to be a combination of idealism and realism. According to Ikenberry (1974), "Essentialism has dominated education since ancient times and continues to be the dominant worldwide philosophy" (p. 210). Basic principles which summarize the essentialist position include:

1. Education is by nature constant and timeless.
2. Education should concentrate on the development of the mind through knowledge and reason.
3. Education should only be concerned with the pursuit of truth, which is universal.
4. Education should prepare students for life by giving them the basics or essentials of knowledge.
5. Education is comprised of basic content or essential knowledge that should teach students about the permanencies of the world—both spiritual and physical.

The central tenet of the philosophy is the emphasis on a foundation of knowledge as the most important function of education. In establishing this knowledge base, there is support for the liberal arts—English, mathematics, science, history, foreign languages, and other traditional, basic subjects. According to Wilds and Lottich (1970):

> While . . . significant variations in philosophy [exist] among the essentialists, they are as one in prescribing the following rubrics for their educational programs:
>
> 1. A fixed curriculum
> 2. Certain minimum 'essentials': literature, mathematics, history, and so on
> 3. Preconceived educational values
> 4. Education as individual adaptation to an absolute knowledge which exists independently of individuals (p. 504).

In carrying out the essentialist curriculum, the educational program is subject-centered, formally organized, and courses such as the performing arts, industrial arts, vocational studies, and physical education are often considered frills, or nonessentials. In the essentialist view, the main purpose of the curriculum is to equip students with intellectual powers, and the students' interests are secondary to the pursuit of academic excellence. The purpose of school is to teach basic skills through a uniform curriculum, and learning is measured by rigorous testing, and as a result, students are "sorted" (ability-grouped) based on the test results (Beach and Reinhartz, 1989).

In Box 3-1, the profile of an educator is given as an example of the essentialist approach to curriculum development. As you read the first profile,

---

Box 3-1   **Profile: Essentialism**

As an English teacher I feel it is extremely important for students to read the classics, which stress the great ideas of authors from each of the major periods of literature. The argument is often made that the classics are difficult to read, that they are in the vernacular of a different time and place, and therefore should not be taught. The argument is often supported with the data that the students are reading on the sixth grade level and cannot comprehend these great pieces of literature. It is my belief, however, that I am not wasting my time or the time of my students by having them vicariously experience different cultures in different times and places of the globe. I believe that it is essential that students be exposed to the literature of the ages so that they can more fully understand the great ideas of past civilizations, cultures, and customs. For me these essentials represent the basic foundation for comprehending more recent literary genres and contemporary writing. This study of the great works provides the building blocks for effective written and oral communication skills.

---

identify the critical attributes of the essentialist philosophy expressed by the English teacher.

Progressivism: The second educational philosophy, progressivism, is based on the philosophies of experimentalism and pragmatism. In the view of the progressive educator, students are thinking beings who are capable of solving social problems based on their experience in the world. The architect of progressivism was Dewey (1902, 1906), who defined *experience* as the students' interaction with the environment and believed that the purpose of education is to cultivate problem solving skills. Dewey (1964) clearly expressed the emphasis on experience in this philosophy in his pedagogic creed when he wrote,

> education . . . is a process of living and not a preparation for future living . . . education must be conceived as a continuing reconstruction of experience; . . . the process and the goal are one and the same . . . (pp. 430–434).

Dewey (1906) in *Democracy and Education* further emphasized the concept of experience when he said,

> We thus reach a technical definition of education: it is that reconstruction or reorganization of experience which adds to the meaning of experience and which increases the ability to direct the course of subsequent ability (p. 89).

Therefore, progressivism can be considered an action-oriented philosophy that "sees thought as intrinsically connected with action. The value of an idea is measured by the consequences [results] produced when it is translated into action" (Rosen, 1968, p. 67).

School programs, when viewed through the progressive philosophy, should mirror society and, like society, require social interaction as a part of the curriculum. Thus, learning is an active process which requires that all students participate, and the learning environment should be student-centered, with the teacher serving as a guide or director. As noted by Beach and Reinhartz (1989), the progressive educator believes that experience is the best source of knowledge, and therefore knowledge is gained only by means of experience. According to Atkinson and Maleska (1965) the following principles represent the foundations of the progressive education philosophy:

1. Individual differences among . . . [students] must be recognized.
2. We learn best by doing and by having a vital interest in what we are doing.
3. Education is a continuous reconstruction of living experience that goes beyond the four walls of the classroom.
4. The classroom [or school] should be a laboratory for democracy.
5. Social goals, as well as intellectual goals, are important.
6. A [student] . . . must be taught to think critically rather than to accept blindly (p. 89).

In designing the curriculum for the secondary school, the progressive educator emphasizes the scientific method—identify problem, hypothesize, experiment, collect data, and draw conclusions—to solve social problems. Thus, according to Beach and Reinhartz (1989), "the progressive teacher tends to use an inductive approach to learning" (p. 104). The curriculum, from science to history to language and literature, involves a series of process experiences in which students find themselves; and by using the scientific method, students identify problems and then determine the best methods and strategies for problem solutions.

In the profile in Box 3-2, an example of a progressive view of curriculum development is presented. What are the qualities or characteristics of progressivism that are expressed in the description of the teaching using cooperative learning and problem solving strategies?

Existentialism: The third philosophy, *existentialism*, places a great deal of emphasis on personal freedom and individual responsibility. The basic tenets of the philosophy hold that individuals exist in a world in which they are required to make choices within the context of the "anguish of freedom" (Beach and Reinhartz, 1989). However, according to Ikenberry (1974), "The individualism that is fundamental to existentialism is difficult to envision in the structured environment of American education" (p. 219). For the existentialist, the curriculum development process should provide students with the opportunity to make choices, for it is through the choice-making process that students find meaning in their lives, discover their personal worth and capabilities, and determine their strengths and weaknesses.

The goal of education is to provide opportunities for individual freedom and uniqueness and to help each student achieve self-development and self-fulfillment. As Ikenberry (1974) states, an existentialistic curriculum should not establish preconceived aims for the student, but should:

1. Make students aware of the meaning of life for themselves on a personal level

Box 3-2 **Profile: Progressivism**

At our school teachers use cooperative learning and problem solving strategies. Whether the students are in mathematics, science, or social studies, we encourage them to work in groups and to interact with materials and data to deal with a dilemma or situation which they are given. The group arrives at a decision and offers suggestions for ways to solve the problem—be it scientific (environmental, health), social (societal conditions), and/or governmental (drugs). Stressing a hands-on, collaborative, learner-centered approach when dealing with hypothetical situations provides secondary students with the skills they will need to help solve problems they encounter as they enter the adult world and assume their roles as responsible citizens.

2. Encourage students to develop their own personal ethical value system and philosophy of life
3. Assist students in recognizing their own areas of strength and weakness, and then develop their abilities to the maximum potential
4. Impress on students that the freedom to make decisions requires them to accept a corresponding responsibility for their decisions

Existentialists would not advocate a structured curriculum, for in their view, little attention should be given to systematic learning. According to Tanner and Tanner (1980), to awaken the student existentially,

> the curriculum should provide considerable time for private introspection and the study of moral questions concerning . . . [the human] predicament. . . . Moreover, the subject matter should not be focused on objective knowledge but on the individual. . . . For example, the social studies should deal with the meaning of individual freedom rather than citizenship, social institutions or organized race experiences (pp. 134–135).

In such an educational program, the arts and literature are included in the curriculum as content areas that help the students confront the human condition. However, no content area exists as a rigid course of study.

When existentialist ideas are implemented in a school, they frequently are put into practice in small private schools with homogeneous populations (Tanner and Tanner, 1980), but also take various forms, from totally student-run programs such as A.S. Neill's (1960) Summerhill School, to the use of individualized programs in public schools that utilize learning packets or learning centers.

When developing curriculum within the existentialistic view, subject matter or knowledge of content assists the students to develop self-knowledge, and

Box 3-3 **Profile: Existentialism**

Our school follows a philosophy that treats each student as a lamp to be lighted rather than a vessel to be filled. We recognize the uniqueness of each student. In our school students have opportunities to improve their self-concepts and to learn about their strengths and weaknesses as they interact with peers and adult role models. The teachers, under the guidance of the principal, plan school projects and activities directed toward helping all students experience success. The "I am special" and "I can do" attitudes develop over time as students in their day-to-day activities experience personal satisfaction and growth along with academic success. Teachers plan instructional activities that are based on self-improvement plans for students and are designed to provide a sense of worth and accomplishment.

the teacher functions as a facilitator who guides students in making choices, thereby helping them to develop the confidence to think for themselves (Beach and Reinhartz, 1989). Such a curriculum design and delivery system would favor individual projects or small group activities that foster individual creativity, freedom, and decision making. According to Ikenberry (1974),

> Special provisions are made in the curriculum to meet individual differences in ability, interest, need, aptitude, personality, and character. . . . The existentialist teacher . . . plans cooperatively with each student . . . [and] never imposes his [or her] goals upon his [or her] students, but guides each student in a non-directive manner, to develop his [or her] own life goals and commitments (p. 220).

The existential curriculum allows, even encourages, the student to search for personal identity and meaningfulness within the school framework.

The profile in Box 3-3 provides a description of a school that is implementing aspects of the existential philosophy. As you read the profile, describe the qualities of existentialism that are represented in the description of the school.

Although three distinct educational philosophies have been presented here, Wiles and Bondi (1989) assert that, ". . . few educators hold a pure version of any of these philosophies, for schools are complex places with many forces vying for prominence" (p. 51). Frequently, what happens in approaching curriculum development is that educators combine, blend, or selectively apply portions of different philosophies, which results in *eclecticism*, or an eclectic approach. In working with curriculum in their classrooms, the eclectic position is most attractive to teachers as they apply philosophic preferences according to the situation(s) and condition(s). Bigge (1982), however, notes that while "eclecticism has its strengths, it provides no defensible, systematic basis for knowing when to use discrete aspects of respective positions"; however, eclectic compromise can be reached by "selecting aspects of opposing theories and taking a position somewhere between them" (p. 3).

Table 3.1   THREE PHILOSOPHIES OF EDUCATION: AN OVERVIEW

Philosophy	Instructional Focus	Curriculum	Methodology	Nature of Learner
Essentialism	The world of ideas, cultivation of knowledge, pursuit of academic excellence	Subject matter of the academic disciplines (the liberal arts, math, science, etc.)	Drill and practice, memorization	Thinking, rational individual
Progressivism	Cooperative learning, problem solving, emphasis on experience	Comprehensive core, interdisciplinary, problem-focused	Interactive groups, reflective thinking	Responsible, socially oriented, interested in good of mankind
Existentialism	Search for meaning, emphasis on personal development	Moral philosophy, individual choice of content selection	Learning centers, individualized instruction	Highly individual; choice maker unfolds

The influence of educational philosophy on practice cannot be underestimated, and Tanner and Tanner (1987) reemphasize the importance of philosophy when they state that

> the philosophy one subscribes to determines the use to which the behavioral sciences are put in connection with (1) the nature of the learner, (2) the nature of the society, and (3) the design of the curriculum (p. 344).

An overview of each educational philosophy is presented in Table 3.1 above, which outlines the implications for curriculum development in secondary classrooms. The philosophical tenets identified in Table 3.1 can be used to examine instructional goals. They can then seek to determine if there are conflicting views regarding:

1. The type of educational experiences the curriculum should provide
2. What content or knowledge seems most helpful
3. The nature of the learner

WHAT IS YOUR PHILOSOPHY?

Now that you have read about the three major educational philosophies, what is your orientation? Read carefully each of the 36 statements in the Philosophical Preference Checklist shown in Box 3-4 and circle the number that best describes your feelings. If you agree with the statement strongly, circle the number 5. If you disagree strongly, circle the number 1. If your feelings are in between these two extremes, circle one of the other numbers. Do not spend

BOX 3-4 Philosophical Preference Checklist

Directions: Using the 1–5 rating, mark a 1 if you strongly disagree and a 5 if you strongly agree.

	STRONGLY DISAGREE				STRONGLY AGREE
1. Effective teachers pose a lot of questions and encourage students to ask questions.	1	2	3	4	5
2. The purpose of schools is to improve society by finding solutions to problems.	1	2	3	4	5
3. Effective teachers frequently use an inquiry technique.	1	2	3	4	5
4. Teacher demonstrations and class recitations are important strategies to promote learning.	1	2	3	4	5
5. Students should be allowed to develop the rules which govern their educational process.	1	2	3	4	5
6. To be relevant, curriculum should reflect the laws of nature.	1	2	3	4	5
7. The school curriculum should include and emphasize social problems and issues.	1	2	3	4	5
8. The students' experiences and opinions help them to understand the truth.	1	2	3	4	5
9. The main role of the teacher is to facilitate learning.	1	2	3	4	5
10. In order to promote learning the teacher should be the subject matter specialist in the classroom.	1	2	3	4	5
11. The most effective teaching strategies are lecture and discussion.	1	2	3	4	5
12. Schools should provide a curriculum which is a "smorgasbord" for students to select from.	1	2	3	4	5
13. The main role of the student is to receive and process information.	1	2	3	4	5
14. Active involvement of the students is the key to learning essential concepts and process skills.	1	2	3	4	5
15. The main purpose of education is to foster the intellectual competencies of students.	1	2	3	4	5
16 Good teachers present and interpret information for their students.	1	2	3	4	5
17. There are basic skills that all students must learn.	1	2	3	4	5
18. A subject-centered approach is the most effective curiculum in the schools.	1	2	3	4	5
19. Students should be actively involved in providing input into projects and school programs.	1	2	3	4	5
20. Teachers serve as role models for their students.	1	2	3	4	5

BOX 3-4 Philosophical Preference Checklist — Continued

	STRONGLY DISAGREE				STRONGLY AGREE
21. The most productive learning takes place in a less structured, more informal environment.	1	2	3	4	5
22. The curriculum should be organized around the needs and interests of the students to provide choices in the classroom.	1	2	3	4	5
23. The most effective learning focuses on the needs and interests of the students.	1	2	3	4	5
24. Knowledge and truth are changing and are determined by circumstances and situations.	1	2	3	4	5
25. The common consensus of society is the best determiner of contemporary standards of behavior (morality).	1	2	3	4	5
26. Knowledge is acquired mainly through the senses.	1	2	3	4	5
27. There is a basic set of knowledge and skills that every student should learn.	1	2	3	4	5
28. One role of the school is to facilitate a reflective nature and self-awareness.	1	2	3	4	5
29. Change is an ongoing, ever-present process.	1	2	3	4	5
30. The inquiry approach is the best way to teach most subjects.	1	2	3	4	5
31. The essence of education is knowledge and skills.	1	2	3	4	5
32. The school should provide group thinking opportunities that encourage cooperation rather than competition.	1	2	3	4	5
33. The school should provide an atmosphere of mental discipline that fosters individual intellectualism and creative thinking.	1	2	3	4	5
34. The school should provide the students with opportunities to explore problems that face mankind within a context that allows the students to make choices and to consider the consequences of their actions.	1	2	3	4	5
35. The primary concern of education should be the development of the uniqueness in each student.	1	2	3	4	5
36. The teacher should provide an education for the "whole child," centering attention on the needs and interests of the student.	1	2	3	4	5

(continued)

BOX 3-4 **Philosophical Preference Checklist — Continued**

Scoring: The following sets of items from the checklist relate to the three major philosophies of education:
Essentialism: 4, 6, 10, 11, 13, 15, 16, 17, 18, 27, 31, 33.
Progressivism: 2, 3, 7, 9, 14, 19, 20, 25, 29, 30, 32, 36.
Existentialism: 1, 5, 8, 12, 21, 22, 23, 24, 26, 28, 34, 25.

1. For each set of items (e.g., the 12 statements for essentialism) add the value of the answers circled. In a single set of numbers, the total should fall between 12 (all 1s) and 60 (all 5s).
2. Divide the total score for each set of items by 3 (example: 60/3 = 20).
3. Plot the scores on the graph in Box 3-5.

time analyzing each statement, but simply read it and respond with your first inclination.

Once you have made a decision about each statement, check the key at the end of the list to determine the number of statements that are included in each philosophical orientation (essentialism, progressivism, existentialism). Plot your results on the Personal Philosophy of Education Graph in Box 3-5.

Analyze your graph. What philosophical orientation do you have? As a curriculum developer planning secondary programs, how will this information influence or affect your job? What information do you have now that you did not have before? Do you have a dominant philosophy or does your graph show approximately equal points that represent an eclectic philosophy of education?

This chapter ends with encouraging news for secondary educators as you reflect on what you believe about adolescents, what they should learn, and how they should be taught. The exercises in reflective thinking are valuable as you work with others to find answers to the pressing educational questions and deal with controversial issues regarding the social as well as intellectual needs of secondary students.

SUMMARY

Philosophy and how it influences or impacts the curriculum development and planning process was the focus of Chapter 3. Philosophy is described as one of the foundations of the secondary curriculum development process (see Figure 3.1) and provides definition for what we do and what we say. Our identity as educators is revealed through our philosophy, and it is these "we believe . . ." statements that help educators make decisions about programs, procedures, personnel, and students. Asking ethical questions forces educators to focus on the following:

BOX 3-5 **Personal Philosophy of Education Graph**

```
20
19
18
17
16
15
14
13
12
11
10
 9
 8
 7
 6
 5
 4
 3
 2
 1
```

ESSENTIALISM   PROGRESSIVISM   EXISTENTIALISM

1. What is a philosophy and how is it formed and developed?
2. What are the three major areas of philosophy, and why are they important?
3. What is philosophy's role in curriculum development?
4. What are the major educational philosophies, and what are their origins?
5. What is your philosophy of education related to curriculum development?

The study of philosophy as presented in Chapter 3 provides an overview that sets the stage for finding out what we believe and encourages us to think seriously about our responsibilities. The chapter presented a conceptual model that highlights the role of philosophy in the curriculum development process.

This chapter also described the three areas of philosophy — epistemology, ontology, and axiology — as well as three major philosophies of education —

essentialism, progressivism, and existentialism. Taken together, these elements help provide guideposts in the development of a personal philosophy of education. The chapter concluded with an activity that helps the reader assess his or her educational philosophy.

YOUR TURN

3.1 Complete the Philosophical Preference Checklist (Box 3-4) and determine your philosophical orientation(s) by plotting your scores on a graph. Does your score accurately reflect what you believe about the means and ends of education? Compare your scores with at least two other educators.

3.2 Take one of the profiles provided in the chapter and rewrite it so that it represents your philosophy according to the Checklist.

3.3 One's philosophical orientation influences the curricular approach taken and the methods used in a classroom. Based on what you know about your philosophical orientation and your teaching area(s), how would you answer the following questions?
   (a) What basic themes or topics should be studied in your field?
   (b) To what degree should underrepresented groups be included in the curriculum in your field(s)?
   (c) What are students supposed to get out of your subject?

3.4 "All educational questions," according to Beckner and Cornett (1972), ". . . are rooted in philosophy and have implications for education." Using this quote, how would you address the following issues in planning for the curriculum of the next decade?
   (a) AIDS education
   (b) Sex education
   (c) Catastrophic illness (euthanasia)
   (d) Discrimination
   (e) Environmental issues
   (f) Natural disasters
   (g) Global interdependence

3.5 Check curriculum guides or other documents generated by a school district and review the philosophy or mission statement. List all the "We believe . . ." statements regarding the purpose of education, the role of the school, the role of parents, students, the learning environment, teaching approaches, grouping and/or individualized instruction. Analyze each and label according to which philosophical orientation each statement reflects.

3.6 Evaluate the philosophy or mission statement of a school using the following questions and criteria.
   (a) Is the statement consistent with the purposes of the larger community?
      To a great degree   *Somewhat*   *Not at all*
   (b) Is attention given to the intellectual, moral, and social development of students?
      To a great degree   *Somewhat*   *Not at all*
   (c) Are there provisions for helping individual students grow and develop?
      To a great degree   *Somewhat*   *Not at all*

(d) Is the nature of learning and knowledge applied to students and their individual development?

To a great degree   *Somewhat*   *Not at all*

(e) Is the philosophy of the school evident in daily practice in the classroom?

To a great degree   *Somewhat*   *Not at all*

(f) Is there a relationship with other educational agencies (colleges, libraries, museums)?

To a great degree   *Somewhat*   *Not at all*

(g) Is change evident (stated, or not stated but implied) and possible as the school moves into the next century?

To a great degree   *Somewhat*   *Not at all*

REFERENCES

Armstrong, D.G. (1989). *Developing and documenting the curriculum*. Boston: Allyn and Bacon.

Atkinson, C. & Maleska, E.T. (1965). *The story of education* (2nd ed.). Philadelphia: Chilton.

Beach, D.M. & Reinhartz, J. (1989). *Supervision: Focus on instruction*. New York: Harper & Row.

Beckner, W. & Cornett, J.D. (1972). *The secondary school curriculum: Content and structure*. San Francisco: Intext Educational Publishers.

Bigge, M.L. (1982). *Educational philosophies for teachers*. Columbus, Ohio: Charles E. Merrill.

Blanchard, K. & Peale, N.V. (1988). *The power of ethical management*. New York: William Morrow Co.

Bruner, J. (1960). *The process of education*. Cambridge, Mass.: Harvard University Press.

Dewey, J. (1964). *John Dewey on education: Selected writings*. R.D. Archambault (Ed.). New York: Random House.

Dewey, J. (1906). *Democracy and education*. New York: Macmillan.

Dewey, J. (1902). *The child and the curriculum*. Chicago: University of Chicago Press.

Ikenberry, O.S. (1974). *American education foundations: An introduction*. Columbus, Ohio: Charles E. Merrill.

Knight, G.R. (1989). *Issues and alternatives in educational philosophy*. Berrien Springs, Mich.: Andrews University Press.

McNeil, J.D. (1976). *Designing curriculum: Self-instructional modules*. Boston: Little Brown.

Neill, A.S. (1960). *Summerhill*. New York: Hart.

Reinhartz, J. (Spring 1980). Stemming the tide: A case against spontaneous curriculum generation. *Alpha Delta Kappan, 10*, 2, 6–8.

Rosen, B. (1968). *Philosophic systems and education*. Columbus, Ohio: Charles E. Merrill.

Saylor, G. & Alexander, W.M. (1974). *Planning curriculum for schools*. New York: Holt, Rinehart & Winston.

Silberman, C.E. (1970). *Crisis in the classroom: The remaking of American education*. New York: Vintage Books.

Tanner, D. & Tanner, L. (1987). *Supervision in education: Problems and practices*. New York: Macmillan.

Tanner, D. & Tanner, L. (1980). *Curriculum development: Theory into practice* (2nd ed.). New York: Macmillan.

Wilds, E.H. & Lottich, K.V. (1970). *The foundations of modern education* (4th ed.). New York: Holt, Rinehart & Winston.

Wiles, J. & Bondi, J. (1984). *Curriculum development: A guide to practice* (2nd ed.). Columbus, Ohio: Charles E. Merrill.

Wiles, J. & Bondi, J. (1989). *Curriculum development: A guide to practice* (3rd ed.). Columbus, Ohio: Charles E. Merrill.

Zais, R.S. (1976). *Curriculum principles and foundations*. New York: Harper & Row.

Chapter
4

Social Foundations of Curriculum Development

As discussed in previous chapters, which discussed contemporary trends and historical foundations, curriculum development and the instructional process do not occur in a vacuum. The cultural and social emphases at a given moment in time provide the context in which schools operate and influence "the nature and organization of curriculum objectives, content, learning activities, and evaluation" (Zais, 1976, p. 156). Through the education process, individuals learn to behave in ways that members of a given society consider appropriate and necessary. These ways of behaving change as the culture and society change, and are reflected in the educational process in schools, although normally at a much slower pace. Educational practices ultimately reflect the expectations of society.

The social foundations of curriculum development perhaps have the most direct impact on curriculum development because of the importance of the social and cultural settings. The social environment, in which educators and curriculum developers function, is complex and, as noted in the 1989/90 *Annual Editions, Education*, the demands of society ultimately affect the schools either indirectly or directly, by . . . major social phenomena. Changes in the social structure . . . have an impact [on] educational systems [which] are integral parts of the broader social system. . . . If the larger social system experiences fundamental change, this is reflected in the curricula and other aspects of the educational systems (p. 222).

An analysis of the needs, problems, trends, and requirements of a particular society and culture helps identify the key issues that must be addressed in the curriculum development process. Counts (1934), one of the early advocates of social considerations in educational planning, notes,

The historical record shows that education is always a function of time, place, and circumstance. . . . It inevitably reflects in varying proportions the experiences, the conditions, and the hopes, fears, and aspirations of a particular people or cultural group at a particular point in history (p. 1).

Since schools are the major institutions organized and operated by society to equip individuals for life in that society, the study of curriculum implies the study of culture and society. As schools assume more and more responsibility for what have traditionally been family functions (i.e., breakfast, after school programs, day care), the school reflects society. High school students reflect the values of a consuming society in their efforts to get jobs and gain economic independence in order to buy cars, clothes, records, tapes, videos, and other material goods. Under these circumstances, Johnson (1967) notes, the only possible source of curriculum is "the total available culture" (p. 132).

If secondary students had no life away from the school, curriculum developers and teachers might have an easier task of planning because they could ignore the influence and impact of the cultural milieu on society and the curriculum. But since students do live in a world bigger than the classroom and school, that world has a tremendous influence, especially on the interests and behaviors of adolescents (Beane, Toepfer, and Alessi, 1986). Teachers, as well as others responsible for curriculum development, must recognize the characteristics of contemporary society and the factors that shape the culture and ultimately shape society. Curriculum specialists also must consider future needs of students, as the students will live in a world different from today's.

Affirming the importance of the role of society in curriculum development, this chapter discusses the nature of culture and society, the social roles of the schools and curriculum, and the social forces that impact curriculum development. The chapter concludes with a brief discussion of social trends and issues affecting the school and curriculum development process. By addressing these very topics and issues, we recognize that students, who are a part of the outside world, become "street smart," and learn many life skills in order to survive. There is also recognition that resolution of current and future social problems rests upon individuals who are skillful, knowledgeable, and have a desire to improve. The school curriculum must therefore be designed to capitalize on the "out of school learning" and draw upon what students have learned as well as their ability to think critically and solve problems.

THE NATURE OF CULTURE AND SOCIETY

From the moment of birth, individuals learn informally as they are "enveloped by the culture into which [they] are born in much the same way that an infant is wrapped in a blanket" (Gutek, 1988, p. 2). This process of learning the requirements, behaviors, attitudes, and content of the culture is referred to as *acculturation*. Students, therefore, acquire their culture by being a part of it, by living in it. As Gutek (1988) notes,

> We acquire our culture by living and participating in it. We have no choice about the matter. We are born into a culture . . . a way of life that is complex . . . [and] while our entry . . . may be simple, our living and learning or taking on the culture is complex (p. 2).

Culture, then, refers to the "patterns and products of learned behavior: the etiquette, language, food habits, religious and moral beliefs, system of knowledge, attitudes and values, as well as the material things and artifacts produced" (Havighurst and Neugarten, 1967, p. 8). In addition, culture has the following general characteristics:

1. Culture is based on ideas, not simply objects or things.
2. Culture is a pattern of learned behavior.
3. Culture is transmitted from one generation to the next.
4. Culture has some general form of organization or core.
5. Culture is continuous and interdependent with individuals.
6. Culture is dynamic and changing.

As students learn their culture, they associate with others—both peer groups and adults. The associations or interactions may be temporary or accidental, or they may be long lasting or permanent. According to Beckner and Cornett (1972) *society* refers to "the more lasting associations which occur because the members share common bonds of sentiment or feeling—similar tastes, interests, experiences and concerns . . . [and] share a mutual or reciprocal service and cooperate for mutual benefits" (p. 70). Society, then, is a collection of individuals who have loosely organized themselves into groups that share common interests or backgrounds. Culture serves as the cement that holds society together based on complex patterns of learned behavior, values, and attitudes.

The values and attitudes shared by most, if not all, Americans—for example, freedom, justice, or patriotism—make up our national culture. These commonalities are frequently expressed in the celebrations associated with national holidays—Thanksgiving, President's Day, the Fourth of July.

The often cited concept of the "melting pot" is an example of how various subcultures were seen as losing their identity to the "American" culture. An English writer named Israel Zangwill (1909) popularized this new view through his drama *The Melting Pot*. In this play, the hero states,

> America is God's Crucible, the great Melting Pot where all the races of Europe are melting and re-forming! Here you stand, good folk, think I, when I see them at

Ellis Island, here you stand in your 50 groups, with your 50 languages and histories, and your 50 blood hatreds and rivalries. But you won't be long like that . . . into the Crucible with you all! God is making the American (p. 37).

The concept of the melting pot and the Americanization process was further aided "by free public education by teaching everybody English and the American social ideals" (Levine and Havighurst, 1989, p. 363). Although the public school was influential in this process, it was not a total success. Many immigrant students had to drop out of school to work and it was not until at least one generation later that some "Americanization" had taken place, yet some groups have never lost their subculture identity.

Educators during this time and even today continue to struggle to provide effective school programs for all immigrants who come to America. The diversity in culture, language, beliefs, and values of these groups has become the thread that when woven forms the American cultural tapestry.

As a part of this national tapestry, there are subgroups or subcultures today that have mores that differ from other groups, based on ethnic background or identity, religion, geographic location, or economic status. These subcultures also have a profound impact on the informal learning of students and even establish a student's view of school, with some subcultures supporting public education more than others.

As a response to the idea of the melting pot, the concept of *cultural pluralism* emerged. Kallen (1924) first proposed the term to describe the United States as a democracy with various nationalities or subgroups cooperating voluntarily. The first attempts at recognizing the cultural diversity of the United States through the curricular efforts of the 1940s and 1950s were followed by the 1954 Supreme Court decision against racially segregated public schools and the Civil Rights Movement of the 1960s. With this pluralistic view of American culture, which affirms diversity, the concept of intergroup relations has become an important issue in the public school curriculum. According to Levine and Havighurst (1989), functions of cultural pluralism include:

1. Providing real opportunities for members of each subculture to achieve satisfaction within their own group and lifestyle
2. Providing quality educational opportunities and training for all subcultures that will enable members to earn a living and not live in poverty
3. Providing access to the labor force or employment on equal terms with other members of society
4. Providing opportunities for youth of all subcultures to be associated with youth of other subcultures in activities of mutual interest
5. Maintaining the freedom of choice of individuals to practice separatism, even though some would sacrifice a standard of living in doing so
6. Allowing subgroups to maintain separate economic systems as long as it does not damage the general welfare of society
7. Allowing the various subgroups to carry on their own educational systems, at their expense

8. Making all subgroups and subcultures responsible for contributions to the general welfare of the greater society

According to Levine and Havighurst (1989), recommendations for more favorable treatment of minority groups reflected in the school curriculum have resulted in teaching units that focus on intergroup relations. These units, which examine the relationships of different ethnic groups to each other, are normally included in a variety of high school social studies and history courses. According to Armstrong (1989), it is believed that students should be aware of the many ways in which all human groups share similarities, not only biologically but culturally, and therefore cultural pluralism embraces many aims, which include:

1. Appreciation and understanding of various cultures in the society
2. Cooperation of the diverse groups in the society's institutions
3. Coexistence of different lifestyles, language, religious beliefs, and family structures
4. Freedom for each subculture to work out its social future (pp. 318–319)

Multicultural studies have been seen as valuable for all students because the acquisition of different perspectives on personal and social problems can be a way of helping to understand the conflicts in values that confront members of our society. Cultural pluralism, therefore, is now generally accepted as a part of the curriculum development process.

SOCIAL FORCES THAT IMPACT CURRICULUM

There are many social forces in contemporary society that have an impact on the secondary curriculum, and educators need to consider these forces in the curriculum development process. Often curriculum planning and development is in response to forces that want to challenge the curriculum and bring about changes; while on the other side, curriculum is also developed according to established protocols to reflect the status quo. In such a tug-of-war, curriculum planning and development seldom emanate from a rationale based on theory, research, and practice; and therefore, the results are often in response to the dominant force, which causes the gap between theory and practice to widen (Reinhartz, 1980).

There are many challenging questions facing educators in the 1990s. What are the changes in society that will most likely affect educational change? How will discoveries in science, or the population demographics, or the transformation of the family structure affect secondary schools and the curriculum? The answers to these questions will impact the secondary curriculum in the next decade and well into the twenty-first century.

The educational process has been and will continue to be confronted with social pressures as long as the school and its curriculum are seen as serving not only the learners, but the needs of society as well. As Tanner and Tanner (1980) note,

> . . . society is both a source and an influence whereby the school develops its objectives and curriculum. In an enlightened society, the school is endowed with the mission of drawing from the social environment the best elements that give promise of enabling the rising generation to build a better society (p. 147).

Given the social forces that are present in society, "those responsible for curriculum planning must decide what kind of skills, knowledge, and attitudes are called for by society's needs" (Beane, Toepfer, and Alessi, 1986, p. 90). Some of the key social forces that impact the curriculum development process include tradition, technology, government, pressure groups, and family structure.

Tradition

Perhaps one of the greatest social forces affecting curriculum development is tradition, which Doll (1986) describes as a "dead hand"—a weight that restrains desirable change. Through tradition, society can maintain the status quo and limit change. One way that tradition inhibits change can be seen in the resistance of rules and procedures to modification. Frequently, policies and procedures that were established by earlier boards and legislative bodies remain "on the books," unchanged, and in effect, even when they no longer are effective or accomplish the original purpose or objective. A second factor that makes tradition a social force is the deeply ingrained notion of right and wrong. Our values have been influenced by our Judeo-Christian history, which has emphasized individual rights and property rights and considered these rights to be immutable (Doll, 1986).

A third factor that works on the side of tradition is our built-in psychological resistance to change. Our own psyches seem to be tradition-bound. As Alfonso, Firth, and Neville (1981) note, "Change is a condition of human existence" (p. 243), but it seems that the older we get, the more we tend to resist change. Hord and colleagues (1987) provide insight into the difficulties associated with change when they describe it as a highly personal process that is accomplished by individuals and involves developmental growth. Doll (1986) further elaborates on the difficulties associated with change when he says, "Human beings resist change so energetically that, in some areas of their lives, they would rather die than shift position" (p. 88). It is the tenacity with which we hold to the past or status quo that makes tradition such a powerful social force.

The secondary school is not immune to the effects of tradition, as seen in the following practices described by Goodlad (1984) and Doll (1986):

1. Regardless of the size, location (urban, suburban, rural), or geographic region, high schools have an amazing similarity in their organization, curriculum or content, and staffing patterns.
2. The organization of instructional time in secondary schools is divided into brief and equal periods.
3. The secondary curriculum content emphasizes a relatively limited

number of educational objectives with particular attention given to the "basics."

4. Students are permitted to select from a range of courses, with a wide variance in programs, especially when considering the electives.
5. In spite of the wide range of abilities and maturity levels found in secondary schools, there is an established and generally uniform means of evaluation and accreditation.
6. Subjects in secondary schools are organized according to the rather rigid guidelines of the Carnegie Unit system, and although courses are added at intervals, removing courses from the curriculum is very difficult if not impossible.

These characteristics, as well as others, are what give high schools approaching the twenty-first century the same general look and feel of high schools at the end of the nineteenth century. Tradition is indeed a powerful force, especially in secondary education.

Technology

One cannot exist in today's world without seeing and feeling the effects of technology, from the grocery store checkout scanner to computerized telecommunications. For example, Forest Hills Central High School in Grand Rapids, Michigan, is one of the top schools in technology. Its telecommunications system, *Practek*, includes a variety of presentations from foreign language newscasts to Cable News Network (CNN), and much more (Cawelti, 1989). Through the use of satellite technology, we are able to witness news events as they happen — to see and hear with our own eyes and ears. An interdependent world economy as well as a world society is developing, and many believe that the school, through its curriculum, should help students examine their own lives and beliefs as well as learn about the ways of other people (Reinhartz, 1980).

Other technological developments are more directly related to classroom instruction. The use of electronic media equipment (e.g., video disc), calculators, and computers will continue to have an impact on the secondary curriculum. The development of teletext and videotext technology, the ability to deliver one-way and two-way communication services electronically, will also impact the educational programs in schools. According to Levine and Havighurst (1989),

> . . . information technology at school . . . will facilitate rote learning and free teachers to concentrate on development of creative problem-solving skills and . . . children [will] become generalists who can work with a fantastic variety of information tools (p. 128).

In addition to having information technology available, students come to school with a greater awareness and understanding of what is happening in the world as a result of the mass media—television, radio, and newspapers. According to Reinhartz (1980),

> Technological advancements bring the expansion of knowledge which presents a dilemma for curriculum developers in the . . . secondary schools. They are forced to seek new answers to Spencer's question: "What knowledge is of most worth?" Will the emphasis be on content, facts, analytical skills, or all three? (p. 6)

In considering the role of technology in the educational process, Beane, Toepfer, and Alessi (1986) present several questions for teachers to consider in the planning process:

- To what extent is the school responsible for introducing learners to technology?
- To what extent should the school involve learners in a critical analysis of the advantages and disadvantages of technology?
- Should the school attempt to develop skills involved in using technology?
- How can technology be used in promoting more effective learning?
- How should the school deal with technology-related learning that young people acquire outside the school (e.g., from television)?
- To what extent should learners use technology (e.g., word processors, computerized spelling checkers) to carry out school activities? (p. 92)

Although technology has created many useful machines and devices to enhance the quality of living, it has also created problems, and as Beane, Toepfer, and Alessi (1986) note, the list of advantages and disadvantages could fill pages. One thing is certain, however: the impact of technology on society and education will continue. It will become a more integral part of our lives, and future students will reap the benefits, as well as the problems, as technology continues to provide the tools to stretch our imaginations.

Government

Governmental agencies, whether national, state, or local, are society's most effective and powerful sources of influence on what is taught in schools. According to Funkhouser, Beach, Ryan, and Fifer (1981), school curriculum requirements are either passed into law by a legislature or approved by a board of education. Although the federal government does not have primary responsibility for education, more and more influence is exerted through appropriations targeted for special programs. The National Defense Education Act of the 1950s is an example of one of the first major federal intervention programs which provided millions of dollars to support mathematics, science, and foreign language instruction. This was followed by the Elementary and Secondary Education Act of the 1960s, which showed continued federal support for educational programs. More recently, the Education Consolidation and Improvement Act of the 1980s demonstrated the federal government's role in education through funding themes for federal dollars to support educational programs in the states.

According to the United States Constitution, state legislatures have been given the primary responsibility for education. These legislative bodies have prescribed, to varying degrees, the curriculum or courses and programs of study for secondary residents, including graduation requirements. However, it is the central education agency of each state that often exerts the greatest amount of pressure to get schools to conform to policies and regulations established by the legislatures. According to Reinhartz (1980), state departments of education exercise control over the textbook selection process, conduct studies in specific curriculum areas, make recommendations for legislative action, license or certify teachers, and administer federal grant and state appropriated funds. These actions directly impact decisions relative to curriculum development at the local level.

The school board at the district level exerts a powerful influence on the education process within a community. This is the front line, where the local board not only hires and fires school personnel—administrators, teachers, support staff—but establishes educational goals and priorities as well. Perhaps more than any other governmental group, the local board most directly reflects the values of the community.

Although there are variations of what each community expects from its schools, Jarolimek (1981) has identified several qualities of education that most Americans would like or expect to see in their schools. These qualities include:

1. In addition to the main concern for academic or intellectual goals, schools should have broad goals that encourage physical, social, emotional, and aesthetic development in young people, including athletic, art, and music programs
2. Schools should develop social and civic responsibility by having students exhibit citizenship skills, help others, do what is right, deal fairly with others, and be loyal to institutions and their country
3. Schools should recognize and account for individual differences by providing different educational programming in order to maximize the educational potential of each student
4. In order for instruction and learning to take place, schools should be orderly, well-disciplined places, with little student permissiveness
5. Schools should ensure that all students attain a minimum level of mastery of basic knowledge, skills, and values
6. Schools should offer educational programs that are relevant to life in society, and in particular, reflect the values and needs of the local community
7. Schools should reflect the good in the culture by providing positive role models who are sensitive and morally uplifting

In addition to incorporating these qualities of education into the local schools, the local district also has to adapt to changes in demographics in the community. Demographic factors which have to be considered include population growth or decline, redistribution of age groups or the population in areas of the district, and mobility, as students move in and out of the district. While many suburban districts have experienced increases in student enrollment, many urban districts have experienced sharp declines in the number of students, and each type of district has had to cope with the problem given the resources of the local community.

Pressure Groups

Pressure groups have, in recent years, exerted considerable pressure on the schools with regard to curriculum and educational programs. These groups are generally concerned with a single issue or a specific area of interest, such as taxes, the role of women in society, patriotism, religion, and professional involvement.

Taxpayer groups, encouraged by California's Proposition 13, have in recent years demanded a fiscally austere, no-frills school budget. Taxpayer groups have lobbied for and won tax rollbacks that have caused schools to limit or stop construction projects, cut back on school personnel, eliminate special instructional programs, and reduce educational services. These groups have discovered the power of the tax dollar, and to bring about what they perceive as fiscal responsibility, they have been successful in limiting the taxing authority of school districts. Limiting funds, or even threatening to limit funds, clearly impacts the kinds of curriculum development and educational programming that can occur in school districts.

The portrayal of the role of women in society has been the concern of several women's groups. Although these different groups may not be unanimous in their concerns, they have sought to have curriculum materials more accurately reflect varied roles of women and their contributions to society. Historically, women have been presented in limited roles in educational materials and seldom seen in a variety of professional positions. Schuster and Van Dyne (1985) document the changes that have occurred in the evolution of the school curriculum to reflect more accurately the contributions of women to society. Table 4.1 traces the stages of curriculum change and describes the impact on curriculum development.

Patriotic groups come in many forms and represent a wide variety of beliefs that range from ultraconservative to ultraliberal. Such groups include the Daughters of the American Revolution, the Veterans of Foreign Wars, the Vietnam War Veterans, and the American Civil Liberties Union. These groups tend to focus attention on textbooks and other instructional materials. Courses involving history, government, sociology, contemporary issues, citizenship, the free enterprise system, and morality have come under the watchful eye of these groups. Curriculum which strays from the "right" interpretation of facts and ideas is subject to intense criticism.

Religious groups have also served as watchdogs of the school curriculum. Although, according to Jarolimek (1981), the Christian fundamentalists have been the most outspoken in their criticisms of the school curriculum, the B'nai B'rith has also taken an active role in the review of curriculum materials. The dilemma that schools are confronted with is in upholding the constitutional requirement of guaranteeing freedom of religion to members of all faiths, even

Table 4.1 STAGES OF CURRICULUM CHANGE

Stages	Questions	Incentives	Means	Outcome
1. Invisible women	Who are the truly great thinkers/actors in history?	Maintaining "standards of excellence"	Back to basics	Pre-1960s exclusionary core curriculum Student as "vessel"
2. Search for missing women	Who are the great women, the female Shakespeares, Napoleons, Darwins?	Affirmative action/ compensatory	Add to existing data within conventional paradigms	"Exceptional" women on male syllabus Student's needs recognized
3. Women as disadvantaged, subordinate group	Why are there so few women leaders? Why are women's roles devalued?	Anger/Social justice	Protest existing paradigms but within perspective of dominant group	"Images of women" courses "Women in politics" Women's studies begins
4. Women studied on own terms	What was/is women's experience? What are differences among women? (attention to race, class, cultural difference)	Intellectual	Outside existing paradigms; develop insider's perspective	Links with ethnic, crosscultural studies Women-focused courses Interdisciplinary courses Student values own experience
5. Women as challenge to disciplines	How valid are current definitions of historical periods, greatness, norms for behavior? How must our questions change to account for women's experience, diversity, difference?	Epistemology	Testing the paradigms Gender as category of analysis	Beginnings of integration Theory courses Student collaborates in learning
6. Transformed, "balanced" curriculum	How can women's and men's experience be understood together? How do class and race intersect with gender?	Inclusive vision of human experience based on difference and diversity, not sameness and generalization	Transform the paradigms	Reconceptualized, inclusive core Transformed introductory courses Empowering of student

Source: Schuster, M., & Van Dyne, S. (1985). Stages of curriculum transformation. In M. Schuster and S. Van Dyne (Eds.), *Women's place in the academy: Transforming the liberal arts curriculum.* Lanham, Maryland: Roman and Littlefield Publishers. Used with permission.

those with no faith at all, while at the same time being sensitive to the concerns of a very dedicated and vocal constituency in the community. An indication of the intensity of this group can be seen in the question of school prayer, which is still very much present today, even though legally it was resolved nearly 30 years ago in *Engel* v. *Vital.*

Professional organizations, especially educational groups, also exert pressure on the educational process. According to Reinhartz (1980), teacher organizations (e.g., National Education Association, American Federation of Teachers) have grown in stature and power in recent years. Not only have these groups been active politically at the national level in support of candidates, but they have been active at the state and local levels through the election process. Through collective bargaining efforts they have impacted school personnel and school programs. Perhaps professional organizations impact the curriculum most directly through the professional commitment of their members and the kinds of professional activities they provide for them.

Family Structure

Perhaps the greatest social force in recent years that has impacted all levels of society, but especially the schools, has been the change in the structure of the family. No longer is the typical American family composed of both natural parents and children, with the mother at home and the father at work. This picture of the family has rapidly changed since the 1970s and is being replaced with a much more complicated and diverse family structure (Beane, Toepfer, and Alesis, 1986). Santrock (1990) concurs when he says, "Children are growing up in a greater variety of family structures than ever before in history" (p. 308).

One of the biggest changes in the family has been the result of mothers entering the work force. More than half of all mothers with children under 5 years old work, and over two-thirds of all mothers with children ages 6–18 are in the labor force (Papalia and Olds, 1990; Santrock, 1990). Although there has been a significant increase in the number of mothers working outside the home, the impact on their children seems minimal. According to Papalia and Olds (1990),

> Fifty years of research do not show an overall ill effect of working in and of itself, although some problems are indirectly related to mother's work, some having to do with substitute child care and some with the mother's task overload. . . . Still, many researchers . . . emphasize the positive effects of a mother's employment on the entire family (p. 476).

The impact of working mothers seems, therefore, to depend on other variables, such as how the mother feels about the work, whether it is full- or part-time, and the overall socioeconomic circumstances of the family rather than the work itself.

In addition to working mothers, another major change in the family structure has been a significant increase in the number of single parent families — headed mostly by women. Papalia and Olds (1990) report that approximately one-fourth of all American children (15 million) live in homes with only one parent. The chart that follows shows by ethnic group the percentage of children who come from single parent families (U.S. Bureau of the Census, 1988).

Ethnic Group	Percentage of Children in Single Parent Homes
White	18
Hispanic	30
African American	53

This data becomes even more alarming when considering that most estimates show that as many as 90 percent of all single parent homes are headed by the mother as custodial parent, even though the number of fathers caring for children has increased by as much as 300 percent in recent years.

The disturbing results of research concerning single parent families and student performance in school indicates that students from one-parent homes (1) tend to achieve less in school, (2) in general like school less than other students do, (3) tend to have more problems with peers in school, (4) are more likely to need disciplinary action at school, and (5) may be at greater risk of having marital and parenting problems (Papalia and Olds, 1990). However, like the research associated with working mothers, there are many other variables, such as parental expectations and socioeconomic levels, which also impact the results of studies of single parent families.

In a related area, the number of students living in stepfamilies has also increased as a result of the high divorce rate. Santrock (1990) indicates that currently over 10 percent of all American households consist of blended families, either stepfamilies or cohabiting adults, and this figure is increasing annually. As a result of the pattern created by the process of marrying, having children, getting divorced, and remarrying, Santrock (1990) notes that there are more elementary and secondary students living in stepfamilies. The most common version of the stepfamily—approximately 70 percent—is the mother, her children from a previous marriage, and the stepfather.

The increasing number of school children growing up in divorced families puts these students at a greater risk for developing behavior problems. According to Papalia and Olds (1990), adolescents have strong reactions to divorce, which are manifested in displays of anger, depression, despair, even guilt; and they feel the strain of having to be the "man" or "woman" of the house. Often the pressures from the divorce cause adolescents to become preoccupied and worry about money, and some even react by becoming very active sexually. Other studies have shown that students bear the marks of divorce years later with feelings of sadness; unmet needs; a sense of powerlessness; missing their fathers, whom they idealized; and becoming anxious about their own love relationships (Papalia and Olds, 1990).

Finally, one additional change affecting family structure has been the development of large numbers of "latchkey" students. According to Maccoby (1984),

> We know little about how parents monitor their children's activities during out-of-school hours when parents are working and no adult is at home. Most schools do not provide after-school programs, and even when they do, children may choose

not to attend. . . . We know that there are "latchkey" children . . . who are instructed to go home and remain at home until their parents return from work (p. 222).

Santrock (1990) describes latchkey children as those who do not see their parents from the time they leave for school in the morning until about 6:00 or 7:00 P.M. They have been given the name "latchkey" because they have a house or apartment key which they take to school and use to let themselves in after school while their parents are still at work. These students are unsupervised for several hours each day, and during the summer months, they may be unsupervised for days at a time.

Some estimates predict that by 1995, with 80 percent of school age children having both parents working, more and more of these students will be left to care for themselves after school. In addition to being vulnerable to physical dangers, they are deprived of nurturing and the fulfillment of other social-emotional needs; and some, particularly adolescents, are left to roam the streets and risk getting into mischief or taking alcohol and drugs (*Stephenville Empire Tribune*, 1990).

However, the totally negative image of these students being lonely and neglected is not entirely accurate and appears to be changing as more is learned about their after-school behavior. The concept of self-care has been proposed as a more accurate view of what happens with these students (Papalia and Olds, 1990). The scenario in Box 4-1 provides a description of what may actually happen with these students.

Clearly, the traditional picture of the nuclear family has changed as a result of working parents, divorce, single parent homes, and latchkey children. Add to these variations in family structure other factors, such as geographical mobility, multifamily homes or communes, and changes in family roles, and a very complex view of the family emerges. These changes in family structure have implications for secondary educators. According to Beane, Toepfer, and Alessi (1986), the following questions are important to consider when planning and developing curriculum for secondary students:

1. What responsibilities should the school assume that were previously expected of the family?
2. What kind of family structure and which variations should be addressed in the secondary curriculum?
3. What learning in the home should complement or supplement the curriculum at school?
4. What is the role of curriculum in developing morals and values previously taught by parents?

As the family structure has changed, so has its role and function in relation to the school curriculum, and curriculum developers need to be cognizant of these changes as they plan curriculum and instructional activities for secondary students.

At a time when the schools are under intense scrutiny and have been subjected to numerous studies and criticisms, it is important to note that social

Box 4-1   **Scenario: Adolescent Self-Care**

Robert, 14, rides the bus home from school each day and after unlocking the apartment door, he puts his books down, checks the mail, and then goes to the kitchen to fix a snack. He then calls and checks in with either his father or his mother, depending on which one is available at work. He lets one of his parents know if he is going to stay at home and do his homework, go to a friend's house, or just watch television. Often he will do chores that have been left for him, such as doing the dishes, carrying out the trash, setting the table for dinner, or starting the evening meal.

Robert's younger sister, Sarah, is 7 and goes to a day-care facility after school. Her parents pick her up on their way home from work. The family has discussed the possibility of Robert caring for Sarah next year after school in order to save some extra money.

One absolute rule that Robert must follow is that no one else can come to the house when his parents are not there. Also, Robert cannot go to a friend's house unless the friend's parent is home. Although supervision by telephone has been awkward, especially as Robert has sometimes disagreed with his parents' wishes, generally Robert has not had any problems in providing self-care after school.

pressures do have an impact on the curriculum development process. According to Armstrong (1989), secondary educators are subject to forces and constraints that operate within social and cultural settings. These influences on curriculum are either direct or indirect. Direct influences come from groups with constituted authority, such as governmental bodies or agencies. Indirect influences are not due to any legal authority but exert power of a *de facto* nature, such as pressure groups.

In recent years, schools have attempted to be more responsive to social concerns in designing a more effective curriculum for students in junior and senior high schools. However, curriculum development in a dynamic world such as exists today is difficult at best. Tradition, technology, governmental bodies, pressure groups, and changes in the family structure all impact the curriculum development process. According to Reinhartz (1980),

> Understanding the forces affecting education and the levels at which decisions are made provides the necessary orientation for the task of improving curriculum of the . . . secondary schools. Perhaps, most importantly, there is a need to build a sound rationale for guiding curriculum development (p. 28).

The rationale can serve as the vehicle to bring some sense and order to the curriculum development process even while the social forces are being felt at all levels. Without a careful and deliberate approach to the process, the result will be haphazard and trendy, at best, as a response to the dominant force at the time.

SUMMARY

Chapter 4 presented the social foundations of curriculum planning and development. The secondary curriculum includes a broad range of subjects and determines what is taught in these subjects and how they are taught. In large part, the curriculum is a reflection of society at a particular moment in time. The members of society in the 1990s are concerned about the structure of the family, teenage pregnancies, school dropouts, drugs, AIDS, and other social issues. In turn, these areas of concern become educational issues because the school curriculum is an integral part of the larger society and is not developed in isolation. The society at a given point in time provides the context for the "what" and "how" of the educational programs.

The first part of the chapter presented an overview of the nature of culture and society, and the role of the school in each. It is from one's culture that patterns of behavior are imitated, learned, and practiced. These behaviors are essential as members of a culture interact in their society. A society is the organizational framework in which individuals with common interests, behaviors, and values associate. Schools are instituted by the society to acculturate its members, and the curriculum forms the script for learning these behaviors and values.

The second part of the chapter focused on the role of the school and curriculum in society. The schools are responsible for educating all the students. Over the past several decades, curricular efforts have been directed toward schooling the masses. As part of this mission, in the early part of the century the "melting pot" concept dominated our thinking, as individuals lost their ethnic identity and became "Americans." More recently the concept of cultural pluralism has been guiding the curriculum planning and development process as well as other aspects of instruction. The latter approach encourages subgroups to retain many of their cultural roots while becoming American citizens. In such a view, one does not have to lose an ethnic identity to become American, but in fact one enriches the American social and cultural tapestry by adding the uniqueness of different languages, values, and/or customs.

Social forces impact the secondary curriculum in many ways. These social forces were described in the last section of the chapter. While the list of forces is not exhaustive, it does contain several illustrations of how social forces impact curriculum development. These forces help to shape the kind of curriculum that is offered in the secondary schools, especially high schools. Some of these social forces are positive and others are negative. Those citizens supporting a particular issue attempt to influence the school curriculum to reflect their concerns. Secondary educators need to be cognizant of these influences and to examine and study each carefully to ensure that the decisions are educationally sound.

Curriculum developers who design an effective secondary curriculum should be aware of and sensitive to these social forces, which attempt to influence what is offered, in what order, and how it is presented. Such pressures, if not examined, could change the focus of the curriculum and ultimately the mission, goals, and objectives that have been established. The social forces will not disappear; in fact, they will likely grow stronger and more intense. Nevertheless, curriculum developers need to confront each issue one at a time and decide which ones are appropriate for the curriculum and for the preadolescents and adolescents in their schools.

YOUR TURN

4.1 Examine the results from the most recent Gallup Poll in the September issue of *Phi Delta Kappan.* In particular, review the responses to the question(s) related to the social issues or concerns that citizens have.
   (a) What are these issues? List them in the order of concern.
   (b) Examine the Gallup Poll issues for the last five years and determine if there are trends that emerge as major issues.

4.2 What are your attitudes about different cultural groups (e.g., Italians, Hispanics, African Americans)? Describe your attitudes in terms of the evidence that you have experienced during your lifetime that contributed to these attitudes. Consider what you have been told, what you have read or seen, and what you have heard from others:
   (a) At an early age
   (b) During adolescence
   (c) As a young adult
   (d) As a mature adult

4.3 Select a high school textbook in any subject area and determine how the book portrays different cultural or ethnic groups. Use the following as a guide for reviewing the textbook.
   Name of textbook

   Author(s)
   Publisher
   Date of Publication
   Subject

   Answer the following questions:
   (a) How does the text portray cultural groups?
   (b) Are any of the examples cited about prominent members of a group?
   (c) Which groups are featured?
   (d) What evidence is found in support of each group (e.g., picture, language used, role models)?
   (e) Are stereotypes used? If so, list them.
   (f) Is there an appreciation for cultural diversity? What evidence can you cite to support your response?

4.4 How do you feel about the following groups? Rate your own feelings.

Group	Comfortable	Uncomfortable
(a) Native Americans		
(b) Drug users/addicts		
(c) Homosexuals		

      (d) Pregnant teenagers
      (e) African Americans
      (f) High school dropouts
      (g) Militant feminists
      (h) Prochoice advocates
      (i) Overweight people
      (j) Antiabortion advocates
      (k) "Skinheads"
      (l) Disabled people
      (m) Elderly people

4.5 Below is a list of social issues. Read the list carefully and prioritize the issues from the most important to you (1) to the second most important (2), third, and so on.

   _____ (a) Child abuse
   _____ (b) Teenage drug use
   _____ (c) High school dropouts
   _____ (d) Sexual promiscuity in adolescents
   _____ (e) Divorce
   _____ (f) Homeless children
   _____ (g) Latchkey students
   _____ (h) Peer pressure
   _____ (i) Home instruction
   _____ (j) Jobs and the economy
   _____ (k) Basic skills mastery
   _____ (l) Use of technology in learning
   _____ (m) Funding for educational programs

Examine your list. What patterns emerge? Have you learned something about your own values and what issues are most important to you?

4.6 Develop a teaching unit for one of your teaching fields or a subject area you enjoy teaching. Incorporate at least three of the top social issues in the previous question in your planning for that unit. For example, if you identified latchkey students as a high concern, how would you teach students about this social concern? How would you help students become more concerned about their own self-care as it relates to this issue?

REFERENCES

Alfonso, R.J., Firth, G.R. & Neville, R.F. (1981). *Instructional supervision: A behavior system* (2nd ed.). Boston: Allyn and Bacon.

Annual editions, Education 89/90 (16th ed.). A look to the future. Guilford, Conn.: Dushkin.

Armstrong, D.G. (1989). *Developing and documenting the curriculum.* Boston: Allyn and Bacon.

Beane, J.A., Toepfer, C.F. & Alessi, S.J., Jr. (1986). *Curriculum planning and development.* Boston: Allyn and Bacon.

Beckner, W. & Cornett, J.D. (1972). *The secondary school curriculum: Content and structure.* Scranton, Pa.: Intext Educational Publishers.

Cawelti, G. (1989). Designing high schools for the future. *Educational Leadership, 47*, 1, 30–35.

Counts, G.S. (1934). *The social foundations of education.* New York: Scribner.

Doll, R.C. (1986). *Curriculum improvement: Decision making and process* (6th ed.). Boston: Allyn and Bacon.

Funkhouser, C.F., Beach, D.M., Ryan, G.T., & Fifer, F.L. (1981). *Classroom applications of the curriculum: A systems approach.* Dubuque, Iowa: Kendall Hunt.

Goodlad, J.I. (1984). *A place called school.* New York: McGraw-Hill.

Gutek, G.L. (1988). *Education and schooling in America.* Englewood Cliffs, N.J.: Prentice-Hall.

Havighurst, R.J. & Neugarten, B.L. (1967). *Society and education* (3rd ed.). Boston: Allyn and Bacon.

Hord, S.M. et al. (1987). *Taking charge of change.* Alexandria, Va.: Association for Supervision and Curriculum Development.

Jarolimek, J. (1981). *The schools in contemporary society: An analysis of social currents, issues, and forces.* New York: Macmillan.

Johnson, M. (April 1967). Definitions and models in curriculum theory. *Educational Theory, 17*, 2, 127–40.

Kallen, H.M. (1924). *Culture and democracy in the United States.* New York: Boni and Liveright.

Levine, D.U. & Havighurst, R.J. (1989). *Society and education* (7th ed.). Boston: Allyn and Bacon.

Maccoby, E.E. (1984). Context of the family. In W.A. Collins (ed.), *Development during middle childhood: The years from six to twelve.* Washington, D.C.: National Academy Press.

Papalia, D.E. & Olds, S.W. (1990). *A child's world: Infancy through adolescence* (5th ed.). New York: McGraw-Hill.

Reinhartz, J. (Spring 1980). Stemming the tide: A case against spontaneous curriculum generation. *Alpha Delta Kappan, 10*, 2, 6–8.

Santrock, J.W. (1990). *Children* (2nd ed.). Dubuque, Iowa: William C. Brown.

Schuster, M. & Van Dyne, S. (1985). Stages of curriculum transformation. In M. Schuster and S. Van Dyne (Eds.), *Women's place in the academy: Transforming the liberal arts curriculum.* Lanham, Maryland: Roman and Littlefield Publishers.

Stephenville Empire Tribune. (July 1990). Stephenville, Texas.

Tanner, D. & Tanner, L.N. (1980). *Curriculum development: Theory into practice* (2nd ed.). New York: Macmillan.

U.S. Bureau of the Census. (1988). *Fertility of American women: June 1987* (Current Population Reports, Series P-20, No. 427). Washington, D.C.: U.S. Government Printing Office.

Zais, R.S. (1976). *Curriculum principles and foundations.* New York: Harper & Row.

Zangwill, Israel. (1909). *The Melting Pot.* New York: Macmillan.

Chapter
5

Foundations of Human Development and Psychology

Knowledge of the nature of human development, needs, and learning is essential to curriculum developers to assist students in making the transition to adulthood. Educators can be more effective in planning and developing curriculum for secondary students when the psychological foundations are a part of the process. According to Beckner and Cornett (1972), "The 'scientific' aspects of teaching are largely dependent upon psychology as a source of knowledge" (p. 107). The application of psychology to curriculum development is important because it serves as both an academic discipline and a technology in improving student learning. In describing psychology, Mathis, Cotton, and Sechrest (1970) state,

> As an academic discipline, psychology is the scientific study of the behavior of human beings and of animals. As a technology, psychology is the means of changing behavior by applying the findings of academic psychology combined with intelligent guesses where knowledge is lacking (p. 1).

Chapter 5 presents the many facets of the psychological foundations used in curriculum planning and development. The conceptual framework introduced in Chapter 2 and referred to in Chapter 3 graphically depicts the importance and role of psychology, particularly the cognitive, social, moral, and physical stages, in educational practices.

The curriculum of the secondary school should be founded on the principles of psychology related to human development, particularly the cognitive, physical, social, and moral stages of development. Knowledge of developmental theories and cognitive abilities of adolescents and preadolescents is crucial to teachers or curriculum planners for secondary schools. Knowledge of moral behavior is equally important in developing an appropriate curriculum for these students. To be effective, secondary educators need a foundation in psychology focusing on students and how they develop and learn.

Curriculum is also shaped by the psychological principles associated with the learning process. In addition to knowing about the developmental aspects of their students, educators need a fundamental understanding of how people learn and process information—knowledge about learning theory. Tyler (1949) suggests that "A study of the learners themselves would seek to identify needed changes in behavior patterns of the students which the educational institution should seek to produce" (p. 6).

This chapter identifies the general principles of development and describes briefly four major theories of development, each having a different emphasis or focus on the developmental process. The chapter also describes specifically the cognitive, physical, social, and moral development of preadolescents and adolescents. The chapter concludes with a discussion of the major theories of learning, with implications for curriculum development and teaching.

GENERAL PRINCIPLES OF DEVELOPMENT

In order to understand the nature of growth and development in the secondary student, it is helpful to view this process within the context of the general principles of human growth and development. These principles apply to the growth and development process from birth through adulthood. These three general principles (Glickman, 1981) include the following:

1. There are common identifiable characteristics of learners within each stage or period of development.
2. Movement from period to period is hierarchical and sequential.
3. The rate of movement within each period and from period to period is highly individual.

These principles guide the development of the preadolescent and the adolescent, and each age group has common identifiable characteristics.

It should be noted that while there are common characteristics for each developmental age group, the range of individual differences generally widens with age and the range of differences is considerably greater by the time students are in the secondary school, particularly high school. Using a continuum may prove helpful to illustrate that the range of differences tends to widen as the students' age increases. For example, the continuum below depicts graphically the range of student cognitive differences in early childhood (ages 3–5). As the line implies, the range of differences (likes, basic needs, etc.) is not as great as it will be later in life.

High ◄————————————————► Low

The next continuum illustrates the wider range of cognitive differences in secondary school students (ages 13–18). As students move through puberty into adulthood, they develop individual interests and unique approaches to solving problems and meeting challenges, which accounts for a very wide range in student differences.

High ◄————————————————————————————————► Low

The characteristics of each age group are summarized in Table 5.1, which presents an overview of the various components of development (physical, social, emotional, and mental) of the K–12 student. In this summary, the increasing range of developmental differences is implied as a function of gender (i.e., girls enter puberty about two years earlier than boys) and individual differences, with each student reaching a particular developmental stage (i.e., adolescence) at his or her own rate.

The range of abilities and the individual differences present a unique challenge for curriculum developers who work with this age group. For example, a ninth-grade student might be developmentally at the concrete operations level in math skills, yet the problem situations that would appeal to a fifth-grade student would not be effective with an adolescent. A math problem about marbles or oranges might be developmentally appropriate for a 10-year-old student, but not a 14-year-old student.

The unique challenge is to make the curriculum or content interesting and relevant to secondary students, while at the same time meeting their cognitive developmental level. For example, the use of technology and interactive computer-video disc instruction might challenge the student to learn math skills while providing an appropriate motivational strategy. Workbooks containing many problems the students must complete have not been very successful in the past, and using more of the same kind of workbook activities without employing varied motivational techniques typically will not work.

The next section provides a brief description of major theories of human development, which provides a perspective for viewing the student and developing instructional programs.

MAJOR DEVELOPMENTAL THEORIES

Depending on the textbook consulted, there are a variety of theories concerning human development. There are four major developmental theories, however, that appear consistently and have implications for curriculum development in the secondary school. These four theories are:

Table 5.1 SUMMARY OF AGE-LEVEL CHARACTERISTICS

	Physical	Social	Emotional	Mental
Kindergarten	Active; large-muscle control; bones soft; boys bigger, girls more mature	Flexible friendships; small, loosely organized play groups; quarrels frequent; dramatic play; little sex-role awareness	Free emotional expression; frequent anger outbursts; fears and jealousy common	Like to talk, vivid imagination
Primary Grades	Active; large-muscle control; eye development incomplete; susceptible to illnesses; accident rate at peak	More selective friendships; small-group activities; quarrels frequent; competition emerges	Sensitive to feelings and to criticism and ridicule; need praise; eager to please	Eager to learn; like to talk; concepts of right and wrong emerge
Elementary Grades	Growth spurt; puberty occurs in some girls; fine motor coordination; poor posture; bones and ligaments soft; boys like rough play	"Gang" age; sex cleavage; team games; hero worship	Peer code-adult code conflict; "character" traits emerge	Curious; wide interests; may be perfectionists; want independence but with support and guidance
Junior High	Growth spurt and puberty; concern about appearance; adolescent awkwardness; limited physical and mental endurance	Peer group takes over; need for conformity; friendships and quarrels more intense; girls more advanced socially	Moody, unpredictable; temperamental; may be opinionated and intolerant; critical of adults	Able to deal with some concepts; tendency to daydream
High School	Physical maturity reached; impact of puberty; self-conscious	Peer group dominant; concern about opposite sex; need for conformity	Adolescent revolt; conflict with parents; moody and preoccupied	Close to maximum mental efficiency but inexperienced; search for a philosophy of life and sense of identity. Conflicts over sex role and occupational identity

Source: Biehler, R. F. (1974). *Psychology applied to teaching* (2nd ed.). Boston: Houghton Mifflin, p. 191. Used with permission.

1. Cognitive development
2. Behaviorism
3. Psychoanalytic
4. Humanism

In addition to these theories of development, which provide a way of viewing the overall development of the learner, there is also a need to examine the area of moral development.

Cognitive Development

The cognitive developmental theory focuses on rational thought and stresses that cognition, or our intellectual ability, unfolds in sequences or stages. Piaget and Bruner are developmental psychologists most often associated with the cognitive development theory. (Piaget, 1967, 1952; Piaget and Inhelder, 1973; Bruner, 1968, 1960; and Bruner et al., 1966.)

Bruner's work has concentrated on perception, learning, memory, and other aspects of cognition in children. With his concept of the "spiral curriculum," Bruner argued that any subject could be taught to any child at any stage of development if it was presented in the proper manner. According to Bruner, all children have a natural curiosity and a desire to become competent at various learning tasks. When a task presented to them is too difficult, however, they become bored. Therefore, tasks must be presented at an appropriate level to challenge the student's current stage of cognitive development. In studying perception in children, he concluded that their individual values significantly affect their perceptions.

Piaget's ideas have been used to form one of the most complete theoretical statements about the development of intelligence and have greatly influenced instruction in classrooms by describing essential cognitive tasks that children master in the K–12 grades. (These tasks will be discussed in greater detail later in this chapter.) Piaget believed that the core of human development is rationality and that intelligence develops from the interaction of heredity and environmental forces. Although he tended to believe that biological forces play a greater role in development, Piaget was more concerned with the *how* of thinking and not so much with the *what*, and therefore his views of human development have helped to explain how students think rather than what they are thinking.

Piaget described the thinking or cognitive process when he established a 4-stage sequence, with specific cognitive characteristics or behaviors occurring in each stage. Although a general time frame is often cited, for Piaget these stages were not linked specifically to chronological age or other benchmarks. For him, each stage was dependent upon specific developmental tasks or behaviors which indicated cognitive ability. Although the first two stages are not directly related to secondary education, they do provide the total developmental perspective.

Piaget's first stage of cognitive development is called the *sensorimotor* stage, which occurs generally from birth to about age 2. During this two-year period of time, the infant organizes and coordinates his or her sensations and perceptions of personal actions and/or the physical environment. One of the major cognitive tasks of this period is recognition of *object permanence*, knowing that an object exists even when not seen. As a result of the development of object permanence as students acquire language, they develop proficiency in describing objects and events.

Piaget's next stage of cognitive development, the *preoperational* stage, generally occurs between the ages of 2 and 7. During this stage, the child's thinking is largely egocentric or self-centered and shows an increase in language and concept (i.e., size, shape, color) development. Toward the end of the stage the child is able to use mental images to represent the world. The child does not understand the law of conservation, and in general thinking is intuitive and impulsive. Children do, however, become good explorers as a result of their increased mobility in their physical environment.

The next stage, *concrete operations*, usually occurs between 7 and 11 years of age. At this time, major cognitive tasks are accomplished because of the child's ability to perform such intellectual operations as conservation, reversibility, and ordering things according to number, size, or class. The child's ability to understand and relate to time and space also matures during this period, although there are still vestiges of egocentric thinking. As a result of improved cognitive skills (conservation and reversibility), children become good investigators of the phenomena that surround them.

The last stage, *formal operations*, normally occurs from age 11 though adulthood. During this period, there is a marked change in cognitive ability due to the person's ability to perform hypothetical reasoning. The student is able to function on a purely symbolic, abstract level, and conceptualization capacities mature. Adolescents begin developing the ability to perform hypothetical reasoning with inductive and deductive logic. For example, students become proficient with "if, then" scenarios. This is observed particularly in science classes. When students conduct laboratory experiments, they are asked to predict the consequences before they have performed the experiment. Students might be asked, "If I vary the intensity of the light, what effect will this have on the growth of plants?" By dealing with the variables and principles simultaneously, students experience formal reasoning and learn to trust the decisions they make. Their confidence increases as they test these ideas through science experiments.

With intellectual skills greatly improved as a result of hypothetico-deductive reasoning and abstract thinking, students become quite adept at manipulating variables when solving problems. They are, however, limited by adolescent egocentrism. The two stages of development that secondary educators must be most concerned with are the concrete operational and formal operations stages. Table 5.2 provides a summary of both concrete and formal operational thought (information processing) along with the behavioral characteristics associated with preadolescent and adolescent development.

Educators working with secondary students will observe these distinct phases as students move from concrete operations in the preadolescent years (sixth and seventh grades) to formal operations in the upper high school grades. Middle/junior high school students present a unique developmental situation because students in the seventh and eighth grades are usually in a transition between the concrete operational level and the formal operational level.

This transitional period, described in Chapter 1 as the focus of the middle school movement, has been supported by the research on brain growth. Epstein (1978, 1974) observes that brain growth occurs in spurts or stages, not smooth, linear increments over time. These growth periods of the brain are similar to Piaget's stages of cognitive development (Brooks, Fusco, and Grennon, 1983). Toepfer (1980) notes that students aged 12–14 achieve a growth

Table 5.2 SUMMARY OF STAGES OF COGNITIVE INFORMATION PROCESSING

Concept/Skill and Stage	Cognition: Information Processing	Characteristics During Preadolescence–Adolescence
Concrete operations	Conservation of matter	The student can conserve number by doing one-to-one correspondence and conserve matter by recognizing that changes in form do not change the amount. If student fails this task, he/she is considered still preoperational and not concrete operational in thinking.
	Reversibility	The student has the ability to reverse mental actions or representations. If the student can perform reversibility tasks, the student is a concrete thinker.
	Classification	The student has the ability to classify or divide objects or pictures into different groups. If the student can classify, he/she is considered to be a concrete thinker who can consider the interrelationships among objects.
Formal operations	Abstract thought	Formal thought is characterized by the ability to conjure up the "if-then" scenarios of hypothetical possibilities. This problem solving ability requires abstract thinking, which tends to improve over time.
	Idealism and imagination	Formal operational thought requires the adolescent to reason beyond the real and limited of concrete operational thought by focusing on possibilities or fantasies of the future.
	Understanding language	Formal thinkers are better than concrete operational thinkers in using and understanding the abstract meanings of words, speech patterns, the use of metaphors, and satire. In addition to having effective verbal skills and understanding oral language, adolescents are more effective writers. They are better at understanding key points when reading material, and they are better at using the rules of oral language.
	Appreciating different points of view	Formal thinkers understand and consider another person's point of view as it relates to issues.

plateau which suggests that they do not necessarily continue to grow and develop new and higher-level cognitive skills as they did during the brain growth spurt at the end of the elementary grades. Reinhartz and Beach (1983) recognize the danger of overchallenging students during the plateau period by presenting concepts students are not able to understand, but this "does not mean that formal intellectual operations should be eliminated" (p. 13).

Such a developmental plateau suggests that curriculum planners should be more concerned with a broader curriculum that encourages personal student involvement rather than the introduction of new, complex concepts. In planning instruction, educators need to recognize that such a curriculum is necessary because the exposure that these transitional students have had to television, movies, reading, and adult and peer relationships have given them more information and provided them with increased curiosity (Alexander and George, 1981). Reinhartz and Beach (1983) summarize the situation when they note that as teachers plan instruction it is important that they ". . . recognize their students' variations in previous experience, knowledge, and potential for higher-level thinking and problem solving, and provide appropriate learning opportunities to foster their cognitive development" (p. 13). It is helpful to the instructional process when teachers and other educators recognize the transitional process in the cognitive development of middle/junior high school students.

Once students reach the ninth or tenth grade in school, their cognitive development is more advanced, both qualitatively and quantitatively. Piaget refers to this period as formal operations, which represents the "crystallization and integration of all previous cognitive stages" (Helms and Turner, 1986, p. 461). It is also important to note that many adolescents are still concrete operational thinkers (Santrock, 1988); not all adolescents reach or maintain a formal level of cognitive thought and success in all areas. Helms and Turner (1986) generally describe the thought process during this time as flexible, deliberate, and systematic, which resembles scientific thought.

For high school students, this means that most are able to engage in abstract thought, which involves the use of subjective concepts or ideas and enables students to move beyond a concrete, physical analysis of their environment and to even think about ideas or propositions that are contrary to reality. Students develop problem solving abilities through the use of inductive and deductive logic. Box 5-1 presents a scenario which puts Piaget's cognitive theory of human development into practice. In what ways is the curricular program at Brake Middle School using the principles of cognitive development?

Adolescent thought at the formal operational level is characterized by Santrock (1988) as:

1. Being more abstract than concrete and using hypothetical and purely abstract propositions
2. Developing an increased ability in verbal problem solving skills
3. Being full of idealism and possibilities with a comparison of self and others to an ideal standard; thoughts often being flights of fantasy

---

Box 5-1   Scenario: Cognitive View

At Brake Middle School the focus of the curriculum is on developing students' minds by promoting critical thinking skills — getting students to trust their decision making abilities. The teachers and administrators willingly follow the precepts set forth by Piaget and other developmental psychologists, particularly in their belief that knowing and perceiving are a part of the biological maturation process.

In order to implement a curriculum in such an environment, teachers use teaching strategies which involve students in learning and match their developmental levels. Younger students experience scientific phenomena through concrete laboratory experiments or demonstrations. When studying about the environment or other value laden issues, students might play roles by assuming the identity of a character. Older students are presented with "if-then" hypothetical thinking exercises. These exercises encourage students to reason and develop deductive thinking skills. These instructional activities involve many factors and the students are asked to make decisions when confronted with a character role. For example, how can a business executive who works for an oil drilling company that supports oil exploration in Alaska be personally concerned about the environment without having a conflict? Deciding what to say and trying to understand cognitively as well as emotionally the dilemma this character is experiencing is important learning in the overall instructional program at Brake Middle School.

Such experiences encourage students (preadolescents) to think critically as they explore and test all possibilities in resolving a conflict or problem. Students are asked to evaluate the information they are given and to support or justify the decisions they make. In addition, students are encouraged to devise personal strategies for working through each dilemma, situation, or problem. Lastly, they come to understand that people think differently and learn to appreciate this diversity. Through such experiences students learn to think logically and deductively as they move from the concrete operational thinking of the younger child to the formal reasoning of the adolescent. The curriculum helps students learn how to think.

At Brake Middle School every effort is made to provide a nurturing instructional environment in which the preadolescent develops formal reasoning skills. These skills will help them live productive lives because they will learn how to cope and how to identify general properties and values of a given situation. Taken together, these skills contribute to the ultimate objective at Brake Middle School: getting students to think — to be successful problem solvers and to function at the synthesis and evaluation levels of Bloom's taxonomy.

---

4. Involving hypothetico-deductive reasoning which is more planful and deliberate than before
5. Demonstrating a more advanced understanding of language by perceiving the abstract meaning of words, including an understanding of grammar, syntax, metaphor, and satire
6. Using improved writing and speaking skills, including an understand-

ing of key points when reading prose and an understanding of pragmatics—the rules of conversation

7. Being better at considering and understanding another person's point of view

Behaviorism

The behaviorist theory of human development emphasizes the impact of the environment on the individual and the behavior that results. According to Green (1989), "The central tenet of behaviorism is that individuals should be studied . . . in terms of observable characteristics" (p. 115). Behaviorism is built on the foundation established by Pavlov's work, which distinguished between innate (unconditioned) and learned (conditioned) reflexes. By demonstrating the principle of *classical conditioning*, a procedure by which a neutral stimulus comes to elicit a response by being paired with a stimulus that regularly evokes the response, he advanced the scientific analysis of behavior significantly (Green, 1989). Through the classical conditioning process, responses or behaviors can be acquired or eliminated.

Behaviorism has been further developed and systematized by Watson (1924), Thorndike (1933, 1931) and Skinner (1968, 1953, 1948). Watson "took an extreme . . . position in maintaining that he could, irrespective of talent, tendency, and ability, train healthy infants to become whatever he might select—doctor or lawyer, beggar or thief" (Green, 1989, p. 117). Thorndike proposed the *law of effect*, which focused on goal-oriented behavior. The law of effect

> holds that responses increase or decrease in likelihood as a function of the effects they produce. Sometimes the effects make the previous response more likely to occur in the future; sometimes they make the responses less likely (Green, 1989, p. 117).

The law of effect added to our understanding of learning in that it provided an explanation for how the likelihood of a response is impacted by the consequences of the response.

Skinner built upon Thorndike's work to help explain the acquisition of new behaviors. Skinner's view of learning is built upon the idea of *operant conditioning*, which is very different from classical conditioning. Operant conditioning, often associated with reinforcement, emphasizes the individual's operating or acting on the environment, with behavior controlled by external consequences. In such a view of development, an individual's behavior results from the controlling forces in the environment. According to Skinner, as we operate on our environment, the consequences of our actions shape our development (who and what we are), and the consequences can be *rewarding* or *punishing*.

Box 5-2 provides an application of behaviorism in an educational program. This theory of human development is described as it is used in a hypothetical school situation in the Oakwood School District. It emphasizes the use of rewards in the school environment to shape learning behavior. Think about the

Box 5-2   # Scenario: Behaviorist View

As a result of the rhetoric concerning declining scores on standardized tests, the Oakwood School District now requires graduating seniors to pass a basic literacy test—reading, writing, math, with some general knowledge in science and social studies. The secondary teachers are somewhat frustrated because they are held responsible for the success that students have in passing this basic skills test. They are also aware that rewards work in achieving such short-term goals. The challenge to the faculty is to have as many seniors as possible pass this test. To raise the test scores, the teachers developed a series of drill and practice exercises for each curriculum area (reading and writing, math, science and social studies). These exercises have become a part of the tutorial sessions that are offered at different times (before, after, and during) the school day.

Students, faculty, and parent community volunteers are responsible for monitoring these tutorial sessions as well as answering any questions that the students may have. A drill and practice approach is used to help the seniors prepare for the literacy test. The volunteers ask students questions and the students respond. The volunteers monitoring the tutorial program are not very concerned with the seniors' in-depth understanding of the answers to the questions, but rather how many they answer correctly and what they can remember over the short term. Repetition characterizes this approach. Computer programs, which include many of the practice exercises, have been developed. Many of the seniors prefer to use this approach because they get immediate feedback and move at their own pace.

In addition, a reward system has been devised to help motivate the students to attend the tutorial practice sessions. Seniors earn points that can be cashed in for prizes such as records, tapes, posters, movie tickets, and food coupons (pizza, burgers, nachos). Many of these items are donated by local businesses.

It is hoped that through the drill and practice exercises (responding to a core of questions prepared for each curriculum area), coupled with an incentive/reward system, the seniors will attend the sessions and a higher percentage of them will pass the literacy test. The organizers of this program are confident that if the seniors attend, they will gain enough "basic" information (facts, names, dates, skills) to pass the test. In fact, the teachers have already made plans to develop a similar program to help seniors get higher scores on their college entrance tests, and the district is planning to implement a drill and practice approach with a reward system to improve PSAT, ACT, and SAT scores.

different ways, if any, that the teachers are getting the seniors to pass the basic literacy test.

Psychoanalytic Theory

The psychoanalytic theory emphasizes the personality of an individual as the driving force behind the developmental process. This theory views development as the transformation of an individual from the expression of "animal desires," which are governed by passions and emotions, into socially acceptable, rational behavior.

Freud (1920, 1910) was instrumental in the development of this theory with his description of the agencies of the mind—id, ego, and superego—and his identification of five stages of psychosexual development. Freud viewed the *id* as the instinctual, biological part of personality that we inherit. He considered it to be the most primitive part of personality because it is governed by the pleasure principle—maximize pleasure and minimize pain (Crain, 1985). Freud described the id as a bundle of sexual and aggressive instincts or drives that are primarily unconscious and that dominate our lives. He believed that as a result of these unconscious drives, we are not aware of the motivation for much of our behavior.

The *ego*, according to Freud, is the part of personality that comes in contact with the environment. It is the rational part of personality, and as it develops, it shapes our behavior in ways that are socially acceptable, within the boundaries of reality. Crain (1985) says that "If we were ruled by the id, we would not live for long. To survive, one cannot . . . simply follow one's impulses. We must learn to deal with reality [and] . . . The agency that . . . considers reality is called the ego" (p. 151). The ego is sometimes called the executive branch of personality because it houses the individual's higher mental functions, such as reasoning, problem solving, and decision making. Although Freud recognized the importance of cognitive functions, he nonetheless believed that these always come into conflict with the id, and usually lose.

The *superego* is considered the moral branch of personality and begins to develop at about age 5. As the superego develops it helps individuals incorporate the values taught by religion, society, and family. The superego houses the conscience and the ideal ego, or ideal self. Within Freud's view, development is the result of the interaction of these three personality components and their relationship with others and the environment.

Freud also identified five distinct periods of development, which he called the *psychosexual stages*. These five stages and the characteristic behaviors associated with each are shown in Table 5.3. The last two stages are the most applicable to preadolescent and adolescent development.

Another individual who contributed significantly to psychoanalytic theory is Erikson (1968, 1963, 1950) who proposed the *psychosocial stages* of development. Erikson agrees that development occurs through a combination of biology and culture, which he says results in psychosocial rather than psychosexual stages. Erikson proposes eight stages which extend from infancy through late adulthood. Each stage of development centers around a "crisis" produced by an emotional concern that is generated by the biological pressures within individuals and the sociocultural expectations outside individuals. These conflicts are resolved in either a positive or a pessimistic way. For development to proceed smoothly, each earlier conflict or crisis must be resolved satisfactorily. Table 5.3 compares Erikson's stages of psychosocial development with Freud's stages of psychosexual development by identifying each stage and providing a description of the typical behavior or crisis that must be resolved.

As noted in Table 5.3, the first three stages for Freud and Erikson involve

Table 5.3   A COMPARISON OF THE DEVELOPMENTAL STAGES OF FREUD AND ERIKSON

Freud's Psychosexual Stages	Age	Erikson's Psychosocial Stages
Oral Stage: Pleasure derived from mouth (sucking, eating, biting, etc.). Unfortunate experiences may cause a fixation that leads to greed, possessiveness, or verbal aggressiveness.	Birth–1	*Trust vs. Mistrust:* Adequate care and general affection lead to a view of the world as safe and dependable and a sense of trust in the environment.
Anal Stage: Pleasure comes from urination and bowel movements. Unfortunate experiences may cause a fixation that leads to messiness, extreme cleanliness, or frugality.	2–3	*Autonomy vs. Shame and Doubt:* The development of a sense of identity and self-worth. Child trys out skills at own pace and in own way, which leads to autonomy. Overprotection or control may lead to self-doubt.
Phallic Stage: Curiosity directed toward self and others. Genital region provides greatest sensual satisfaction. Unfortunate experiences may cause a fixation which can lead to unclear sex roles. Parent of opposite sex is taken as object of sensual satisfaction, which leads to a tendency to regard same-sexed parent as a rival (Oedipus and Electra complexes). Unfortunate experiences may lead to competitiveness.	4–5	*Initiative vs. Guilt:* Freedom to engage in activities and to learn and develop competence. Restriction of activities or fear of failure may lead to feelings of guilt.
Latency Period: Tranquil period with refinement of self-concept and increased social (peer group) interaction. Satisfaction of sensual needs is done vicariously. Resolution of Oedipus and Electra complexes.	6–11	*Industry vs. Inferiority:* Learns the value of work by being permitted to make and do things and by being praised for accomplishments. Limitations on activities and criticism of what is done may lead to feelings of inferiority.
Genital Period: Beginning of romantic love with the discovery of new sexual feelings and sexual maturation. Integration of sensual tendencies from previous stages into unitary and overriding genital sexuality.	12–18	*Identity vs. Role Confusion:* Experimentation with roles and recognition of the continuity and sameness in one's personality, even when in different situations and when reacted to by different individuals. Inability to establish stable traits and acceptable roles may lead to role confusion.

Modified from: Biehler, R. F. (1974). *Psychology applied to teaching* (2nd ed.). Boston: Houghton Mifflin, p. 109.

infancy, toddlerhood, and preschool years and form the foundation for a sense of achievement and self-worth by trusting in the environment. The *industry vs. inferiority* stage covers the middle childhood and preadolescent years—a tranquil period of time in which coping mechanisms develop. The student is involved in the extensive acquisition of knowledge and the development of physical as well as intellectual skills, which bring a feeling of competence to the individual and serve to help order life and make things work.

The next stage, *identity vs. role confusion*, corresponds with the adolescent years. This stage is roughly associated with Freud's genital stage, which involves the discovery of new sexual feelings and heterosexual attractions, and centers on the establishment of a stable personal identity. The central ingredient for this period is the development of an "accrued confidence" and a clear path toward a vocation. According to Erikson (1968), "The growing and developing youths, faced with . . . adult tasks ahead of them are now primarily concerned with how they appear in the eyes of others as compared with what they feel they are" (p. 261). Erikson does not always see a positive resolution to each stage. However, in a healthy solution to a stage crisis, a positive resolution of the conflict should always be desirable and dominant.

The scenario presented in Box 5-3 describes several ways that the psychoanalytic theory of development is applied in a secondary school setting. This scenario emphasizes the importance of helping students develop their personality.

Humanism

The fourth and final developmental theory is humanism, which places a strong emphasis on the role of self and self-concept in the development of the individual. The humanistic view recognizes the importance of a student's self-concept, how he or she generally perceives himself or herself, as a key organizing principle. This developmental theory was described by Maslow (1971, 1968, 1954) and supported by the work of Rogers (1969, 1961).

Maslow proposed a theory of *need gratification*, which he saw as "the most important single principle underlying all development . . . that binds together the multiplicity of human motives" (1968, p. 55). He believed that individuals are wanting beings and no sooner than one desire is satisfied, another takes its place. Maslow elaborated on this theory by arguing that each person has a hierarchy of needs that must be satisfied. These needs range from basic physiological requirements to love and self-esteem. Figure 5.1 illustrates each level of the hierarchy of needs.

Biehler (1974), interpreting Maslow's hierarchy, says,

> . . . when a person has the lower needs (physiological, safety, belongingness and love, esteem) satisfied, he [or she] will feel motivated to satisfy the higher . . . needs (self-actualization, knowing and understanding, aesthetic) — not because of a deficit but because of a desire to gratify higher needs. Being needs are the basis for self-actualization (p. 411).

Self-actualization, the highest need of the hierarchy, refers to the full attainment of one's talents, abilities, and potential. It is the relatively rare individuals who have the lower needs sufficiently satisfied so that they can develop the motive or drive for self-actualization. Maslow found that self-actualized persons attain a certain degree of independence from society and are much less conforming. They seem less molded and shaped by the social environment and

Box 5-3   Scenario: Psychoanalytic View

As students progress from elementary school to middle or junior high school and later to high school, they begin to develop unique personalities. They learn how to behave, what to say in social settings, and how their behavior affects others. Preadolescence and adolescence are stages when students begin to experiment with different personality behaviors, often just to get a response from others. This frequently creates conflicts between students and adults. As more and more parents or guardians work and students are left on their own they must learn to resolve dilemmas that arise. Often the only adults available in an adolescent's life are teachers. The schools, especially teachers, are being asked to serve as models and to help students resolve problems and conflicts.

Recently, a problem has developed in a local high school. Students are having difficulty resolving minor conflicts in and outside the classroom. It seems that not a day goes by but at least 20 students are in the office for misbehavior, poor conduct, and/or disrespectful behaviors to their peers and/or teachers. Many of the episodes can be attributed to "personality conflicts" as students are trying to establish a sense of identity. As a result, the following questions have arisen: How can these students be helped? What steps should be taken?

Under the leadership of the principal, and with the sanction of the central office, the faculty, staff, parents, and students, a plan has been developed for "teaching" students acceptable behavior with their peers and adults. The counselors in the building have developed modules and case studies for teachers to use during the "socializing hour" once a week. Video tapes are a part of the modules, and they portray students "acting out" various behaviors. Students can see the same person as he or she takes on a new "personality" in the episodes. The students then analyze the tapes, both from the standpoint of the person behaving in a certain way and from the perspective of the person on the receiving end (parent, teacher, friend, etc.). Inservice has been provided for the teachers to help them become familiar with these modules and case studies and to learn how to use them with students in their classes.

How do you help these students to go beyond their ego and consider others and their feelings? The modules identify the key concepts to be achieved along with the objectives. Suggested strategies are included as well. Placing students in conflict situations with their peers and adults helps these students think through the process rather than acting on instinct, which often results in fights, verbal abuse, and hurt feelings. These modules are designed to help students explore alternative behaviors and begin to act responsibly. Students have the opportunity to learn appropriate roles and responses when interacting with others, rather than relying on their feelings at the moment.

In addition, students who continue to behave in inappropriate ways (e.g., get in fights, argue with teachers) are asked to participate in a session where they present their "side" to a panel of their peers. The students serving as peer reviewers receive 15 hours of training from the counselors. The students' role on the panel is to listen and help the student having difficulty present all aspects of the conflict in an attempt to obtain resolution. No teachers attend these sessions and all students must maintain strict confidentiality.

Box 5-3 **Scenario: Psychoanalytic View — Continued**

By having a curriculum that focuses on learning opportunities which help resolve conflict as well as having an opportunity to present their cases to an impartial group of peers, adolescents develop confidence and learn to trust their own judgments. Confidence building and handling conflict are essential in helping each student develop his or her personal identity.

remain more spontaneous, although rarely behaving in unconventional ways (Crain, 1985). Maslow distinguished self-actualized people from most in that they are unusually healthy psychologically, perceiving everyday life realistically, and accepting it without defensiveness.

The applications of Maslow's theory of development suggest that educators should make sure that the lower level needs of students are met. According to Biehler (1974), by meeting lower level needs,

> . . . students will be more likely to be primed to seek satisfaction of the needs to understand and know in [their] classes if they are physically comfortable, feel safe and relaxed, have a sense of belonging, and experience self-esteem (p. 414).

The more we are able to help students satisfy basic needs, the more likely we will be able to foster motivation for higher needs and promote healthy development. Growth, as a part of development, is the result of a never-ending series of

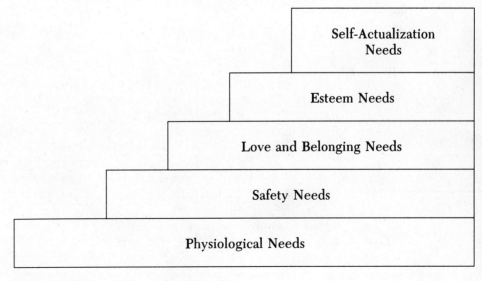

Figure 5.1 Maslow's Hierarchy of Needs

situations offering freedom of choice between the attractions and dangers of safety and growth (Biehler, 1974).

Rogers (1969, 1961) has added to the humanistic theory of development by applying his principles of psychotherapy to educational settings. He saw the child's *perception* of the world as more important in understanding his or her development than his or her actual behavior. In studying the self, Rogers believed in utilizing both direct observations and psychological tests to measure growth. He further suggested that individuals — teachers and students — could gain a greater understanding of themselves through intensive group experiences, which he called *learner-centered* teaching. This approach is essentially an ultimate version of the discovery approach to teaching (Biehler, 1974). For Rogers, learner-centered teaching helps the participants to explore their attitudes and interpersonal relationships. Box 5-4 describes Prest High School as it is now and as it was before a humanistic approach was applied to the school situation. In many respects, the curriculum is student and faculty centered. Can you identify the concepts of humanism in the scenario? If so, what are they?

In summary, cognitive development, behaviorism, psychoanalytic theory, and humanism are the four main theories of human development. No single theory adequately explains human development and behavior, but each one contributes significantly to our understanding of development and provides insights for curriculum developers when establishing educational programs for preadolescents and adolescents. Those who are concerned about the total development of the junior and senior high school student will be able to draw upon the concepts of all the theories to produce a well-rounded educational program.

MORAL DEVELOPMENT

In addition to the four developmental theories discussed previously, it is also appropriate to briefly discuss the moral development of students, particularly preadolescents and adolescents. Moral development concerns rules and conventions about what people should do in their interactions with other people. In studying these rules, developmental psychologists examine three different domains of moral development — thought, action, and feeling.

In addition to studying the cognitive development of children, Piaget also studied the development of moral reasoning. Piaget recognized and acknowledged that an individual's cognitive development was paralleled by the person's moral development. He saw moral development as involving the acceptance of social rules and concern for equality and justice in relationships. According to Helms and Turner (1986), Piaget considered morality to be a set of rules handed down from adults to children and "through training and practice, children learn to respect these standards of conduct" (p. 381). Piaget (1965) proposed three stages of moral development, which include the premoral period, the period of moral reciprocity or moral realism, and the moral relativity period.

Box 5-4 **Scenario: Humanistic View**

The students and faculty at Prest High School are proud of their school and themselves for their contributions toward making their school a "nice place." They have made a concerted effort to foster student and faculty harmony as well as personal development. The key ingredient in this school is a sense of well-being: students feel good about themselves and teachers eagerly share their knowledge as they teach.

Teachers are dedicated to helping each student achieve his or her maximum potential. They believe that every student has at least one special talent to be developed. As a result, students are anxious to tell you about themselves — what they have learned, accomplished, and/or hope to achieve next year. As the students deal realistically with everyday life, needs, and demands, their spontaneity is genuine. This caring, "I am special" attitude permeates the whole school.

This has not always been the case. Just five years ago, parents, teachers, and students were unhappy, dissatisfied, and, to some degree, rebellious. Rules were not followed and there was a general attitude of not caring. Absenteeism by both faculty and students was very high. It was clear that neither the students nor the faculty wanted to be at Prest High School. Students did not see the school as a good place to be and develop their potential.

Under great pressure from several sources, the school board decided to make some changes after meeting and talking to several groups including students, parents, and teachers. First, a learner-centered approach was developed and implemented in the instructional program. The focus of instruction became the students rather than behavioral outcomes. Teachers were given time during the school day to visit other schools where such programs had been implemented. Teachers were also provided with ongoing support from the principal and central office staff. When possible, students participated in group activities so that they could explore attitudes and interpersonal relationships. Students had many opportunities to consider their strengths and shortcomings. Through such opportunities, they were in a better position to analyze who they were and where they wanted to go. In addition, teachers increased their praise vocabulary and went out of their way to let students know when they were correct and offered suggestions in a positive way when students were not correct.

After five years of working together, Prest High School has became what it is today. Ask any student or teacher how they feel about the school, and they will tell you that they are happy to be at school and that they think they are learning what they need to know to be successful in their own ways.

In the *premoral period* (birth to 7 years), the child initially focuses on the self and is highly egocentric. In the first two years, the child has little awareness of rules and is not capable of making moral judgments because of limited cognitive development and a high degree of egocentrism. In the latter part of the premoral period, there is a shift from the self to a focus on authority. Rules which govern the child's behavior come from a parent or other authority figure, and the child believes that any deviation from the rules will result in some form of punishment. Children often focus on the consequences of their actions rather than their intentions.

In the second period, *moral reciprocity* or *moral realism* (8 to 11 years), the student moves from an exclusive focus on authority to more prosocial behavior and a concern for interactions with others in specific situations. During this period the student develops a sense of autonomy, and according to Schiamberg (1988), moral behavior is influenced by the student's recognition of the following:

1. Social rules are not absolute and can be challenged when necessary.
2. It is not always wrong to break the rules.
3. In understanding the behavior of others, feelings and viewpoints should be considered.
4. The nature of the rule that was broken, the intentions of the person, and the type of correction (retribution or restitution) should be taken into account if there is to be any punishment.

One of the dangers of this period is that the student may become inflexible in moral reasoning and develop an "eye-for-an-eye" level of morality in dealing with others.

The *moral relativism* period (age 12 though adolescence and adult years) normally begins during the high school years and continues into adulthood. It should be noted, however, that Piaget recognized that not every individual attains this stage of moral development, since moral development is tied to cognitive development and not all individuals attain the formal level. At this stage, individuals view rules as products of mutual consent and respect based on certain principles, and they can make realistic applications of moral values in specific situations by taking all factors into account. Moral decisions therefore tend to be based on the highly specific situation and the circumstances involved and have a social, logical, and cooperative quality.

Kohlberg (1981, 1968) proposed an expanded theory of moral development. He believed that moral development was based on moral reasoning, which unfolds in three different levels with two stages in each level. The first level (birth to 9) is called *preconventional morality*, where the child shows no internalization of moral values and little conception of socially acceptable or moral behavior. In the first stage of this level—obedience and punishment orientation—children generally obey rules in order to avoid punishment. Children normally conform to rules imposed on them by persons in authority. In the second stage—naively egoistic orientation—children are motivated to behave correctly because they believe they will earn some concrete or tangible reward.

In Kohlberg's second level, *conventional morality* (ages 9 through 15), students learn the nature of authority in society as well as in the family. In the third stage—good boy-nice girl orientation—students exhibit considerable conformist behavior, and they learn to recognize that they must abide by the rules in order to receive approval. This conformity in their behavior fosters an internal awareness of rules and therefore promotes respect for others, especially those in authority. In the fourth stage — law and order orientation — the focus shifts to organizations and institutions in society which provide rules that guide or govern behavior. The school and church, as well as many youth organizations (e.g., scouts) often codify appropriate behavior for students.

Sometimes, an intervening stage will occur between stages four and five (Helms and Turner, 1986). In this intermediate stage, the student may begin to seriously question society's definition of what is right and wrong. This questioning of the accepted behaviors, while rejecting conventional morality, does contribute to self-realization. Since this intervening stage corresponds with the preadolescent and adolescent years and the struggle for independence from adult supervision, it is not surprising that students would also question and reject some of the values of their parents.

The third and final level of Kohlberg's moral development theory is called *postconventional morality* (age 16 through adulthood) and represents the highest level of moral reasoning. At this level, morality is completely internalized — not based on the standards of others — and the individual reaches a mature understanding of moral behavior. In the fifth stage — contractual legalistic orientation — individuals, especially teenagers and young adults, select moral principles to guide their personal behavior. Students are also careful not to violate the rights and wills of others. The sixth stage — universal ethical principle orientation — marks the onset of a true conscience, which prompts individuals to select the most appropriate forms of behavior that will affirm their rights as well as the rights of others. Kohlberg believed that relatively few people attain stage six of moral reasoning.

As indicated in the previous discussion, Kohlberg's stages four through six and Piaget's third stage seem to have the greatest significance in the development of curriculum for preadolescents and adolescents. By asking students about moral issues and listening to their responses, secondary teachers can gain insight into their students' level of moral reasoning. The procedure of presenting students with moral dilemmas, as suggested by Kohlberg, can provide a basis for classroom discussions on such issues as suicide, the right to life and the right to die, and drug use. Teachers can, for example, use Shakespeare's *Romeo and Juliet* to discuss such themes as love, disobedience to parents, and suicide. Such discussions not only appeal to the developmental interests of the students but also serve to raise students' levels of moral reasoning. When working with adolescents teachers should also be careful not to overemphasize classroom rules and procedures, since they may apply only to school circumstances and students need to deal with issues and problems, including their own behavior, in a broader context (Reinhartz and Beach, 1983).

Curriculum writers need to be knowledgeable, not only of the general principles of human development but also of the basic theories of human development, as they plan learning activities for secondary students. Moral development is also an important aspect of development included in this chapter because it is especially significant for curriculum developers when considering programs for middle, junior, and high school students.

SUMMARY

Chapter 5 presented the role of psychology in planning and developing curricular programs for secondary students. The content of the chapter included the various ways the psychological principles are associated with the learning process and how they shape the curriculum. In addition, the three general principles of development were discussed as the overriding framework for development. These principles suggest that as people grow and develop, there is an individual pattern for rate and movement from stage to stage, and as we mature, the range of abilities among individuals widens.

The majority of the chapter was devoted to a description of the four major developmental theories: cognitive, behavioristic, psychoanalytic, and humanistic. Each theory, or view of how human beings develop, was presented in great detail and a scenario accompanied each. The scenario provided an application of each theory in a real or contextual setting. The chapter ended with a discussion of moral development, particularly as it relates to the preadolescent and adolescent student.

Based on the information and descriptions in the chapter, it should be evident that there is no single theory for explaining the physical, cognitive, social, and moral development of preadolescents and adolescents. By presenting a variety of theories and perspectives, curriculum developers have an opportunity to study each and determine how each contributes in a meaningful way to understanding the secondary student, which in turn facilitates planning for a meaningful and relevant curriculum.

YOUR TURN

5.1 Review the three educational philosophies (essentialism, progressivism, and existentialism) in Chapter 3 and the different developmental theories (cognitive, behavioristic, psychoanalytic, and humanistic) and determine which developmental theory is compatible with which philosophy or philosophies. It might be helpful to review the "Profiles" in Chapter 3 and the "Scenarios" in this chapter.

5.2 Review the school mission statement that follows and list all of the ways that psychological foundations are reflected or involved in the school curriculum. Although not necessarily named specifically, some references are made concerning aspects of the psychological foundations. What aspects can you find?

The educational practices at Hilton Middle School are based on the belief that students, who are in transition between childhood and adolescence, have special physiological, psychological, emotional, and intellectual needs. This transitional period is characterized by accelerated development and wide variations among students. To effectively meet the needs of each student, a unique educational environment is required.

The curriculum of the middle school should be designed to meet the individual needs of students in grades 6–8. For a student to experience psychological, physiological, emotional, social, and intellectual growth, he or she must be an active learner. Each student must, therefore, take responsibility for learning. There must be freedom within the classroom environment so that students can make decisions, explore, gather information, and interact with peers and adults. The students need to become explorers, discoverers, inquirers, and performers. They must be allowed to do their own learning according to their development. As a consequence of such experiences, students develop competence, trust, and confidence in themselves and in what they can do. They begin to move toward independence through self-awareness and learn not to be afraid of taking the initiative.

Developing curriculum for the middle school is a cooperative venture. Curriculum planning sessions involve educators, students, and members of the community. A survey of the community's needs, desires, and aspirations is conducted annually to help in the curriculum development process. This study has revealed the community resources which serve as natural starting points for learning. As the cultural and social characteristics of the community become evident, the educational activities are linked more closely with the student's home experiences. Within an integrated day framework, the teacher primarily plays the role of guide or facilitator. He or she establishes a learning environment that provides a broad base of experiences, so that each student can match his or her learning style and pace with the learning situations. The school, through the curriculum, is guided by the belief that students should have every opportunity to learn to think for themselves. Also, the students must have opportunities to develop their individual talents and potentials. Therefore, the school helps each student become more than he or she thought possible.

5.3 Return to Table 3.1 in Chapter 3, add a fourth column called "The Psychological Perspective," and provide appropriate descriptions.

REFERENCES

Alexander, W.M. & George, P.S. (1981). *The exemplary middle school*. New York: Holt, Rinehart & Winston.

Beckner, W. & Cornett, J.D. (1972). *The secondary school curriculum: Content and structure*. Scranton, Pa.: Intext Educational Publishers.

Biehler, R.F. (1974). *Psychology applied to teaching* (2nd. ed.). Boston: Houghton Mifflin.

Brooks, M., Fusco, E. & Grennon, J. (May 1983). Cognitive levels matching. *Educational Leadership, 40, 8, 5*.

Bruner, J.S. (1968). *Toward a theory of instruction*. New York: Norton.

Bruner, J.S. (1960). *The process of education*. Cambridge, Mass.: Harvard University Press.

Bruner, J.S. et al. (1966). *Studies in cognitive growth*. New York: Wiley.

Crain, W.C. (1985). *Theories of development, concepts and applications* (2nd ed.). Englewood Cliffs, N.J.: Prentice-Hall.

Epstein, H.T. (1978). Growth spurts during brain development: Implications for educational policy and practice. In *Education and the brain*. J. Chall (Ed.), 79th Yearbook, Part II. National Society for the Study of Education. Chicago: University of Chicago Press.

Epstein, H.T. (1974). Phrenoblysis: Special brain and mind growth periods: Human brain and skull development, *Developmental Psychology, 7, 3, 217–224*.

Erikson, E.H. (1968). *Identity: Youth and crisis.* New York: Norton.

Erikson, E.H. (1963). *Childhood and society* (2nd ed.). New York: Norton.

Erikson, E.H. (1950). *Childhood and society.* New York: Norton.

Freud, S. (1920). *A general introduction to psychoanalysis* (J. Riviere, trans.). New York: Washington Square Press, 1965.

Freud, S. (1910). *The origin and development of psychoanalysis.* New York: Henry Regnery (Gateway Editions, 1965).

Glickman, C.D. (1981). *Developmental supervision: Alternative practices for helping teachers improve instruction.* Alexandria, Va.: Association for Supervision and Curriculum Development.

Green, M. (1989). *Theories of human development.* Englewood Cliffs, N.J.: Prentice-Hall.

Helms, D.B. & Turner, J.S. (1986). *Exploring child behavior.* Monterey, Calif.: Brooks Cole.

Kohlberg, L. (1981). *The philosophy of moral development.* New York: Harper & Row.

Kohlberg, L. (September 1968). The child as a moral philosopher. *Psychology Today, 2,* 4, 25–30.

Maslow, A.H. (1971). *The farther reaches of human nature.* New York: Viking.

Maslow, A.H. (1968). *Toward a psychology of being* (2nd ed.). New York: Van Nostrand Reinhold.

Maslow, A.H. (1954). *Motivation and personality.* New York: Harper & Row.

Mathis, B.C., Cotton, J.W. & Sechrest, L. (1970). *Psychological foundations of education.* New York: Academic Press.

Piaget, J. (1967). *Six psychological studies.* New York: Random House.

Piaget, J. (1965). *The moral judgement of the child.* New York: Free Press.

Piaget, J. (1952). *The origins of intelligence.* New York: International Universities Press.

Piaget, J. & Inhelder, B. (1973). *Memory and intelligence.* New York: Basic Books.

Reinhartz, J. & Beach D.M. (1983). *Improving middle school instruction: A research-based self-assessment system.* Washington, D.C.: National Education Association.

Rogers, C.R. (1969). *Freedom to learn.* Columbus, Ohio: Charles E. Merrill.

Rogers, C.R. (1961). *On becoming a person.* Boston: Houghton Mifflin.

Santrock, J.W. (1988). *Children.* Dubuque, Iowa: Brown.

Schiamberg, L.B. (1988). *Child and adolescent development.* New York: Macmillan.

Skinner, B.F. (1968). *The technology of teaching.* New York: Appleton-Century-Crofts.

Skinner, B.F. (1953). *Science and human behavior.* New York: Free Press.

Skinner, B.F. (1948). *Walden two.* New York: Macmillan.

Thorndike, E.L. (1933). A proof of the law of the effect. *Science, 77,* 1989, 173–175.

Thorndike, E.L. (1931). *Human learning.* New York: The Century Company.

Toepfer, C.F., Jr. (March 1980). Brain growth periodization data: Some suggestions for reorganizing middle grades education. *High School Journal, 63,* 6, 224–226.

Tyler, R. (1949). *Basic principles of curriculum and instruction.* Chicago: University of Chicago Press.

Watson, J.B. (1924). *Behaviorism.* New York: Norton.

Chapter
6

Characteristics of Secondary Students

*I*n addition to a knowledge of the general principles of development and the various developmental theories, educators working with preadolescents and adolescents also need a knowledge of the developmental characteristics of these students. Developing and improving instruction at the secondary level is predicated on an understanding of the nature of the student population in grades 7–12. Popham and Baker (1970) support this assertion when they say,

> The learner—the high school student . . . is the first basic data source of possible objectives. We should have some idea of the abilities of the learner so that we can decide what he[/she] is likely to know already. In addition, we might use the learner's own interests and needs as a possible basis for curricular decisions (p. 49).

Recognizing typical behavior and special needs of middle, junior, and senior high school students is central to curriculum development.

Planning and developing curriculum would be incomplete without considering the learners. This chapter does just that—describes the characteristics of the students in grades 7–12. Curriculum planners need knowledge and understanding of the developmental characteristics of secondary school pupils. This knowledge comes from a variety of sources, but the best way educators can obtain information is by observing students and having them complete personal interest inventories as well as cognitive inventories. Another source of data about specific students is the cumulative record or folder. This information about individual students can be valuable to the curriculum developer and the teacher at the classroom level in planning instruction. Another more global or generic source of information about secondary students comes from the research and writings of educational psychologists and human development specialists.

Chapter 5 described the major developmental theories and how each of the different views of development shapes perceptions about students. This chapter presents in detail the physical, physiological, cognitive, and social aspects of preadolescents and adolescents. The following sections describe the gender differences in cognition and the social development of adolescents. The chapter also contains a brief discussion of three theories of learning (faculty psychology, behaviorism, and cognitive field) and how each views student learning. The chapter concludes with a description of the basic developmental tasks of adolescence, including some special needs of junior and senior high school students which have implications for curriculum development.

PHYSICAL AND PHYSIOLOGICAL CHARACTERISTICS

During the preadolescent years, students experience a resting period followed by a period of rapid growth in height and weight called the adolescent growth spurt. Until the end of the elementary grades, boys tend to be taller and heavier than girls, but during the middle and junior high school years (ages 11–14) girls forge ahead. This growth spurt normally starts sometime between 10 and 13 in girls and may be as much as two years later in boys. Girls, as they enter junior high school, begin to slim down compared to the later elementary years.

During this transition period from childhood to adolescence girls are normally taller than boys. Students of either gender whose maturation rate is noticeably ahead or behind the average are likely to be self-conscious and experience varying degrees of anxiety. Students in this period often appear awkward and clumsy due to the uneven growth of different parts of the body and are self-conscious about their physical appearance. These students frequently have enormous appetites—they will eat anything in sight, but there are times when they will also be finicky about what they eat.

The junior high school preadolescent enters adolescence with the onset of puberty. This is a time period that many refer to as being governed by hormones, and it is true that hormones begin to exert tremendous influence on the physiological development of the student. For Schiamberg (1988), puberty refers to "specific sexual changes that result in reproductive capability *and* other biological changes that lead up to reproductive capability (the adolescent growth spurt, and accompanying changes in respiration, circulation and body composition)" (p. 646). All of these physiological changes are triggered by hormones. According to Marshall (1978), there are five indicators related to puberty:

1. Rapid acceleration in growth which produces dramatic changes in both weight and height (growth spurt)
2. Changes in the distribution of muscle and body fat (body composition)
3. Increased physical strength and motor skill performance due to changes in respiratory and circulatory systems
4. Development of male and female sex organs (gonads) that leads to reproductive capability (sexual maturity)
5. Development of secondary sex characteristics (breasts in females, growth of facial hair in males, etc.)

The physiological changes which occur during adolescence are outwardly evident and can be the most obvious of the developmental processes that take place in students during this period. Mussen, Conger, Kagan, and Huston (1990) provide the following summary of the physiological events that lead to maturation in adolescent boys and girls:

Although there may be some individual—and perfectly normal—variations in the sequence of events leading to physical and sexual maturity in boys, the following sequence is typical:

1. Testes and scrotum begin to increase in size.
2. Pubic hair begins to appear.
3. Adolescent growth spurt starts; the penis begins to enlarge.
4. Voice deepens as the larynx grows.
5. Hair begins to appear under the arms and on the upper lip.
6. Sperm production increases, and nocturnal emission (ejaculation of semen during sleep) may occur.
7. Growth spurt reaches peak rate: pubic hair becomes pigmented.
8. Prostate gland enlarges.
9. Sperm production becomes sufficient for fertility; growth rate decreases.
10. Physical strength reaches a peak.

Although, as in the case of boys, there may be normal variations in the sequence of physical and sexual maturation in girls, a typical sequence of events is as follows:

1. Adolescent growth spurt begins.
2. Downy (nonpigmented) pubic hair makes its initial appearance.
3. Elevation of the breast (the so-called bud stage of development) and rounding of the hips begin, accompanied by the beginning of downy axillary (armpit) hair.
4. The uterus and vagina, as well as labia and clitoris, increase in size.
5. Pubic hair grows rapidly and becomes slightly pigmented.
6. Breasts develop further: nipple pigmentation begins; areola increases in size; axillary hair becomes slightly pigmented.
7. Growth spurt reaches peak rate and then declines.
8. Menarche (onset of menstruation) occurs.
9. Pubic hair development is completed, followed by mature breast development and completion of axillary hair development.

10. Period of "adolescent sterility" ends, and girl becomes capable of conception (up to a year or so after menarche) (p. 575).

Again, it is important to emphasize the individual rates of development and maturation. For example, the development of adolescent boys is such that some appear physically like grade school boys, some are in the transitional phase from childhood to sexual maturity, while still others are physically and sexually mature and have the appearance of much older males (Mussen, Conger, Kagan, and Huston, 1990; Schiamberg, 1988). This same variation is also evident in adolescent girls, although the range of physical differences is not quite as evident. These physical changes may also exert significant influence on the general psychological development and the extent to which boys and girls become self-conscious of their physical appearance.

COGNITIVE CHARACTERISTICS

Cognitive development in adolescence occurs in two areas: quantity and quality. Schiamberg (1988) defines quantitative changes as altering "the total amount of a particular skill or ability . . . (e.g., increasing precision in the use of words to label objects, people, or actions)" and qualitative as changing ". . . the manner or process of cognitive functioning," such as using abstract labels (love, justice, freedom) without referring to concrete examples (p. 671). As mentioned previously, the preadolescent is in a transitional stage between concrete and formal thought and has reached a plateau in learning. There is evidence (Cole and Hall, 1970) to suggest, however, that during early adolescence, there is an increase in the intellectual growth rate which allows the individual to learn more.

The mind is quite creative and imaginative during the adolescent and young adult years. According to Beckner and Cornett (1972), "Abilities in some areas become more pronounced, while in others there may be little improvement" (p. 115). As a result, ability tests which provide some indication of success in particular fields, such as medicine, engineering or the arts, can be given to teenagers. As indicated throughout the chapter, there is a wide range of individual differences.

In addition to intellectual development of a quantitative nature, curriculum developers must consider the qualitative changes that occur as well. Sund (1976) notes that ". . . the type of reasoning manifested is systematic and involves logically complex processes" (p. 48). The types of adolescent thought can be seen in the advanced problem solving abilities. Cole and Cole (1989) and Keating (1980) have identified five basic types of adolescent thinking that distinguish it from the thought of elementary (middle childhood) students. These types of adolescent thinking include:

1. Thinking about possibilities
2. Thinking ahead
3. Thinking through hypotheses

4. Thinking about thought

5. Thinking beyond conventional limits

As a result of this improvement in intellectual ability, the adolescent can solve many types of problems that require the use of higher levels of logical operations. Students at the formal operational level use their minds to a greater degree because higher levels of reasoning require the application of rules and logical patterns of thought. Students at this level are no longer limited to concrete problems, but can think abstractly and form multiple hypotheses. They can solve complex verbal problems and perform sophisticated logical operations. According to Sund (1976), ". . . the formal mind utilizes several operations to resolve problems and to apply hypotheses to their solutions" (p. 49) and these operations include:

1. Reasoning abstractly

2. Thinking hypothetically and deductively

3. Syllogistic reasoning

4. Reflexive and propositional thinking

5. Thinking idealistically and conceiving of utopia

6. Understanding advanced language concepts

7. Controlling variables and establishing hierarchical classification systems

Because these cognitive skills are important in the development of curriculum for secondary students, each of these intellectual operations will be described briefly in the section that follows.

Reasoning Abstractly Adolescent thought becomes more like adult thought with the ability to carry on a series of logical mental processes. The student demonstrates abstract reasoning ability by constructing make-believe situations, comprehending legalistic arguments and complex literary criticism, and solving verbal mathematical problems. For example, Santrock (1988) describes this abstract problem solving ability by noting,

> While the concrete operational thinker would need to see the concrete elements A, B, and C to make the logical inference that if $A > B$ and $B > C$ then $A > C$, the formal operational thinker can solve this problem merely through verbal presentation (p. 522).

Students who have abstract thinking ability can hold a large amount of information in their minds while performing mental operations on the information.

Thinking Hypothetically and Deductively Formal thinkers are more likely to think in hypothetical-deductive ways. The thought process is more scientific in nature because the adolescent formulates hypotheses or guesses, deduces conclusions, and tests solutions in a deliberate way. Santrock (1988) notes that ". . . in solving a problem an individual develops hypotheses or hunches about what will be a correct solution to the problem and then in a planned manner tests one or more of the hypotheses, discarding the ones that do not work" (p. 523).

Syllogistic Reasoning   Syllogisms are special situations involving hypothetical-deductive reasoning. Students using syllogistic reasoning can evaluate and determine if a syllogism is true. In the example below, the formal thinker would be able to evaluate the statements and determine if the syllogism is true.

  a. Cats meow.
  b. The animal meowed.
  c. The animal is a cat.

In evaluating the syllogism, the formal thinker would realize that the premise which establishes the sound that the animal makes, "Cats meow," may not be sufficient if other animals can be said to make the same sound. According to Sund (1976), the ability to check the validity of a syllogism ". . . enables formal thinkers to further broaden their conceptualizations and perceive problems from various vantage points enabling better resolution of them" (p. 50).

Reflexive and Propositional Thinking   The student is able to reflect over a series of operations and identify their functions in the thinking process. The adolescent can also answer a series of if-then questions such as:

  a. If X then Y.
     If it is sleeting, then the roads are slick.
  b. If Y then X.
     If the roads are slick, then it is sleeting.
  c. If not X then not Y.
     If it is not sleeting, then the roads are not slick.
  d. If not Y then not X.
     If the roads are not slick, then it is not sleeting.

Adolescents are able to relate any of the propositions in the mind and, by reasoning, act on them and discard any inappropriate or inaccurate ones.

Thinking Idealistically and Conceiving of Utopia   The adolescent, because of the abstract nature of formal operational thought, is capable of thinking in idealistic ways not only about what is but about what is possible. The students can think of things not present, can describe an idealistic society, and often adolescent thought is transformed into fantasy with views of future possibilities. Santrock (1990) notes that, "It is not unusual for the adolescent to become impatient with these new found ideal standards and to be perplexed over which . . . to adopt" (p. 495). As adolescents engage in speculation about ideal qualities and characteristics, they begin not only to think of the ideal self, but to speculate on these qualities in others as well.

Understanding Advanced Language Concepts   As a result of an increased ability to use abstract verbal concepts, adolescents are able to make sense out of complex language in the way they were able to ascertain the influences and relations among familiar words during childhood. Students are able to understand and interpret works of literature such as *Moby-Dick* or *Gulliver's Travels* as more than just adventure stories. "They realize that reading a word, line or sentence at a time may not result in comprehension of the author's message. The ideas have to be mentally combined and considered as a whole" (Sund, 1976, p. 51). In addition, adolescents are generally better at analyzing the function of a word (e.g., noun, verb, adjective) in a sentence.

Other areas in which adolescents have more advanced understanding of language include conversation and the use of metaphors and satire. Adolescents are better conversationalists because of their understanding of the *pragmatics* of language—the rules of conversation. Students are able to comprehend the symbolic meanings of metaphors such as "cool as a cucumber" because they are more aware of multiple meanings and multiple levels of meaning (Elkind, 1984). Students are also able to understand the satire of literature, politics, or caricature, when the author or creator uses "irony, wit, or derision to expose folly or wickedness" (Santrock, 1990, p. 495). Adolescents in general and junior high school students in particular become very proficient in the use of satire in making up names or labels for teachers and/or other students.

The written language of adolescents is also different from earlier forms. Because writing is a complex process, it is not surprising that students who function at the formal operational level are better at organizing ideas and putting them in a structured, written form. As a result, "adolescents' essays are more likely to include an introduction, several paragraphs that represent a body of the paper, and concluding remarks" (Santrock, 1988, 526). New structures and word meaning begin to take shape during adolescence, and the change in the structure and use of language is an important factor in cognitive development (Cole and Cole, 1989).

Controlling Variables and Establishing Hierarchical Classification Systems As cognitive thought develops, adolescents begin to realize that in solving complex problems, they must control all factors and then change only one variable at a time in order to observe its influence on the reaction or situation. Students are also able to establish criteria for a hierarchical classification system and build and use keys to classify, identify, or locate organisms or objects.

GENDER DIFFERENCES IN COGNITION

In addition to the physiological differences that exist between males and females during adolescence, some cognitive differences appear as well. According to Helms and Turner (1986), "Males seem to perform better on tests of mathematical reasoning and visual and spatial problems; females tend to excel in tasks involving verbal abilities" (p. 451). Schiamberg (1988) confirms these differences in cognitive abilities, but suggests that part of the lack of scientific ability for girls may be due to cultural values, societal expectations, and sex-role stereotypes. Meehan (1984) found that males and females solve the same kinds of formal operations problems, but notes that some studies do show that males tend to be superior in formal operations. According to Cole and Cole (1989), "Current evidence favors the idea that the capacity to solve formal operational problems develops equally in males and females, but the realization of this ability in solving particular problems depends upon a person's past experience" (p. 566). The data suggest that curriculum planners should be aware of these gender differences and recognize the various explanations for the cognitive differences.

SOCIAL DEVELOPMENT

During preadolescence, gangs continue to be a major part of social interaction, although there tends to be more loyalty to the gang for boys than for girls. Girls, in their social development, begin to form close friendships within a small group of two or three. There is an increased interest in team sports, movies, television, as well as radio, records, and tapes; there are, however, marked differences in interests between boys and girls. In the preadolescent, middle school, and junior high years, girls accelerate in their physical development and there is often a teasing or playful antagonism between boys and girls. Students in this period begin to value the opinions of their peers and older students more than adults. Mood swings are often prevalent, with the student desperately wanting to please adults one minute and becoming rebellious, overcritical, and uncooperative the next. Students in this stage of development vascillate between being a child one minute and being more adult-like the next.

Box 6-1 provides a profile of a junior high student. In what ways does Todd represent the typical preadolescent? What are the changes that Todd is experiencing? How is he different from the younger child? Older teenager?

For the adolescent student in high school, there is a preoccupation with acceptance by the peer or social group coupled with a concern of being ridiculed, unpopular, or rejected. The social interaction patterns of high school adolescents frequently result in the formation of cliques—highly exclusive, small groups of friends who share common interests, have similar attitudes and economic backgrounds, and exhibit a strong emotional attachment for each other. The pressure to be accepted by peers, to become part of a clique, often results in adolescents experimenting with behaviors, "going along," or doing things that they normally would not do. There is also a high interest in physical attractiveness and students often experiment with fads related to such areas as fashion and/or hair style.

Because they are breaking away from direct adult supervision and beginning to assert their independence, adolescents often exhibit a know-it-all attitude. Even as they assert their independence from parents, adolescents look to other adults whom they admire as role models. For junior and senior high school students, teachers often serve as adult role models. As high school students begin to establish a sense of self and search for their own set of values, they frequently look for answers in philosophical, moral, and ethical situations and become more interested in the discussion of these issues in class.

Box 6-1 Junior High School Student Profile

Todd is a 13-year-old junior high school student. He is the oldest in his family and has two younger brothers and a younger sister. Todd is good-natured and easy going. When asked what his favorite things to do are he replies, playing basketball, soccer, and Nintendo. He is currently playing baseball in the summer sports program in his city, but that, he says, is not his favorite. He also enjoys waterskiing in summer and snow skiing in winter.

Todd says that he watches TV about 20 hours a week. He watches cartoons on Saturday, and his favorite shows are "The Simpsons," "Funniest Home Videos," "McGyver," and various sports programs, especially the NCAA basketball tournament. Todd is currently taking guitar lessons and enjoys music. He listens to the radio, and for his birthday received a compact disc player.

Todd admits that he has begun spending more time with his friends or alone in his room. He has noticed that he is having more arguments with his parents and brothers and sisters. Although he has good grades at school, he admits some could be better, but he really doesn't try hard. Next year will be really hard for him he thinks because of the subjects he will be taking.

Although he is athletic, Todd is still short for his age. He has not gone through his growth spurt, so he is self-conscious about his appearance. His best friend, Matt, has already grown 2 inches in the last six months and Todd wants to "catch up." Todd has several groups of friends he enjoys being with, but almost all of them are boys. He has friends on his sports teams, friends at school, and friends in scouting. He moves easily from group to group. He was born in September and he did not start school until nearly a year after some of his friends, so he is older than most. He is looking forward to getting his driver's license and getting a part-time job.

The profile presented in Box 6-2 recounts the social and, to some degree, the cognitive characteristics of a high school student. Amy, like other 16-year-old girls, has many interests including sports and teen fashion reading material. In what ways is Amy like other high school girls? In what ways is Amy different?

High school students are often preoccupied with what other people think about them and often feel that others are obsessed with the same feelings and views that they have. This concern with what other people think is called *adolescent egocentrism*, and it is another important factor affecting social development (Elkind, 1980, 1967). The egocentrism is manifested in two main ways: first in the form of the *imaginary audience*—the belief that others are constantly watching. Adolescents see themselves as the center of attention with everyone constantly focusing attention on them. The imaginary audience is particularly pronounced when an adolescent student enters a crowded room and feels that everyone in the room is watching.

The second consequence of adolescent egocentrism is called the *personal*

Box 6-2   # High School Student Profile

Amy is 16 years old and the youngest of three children in her family. Her brother is a high school senior, and her older sister, now 21, is married and lives in another state. Her parents, married for 25 years, are both employed, so Amy enjoys the benefits of a middle-class family. Although her mother has worked since Amy was in elementary school, this has not been a problem for Amy since she had older family members at home.

Amy's interests involve many outdoor activities. She enjoys walking, jogging, playing tennis, and swimming. Amy is active in high school activities such as pep squad, one-act plays, and academic clubs and contests. She also enjoys going shopping for clothes and has just gotten a part-time job as a lifeguard at the local swimming pool in order to earn money for clothes and other things she wants to buy, like tapes and compact discs.

At home, she enjoys listening to the radio and reading magazines such as *Teen*, *Sassy*, *Glamour*, and *Seventeen*. She is selective about the television programs she watches, but her current favorites are daytime soaps, "Designing Women," "Oprah," and "Quantum Leap." She also talks frequently on the telephone to friends, especially to her best girlfriend and her new boyfriend, whom she met at work. Amy is very competitive in athletics and competes in tennis tournaments and track meets.

Amy confides in her close friends more than she does in her parents. Her occasional mood swings cause conflicts with her family as she asserts her sense of independence. Although she has her driver's license, she does not have her own car, but uses her brother's or a parent's car. She wants her own car and hopes she will get one next year.

---

fable, which is a fantasy that the student constructs and tells about himself or herself. Personal fables are often expressed in diaries with the belief that they have universal significance. Boys, as they talk about athletic ability or relationships with girls, often fantasize and exaggerate, which is a form of the personal fable. Girls also construct stories to tell about themselves, such as dating some special boy or seeing themselves in a special situation. According to Helms and Turner (1986), "The personal fable, like the imaginary audience, is overcome when adolescents are able to see themselves and others in a more realistic light" (p. 459).

SPECIAL NEEDS OF ADOLESCENTS

Because of the developmental changes that occur in adolescence, students in this stage of development have special needs. These needs include acceptance by peers, adult guidance without nagging or criticizing, a sense of security while seeking both independence and dependence, and opportunities for greater responsibility, including the opportunity to make money. According to Beane, Toepfer, and Alessi (1986), "If curriculum is to help learners pursue a full and happy life, educators must consider how it will contribute to meeting basic human needs and how, in turn, those needs affect what happens in school" (p. 100).

In developing curriculum plans and establishing school programs, one of the most specific approaches to considering preadolescent and adolescent needs is the concept of developmental tasks. For Havighurst (1972), "A developmental task is a significant accomplishment that an individual must achieve by a certain time if he [or she] is going to meet the demands placed on him [or her] by society" (p. 29). A major developmental task of the preadolescent is the organization of knowledge of social and physical reality—the classifying and systematizing of knowledge while becoming proficient in the fundamental skills of reading, writing, and calculating. For the adolescent the major developmental tasks include:

1. Achieving new and more mature relations with age-mates of both sexes
2. Achieving a masculine or feminine social role
3. Accepting one's physique and using the body effectively
4. Achieving emotional independence of parents and other adults
5. Preparing for marriage and family life
6. Preparing for a career
7. Acquiring a set of values and an ethical system as a guide to behavior —developing an ideology
8. Desiring and achieving socially responsible behavior

Perhaps one of the most important questions educators should ask is, "Given all of these special needs and developmental tasks, do I like preadolescents and/or adolescents enough to work with them?" The response is important in shaping our view of the world and, therefore, the curriculum for these students. The following questions should help secondary educators assess the degree to which they know their students by focusing on the unique developmental aspects and characteristics of the preadolescent and adolescent student.

1. Do I understand the physical and emotional changes that occur during preadolescence and adolescence?
2. Do I provide opportunities within the curriculum which foster independence and responsibility in each student?
3. Do I show warmth and humor as I work with junior high and/or high school students?
4. Do I refrain from nagging, condemning, or talking down to students, and am I careful to review curriculum materials that would have the same effect?
5. Do I provide opportunities in the curriculum and classroom activities for students to feel a sense of belonging to the class or peer group?
6. Do I plan for multiple levels of learning within the curriculum to accommodate the wide range of individual differences?
7. Do I incorporate curriculum materials that help students overcome

self-consciousness about physical changes, awkwardness, and rest-
lessness?

8. Do I provide materials in the curriculum that help students deal
   effectively with the pressure by peers to conform to certain
   behaviors?

9. Do I encourage students, through my own actions, as well as through
   the curriculum and classroom activities, to be life-long learners?

10. Do I provide opportunities in the curriculum to go beyond the basics
    and discuss or make decisions based on a value system?

If you answered "yes" to the majority of these questions, then you have an
understanding of the complexities of adolescent development and the kinds of
educational programming that should be provided in the schools. If you did not
agree with at least 50 percent of the statements, then more consideration
should be given to the psychological foundations of curriculum development.

THEORIES OF LEARNING

A theory of learning also serves as a foundation for curriculum development.
Many, if not most, of the things teachers do in their classrooms can be traced to
a specific theory of learning. This foundation area helps answer the questions:
"How do students best learn the content?" and "Are the goals and objectives
appropriate for the level of students?" (Beach and Reinhartz, 1989). Although
there are a variety of definitions of learning currently used, a generally accepted definition is "a process by which behavior is either modified or changed
through experience or training" (Dembo, 1981, p. 1). While space does not
allow for a full discussion of learning theories—entire books and courses are
devoted to the subject—it does serve our purpose to briefly describe three
major categories of learning theories to illustrate how they impact the curriculum development process. The three major categories or themes of learning
theory include: behaviorism (stimulus-response/S-R or operant conditioning),
cognitive-field or gestalt psychology, and faculty psychology (Bigge, 1982).
Each one will be discussed briefly and with examples of how they apply to
classroom instruction.

According to *behaviorism* or the S-R theory, people learn primarily through
a process called operant conditioning. In this process, a learning stimulus or
prompt produces a response from the student, and approximately correct responses are rewarded until the learner can give a correct response. Then the
correct response is rewarded or reinforced. The reinforcement strengthens the
connection between the "stimulus" or prompt (i.e., question) and the "response" (answer or correct behavior). As students learn the content or concepts
imbedded in the curriculum, each correct response they make is followed by
praise or reinforcement so that learning is encouraged and/or rewarded. Many
objectives of the curriculum, particularly those that involve recall and compre-

hension, often focus on this learning theory. According to Bigge (1982), the S-R theory impacts the curriculum in that it views learning as

> . . . nonpurposive habit formation. . . . Thus . . . learning is a more or less permanent change of behavior that occurs as a result of conditioning. . . . Consequently, the problem of the nature of the learning process is centered in a study of the relationships of processions of stimuli and responses and what occurs between them (pp. 88–89).

Examples of curriculum applications of the S–R/behaviorist learning theory include the following:

1. Motivational strategies that include the use of rewards (e.g., free time, coupons, etc.) for completion of instructional tasks
2. Programmed or computer assisted instruction (formatting the content to provide prompts, acknowledge correct responses, and reinforce with a praise statement)
3. Student management techniques that reinforce appropriate classroom behavior (assertive discipline and behavior modification)
4. Extensive use of questions during instruction to actively solicit student participation in the lesson (large numbers of questions, especially recall questions, are used to prompt students' responses and actively involve students in the lesson)

According to Zais (1976), when viewed in the larger context of associationist theory, individual behavior, personality, and knowledge are systems of many S-R bonds.

> Each time a teacher makes an assignment or asks a question . . . his [or her] purpose is to build or strengthen a desired S-R bond and thereby contribute to the learning of a more complex totality . . . learning is a process of building simple units into complex wholes; it is analogous to constructing a brick building (p. 252).

Because much of the curriculum content is viewed as building upon prior factual knowledge, the behaviorist/associationist view has exerted more influence on curriculum development than any other theory of learning. However, advanced cognitive functions, such as problem solving, insight, and higher order thinking, have been given little attention by this particular theory.

The *cognitive-field* or gestalt theory is another explanation of how people learn. The cognitive-field theory is based on the works of a German psychologist, Kohler (1929), who used the term *gestalt* to refer to a pattern or configuration — an undivided, articulated whole. In this view, "learning is not a piecemeal, trial-and-error progression . . . [but] the sudden restructuring of integrated wholes — in other words, *insight*" (Zais, 1976, p. 254). Cognitive-field theory is based on ideas expressed in gestalt psychology and includes the following principles.

1. Stimuli occur in complex patterns that are never completely reproducible, rather than in isolation as implied by the S-R theory.
2. Individuals respond to whole patterns of stimuli rather than to simple stimuli

within a pattern, and the response is based on the organization of the stimuli within the pattern and the individual's perception of it.

3. An individual's perception is influenced by his or her perceptual field, a perception of self and previous and immediate perceptions of the environment.

4. As individuals respond to patterns of stimuli, their whole being is changed by the experience, which influences any future responses to the patterns of stimuli.

5. Individual goals influence learning and behavior and, therefore, human behavior cannot be entirely controlled by the environment. The way the individual responds to the pattern of stimuli is shaped by the goals held.

6. Human learning occurs through insight rather than through the painfully inefficient trial-and-error and conditioning procedures (Dumas and Beckner, 1968).

The cognitive-field or gestalt approach to learning acknowledges the importance of the learner's values, attitudes, and prior experiences as he or she interacts with fields or configurations to see "wholes," not small, simple units. For the field psychologists, learning proceeds from whole to parts and

> "Seeing" wholes . . . necessitates a grasp of the relationships that exist among the parts, for it is these relationships that endow the whole with its distinctive qualities. . . . Consequently, the field psychologists maintain that the whole is more than the sum of its parts and . . . that it precedes the parts, knowledge of which is derived from the whole (Zais, 1976, p. 256).

Curriculum development based on the cognitive-field theory, differs significantly from the behaviorist view. The field theorist begins with major concepts or ideas related to themes or problems. These major concepts are presented in such a way as to emphasize or highlight the structure of the whole, the dominant theme. History viewed this way becomes the study of periods of expansion, great economic depressions, or major world conflicts rather than a series of isolated events presented in chronological order, often out of context. Applications of the cognitive-field or gestalt theory to curriculum development include:

1. Use of laboratory or role playing activities in discovery learning situations (playing a game that simulates the stock market crash)

2. Use of a problem solving curriculum to foster critical thinking (using a study of pond water contamination as a means of studying principles of ecology and environmental issues)

3. Concept mapping or the presentation of ideas within a framework of the whole to teach content (looking for major themes within a story)

4. Developing units of study that focus on higher order thinking (analysis, synthesis, and evaluation) and the development of self-concept

The most important aspect of the cognitive-field theory involves insights, either developing new ones or changing old ones. Learning is shaped by the prompts or stimulus as well as who the learner is and what he or she brings to the situation. In this framework of learning, reinforcements, particularly external ones, are not necessarily important.

Although not nearly as influential in education and the development of curriculum, the *faculty psychology* view of learning still has an impact on classroom instruction. The central idea is mental discipline—the mind, which is envisioned as a nonphysical substance that lies dormant until exercised (Bigge, 1982):

> The faculties of the mind such as memory, will, reason, and perseverance are the "muscles of the mind" [and] like physiological muscles, they are strengthened only through exercise, and subsequent to their adequate exercise they operate automatically (p. 24).

Thus, within this view, learning is a matter of exercising and strengthening the mind or disciplining the faculties to produce intelligent behavior.

Curriculum development within this framework views the mastery of content as "hard work." Curricular activities frequently used in this theory include:

1. Rote memorization (memorizing formulas, definitions, multiplication tables, poems, or speeches)
2. Structuring the content to be learned in manageable amounts, and organizing material factually and in sequence or order
3. Content and curricular materials relatively fixed with an almost exclusive emphasis on basic skills
4. Using mnemonic devices to help structure learning so that it can be easily recalled

SUMMARY

Chapter 6 focused on the psychological foundations of curriculum planning and development. The application of psychology—the knowledge of human development, needs, and learning—is critical to curriculum development because it helps to facilitate student learning. The chapter discussed the importance and role of psychology in educating secondary students, specifically the cognitive, social and moral, and physical stages. Chapter 5 provided the rationale for studying psychology, along with the principles associated with the learning process, as a prerequisite for developing curriculum for preadolescents and adolescents.

The general principles of development, the four major development theories (cognitive, behavioristic, psychoanalytic, and humanistic), moral development, preadolescent and adolescent physical growth and development, intellectual growth and development, and theories of learning were discussed in detail. It is evident from this discussion that there is no single theory for explaining how people develop and learn behavior. By presenting a variety of theories and perspectives, curriculum developers have an opportunity to study each of these theories and determine how each contributes to the curriculum development process.

YOUR TURN

6.1 Think back to your own adolescent period. Do you remember the physical changes that you experienced as a result of the changes you were going through? At what age did you experience the onset of puberty? Do you remember how you felt? Had you been prepared for this change by parents? School? Peers or classmates?

6.2 Interview a junior high school boy and girl. Specific areas to focus on include likes and dislikes about school, the opposite sex, hobbies, movies and television programs, and "best friends." Are the boys different from the girls? How?

6.3 Interview the parent of an adolescent (15–16 years old). Focus on areas such as the student's attitude toward parents and other adults, school (grades and subjects), work, best friends, hobbies, and the parent-adolescent interaction.

6.4 Given the descriptions of cognitive capabilities of adolescents, develop a concept in your field of study that would challenge adolescent students to use formal operational thinking in the instructional process. Identify the specific formal operations that the activity requires.

REFERENCES

Beach, Don M. & Reinhartz, J. (1989). *Supervision: Focus on instruction*. New York: Harper & Row.

Beane, J.A., Toepfer, C.F., Jr. & Alessi, S.J., Jr. (1986). *Curriculum planning and development*. Boston: Allyn and Bacon.

Beckner, W. & Cornett, J.D. (1972). *The secondary school curriculum: Content and structure*. Scranton, PA.: Intext Educational Publishers

Bigge, M.L. (1982). *Learning theories for teachers*. New York: Harper & Row.

Cole, L. & Hall, I.N. (1970). *Psychology of adolescence* (7th ed.). New York: Holt.

Cole, M. & Cole, S.R. (1989). *The development of children*. New York: Scientific American Books.

Dembo, M.H. (1981). *Teaching for learning: Applying educational psychology in the classroom* (2nd ed.). Santa Monica, Calif.: Goodyear.

Dumas, W. & Beckner, W. (1968). *Introduction to secondary education: A foundations approach*. Scranton, Pa.: Intext.

Elkind, D. (1984). *All grown up and no place to go*. Reading, Mass.: Addison-Wesley.

Elkind, D. (1980). Strategic interactions in early adolescence. In J. Adelson (Ed.), *Handbook of adolescent psychology*. New York: Wiley.

Elkind, D. (1967). Egocentrism in adolescence. *Child Development, 38*, 4, 1025–1034.

Havighurst, R.J. (1972). *Developmental tasks and education* (3rd ed.). New York: David McKay.

Helms, D.B. & Turner, J.S. (1986). *Exploring child behavior*. Monterey, Calif.: Brooks Cole.

Keating, D. (1980). Thinking processes in adolescence. In J. Adelson (Ed.), *Handbook of adolescent psychology*. New York: Wiley.

Kohler, W. (1929). *Gestalt psychology*. New York: Liverwright.

Marshall, W.A. (1978). Puberty. In *Human growth (Vol 2): Postnatal growth*. N. F. Falkner and J. Tanner (Eds.), New York: Plenum.

Meehan, A.M. (1984). A meta-analysis of sex differences in formal operational thought. *Child Development, 55*, 3, 1110–1124.

Mussen, P.H., Conger, J.J., Kagan, J. & Huston, A.C. (1990). *Child development and personality*. New York: Harper & Row.

Popham, W.J. & Baker, E.L. (1970). *Establishing instructional goals*. Englewood Cliffs, N.J.: Prentice-Hall.

Santrock, J.W. (1990). *Children* (2nd ed.). Dubuque, Iowa: Brown.

Santrock, J.W. (1988). *Children*. Dubuque, Iowa: Brown.

Schiamberg, L.B. (1988). *Child and adolescent development*. New York: Macmillan.

Sund, R.B. (1976). *Piaget for educators*. Columbus, Ohio: Charles E. Merrill.

Zais, R.S. (1976). *Curriculum principles and foundations*. New York: Harper & Row.

PART THREE

THREE

Curriculum Development Process

Part Three, Curriculum Development Process, includes distinct areas which focus on (1) curriculum planning and development and (2) models of curriculum development. The essence of the theory and practice of curriculum planning and building is an integral part of Part Three.

The two chapters contained in this part are the heart of the secondary curriculum development process. Chapter 7 provides the building blocks for curriculum planning and development. It presents several factors that educators should consider when developing curriculum for secondary students. The question "What knowledge is of worth?" continues to confront educators. In addition, Chapter 7 discusses the components of the curriculum and how they are organized and sequenced, as well as the sources to consult, organization of the material, and dimensions of curriculum. To help put all this information into perspective, various curriculum designs are also provided.

Part Three would not be complete without a discussion of the models of curriculum development. Chapter 8 presents various models that can be used to conceptualize the curriculum development process. These models provide a broader context for understanding the complex nature of planning and developing a curriculum for secondary students. The final phase in the curriculum development process should help teachers and curriculum developers to examine what changes need to be made, what content should be included, and the sequence of content.

Whether a subject-centered, student-centered, and/or problem-centered focus is taken, the planning and development process is dependent on the model of curriculum development selected. Chapter 8 concludes with a discussion of the elements that must be considered when developing a curriculum, and these elements also transcend the type of model that is followed.

Chapter
7

Curriculum Planning and Development

*C*hanges in society over the centuries have brought monumental changes for secondary schools in the areas of who is taught, what is taught, and how it is taught and learned. Teachers, students, and the instructional process have consistently been the focus of efforts to improve the learning process. Many, if not most, of these efforts have involved the curriculum as a component in the improvement of instruction. Curriculum planning and development is not new; educators have been concerned with curriculum development since the beginning of formal education in Grecian times (Wulf and Schave, 1984). As indicated in Chapter 4, during the last half of the twentieth century curriculum developers have encountered many radical social changes (family structure, scientific and technological revolution, equity movement, etc.) that have impacted the schools. Faced with these new challenges, educators have sought curricular approaches that will help them meet the needs of all learners as well as the demands imposed by society.

This chapter describes several factors that educators must consider in planning curricular programs for preadolescent and adolescent populations. Both the theoretical and practical aspects of curriculum planning and development are presented. In addition, the components, sources, organization, and dimensions of the curriculum are discussed. The chapter ends with descriptions of various types of curriculum designs. After reading this chapter, a secondary educator should have a general overview of what is included in curriculum planning and development.

VIEWS OF CURRICULUM DEVELOPMENT

Many ideas have been generated concerning the best way to develop curriculum. For Wiles and Bondi (1989), curriculum development is a comprehensive process which ". . . (1) facilitates an analysis of purpose, (2) designs a program, (3) implements a series of related experiences, and (4) aids in the evaluation of the process" (p. 87). Taba (1962), however, depicts curriculum development as "a task requiring orderly thinking . . . to examine both the order in which decisions are made and the way in which they are made to make sure that all relevant considerations are brought to bear on these decisions" (p. 11–12). We see curriculum development in the broadest sense — a comprehensive plan that has three phases: planning, implementation, and evaluation. Curriculum change and betterment are implied and incorporated in such a view. Therefore, for us, curriculum development is synonymous with curriculum improvement.

When considered as a whole, these various views comprise curriculum development. Traditionally, curriculum development has had a subject matter or academic discipline focus. More recently, curriculum development has had an integrated, holistic approach, with a focus on the education of the "total individual."

As a result of these two different views, the continuum of curriculum development is broad; at one end is the very rigid view that is characterized by a subject-centered or discipline-based curriculum. Such a view emphasizes the content, facts, or knowledge to be learned. At the other end of the continuum is the open-ended design, characterized by a student-centered focus that views learning from a holistic perspective. This curriculum is one that emphasizes the needs of the individual learner and self-realization or self-actualization (see Chapter 5). In the middle of the continuum is the problem-solving approach. This view of curriculum is more pragmatic, and learning involves students solving the problems and issues facing mankind. Figure 7.1 represents the continuum of the views of curriculum development.

The discipline-based end of the continuum follows a more traditional approach to educational programming for secondary students. As indicated in Chapter 2, the subject-centered curriculum has been emphasized during various time periods of the last century. One such period was after the launching of Sputnik in 1957 and another was during the 1980s as a result of the school reform movements (see Chapter 1). This view of curriculum development embodies the essentialist philosophy discussed in Chapter 3.

At the other end of the continuum is the open-ended curriculum design, which begins with the needs and interests of the students. The student is the source for program planning rather than the predetermined set of facts and skills of an academic discipline. When designing educational programs, the

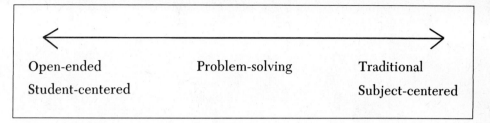

Figure 7.1 Continuum of curriculum development theories

focus is on individual learners—their cognitive, social, physical, and moral development (see also Chapter 5). Such a view of curriculum development was the case during the late 1960s and early 1970s, with various forms of individualized instruction, such as learning centers. More recently, this view of curriculum development can be seen in the whole language approach to English language arts, which focuses on the language abilities and interests of the student. The open-ended curriculum incorporates many of the beliefs of the existentialist philosophy (see Chapter 3).

The problem solving curriculum, occupying the central portion of the continuum, was advocated by Dewey (1938) in his writing *Experience and Education.* This theory has been evident in many instructional programs of the progressive education movement throughout the United States. A problem-solving curriculum is of interest and is particularly appropriate as new social concerns (AIDS, drugs, teen pregnancy, and teen suicide) have dominated the news in the last decade and continue to confront curriculum developers into the twenty-first century. Such a curricular focus requires educators to include problem-solving strategies in the instructional programs as students learn to cope with the social dilemmas of the day. In this view of curriculum development, preadolescents and adolescents must be given coping strategies, as well as the content of an academic discipline, in order to deal realistically with contemporary situations in their lives.

FACTORS TO CONSIDER WHEN DEVELOPING A CURRICULUM

How do you develop a curriculum? What questions and factors should be addressed when developing curriculum? Regardless of the curricular focus, there are factors that must be considered and questions that must be resolved in the curriculum planning and development process. These factors and related questions will be addressed in this section on developing curriculum. Any plan for learning, that is, the curriculum, contains a structure or basic organization. The vision of the curriculum, also known as a philosophy—those beliefs about people and the world (see Chapter 3)—is translated into a series of learning experiences for students. These learning experiences translate one's beliefs about the how and what of learning into a curriculum that is implemented. The value laden questions posed by curriculum theorists of the past remain viable today and can serve as a guide in developing educational programs. A list of such questions has been presented by Beach and Reinhartz (1989) and includes:

1. What is society's philosophy of public education in the United States?
2. What goals should the public schools hope to achieve?
3. What types of jobs will be available for students graduating in the year 2000?
4. What knowledge and skills are needed for the present and the future?
5. What and how much are students capable of learning?
6. What type(s) of knowledge can students accommodate and assimilate?
7. How can schools provide an educational program (curriculum) for students who have different interests, abilities and disabilities, skills, likes and dislikes, and socioeconomic backgrounds?
8. What is the structure of each content area or discipline?
9. Is the subject hierarchical, sequential, and/or spiral in nature?
10. What skills are inherent in the subject?
11. At the developmental level will the . . . student best be able to assimilate facts, concepts, generalizations, and principles? (pp. 100–101)

Responding to these questions can provide a starting point for the curriculum planning and development process. Each response helps determine the means and ends of secondary education and establishes priorities for the instructional program.

The aims of the curriculum can also serve as a beginning point when developing curriculum. Although developed in 1918 by the Commission on the Reorganization of Secondary Education, *Cardinal Principles of Secondary Education* (1918), for example, still serve as aims for many, if not most, secondary students. These aims include: (1) maintenance of good health, (2) developing command of fundamental skills, (3) being worthy members of a family, (4) developing a vocation, (5) being good citizens, (6) using leisure time well, and (7) developing individuals with ethical character. Whatever questions are asked and responses given, these factors are crucial in providing direction for the curriculum planning and development process.

While the definitions of curriculum and the educational programs have reflected the social, political, and psychological forces and movements over the decades, the basic steps in the curriculum planning and development process have remained relatively constant (Wiles and Bondi, 1989). It seems clear that no matter what curriculum is developed, the steps in the process (analysis, design, implementation, and evaluation) have been used routinely. Within these four steps, goals are set, learning experiences are identified, content is selected, and the program as well as the outcomes are evaluated.

The question that Herbert Spencer (1860) asked, "What knowledge is of most worth?" continues to confront educators today. This fundamental question can serve as the starting point for curriculum planning and development. Although the question is simple, it has generated fierce controversy and conflict. According to Apple (1990), the question is not only an educational one, but ". . . inherently ideological and political" (p. 526). He continues by suggesting that a better way to phrase the question is "Whose knowledge is of most worth?" In this question, Apple makes it abundantly clear that curriculum planning and development is not only academic but political as well. As secondary educators become involved in curriculum planning, Apple cautions them to be aware of the political nature of the curriculum, which tends to dominate the news and headlines.

An early proponent of curriculum planning and development, Briggs (1926) posed 14 questions that have consistently provided direction for curriculum developers. In guiding the curriculum development process for secondary schools, the questions posed include:

1. What are the desired ends of secondary education?
2. What is the good life?
3. To what extent shall secondary education modify the character and actions of future citizens?
4. For what ends are the secondary schools responsible?
5. What subject areas are most vital in attaining these ends?
6. What should be the content of these subject arrangements?
7. How should the material be organized?
8. What is the responsibility of each level of schooling?
9. What is the relative importance of each course of study?
10. How much time should be allotted for each subject?
11. How long should secondary education be continued at public expense?
12. What is the optimum length of the school day? School year?
13. What is the optimum work load for each student?
14. What are the most probable future needs of the students?

Responses to these questions and the resulting decisions will facilitate the planning and development of the curriculum.

Decisions regarding the curriculum are made at five levels: (1) classroom, (2) school building (campus), (3) district, (4) state, and (5) national (Wiles and Bondi, 1989; Zais, 1976). Figure 7.2 illustrates these five levels of decision making relative to the curriculum planning and development process. The levels of decision making shown in Figure 7.2 are wide and varied, yet each has a profound effect on the type and nature of the school instructional program. For example, legislative funding themes at the national level as well as budget constraints at the local or district level both impact curricular programs. For Eisner (1990), subject matter specialists, professional organizations, along with textbook publishers have had and will continue to have a strong impact as well as a stabilizing influence on the secondary curriculum.

By having a general idea of what is meant by curriculum development and considering the many factors involved in the curriculum development process, curriculum developers are in a better position to begin the curriculum building process. The following section will present a brief discussion on the components of all curricular programs.

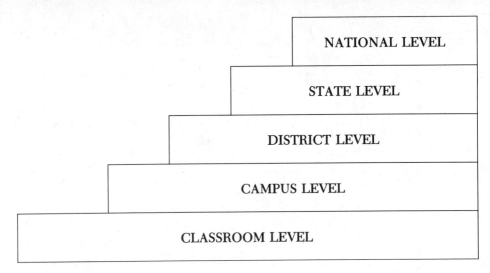

Figure 7.2 Levels of curriculum decision making

COMPONENTS OF A CURRICULUM

Any curriculum contains components, parts, or elements which result in an educational program. The specific name given to these components varies depending on the educators, their philosophy of education, and the location of their school district. Each part is important but is not always given equal emphasis. The components include: (1) aims, goals and objectives; (2) subject matter; (3) strategies and learning experiences; and (4) evaluation approaches. The way these parts are organized and sequenced forms the design of the curriculum. When considering all four parts, subject matter generally receives more emphasis than the other three (Ornstein and Hunkins, 1988). The interaction between the components, described by Giles, McCutchen, and Zechiel (1942), suggests that decisions about one part are dependent on decisions about another and shows a relationship among the various components (Ornstein and Hunkins, 1988).

The curriculum is also influenced by philosophical underpinnings—the "We believe. . . ." statements. These statements, rooted in educational philosophy, help articulate the nature, scope, and sequence of the parts that form the curriculum design. With such philosophical underpinnings, the influence of societal needs and demands, along with the psychological foundations as givens, the rest of this section will explore other aspects of curriculum development: the structure, the sources for planning, the organization, and the dimensions.

Structure

The structure of the curriculum is determined by a four-step process mentioned earlier in this chapter. These steps help curriculum developers see what form the educational program of the school will take. These four steps (Wiles and Bondi, 1989; Ornstein and Hunkins, 1988) include:

1. *Analysis* involves examining the situation/problem, and using a visionary screen, identifying the ultimate goals, which are then translated into instructional objectives.
2. *Design* is an orderly plan to put curriculum into action. The plan is clear and communicates what will be done, the order in which it will be taught, and the time frame for the curriculum to be implemented.
3. *Implementation* requires a system of management to put the curricular program in place in the school or classroom.
4. *Evaluation* is the looking back step which encourages the curriculum developer to gain feedback about the program being piloted/ implemented.

Analysis, design, implementation, and evaluation are basic if a curriculum is to respond to key questions and remain relevant for secondary students.

Sources

Where do curriculum planners get their ideas for generating new educational programs and to modify the existing ones? Doll (1986) identifies four sources for designing curriculum: (1) science, (2) society, (3) external verities, and (4) divine will. These are similar to sources first mentioned by Dewey (1902) and Bode (1927)—knowledge, society, and learners—and made popular by Tyler (1949). Ornstein and Hunkins (1988) provide an additional list of five items that can serve as sources for curriculum development. These sources include the following:

1. Science as a source
2. Society as a source
3. Eternal and divine sources
4. Knowledge as a source
5. Learner as a source

Often these sources get out of balance; one becomes more important to the exclusion of the others. When there is imbalance, all the other sources are ignored, the curriculum design takes on features that make it liked by some and disliked by most. If the emphasis is on the learner, a dichotomy develops and the concern for subject matter knowledge tends to decline. The challenge for curriculum developers is to keep these sources in proper perspective without losing the overall focus of the curriculum.

Organization

The organization displays in visual form how the parts of the curriculum fit together and how the curriculum "looks." One organizational plan is characterized by delineating the scope and sequence of a specific topic or course. Box 7-1 is an example of such a scope and sequence for the topic of energy. The major concepts are presented in the order in which they are taught. The outline is organized using a simple to complex approach.

Additionally, an organizational plan can also include the sequence and continuity of concepts; however, concepts spiral over the long term, according to Bruner (1959), both in depth and level of understanding throughout the K–12 curriculum. Box 7-2 is an example of a geography curriculum that spirals through the K–12 social studies curriculum of the school program. Geographic content such as map skills, interactions, physical features, and cultural differences are introduced and then developed and expanded to meet the appropriate cognitive developmental needs of students. These themes are repeated as they spiral throughout the K–12 geography curriculum.

There is evidence to suggest that there is little interaction among the various curriculum areas, which results in little attention given to the overall curriculum design. As Ornstein and Hunkins (1988) say, "Most school curricula, regardless of school level, are not really closely related either vertically or horizontally" and as a result, most curriculum design looks like "a patchwork quilt" (p. 168). Komoski (1990) contends that school curriculum is fragmented and lacks connectedness. He advocates a systematically balanced, whole curriculum approach. That is why it is essential to have a curriculum that has many parts which are integral to the main mission of the school's overall program rather than a disjointed collection of courses grouped together.

Dimensions

There are intangible dimensions at play which make the curriculum either work or not work, both in the short or long term. The following dimensions should be considered as educators organize the curriculum.

Scope Decisions need to be made about how much content will be presented with how much depth. The breadth and depth issues are coupled with such questions as "What activities should be used and for how long?" For Saylor and Alexander (1954), scope ". . . is the breadth, variety and types of educational experiences that are to be provided pupils as they progress through the school program . . . the what of the curriculum" (p. 248). The scope of a content area poses one of the most difficult challenges for curriculum developers because there are no precise right or wrong answers, only relative ones. Wulf and Schave (1984) list McNeil's (1981) five kinds of criteria for guiding the selection of learning activities. These five criteria include: (a) philosophical — values for judging learning activities; (2) psychological — beliefs about learning which determine how activities are presented; (3) technological — skills to identify

Box 7-1 **Energy Education: Scope and Sequence**

I. Nature of energy
  A. Energy
    1. Kinetic
    2. Potential
  B. Forms of energy
    1. Mechanical
      a) Moving energy
      b) Ways produced
    2. Heat
    3. Electrical
      a) Production
      b) Delivery
    4. Radiant
    5. Chemical
    6. Nuclear energy
      a) Known as atomic energy
      b) Natural radioactivity
        i. Fluorescent
        ii. Invisible rays
      c) Radioactivity
        i. Alpha and beta particles
          a. Unstable nuclei
          b. New elements formed
        ii. Gamma rays
          a. High energy X-rays
          b. Penetrating power
        iii. Chemical change of radioactive elements
          a. Half-life
          b. Carbon 14 dating
        iv. Ways to detect and measure radioactivity
      d) Nuclear fission
        i. Cyclotron, cosmotron, and synchroton
        ii. Critical mass
        iii. Atomic bomb
          a. Nagasaki, Japan
          b. Shock wave
          c. Flash effect
          d. Radioactive fallout
        iv. Nuclear reactor (atomic pile)
      e) Nuclear fusion (hydrogen bomb)

II. Transferring and conserving energy
  A. Energy changes, for example: electricity

continued

Box 7-1 Energy Education: Scope and Sequence — Continued

coal⟶water to steam⟶steam turns turbines⟶
(chemical)   (heat)   (mechanical)

turbines run generator⟶energy
(mechanical)   (electrical)

B. Energy is not destroyed: law of conservation of energy

III. Relationship of matter and energy
  A. Einstein's formula, $E = mc^2$
    1. E = amount of energy
    2. m = mass
    3. c = speed of light (300,000 kilometers or 186,000 miles/second)
  B. Single law: law of conservation of energy and matter

IV. Work
  A. Simple machines
    1. Screw
    2. Lever
    3. Wedge
    4. Pulley
    5. Inclined plane
    6. Wheel and axle
  B. Force $\times$ distance = work done
  C. Mechanical advantage

V. Energy in nature
  A. Sun — solar energy — radiant and grass-growing
  B. Food chain and webs — plants produce food
    1. Photosynthesis
    2. Community/habitat
      a) Herbivores (producers)
      b) Carnivores (consumers)
      c) Energy pyramids
    3. Food stores
  C. Energy in prehistoric times
    1. Dinosaurs
    2. Vegetation
    3. Sedimentation
    4. Fossil fuels: coal, oil, and natural formation
  D. Pond ecosystem
  E. Tidal pool ecosystem
  F. Marine ecosystem
  G. Desert ecosystem

VI. Man and planet earth
  A. Power production

Box 7-1　**Energy Education: Scope and Sequence—Continued**

    B. Environment
       1. Pollution (pollutants)
       2. Diseases
       3. Ecological pyramid (biomass)
    C. City ecosystem
    D. Energy use and abuse
       1. Attitudes
       2. Energy conservation

Box 7-2　**K–12 Geography Spiral Curriculum**

Kindergarten:　Identification—names, location, distance, and relative sizes
　　　　　　　　Direction—right, left, up, down, etc.
　　　　　　　　Relative location
　　　　　　　　The globe as a model
　　　　　　　　Characteristics of places

Grade 1:　Identification—state and country
　　　　　Characteristics of the community
　　　　　Location—home, school, and community
　　　　　Topography of school
　　　　　Weather, seasons
　　　　　The map as a representation of the local environment

Grade 2:　Identification and placement on maps and globes—neighborhood, community, state, and country, and routes
　　　　　Map keys, symbols, legends
　　　　　Cardinal directions
　　　　　Local landforms
　　　　　Seasonal change
　　　　　Interdependence with and between space

Grade 3:　Relative location—community, state and country
　　　　　Comparison and contrast of environmental situation (urban and rural)
　　　　　Intermediate directions
　　　　　Map scale and grid
　　　　　Compass rose
　　　　　Interdependence of people in communities

continued

Box 7-2   K – 12 Geography Spiral Curriculum — Continued

Grade 4:   Identification and placement of state, national, and global physical and
                    political features
               Regions
               Adaptation to environment
               Interpretation of graphic models (pictures, tables, graphs, etc.)
               Regional concept used
               Comparison of regions and people
               Systems of transportation

Grade 5:   Comparison, contrast, and interrelatedness
               The atlas
               Latitude and longitude
               Where and why relationships
               Decision making and environmental and global issues

Grade 6:   Cultural geography
               Demography
               Historical geography
               Sun-earth, human-land relationships
               Trade routes
               Cultural characteristics (language, nationality, religion, etc.)
               Plotting distributions

Grade 7:   State/regional geography course (year)
               Human interaction with environment
               Comparative analysis of areas
               Diversity of populations
               Geographic elements
               Resolution of problems

Grade 8:   National/continental geography course (year)

Grades 9 – 12: World geography course (year)
               Geographic influences on state/regional history (physical and cultural
                    characteristics)
               Geographic influences on national history
               Geographic influences on world history
               Human-environment relationships
               Geography of oceans
               Systematic and regional analysis
               Interpretation and management of problems

Source: Reinhartz, D. & Reinhartz, J. (1990). *Integrating geography across the curriculum*. Washington, D.C.: National Education Association, pp. 21 – 22. Used with permission.

precise learner behaviors and derived from conducting a task analysis; (4) political—concerns which result in fulfilling legal requirements; and (5) practical—costs which must be considered. The scope of the curriculum provides answers to the age old question "What should the school teach?" and gives form to the curriculum or the school program.

Integration   In addition to determining the scope of a curriculum, there is the challenge of determining what related areas of a study can be integrated to make learning more meaningful. Integrating knowledge requires a linear curriculum organization that illustrates how the common threads of knowledge are linked, intertwined, and related. Integration encourages an appreciation for the interconnectedness of knowledge. The current whole language movement is an example of a broader scope that integrates reading and other elements of the language arts into all of the content areas.

Sequence   The sequence of the curriculum deals with the order in which the content, skills, and experiences are organized and taught in the school program. For Saylor and Alexander (1954) the sequence is ". . . the when in curriculum planning" (p. 249). Deciding the order requires examining the content and skills to be taught and identifying the steps required to arrive at the long-term goal of understanding. These steps are determined by how the subject matter is structured and how the learners process information (Ornstein and Hunkins, 1988). The psychological principles discussed in Chapter 5 provide the basis for sequencing content, skills, and experiences for secondary students. Suggestions for determining the order of the curriculum include: (1) learning proceeds from simple to complex, from the concrete to the abstract; (2) having prerequisite skills and knowledge is critical for learning to occur; (3) deductive (general to particular) learning introduces the organizer or general overview first with attention given to particulars, parts, or experiences later; and (4) chronological learning organizes present content and skills in the order in which they occurred in the world (Smith, Stanley, and Shores, 1957). For example, in secondary mathematics, students may be required to have both algebra I and geometry before they can take algebra II. Each content area is unique in sequencing, but in sequencing between the grade levels, "A breadth of activities of beginning and intermediate competency levels should be offered in the middle/junior high school with more advanced experiences offered in high school" (Funkhouser, Beach, Ryan, and Fifer, 1981, p. 47).

Continuity   Continuity deals with the repetition of concepts. This dimension of the curriculum planning process was advocated by Bruner (1959), who introduced the idea of the spiral curriculum. Bruner believed that there are fundamental ideas that are central to the understanding of each subject area which forms the structure of the discipline. These basic ideas are "developed and redeveloped in a spiral fashion, becoming deeper and wider, as the child progresses through the higher grades . . . [and therefore] the concept of the spiral curriculum relates not only to the vertical integration or deepening of knowledge but also to the horizontal integration or widening of knowledge" (Tanner and Tanner, 1980, pp. 541, 462). Concepts are introduced at the appropriate cognitive developmental level and then studied in greater depth later as the students move through the secondary grades.

TYPICAL CURRICULUM DESIGNS

Curriculum designs are blueprints for learning. For Wiles and Bondi (1989), a curriculum design is

> . . . a plan [which] clearly identifies what is to be done, the order, . . . a time estimate, . . . various responsibilities for parts of the plan, and the anticipated results of these efforts. Collectively, these parts of the plan serve to communicate to all persons involved what is to happen (p. 18).

Three designs will be discussed and they are (1) discipline-based or subject-centered, (2) student-centered, and (3) problem solving. Each design will be explained briefly. In addition, some of the modifications and adaptations of these three basic designs were presented earlier in the chapter and will be presented in further detail.

Discipline-Based or Subject-Centered Design

This curriculum design continues to be the dominant form found in secondary schools. The discipline-based design is known by many labels, but the focus is on the content or concepts that are to be taught and learned. Its popularity can be attributed to a number of factors including: (1) the content of the discipline can be measured using standardized, normed testing programs; (2) textbooks are written along disciplinary lines and they easily communicate the fundamental knowledge of each area; and (3) the influence exerted by professional subject matter specialists and professional organizations has proven very successful during the past few decades.

When using the discipline-based design as a framework, the curriculum can be described as a collection of subjects which ". . . represents a specialized and unique body of content" (Ornstein and Hunkins, 1988, p. 172). Each discipline has its own structure, set of principles, body of knowledge, skills, vocabulary/language, mode of inquiry, processes, and relationships. The idea of the discipline having its own structure was first introduced by Bruner. In his book *The Process of Education*, Bruner explains this idea fully. In addition, he believed that "any subject can be taught in some effectively honest form to any child at any stage of development" (1959, p. 33).

This design organizes the curriculum into compartments with a single discipline filling each compartment, such as English, history, and mathematics. This structure leads critics to say that the discipline-based curriculum design has reinforced the notion that knowledge of each discipline is taught in separate units and in isolation from each other. The emphasis in this design is on a single discipline and its characteristics, and there is little if any interaction between and among the disciplines. Another shortcoming of the discipline-based design is that it ignores such areas as personal concerns, social problems, and ethical issues.

The proponents, on the other hand, believe that the discipline or subject matter design reflects the real world by approaching each discipline from a specialist's perspective. For example, history can be made more meaningful if it is taught with a historian's perspective. Likewise, mathematics and biology can be taught more effectively when taught by people who have the perspective and training of mathematicians and biologists.

Within the discipline-based curriculum design there are two major variations, the broad field and the correlation curriculum designs. The broad field design is an attempt to deal with the critics who say there is little interaction among disciplines. The broad field design brings two or more disciplines together under one general area of study. For example, one broad field design that is found in the secondary schools is physical science. Physical science is a broad field which draws its content from at least two areas of science — chemistry and physics, and sometimes astronomy is also added. At more advanced high school levels, such humanities courses as "History of Western Thought" combine the study of history, sociology, philosophy, and literature.

The second variation of the discipline-based perspective is the correlation curriculum design — linkages between disciplines. For example, the issue of environmental pollution involves several disciplines — life science, earth science, history, geography, and even mathematics — and these areas can be brought together temporarily to deal with this issue in a comprehensive manner. It is common for middle/junior high schools to have a topic or theme of study for a week or two, and all of the subject areas link together to contribute to the understanding of the topic or theme. Correlation curriculum design attempts to introduce concepts from other disciplines as a means of approaching a problem in order to find a solution. As pointed out, the disciplinary linkages are temporary, so the correlated disciplines retain their original identities while studying the problem under consideration. Because of its flexibility and reduced structure, the correlation design enjoys less popularity, especially at the high school level.

Student-Centered Design

When thinking about student-centered curriculum design, the name of John Dewey comes to mind. However, Frances Parker was an early progressive who was responsible for the learner or child-centered curriculum, which he implemented in Quincy, Massachusetts, when he was the superintendent of schools (Ornstein and Hunkins, 1988). Dewey, like Parker, viewed education as a process which served a social function.

It is the student or the learner, not the discipline or content, that serves as the beginning point for building this curriculum design. The student is the source for the curriculum, but as such provides little guidance for curriculum developers compared to subject matter and social concerns, controversial as these might be (Tanner and Tanner, 1980). Because the focus of the curriculum is the learner, the student-centered design is organized around a common set of learning experiences. One view would have the student left alone to develop his or her intellect or capacity for self-expression. Dewey, however, viewed this as ridiculous (Tanner and Tanner, 1980) and felt that a student "who was denied the guidance of a teacher was not having an enriching experience; on the contrary, he [or she] was being impoverished" (p. 295).

A frequently cited weakness of this design is that it lacks a definite structure. There are no key organizers, no definitive principles to guide the planning process except that students should have ". . . freedom *from* teacher domination, freedom *from* the millstone of subject matter, [and] freedom *from* adult imposed curriculum goals" (Tanner and Tanner, 1980, p. 294). Perhaps more damaging is the lack of commercial materials, including textbooks, which advocate a student-centered approach to curriculum planning and learning. As a result, this design has been difficult to implement in secondary schools because the discipline-based curriculum has dominated.

Problem-Centered or Problem-Solving Design

The third curriculum design focuses on school and individual problems. As society changes, so do the values, traditions, and concerns. The problem-centered curriculum design places the students in a problem situation or a dilemma, and they must find a solution. Unlike the student-centered design, the curriculum is planned for the students—the problem situations have already been identified and developed. This problem-solving approach has two advantages: (1) problems cross several disciplines and (2) the learners' abilities and needs are acknowledged and accommodated.

Most curriculum developers view the problem solving design as "a total process beginning with the definition of the problem and ending with action, that is, implementing the decision" (Tanner and Tanner, 1980, p. 401). Since problems seldom fall within one content area, the problem-centered design led to the development of the core curriculum. The problem under consideration provides the beginning point and the context for learning specific content.

Like the other two designs, the problem-centered curriculum has been identified using many different names throughout the recent past. Life situations, core curriculum, and social problems design are but a few of the more popular variations.

The problem-centered design, which uses life situations, helps students gain a deeper understanding about real problems and how to solve them. Problem-solving skills—identifying the problem, critically analyzing it, gathering appropriate information related to it, testing hypotheses, drawing conclusions, and acting on the information—are learned and applied to hypothetical world problems, and this can have a long lasting effect on students when they become responsible, productive citizens.

As strong as this design may be in helping students prepare for their roles as adults, there are some shortcomings. For one, there is no common body of knowledge taught and learned by all students, which is a significant departure from the discipline-based curriculum and makes assessment of common knowledge difficult. Secondly, as teachers select the problems for study they must be prepared in ways that integrate several disciplines in a comprehensive manner. Lastly, teachers do not feel adequately prepared to integrate content areas at the secondary level.

Depending on the social and intellectual climate of the time, the problem-centered curriculum enjoys some popularity. Although it has never been a dominant curriculum design for secondary schools, it is reflected in some of the course titles, such as "Contemporary Issues" and "Environmental Concerns."

From the brief discussions of the three major curriculum designs—discipline-centered, student-centered, and problem-centered—it is evident that each has strengths and weaknesses. It seems appropriate, however, to design a secondary curriculum that incorporates aspects of two, or perhaps all three of these. Even if, for example, the curriculum is discipline-based, there will be opportunities to consider and incorporate the interests of the students. In addition, there should be opportunities for the students to solve problems by applying the knowledge or content being presented. Being placed in a problem-solving situation will help students understand and appreciate the concerns that historians, geologists, mathematicians, and writers face when exploring their disciplines.

The basic curriculum designs parallel the basic views of curriculum development presented earlier in the chapter. These typical designs serve as guides when developing educational programs for the secondary schools.

SUMMARY

Chapter 7 provided an overview of what is involved in the curriculum planning and development process. It specifically identified the factors to consider in the planning and development process. Fundamental questions relative to what knowledge is important continue to keep educators focused on what should be included in the curriculum of the secondary school.

The general components of the curriculum—structure, sources, organization, and dimension—were discussed briefly. This information provides the building blocks for what is to come—the writing of the curriculum. The basic curriculum development designs presented at the end of the chapter serve as formats for the curriculum documents that are developed, which in turn guide the total teaching-learning interaction in junior and senior high schools.

YOUR TURN

7.1 In 1860 Herbert Spencer identified the following five areas as being knowledge that was of most worth. Examine these five areas closely and, based on your understanding of the characteristics of secondary students today (review Chapter 6), make recommendations for additions, deletions, or other revisions under the heading "What Knowledge Is of Most Worth for the Twenty-First Century?"

(a) Knowledge which leads directly to self-preservation and produces physical well-being (i.e., physiology, biology, health, chemistry)

(b) Knowledge which leads indirectly to self-preservation through the building up of sufficient vocational capacity (i.e., practical and applied sciences, mathematics)

(c) Knowledge which leads to parenthood and the rearing of offspring (i.e., biology, physiology, and psychology)

(d) Knowledge which leads to leisure and the enjoyment of finer things of life (i.e, fine arts, psychology, health, and recreation)

(e) Knowledge which leads to citizenship and which helps one to become a good neighbor and a useful member of the community (i.e., political, social, and economic sciences)

7.2 Read the passage below by Walter R. Coppedge (1970) and then answer each of the questions that follows.

> We don't acquire our really important learning in packages. As interested explorers we are not concerned about boundaries which mark those august empire states called disciplines—separating literature from history, sociology from psychology, chemistry from biology, and so on. But as educators, we begin to be concerned about passports, visas, and entry and exit permits, failing to realize that the student wants to explore life in its mysterious wholeness rather than in the exclusive little principalities of subject areas. (What the world is coming to. *Journal of Phi Delta Kappan, L11,* 2, 75–78)

(a) Do you agree with the author that we don't acquire really important learning in discrete "packages?"

(b) Do you agree with the author that we treat disciplines or subjects as "empire states"?

(c) What does the author mean by passports and visas? Were your teachers captives of separate empires? Were they concerned with passports and visas between empires?

(d) Were you comfortable exploring the separate domains, or would you prefer to demolish the walls? Do something in between? What?

(e) What implications does this metaphor have for you as an educator or curriculum developer? Are you prepared to help students explore life in "its mysterious wholeness"?

REFERENCES

Apple, M.W. (March 1990). Is there a curriculum voice to reclaim? *Phi Delta Kappan, 71,* 7, 526–530.

Beach, D.M. & Reinhartz, J. (1989). *Supervision: Focus on instruction.* New York: Harper & Row.

Bode, B.H. (1927). *Modern educational theories.* New York: Macmillan.

Briggs, T.H. (1926). *Curriculum problems.* New York: Macmillan.

Bruner, J.S. (1959). *The process of education.* Cambridge Mass.: Harvard University Press.

Commission on the Reorganization of Secondary Education. (1918). *Cardinal principles of secondary education.* Washington, D.C.: National Education Association.

Dewey, J. (1938). *Experience and education.* New York: Collier Books.

Dewey, J. (1902). *The child and the curriculum.* Chicago: University of Chicago Press.

Doll, R.C. (1986). *Curriculum improvement* (6th ed.). Needham Heights, Mass.: Allyn & Bacon.

Eisner, E.W. (March 1990). Who decides what schools teach? *Phi Delta Kappan, 71,* 7, 523–526.

Funkhouser, C.W., Beach, D.M., Ryan, G.T. & Fifer, F. (1981). *Classroom applications of the curriculum: A systems approach.* Dubuque, Iowa: Kendall Hunt.

Giles, H.H., McCutchen, S.R. & Zechiel, A.N. (1942). *Exploring the curriculum.* New York: Harper & Row.

Komoski, P.K. (February 1990). Needed: A whole-curriculum approach. *Educational Leadership, 47,* 5, 72–77.

McNeil, J. (1981). *Curriculum: A comprehensive introduction.* Boston: Little Brown.

Ornstein, A.C. & Hunkins, F.P. (1988). *Curriculum: Foundations, principles and issues.* Englewood Cliffs, N.J.: Prentice Hall.

Saylor, J.G. & Alexander, W.M. (1954). *Curriculum planning for better teaching and learning.* New York: Holt, Rinehart & Winston.

Smith, B.O., Stanley, W.O. & Shores, H.J. (1957). *Fundamentals of curriculum development* (rev. ed.). New York: Harcourt, Brace & World, Inc.

Spencer, H. (1860). *Education, intellectual, moral, and physical.* New York: Appleton-Century-Crofts.

Reinhartz, D. & Reinhartz, J. (1990). *Integrating geography across the curriculum.* Washington, D.C.: National Education Association.

Taba, H. (1962). *Curriculum development: Theory and practice.* Harcourt, Brace & World, Inc.

Tanner, D. & Tanner, L.N. (1980). *Curriculum development theory into practice* (2nd ed.). New York: Macmillan.

Tyler, R.W. (1949). *Basic principles of curriculum and instruction.* Chicago: University of Chicago Press.

Wiles, J. & Bondi, J. (1989). *Curriculum development: A guide to practice* (3rd ed.). Columbus, Ohio: Charles E. Merrill.

Wulf, K.M. & Schave, B. (1984). *Curriculum design: A handbook for educators.* Glenview, Ill.: Scott Foresman.

Zais, R.S. (1976). *Curriculum principles and foundations.* New York: Harper & Row.

Chapter
8

Models of Curriculum Development

Selecting a model for planning and curriculum development is not an easy task. The literature is replete with various models of curriculum development, and in fact these models continue to evolve as new information becomes available about effective schools and the teaching-learning process. Although models continue to evolve, a model is a way to determine the ingredients or components of what should be included in the curriculum. This chapter discusses several models that can be used to facilitate the curriculum development process. We believe that it is easier to conceptualize the curriculum development process if presented within the framework of linear, circular, and multidimensional models. Secondly, the steps can be discussed and analyzed individually and their relationship and interaction can be shown within the overall system of the model.

The previous chapter dealt with the three most common designs used as a framework to plan curriculum. Regardless of the design, there are generally two approaches used when developing curriculum: the technical or scientific approach and the nontechnical-nonscientific approach. Ornstein and Hunkins (1988) note that a technical-scientific approach to curriculum development enables ". . . us to comprehend curriculum from a . . . broad view and to understand it as a complex unity of parts organized to serve a common function—the education of individuals" (p. 192). Both approaches are presented, but the technical models are described in detail because they provide educators with multiple options for planning and developing curriculum for contemporary secondary classrooms.

TECHNICAL-SCIENTIFIC MODELS

Six technical-scientific models of curriculum development will be discussed in this section. These models include the Tyler model, the Taba model, the Saylor and Alexander model, the Wulf and Schave model, and the Goodlad and Hunkins models.

Tyler Model

The Tyler (1949) model is one of the best examples of the technical-scientific approach. Originally published as a syllabus for a course he was teaching, Tyler's *Basic Principles of Curriculum and Instruction* was intended to present "a rationale for viewing, analyzing and interpreting the curriculum and instructional program of an educational institution" (p. 1). Tyler in the 1940s and early 1950s refined his inventory of questions to four, which continue to guide the design of curriculum. The questions that Tyler posed provide a focus and direction for the curriculum planning and development process and include:

1. What educational purposes shall the school seek to attain?
2. What educational experiences can be provided that are likely to attain those purposes?
3. How can these educational experiences be effectively organized?
4. How can we determine whether these purposes are being attained?

According to Komoski (1990), Tyler provided "a valid set of systematic parameters of curriculum wholeness . . . in the form of these four inescapable questions" (p. 73). Komoski has rephrased the original four questions and added a fifth to relate to the classrooms of today. These five questions are:

1. What educational purposes is this school, district, or state seeking to attain?
2. Are we providing a range of learning experiences that are likely to facilitate the attainment of our school's educational purposes?
3. Are we effectively organizing those learning experiences and making them readily available to learners?
4. How well are we determining that the school's educational purposes are being attained (by means of those learning experiences we have provided, organized, and made available to learners)?
5. Are we striving to maintain dynamic interrelatedness (i.e., wholeness) among curricular activities called for by the first four questions by continuously re-asking and re-answering those questions? (p. 73)

Komoski, like Tyler, views curriculum as a dynamic process that functions as a comprehensive system, and these questions help guide the planning process.

Although Tyler did not present his model graphically, many curriculum theorists have created their own version of Tyler's four basic questions dealing with (1) the purposes of education, (2) the selection of experiences related to the purposes, (3) the organization of the experiences, and (4) evaluation of the purposes. According to Tanner and Tanner (1980) the Tyler model was derived from the progressive educational thought of the early twentieth century, but Tyler was the one who fully elaborated on the paradigm. Popham and Baker (1970) have taken the four basic steps described by Tyler and developed a diagram of the model. Figure 8.1 represents our view of Tyler's model of curriculum development.

The Tyler model helps answer the question "Where does curriculum come from?" Building upon Dewey's three sources of curriculum—the learner, society, and organized subject matter—and Taba's sources of data for planning—studies of society, studies of learners, and studies of subject matter content—the model suggests that there are three main sources for developing curriculum: society's values, the needs of the students, and the subject matter specialists. Together these three sources help curriculum developers determine the educational purposes of secondary schools. According to Funkhouser, Beach, Ryan, and Fifer (1981), "These three data sources . . . are the first considerations in determining what will ultimately be measured in judging the effectiveness of schooling" (p. 13). In addition, these sources help to set the scope—what is ultimately taught in school—and the sequence—the order of presentation—of the school curriculum and produce the broad, general goals of secondary education.

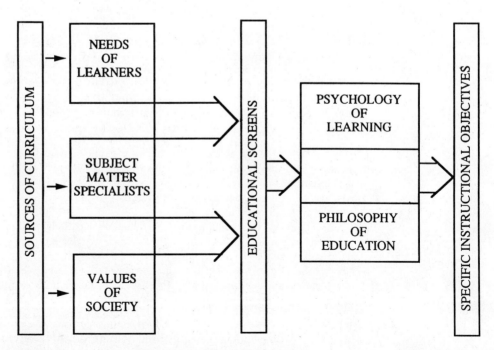

Figure 8.1 Tyler's model of curriculum development

Once the goals or general aims have been identified, they are ". . . 'sifted' through educational philosophy and educational psychology screens to produce instructional objectives expressed in more precise terms" (Beach and Reinhartz, 1989, p. 101). The first screen, philosophy, influences what goals are selected and how they are implemented in the curriculum. (See Chapter 3 for more detail about the role of philosophy in developing curriculum.) The second screen, psychology, addresses the question concerning how students learn best. It also answers the question "Are the general goals compatible with the developmental levels and characteristics of the learners?" (For more detailed information on the role of psychology in curriculum development, and characteristics of secondary students, see Chapters 5 and 6.)

The final step in the Tyler model is writing and selecting precise instructional objectives. It is at this step that the general goals are reduced to specific instructional objectives that are translated into specific learning experiences. It is during the goal reduction step that teachers directly implement curriculum development in their classrooms.

Tyler was unique in his recommendations that evaluation be used to reconsider the purpose of education. His four-step, question-oriented curriculum design helped to introduce the use of measurable behavioral objectives into the curriculum planning process. Although Tyler did not specifically intend his model to be used primarily by central office personnel, the effect has often been a "top-down" development process.

Taba Model

Another generally accepted model of curriculum development was presented by Taba. According to Ornstein and Hunkins (1988) Tyler was "highly influenced by Hilda Taba, his colleague for over 20 years at Ohio State and the University of Chicago" (p. 78). However, unlike Tyler's model, Taba's (1962) was an inductive approach that teachers could use to develop curriculum first for their own classrooms. It was later, during the 1950s and 1960s, that Taba took the questions presented earlier and expanded them and expressed them as steps. Zais (1976) refers to these steps as the inverted model of curriculum development because Taba advocated beginning the process at the classroom level with planning done by teachers for their students.

Taba encouraged teachers to approach curriculum development in a systematic way using a five-step model of curriculum planning and development. The five steps include "(1) creation of teaching units by classroom teachers, (2) testing the experimental units in the classroom, (3) revision and consolidation of the units, (4) development of a framework or overall curriculum design, and (5) dissemination of the units to others" (Beach and Reinhartz, 1989, p. 97). It is only after the curriculum is implemented and tested at the classroom level that it would be appropriate for determining an overall design applicable to other instructional situations. In 1962 Taba presented her five-step model, a revised version of Tyler's four questions. Step one of Taba's model (creation of teaching units by classroom teachers) has seven components. As teachers plan units of instruction for their classrooms, the following seven components are to be used in the planning process:

1. Diagnosis of needs
2. Formulation of objectives
3. Selection of content
4. Organization of content
5. Selection of learning experiences
6. Organization of learning experiences
7. Determine what to evaluate and the means of doing it

Taba strongly advocated the "grass roots" or classroom level of curriculum development and her five-step model, with its seven components for unit development, has been widely adopted by teachers to structure teaching and learning for their classrooms.

Saylor and Alexander Model

A third model for developing curriculum, which can be classified as technical-scientific, was proposed by Saylor and Alexander (1981). Rather than focus on the sources of curriculum development, Saylor and Alexander begin the process with goals and objectives and end with curriculum evaluation. In between they are concerned with design and implementation. Figure 8.2 depicts their

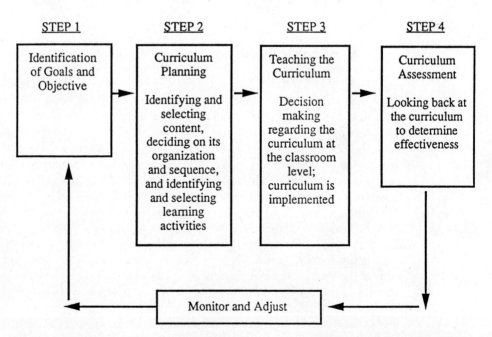

Figure 8.2 Saylor and Alexander's model of curriculum development (*Modified from:* Saylor, J.G. & Alexander, W.M. (1974). *Planning curriculum for schools.* New York: Holt, Rinehart & Winston.)

four-step model with a modification component. The following is a description of each of the four steps in the Saylor and Alexander model.

Step 1   The development process begins with the identification of the goals and objectives. After the major goals and objectives are identified, the curriculum domains are addressed. For each goal, a domain is identified. The four major curriculum domains are personal development, human relations, continued learning skills, and specializations. The authors caution that these may not be the only domains to consider.

Step 2   This step involves decisions about curriculum designs, which require planners to consider characteristics of a "good curriculum." This requires decisions to be made about the content, its organization, and the learning experiences. What focus will be emphasized: the discipline, the students, and/or societal/personal problems?

Step 3   Another name for this step is teaching. It is here that the curriculum is implemented in the classroom. This step requires the planners to consider the instructional process so the curriculum can be taught.

Step 4   The final step involves an evaluation of the curriculum. Teachers as well as curriculum developers select the techniques that will be used to determine the effectiveness of the curriculum plan. Decisions are then made about whether to retain, change, or eliminate the educational program.

Wulf and Schave Model

In the early 1980s Wulf and Schave developed a different model for planning and developing curriculum. They recommend a systems approach which involves group interaction and group goals to develop a meaningful curriculum. This approach is divided into three distinct phases:

1. Problem definition
2. Development
3. Evaluation

Wulf and Schave (1984) recommend that these phases be followed in sequence so that the most coherent learning outcomes can be achieved. The three phases are described in greater detail in the section that follows.

    I. Problem definition phase
       A. Identify problem/purpose: There is a connection between the content and the participants of the group.
       B. "Needs" of participants should be reflected in the project.

    II. Development phase
       A. Six elements of curriculum design include:
          1. Content is selected using information from research, theory, experts, and/or needs assessment.

2. Learner goals are identified in light of content identified.
3. Instructional objectives are reduced from the goals.
4. Lessons are generated.
5. Appropriate materials for use with the lessons are identified.
6. The learning environment to implement the newly designed curriculum is identified.

III. Final Phase
    A. Evaluation
    B. Feedback

The Wulf and Schave model can be used at both the district and classroom levels. Each phase provides direction for program development.

Goodlad and Hunkins Models

Two lesser used technical-scientific models of curriculum development have been proposed by both Goodlad and Hunkins. The Goodlad proposal is unique in that it is not a linear model, but it is symmetrical. His model, as shown in Figure 8.3, draws its educational aims ". . . from the analysis of the values of the existing culture" (Ornstein and Hunkins, 1988, p. 196). Figure 8.3 provides a representation of how the Goodlad model operates. Because of its symmetry, there is a balance between funded knowledge and conventional wisdom as data sources. In addition, in looking at the conceptual framework, it is not easy to determine the starting point, but what is clear is that values of both society and students occupy an equally important position in getting the curriculum development process started. The components of educational aims and behavioral objectives, along with outcomes, are shared with the other models.

The Hunkins curriculum development model also has components similar to those studied earlier (i.e., curriculum implementation and evaluation), but includes several different components as well. In all, there are seven stages which include:

1. Curriculum conceptualization and legitimization
2. Curriculum diagnosis
3. Content selection
4. Experience selection
5. Implementation
6. Evaluation
7. Maintenance

Figure 8.4 shows the relationships of these seven stages. The Hunkins model is somewhat different from the models of curriculum development that have been discussed previously. It has a feedback loop as well as conceptualization and management and maintenance stages (Ornstein and Hunkins, 1988). As seen in Figure 8.4, the feedback loop makes the model circular and the conceptualization and management stage encourages curriculum developers to raise philosophical questions in the process, causing them to consider their philosophical

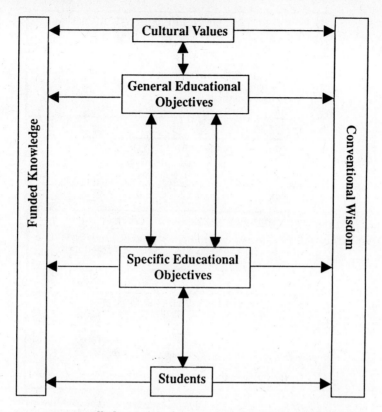

Figure 8.3 Goodlad's model of curriculum development (*Modified from:* Goodlad, J. L. & Richter, M. N. (1966). *The development of a conceptual system for dealing with problems of curriculum and instruction.* Los Angeles: University of California Institute for Development of Educational Activities.)

orientations—essentialism, progressivism, existentialism—early on. Curriculum maintenance, perhaps implied in the other models, occupies a well-defined step in the Hunkins model. By giving attention to maintenance of the curriculum, there is an ongoing assessment of the instructional program built into the model.

NONTECHNICAL-NONSCIENTIFIC MODELS

Other curriculum development models have a totally different orientation. They focus on the learner more and are less concerned with product and output. Curriculum developers using this approach find that the curriculum evolves daily, and therefore is not sequentially planned in advance. These models, used in the early 1970s, have never had a large following nor gained much attention. Nevertheless, it seems appropriate to discuss at least two of

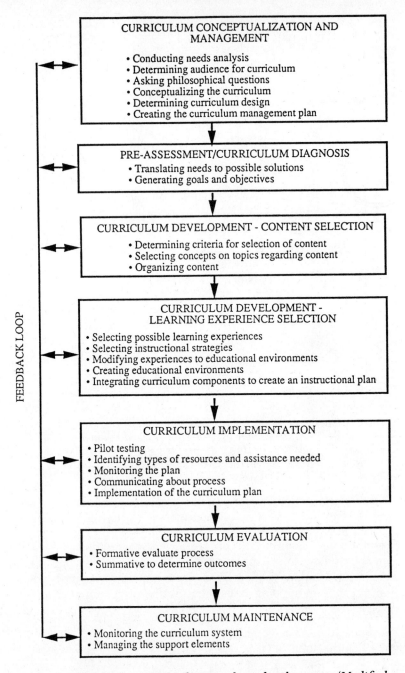

Figure 8.4 Hunkins's model of curriculum development (*Modified from:* Hunkins, F.P. (1980). *Curriculum development program improvement.* (Columbus, Ohio: Charles E. Merrill)

these models because of their contrast with the more content-focused models. The two models include an open classroom model and the Weinstein and Fantini models.

Open Classroom Model

This model is based on the open classroom philosophy. The emphasis is on activity and getting students involved in the learning process rather than having them learn passively. The open classroom curriculum development model relies on spontaneity and therefore does not entail a great deal of preplanning. It relies heavily on the learners to provide the direction for content and learning activities in the curriculum. Strategies frequently used in the model include learning packets or activity stations. The physical characteristics of the classroom also play a large part in the structure and design of the curriculum, in that desks are not in rows and the environment is not as structured.

Weinstein and Fantini Model

This model, developed during the 1970s as well, presents teachers with a means of generating new curriculum content by dealing with the current topic in a special way. Figure 8.5 provides a framework for this model. In this model, the identification of the learners and the determination of their concerns are the beginning points. Weinstein and Fantini (1970) are interested in helping students gain control over their lives. This model does have a clear beginning point and that is the learners. It is their concerns and ideas which drive the curriculum development process to its conclusion and the learning outcomes. In the end, the educational aims, which ultimately liberate the learners, are the major focus. The content results from traditional sources or from enriching experiences. For this model, the content is organized into three categories: (1) experiences of those growing up, (2) affective dealing with the interests of the learner, and (3) the type of content that is experiential.

When you compare various models of curriculum development, it is evident that Tyler and Taba outlined a series of steps that curriculum developers have found easy and practical to use in constructing educational programs, especially at the secondary level where content is the major focus. The Saylor and Alexander model focuses on the critical elements, rather than preliminary data or activities, so design, implementation, and evaluation become the essential ingredients. The other models (i.e., Goodlad, Hunkins, Weinstein and Fantini) have components that may fit the various designs and philosophies better and have therefore been included as options to consider when developing curriculum.

As we enter the 1990s, curricular concerns of (1) philosophy and goals, (2) instructional systems, (3) development of materials, (4) management and alignment of curriculum and instruction, and (5) teacher training have become the emerging themes. Each concern requires educators to make decisions. Often these curricular concerns are stated as questions as indicated in Chapter

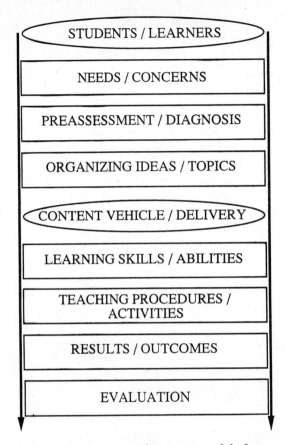

Figure 8.5 Weinstein and Fantini's model of curriculum development (*Modified from* Weinstein, G. & Fantini, M.D. (1970). *Toward humanistic education.* New York: Praeger.)

7. These concerns and questions help determine the best model of curriculum development to employ.

The general overview of the six technical-scientific curriculum development models, along with the options, provides some idea of the many variations available. Different curriculum theorists view curriculum development in very specific terms and each tries to sway educators to use their model. All the models provide a forum for discussion and debate.

ELEMENTS TO CONSIDER IN CURRICULUM DEVELOPMENT

Regardless of the model used, when developing curriculum, there are several elements to consider. This section describes the specific elements that can be included. These elements include: (1) selecting the content: where consideration is given to significance, validity, and interest; (2) organizing the content: where consideration is given to ordering; and (3) selecting the learning experiences: where consideration is given to the learners and to the nature of focus, motivation, and participation. The first two elements deal with the scope and sequence, the what and the when. The third element deals with how the content will be presented.

Selecting and Organizing the Content

The scope of information for a specific subject can be enormous. Without a system for selecting and organizing the content, the sheer volume makes curriculum development unmanageable. Regardless of the model used and/or one's philosophical orientation, all curricula of the secondary school have content. These considerations—model and philosophical orientation—can and do influence what content is selected and how it is organized.

Feyereisen and colleagues (1970) emphasize the need to use the goals and objectives as a way to determine which knowledge is significant. As they note,

> The education received in school is not meant to perpetuate an academic discipline, prepare students for college, or train bricklayers. All these things may be accomplished, but its chief mission is to provide graduates who are capable of becoming active, participating, contributing members of society. To achieve this goal the individual must learn to live with himself [or herself] and others and must have a system of values to guide him [or her]. Therefore, if this is the ultimate purpose of education, we must start by defining the needs of the individual, the nature and needs of society, and the system of values from which derive the objectives of the curriculum. The means should not determine the ends. . . . In addition, the inclusion of a variable such as knowledge areas would also predestine the content, curriculum organization, scope, and sequence variables . . . (p. 138).

Curriculum developers may want to consider specific criteria as guides in selecting and organizing the content. These criteria help determine what information, skills, and facts are compatible with the identified goals and purposes of the overall curriculum. The criteria are significance, validity, interest, and utility. A brief description of each follows.

Significance is a criterion that is difficult to determine for all curriculum areas. The curriculum planners determine what content is significant. If the design is student-centered, significance is defined in terms of the experiences and content that would be meaningful to the students. However, by the mid 1980s, knowledge had increased considerably. To assist curriculum planners with the selection and organization of the content, the focus has been on the goals and objectives.

Validity can be explained in terms of the content's authenticity and coincides with the goals and objectives. Is this information appropriate given the goals and objectives of the program?

Interest is most compatible with student-centered curriculum design. Students' interests will vary depending on their maturity level and the social conditions of the times.

Utility is concerned with how useful the content is as judged against the curriculum design that is used. For a problem-centered curriculum, usefulness is measured against its application to social and political situations. Usefulness within a student-centered curriculum would be determined by its effect on increasing a student's self-identity.

Selecting the Learning Experiences

The experiences that are selected for the curriculum become the means by which the content is communicated to students. Curriculum experiences represent the teaching methods and strategies used in the classroom to learn about the content. Tyler (1949) used the term "learning experiences" in describing the basics of curriculum development.

These elements listed will find their way into any of the various models and philosophical orientations. What happens is that each element may "look" different in the curricular program depending on one's philosophical beliefs and the organizing model that is used to develop the curriculum.

It should be noted that there is no "best" curriculum development model. It is no secret that curriculum planners have used the Tyler model for years because it has proven so successful in meeting the needs of the school and students. This does not mean, however, that it represents the best model. For curriculum developers, it is a matter of selecting the model that meets the needs of the district, the students, and the desired goals and objectives of the educational program. Tyler (1949) accurately describes curriculum planning and development as a continuous cycle of planning, replanning, redevelopment, and reevaluation which produces . . . "an increasingly more effective educational program rather than depending so much upon hit and miss judgement as a basis for curriculum development" (p. 123). Clearly, the process of selecting an appropriate model for curriculum planning and development and then to implement that model through various "cycles" is a complex process with many different variables. It is important to begin with a good framework, so that you can successfully attach all of the other components required for successful implementation of an educational program: the curriculum. The model serves as the foundation, the undergirding framework for all that follows in curriculum planning and development.

SUMMARY

Chapter 8 is devoted to the topic of models for developing curriculum. When developing a curriculum for secondary students, there are several models to consider and this chapter presented two basic approaches: the technical-scientific and the nontechnical-nonscientific.

Six technical-scientific models are discussed (Tyler, Taba, Saylor and Alexander, Wulf and Schave, Goodlad, and Hunkins). In addition, nontechnical-nonscientific (open classroom and Weinstein and Fantini) are presented as options to consider.

The models vary from each other largely in the degree of specificity demanded in the curriculum development process. For example, the Taba model includes more steps than the model suggested by Tyler, thus providing more guidance for teachers and curriculum developers. By presenting several versions of the curriculum development process, the practical side of program planning and development is outlined.

The chapter concluded with a brief discussion of elements which are basic to all curricular models. These basic elements — selecting and organizing content, determining its significance and validity, and then considering the interests of students and selecting learning experiences — to some degree can be found in each model. The selection and organization of the content, along with the selection of learning experiences, is influenced by the philosophical orientations of the planners as well as the desired outcomes advocated by the community. The model of curriculum that is selected by a specific school district will likely be compatible with the philosophy and expected outcomes outlined in the district's mission statement.

YOUR TURN

8.1 You have been approached by a group of citizens — educators, business people, lawyers, accountants — to direct a science curriculum project. The science project would entail developing a science curriculum for grades 7–9 which will focus on the superconducting super collider technology. Consider responding to the following questions to help you get the project started.
  (a) What curriculum development model would be appropriate for you to use? Why?
  (b) How will you select the content, the units of study, for the project?
  (c) How will you sequence the curriculum?
  (d) What learning activities will you select?
  (e) What guidelines will you provide the curriculum writers (science teachers, science specialists, curriculum consultants) to ensure that all steps, components, and elements of the curriculum development process are followed?

8.2 You are part of a panel exploring a curriculum which is integrative in nature. You have been asked to present the argument in favor of what Komoski (1990) calls a "whole curriculum." You are cautioned that in attendance there will be educators, parents, and community leaders who are diehard supporters of a discipline-based curriculum for the secondary schools. Use the following as a guide to help you prepare your response.
  (a) Read the complete Komoski article contained in the references.
  (b) What evidence will you use to support your view of a "whole curriculum"?
  (c) What curriculum model will you cite in order to develop an integrative secondary science program?
  (d) What example will you use to work through one of the curriculum development models to illustrate how the "whole curriculum" operates?
  (e) What activity will you use to get the audience to experience such a curriculum?

8.3 You have been asked to develop a drug education curriculum for the middle schools. Using the Tyler model, establish a protocol or procedure that you could use. Illustrate how the model works. Write out your plan by following the model (see Figure 8.1).

8.4 Once the drug education curriculum is formulated for the district, teachers will need assistance in bringing the curriculum to the classroom level. Using Taba's seven components, plan a unit of instruction for a life science or health class.

8.5 Your school district has been criticized by citizens in the community for not involving more of them in the educational planning process. To deal with this controversy regarding community involvement, you as the director of secondary education are asked to select a model of curriculum development which either involves the community directly or suggests ways to involve them. Using a visual of the curriculum model, describe the curriculum process that you plan to use and clearly indicate the role of community members. After identifying the basic curriculum development model and drawing the schema, explain each step fully so that you can present it at the next school board meeting.

8.6 When you have a meeting with teachers who are writing the English language arts curriculum for high school, you want to encourage them to use a whole language approach. Before the meeting, review this approach and write out all of the steps so that you will have a rehearsal in preparation for the actual meeting. Consider ways to involve participants in various ways.

8.7 As a curriculum developer, you are an agent of change. Put in writing how you will feel initiating change in your school district, which is basically operating as it did 25 years ago, even though student performance on national achievement tests, as well as state tests, has continued to decline. In addition, there has been a changing student population. How will you deal with these situations? What meetings will you plan? With whom? What strategies will you adopt or employ? Write out the questions you can expect and note your responses.

REFERENCES

Beach, D.M. & Reinhartz, J. (1989). *Supervision: Focus on instruction*. New York: Harper & Row.

Feyereisen, K.V. et al. (1970). *Curriculum renewal: A systems approach*. New York: Appleton.

Funkhouser, C.W., Beach, D.M., Ryan, G.T. & Fifer, F. (1981). *Classroom applications of the curriculum: A systems approach*. Dubuque, Iowa: Kendall Hunt.

Goodlad, J.L. & Richter, M.N. (1966). *The development of a conceptual system for dealing with problems of curriculum and instruction*. Los Angeles: University of California Institute for Development of Educational Activities.

Hunkins, F.P. (1980). *Curriculum development program improvement*. Columbus, Ohio: Charles E. Merrill.

Komoski, P.K. (February 1990). Needed: A whole-curriculum approach. *Educational Leadership*, 47, 5, 72–77.

Ornstein, A.C. & Hunkins, F.P. (1988). *Curriculum: Foundations, principles and issues*. Englewood Cliffs, N.J.: Prentice Hall.

Popham, W.J. & Baker, E.L. (1970). *Establishing instructional goals.* Englewood Cliffs, N.J.: Prentice Hall.

Saylor, J.G., Alexander, W.M. & Lewis, A.J. (1981). *Curriculum planning for better teaching and learning* (4th ed.). New York: Holt, Rinehart & Winston.

Saylor, J.G. & Alexander, W.M. (1974). *Planning curriculum for schools.* New York: Holt, Rinehart & Winston.

Taba, H. (1962). *Curriculum development: Theory and practice.* New York: Harcourt, Brace & World, Inc.

Tanner, D. & Tanner, L.N. (1980). *Curriculum development theory into practice* (2nd ed.). New York: Macmillan.

Tyler, R.W. (1949). *Basic principles of curriculum and instruction.* Chicago: University of Chicago Press.

Weinstein, G. & Fantini, M.D. (1970). *Toward humanistic education.* New York: Praeger.

Wulf, K.M. & Schave, B. (1984). *Curriculum design: A handbook for educators.* Glenview, Ill.: Scott Foresman.

Zais, R.S. (1976). *Curriculum principles and foundations.* New York: Harper & Row.

FOUR

Curriculum Development for the Secondary Classroom

P art Four includes information about organizing the curriculum specifically for the classroom level. Up to this point, the broad picture was provided. In Chapter 9, detailed information about the curriculum development process is included. Using the task analysis process (**TAP**) to guide the classroom level planning, activities and steps are carefully delineated to aid educators in the planning process.

A textbook with a focus on secondary curriculum would not be complete without a discussion of ways to evaluate the effectiveness of curricular programs. Chapter 10 presents different models and rationales that can be used to evaluate the curriculum at various levels of the secondary program. This final phase in the curriculum development process helps determine what changes need to be made, what content or programs should be removed, and what programs should be retained or strengthened.

Chapter
9

Curriculum Planning
and Development

Organizing the Curriculum
for Instruction

*P*lanning is central to curriculum development and is crucial to the teaching-learning process. However, when the term *planning* is mentioned, the matrix in a teacher's plan book is what often may come to mind. For us, planning for instruction goes beyond this matrix or "to do" list and involves a comprehensive process that occurs at multiple levels — district, campus, grade, and classroom — and involves teachers at each and every level. We concur with Zahorik's (1970) view that detailed and thorough planning gives direction to teaching, which produces worthwhile learning. When preservice and inservice teachers consider the curriculum, they need to know about (1) long-term goals and instructional objectives, (2) the scope and sequence of the content, (3) the activities and teaching strategies that are appropriate for the learners and the content, and (4) ways to evaluate the success of the planning efforts. The curriculum planning process thus becomes the foundation or cornerstone of the instructional process and although hidden from view, it is "one of the most important functions of teaching" (Arends, 1988, p. 86).

Although complex, planning is often a private process that requires individual educators to make a series of decisions relative to instruction (Ornstein, 1990). Curriculum planning precedes the teaching-learning process and because it occurs outside the classroom, it is not easily observed. Because planning is nonobservable and first done mentally, it is a process that is often difficult for beginning teachers to learn from experienced teachers (McCutcheon, 1980; Yinger, 1980). Educators must therefore make every effort to be involved directly in the curriculum planning and development process to fully recognize its importance. Theory, research, and common sense, however, suggest that engaging in the planning process also improves student learning (Arends, 1988).

With the publication of numerous reports on education in the 1980s, more attention was directed to academic excellence and a concern for the basics. These reform reports brought greater attention to the curriculum development process and a renewed interest in curriculum as a body of knowledge or content to be learned. However, as described in Chapters 7 and 8, we view curriculum planning and development as both a process and a product (content). The curriculum is determined by the principles, concepts, or content of a particular body of knowledge, or academic discipline. To improve the curriculum, educators adjust both the ways in which content is determined (process) and the kinds and numbers of concepts taught, as well as the sequencing of content.

Bruner (1960) emphasized the importance of the structure of knowledge in the curriculum development process and provided four justifications for teaching the structure of knowledge. These justifications include:

1. By teaching fundamental principles (concepts) teachers make the subject more understandable to the student.
2. By placing details and facts within a conceptual or mental framework, students can remember more easily.
3. By helping the students make the connections between and among concepts or see the relatedness of the details or facts, teachers facilitate learning more readily.
4. By examining the subject matter content periodically to determine the relevancy or appropriateness of the concepts or content, teachers present the structure of knowledge.

Within this view of curriculum development, the teaching of the structure of knowledge, as well as the content itself, contributes to more efficient learning. As Nicholls and Nicholls (1978) note, in planning for teaching, "one must teach something to someone, the someone is the pupil and the something is the content" (p. 48). However, there is some overlap between and among content areas and as new knowledge is generated, educators are continually ". . . faced with a problem of defining their discipline and of structuring or organizing the knowledge within the discipline" (Blount and Klausmier, 1968, p. 118). In planning and developing curriculum, the subject matter or content, which includes the knowledge, skills, attitudes, and values to be learned, must be regularly reviewed.

This chapter is designed to assist secondary educators in planning and developing the content of the curriculum for classroom instruction. The chapter identifies issues and aspects of the curriculum development process that occur at the district, campus, and classroom levels. First, resources that can be used in curriculum planning at the various levels are presented. These resources include scope and sequence charts, curriculum guides, and resource units or guides.

The next section of the chapter describes the planning that occurs within the time frames of yearly reporting periods (i.e., semester, six weeks), units, and daily lessons. The task analysis process (TAP) is presented in detail and explained as a part of the lesson planning process. One very important step that is highlighted in task analysis is selection and prioritization of goals and then reducing them to instructional objectives. The chapter also discusses the domains of learning as a part of the process of developing objectives. The chapter ends with a detailed explanation of the remaining steps of the task analysis process. At the conclusion of the chapter, secondary educators should have a better understanding of the curriculum planning and development process, its importance and relationship to the instructional process, and its role at the classroom level, where the students are directly involved.

RESOURCES FOR CURRICULUM PLANNING

When teachers begin to plan for classroom instruction, they need resources to ensure the comprehensiveness and effectiveness of the process. The resources for curriculum planning take various forms, but three of the most frequently consulted planning resources for secondary teachers include scope and sequence charts, curriculum guides, and resource guides. These documents facilitate the planning process and contain information and suggestions that aid the teacher.

Scope and Sequence Charts

One of the first decisions that educators make in planning and developing curriculum at each school organizational level (district, campus, grade, and classroom) is to determine the scope and sequence of the content. Saylor and Alexander (1954) have defined *scope* as the "breadth, variety, and types of educational experiences that are to be provided pupils as they progress through the school program . . . the 'what' of the curriculum" (p. 248). They define *sequence* as "the order in which educational experiences are developed with pupils . . . the 'when' in curriculum planning" (p. 249). Scope and sequence, the what and when of curriculum, are important for each level of educational planning.

These charts help identify key concepts and skills that are taught across grade levels for individual subject areas (i.e., social studies, language, the arts, science, mathematics). This provides a K–12 perspective for the district, or what is called vertical articulation, the view of the content in the grades above and below. For example, a scope and sequence chart for secondary science would indicate the grade level that the particular science course is normally taught (seventh grade life science, eighth grade earth science, ninth grade physical science, tenth grade biology, eleventh grade chemistry, and twelfth grade physics) along with the skills and science concepts that are to be learned within each content area. At the campus level, this chart would be applied to the grades that are housed at a particular campus, and for high school it would typically cover grades 9–12.

Table 9.1 is an example of a scope and sequence chart for high school science, which is a part of the *Guidelines for Science Curriculum in Washington Schools* (1988) published by the Office of the Superintendent of Public Instruction. Included in this chart are specific statements of goals, objectives, and learning outcomes for physics, chemistry, life and earth/space science.

Scope and sequence charts vary with respect to the degree of specificity, but they are useful in providing direction for teachers as they plan instruction for an individual class. At each grade level, teachers focus on the "what," the content to be taught, and the "when," the order in which it would be taught, given the nature of the students at that grade level. Using this resource, teachers establish their own scope and sequence for implementing instruction.

Table 9.1   SPI—SCIENCE CURRICULUM GUIDE 9–12

GOAL #3: DEVELOP AND APPLY RATIONAL, CREATIVE AND CRITICAL THINKING SKILLS.

OBJECTIVE: A. Acquire the ability to collect and process data.

LEARNER OUTCOME: 1. Skill development in gathering data
2. Skill development in organizing and describing data
3. Skill development in comparing and evaluating data

Instructional implications

Physics	Chemistry	Life	Earth/Space

---

1. a. Teacher will provide students with opportunities to decide what information is relevant and to recognize lack of needed information.
   b. Teacher will provide students with problems/situations that contain more information than is needed and lack of some needed information so that the student can discriminate observations from inferences, fact from opinion, etc.

Physics	Chemistry	Life	Earth/Space
Observe electroscope leaves and infer conditions causing changes.	Candle burning. What do you observe? What can you infer?	Observe animal tracks and infer what animal made them.	Observe apparent motions of stars from earth and infer possible models to fit observation.

   c. Teacher will provide students with opportunities to formulate their own questions and gather data to answer questions, designing and conducting their own experiments.

Physics	Chemistry	Life	Earth/Space
Identify and investigate factors believed to affect friction. How to measure friction? How to measure other factors?	Design and construct an Electro Motive Force (EMF) cell to produce a maximum potential difference and current for a specified minimum time.	Identify and investigate factors believed to affect a population of organisms.	Identify and investigate the factors affecting water holding capacity of soil or the speed of flowing water in a stream.

   d. Teacher will provide students opportunities to measure, observe and record, and use numerical scales to order observations and measurements.

Table 9.1 SPI—SCIENCE CURRICULUM GUIDE 9–12 *Continued*

Instructional implications			
Physics	Chemistry	Life	Earth/Space

2. Teacher will provide opportunities for students to:
   a. Serially order data,
   b. Translate data symbols into words, pictures, graphs, etc.,
   c. Hierarchically organize data,
   d. Analyze data for range, average, median, mode, variance, standard deviation, etc.,
   e. Determine products or ratios of relevant quantities,
   f. Describe properties of systems and subsystems,
   g. Describe changes in properties, and
   h. Describe relevant interactions.

Physics	Chemistry	Life	Earth/Space
Represent the motion of an object using data table, words, strobe pictures, graphs, and gestures with hand.	For objects made of one substance, determine the mass and volume of each, and determine the ratio of mass to volume for each.	Describe the sizes of members of the population and the numbers in various size ranges.	Design and apply a classification scheme for rocks. Design how to describe the distribution of area of a sea basin with depth.

3. Teachers will provide opportunities for students to:
   a. Determine whether the quantitative property was more, less, or the same
      (i) from one time to another, or
      (ii) for one part of the system compared with another,
   b. Compare averages of groups of data,
   c. Seek consistency among forms of descriptions of data, and
   d. Compare data and methods of describing data and demonstrate their rationale for explaining the results.

Physics	Chemistry	Life	Earth/Space
How does the work we get out of the pulley system compare with the work put into the system? Show how you decided.	Is the total energy of the system after the reaction the same as it was before the reaction? How do you know?	Are the sizes of the organism in one population significantly different from the size of that organism in another environment? How do you know?	How does annual rainfall in our state prior to eruption of a volcano compare with rainfall after? How did you define average rainfall?

Teacher will have students compare data by use of graphing techniques.

Physics	Chemistry	Life	Earth/Space
Are your graphs, tables, words, and pictures describing the motion consistent with each other? How can you tell?	Are your graphs, tables, words, and pictures of data consistent with Boyle's Law?	Are your graphs, tables, words, and pictures describing the population change?	Are your graphs, tables, words, and pictures describing the precipitation patterns consistent?

Source: Guidelines for science curriculum in Washington schools. (November 1988). Olympia, Wash.: Office of the Superintendent of Public Instruction, p. 65. Used with permission.

Curriculum Guides

Curriculum guides are another useful tool that educators consult in the planning process. A curriculum guide, sometimes referred to as a course syllabus, outlines in some detail the content that is to be covered in a particular subject at a specific grade level. Some states have developed state guides that provide such a content outline for each subject area, while other states require that local school districts develop their own curriculum guides, which are then approved by the state. Curriculum guides that have the most teacher input are often written at the district level and may include, in addition to the content outline, the objectives to be mastered for each subject at specific grade levels. Box 9-1 represents part of a curriculum guide developed locally by the Decatur County Community School Corporation to help teachers plan for instruction in eighth grade mathematics. The topics of problem solving and number sentences are featured in the guide.

As seen in the box, the curriculum guide is designed to provide a topic-by-topic outline of the subject matter and, although not required, student objectives for each concept are also included. In the example provided, the content outline is specific with regard to concepts and skills related to problem solving and number sentences. As Funkhouser, Beach, Ryan, and Fifer (1981) note,

> The organization of the curriculum in such a specific way is designed to answer the questions, "What educational experiences should a student have in a subject matter area during the school year?" and "What should the student learn each day in each subject?" (p. 56).

Although the secondary subject area of mathematics is used to answer those questions here, the same general process would apply to each of the other secondary curriculum areas.

Resource Guides or Units

Another tool used in curriculum planning that secondary teachers find helpful is the resource guide or unit. According to Beach and Reinhartz (1989), the resource guide or unit is a collection of materials, procedures, activities, and, on occasion, objectives that have been recommended for teachers to use to plan each unit and/or lesson. The resource guide is organized in such a way as to be of help to teachers by suggesting ideas, materials, and procedures for teaching various topics in the curriculum. For example, in presenting a unit on the short story using the prescribed content and objectives of the curriculum guide, the teacher would consult the resource guide to determine what student learning activities might be helpful, along with other materials and suggestions that could be used in teaching this particular concept in English.

Frequently, the resource guide or unit is a part of the teacher's edition of the textbook that has been adopted for use in a particular course. Within the teacher's edition, pages are devoted to suggested activities and materials. Although the degree of specificity varies, many, if not most, of the teacher's editions have very specific suggestions with notes to the teacher on how to plan the lesson. Figure 9.1 is an example of three pages from the teacher's edition of the *World History* textbook. This teacher's edition resource guide includes suggestions for books, audiovisual materials, a planning guide, objectives, suggested lesson strategies, a reteaching strategy, and an answer key. This information provides the teacher with what the publisher describes as a "well-orga-

Box 9-1 **Graphing and Relations**

1. Graph the solution sets of equations and inequalities involving integers.

2. Associate ordered pairs of integers with points in a coordinate plane.

3. Graph a set of ordered pairs on a coordinate plane.

4. Interpret the information shown on a graph.

5. Graph the solution set of an open sentence on the form $n + 7 = 12$, $n + 7 < 12$, etc.

6. Identify the kinds of graphs used in the real world.

7. Construct bar and picture graphs.

8. Interpret and construct line graphs.

9. Construct and interpret data on a circle graph.

10. Locate points on a number line including negative rational numbers.

11. Generate a set of ordered pairs from a given rule.

12. Determine a rule for a function given a specific pair of elements.

13. Identify and give examples of: axis, origin, quadrant, abscissa, ordinate, and coordinates.

14. Recognize the domain and range of a function as defined by a set of ordered pairs.

15. Use the function of (n).

16. Distinguish between relations which are functions and those that are not.

17. Graph solutions of compound sentences on a coordinate plane.

18. Graph irrational numbers on a number line.

19. Identify and classify sets according to their relationships to one another.

Source: *The mathematics program of the Decatur County Community School Corporation.* (August 1986). Greensburg, Ind.: Decatur County Community School Corporation, p. 33.

nized teacher support system." In addition, this edition has been written to meet state requirements and to provide an evaluation system for teachers.

As seen in the example, Addison-Wesley has provided valuable resource material by including a wealth of detailed information to aid the teacher in planning for instruction. Such assistance in curriculum development is helpful as teachers organize the content and objectives for classroom presentation. In

CHAPTER THREE

Ancient India and China

CHAPTER THREE-PLANNING GUIDE

Skills	Special Features	Worksheets	Review/Evaluation
Thinking Skills: Classifying **Thinking Skills Guided Practice:** Classifying **Texas Student Assessment Program:** Chapter 3	Chapter 3 Timeline Spotlight on Ideas and Developments: The Secret of Silk Making Almanac: Ancient China	**Previewing:** Ancient India and China **Reinforcement:** Locating Places on Maps **Reteaching:** Preparing Timelines **Enrichment:** Analyzing Primary Sources	Section Reviews Chapter 3 Survey Unit 1 Survey **Tests:** Chapter 3 Test; Unit 1 Test Testing Software **Additional Resources** **Transparencies and Activity Book:** 3.1 China and Southeast Asia; 3.2 The Monsoon Lands of Asia **Echoes of the Past** **Essential Ideas** **Tools of Time and Place**

Chapter Themes

Cultural Diffusion

• The Chou conquerors of the Shang Dynasty in China adopted from the Shang artistic techniques, ideas about family and

religion, and a system of writing, passing these achievements down to future generations.

Diversity

• Between 1000 B.C. and 800 B.C., Aryan tribes began moving eastward and south-

Figure 9.1 Teachers' Edition from the *World history* textbook by Addison-Wesley. (Source: Stearns, P.N., Schwartz, D. R., & Beyer, B. K. (1990) *World history: Traditions and new directions.* Teacher's edition. Menlo Park, Calif.: Addison-Wesley, pp. T37–T39. Used with permission.)

ward from the Indus River valley, establishing their customs and their Sanskrit language. In the process, they conquered or displaced the Dravidians, who held onto their own language, customs, and beliefs.

■ LESSON PLANS

SECTION 3–1 (PAGES 47–51)

RISE OF CIVILIZATION IN INDIA

Objectives

After this lesson, students should be able to
— describe the influence of geography and climate on the development of civilizations in India.
— identify the achievements of the Indus Valley civilization.
— analyze reasons for the decline of the Indus Valley civilization.

Vocabulary

subcontinent (47), monsoon (48)

Lesson Strategy

The Development of Civilization in the Indus Valley

(Analysis: Identifying Relationships)

1. Display a physical map of India on an overhead projector. Point out that the first civilization in India, like civilizations of the Middle East, arose in a fertile river valley. Unlike settlements that developed along the Tigris, Euphrates, and Nile rivers, however, the communities that developed in India were somewhat more isolated, less vulnerable to conquest, and had fewer cultural contacts. Among the keys to the study of Indus Valley civilization are India's location as a subcontinent, its physical geography, and its climate.

2. Ask students to study the map and identify the boundaries of the Indian peninsula. (On the north, India is separated from the rest of the Eurasian continent by high mountains, and on the west and east, by water.) Ask students to name the mountain ranges and bodies of water. (Himalaya Mountains and Hindu Kush; Arabian Sea and Bay of Bengal.)

3. Use the map to have students identify significant physical features that may have influenced the development and caused the isolation of Indian civilization. (the northern desert; the Indus and Ganges rivers, and the valleys, deltas, and plains they irrigate; the mountains that separate the Deccan plateau from northern India.) Ask students to cite the advantages and disadvantages of India's landforms. (Advantages include fertile river valleys and plains; water supply from rivers for drinking and irrigating; protection from invaders provided by mountains; trade route to Persian Gulf provided by Indus River. Disadvantages include relative isolation from rest of world due to mountains; disastrous floods from rivers.)

4. Ask students to describe India's climate. (mild to hot temperatures, except in the mountains; either dry or rainy seasons, with monsoons carrying moisture or dangerous, hot, dry winds) Then ask students to cite the advantages and disadvantages of the climate. (Advantages include mild temperature suitable for farming and herding, moisture from southern monsoons. Disadvantages include scorching

Figure 9.1 *Continued*

continued

heat at times, and famine-producing droughts from northern monsoons.)

5. Have students infer what type of society would develop in the river valleys. (agricultural settlements in the river valleys; the rise of urban trade centers with strong governments to plan and organize) Then have the class skim the text to cite significant achievements of the Indus Valley people such as cultivation of cotton, well-planned cities, pictograph writing, strong central government, uniform system of weights and measures, and so on.)

6. Return to the large map of India. Ask the class to speculate how physical geography might have contributed to the destruction of the Indus Valley civilization. (famine or flood, invasion through the mountain passes, volcanic activity in the mountains.)

shape of the Indian subcontinent. Tell students that the diamond is a simple way to remember India's geographic features. Ask students to copy the outline on a piece of paper and to label these places: the northern desert, the Himalayas, the Hindu Kush, the Vindhya Mountains, the Ganges and Indus rivers, the Deccan Plateau, the Eastern and Western Ghats, and the bodies of water that surround India. (Students may refer to the map on text page 48.) To provide a check, have volunteers label the outline map on the chalkboard. Ask students to explain how India's geographical features affected life and settlement on the subcontinent. (Some possible answers include: fertile land and tropical climate led to the growth of agriculture in the river valleys; proximity to the sea led to the rise of seaports and encouraged trade, and so on.)

Reteaching Strategy

Geographic Features of India
(Analysis: Identifying Cause-Effect Relationships)
Draw on the chalkboard the outline of an elongated diamond, roughly following the

Enrichment

For enrichment strategies, see the Planning Guide on page T37 and the annotation on text page 51.

Figure 9.1 *Continued*

addition to the teacher's edition to the textbook, some school districts compile resource guides for teachers. These guides contain suggestions for teaching specific units for each of the content areas. Teachers are asked to submit activities that have worked in the past, and then these ideas are cataloged and bound in a resource guide.

By incorporating suggestions from resource guides into their curriculum planning and teaching repertoire, teachers can establish a systematic approach to curriculum building at the district, campus, and classroom levels. Teachers who utilize the various planning aids presented in this chapter promote a systematic approach to curriculum development. Table 9.2 summarizes the variety of resources from which secondary teachers can select as they complete

Table 9.2   ADDITIONAL RESOURCES FOR PLANNING

Printed Materials	Visual Aids	Learning Opportunities Beyond the Classroom
Books	Transparencies	Field trips
Brochures	Slides	Concerts
Newspapers	Videos, films, filmstrips	Theatrical presentations
Original letters	Television	
Graphs	Pictures	
Banners/posters	Drawings	
Maps	Audiotapes	
Scrolls	Computer programs	
Reports		
Riddles		
Timelines		
Puzzles		
Mazes		

the lesson planning process. The table identifies additional sources for curriculum planning and development and includes three areas: printed materials, visual aids, and experiences beyond the classroom. This is not an exhaustive list, but it does suggest some of the resources that teachers can consult and use to supplement the curriculum planning and development process.

LEVELS OF INSTRUCTIONAL PLANNING

After consulting the scope and sequence charts, the curriculum guides, and the resource guides or units, the next step is writing more detailed plans. The resources are like reference materials that are to be consulted before the actual writing process begins. As Cotton, Sparks-Langer, Tripp-Apple, and Simmons (1989) note, effective teaching practices rest on sound, thorough planning and

> The process of planning is similar to flow charting a computer program. The person [teacher] not only determines what will be taught, but also identifies where decisions will need to be made, what the decisions are, and what they will need to do for each (pp. 47–48).

Classroom teachers can be compared to computer programmers in the sense that just as producing a blueprint or flow chart is essential for the computer program, planning is a prerequisite for effective instruction. To adequately plan the curriculum, overall mission, knowledge of general goals and objectives, student needs, and instructional resources are essential (Ornstein, 1990). Teachers plan the curriculum on several levels. These levels of planning include yearly or semester scope and sequence charts for each subject and grade, unit planning for each reporting or grading period, and lastly, detailed daily lesson plans (Ornstein, 1990).

Year or Semester Scope and Sequence Plans

These large time-frame outlines play a central role in curriculum planning and development. In addition, they provide secondary educators with the content, concepts, skills, and values that are essential.

When attempting to develop the "big picture" of the content for a specific group of students and content area, there are several strategies which may prove helpful. One strategy is to use the textbook, in which the major headings and chapter arrangements can help to focus on the major concepts of the subject area. Another strategy to use in selecting content is to make comparisons—similarities and differences—relationships, and/or classifications. Using the topic of measurement, for example, comparisons can be made within the metric system for length. Comparing the meaning of the prefixes *kilo, deka, deci, centi, milli,* and so on can be helpful in understanding the base ten concept inherent in the metric system of measurement. When studying the civil War, for example, comparisons between the North and the South can be made by considering (1) the number of states, (2) population, (3) losses, (4) industries supporting the war effort, (5) goals or objectives, and (6) purpose(s) for fighting the war.

Another strategy to use to see the big picture when developing the yearly plan is to identify key concepts. The term *concept* is defined as the major ideas of the subject area or, more specifically, as any general idea for which we may continually develop descriptions, provide definitions, and identify examples and nonexamples. A concept may therefore include principles, formulas, interpretations, and relationships. For example, one way that historians may view events or occurrences is by using a relativistic interpretation. Such an interpretation views chance as a principal factor in historical developments. For example, if John F. Kennedy had not been assassinated, Lyndon Johnson would not have become president, and arguably the United States might not have become so deeply involved in Vietnam. Hence, the chance assassination of Kennedy sharply changed global history.

The basic skills that are inherent in the subject area provide a third strategy to employ when developing a yearly content outline. Basic skills of a content area or discipline are subject-specific and are essential to success when studying the subject. In science, for example, the process skills, such as observing, measuring, inferring, experimenting, hypothesizing, and defining operationally, are key to understanding biology, general science, earth science, physical science, chemistry, or physics.

The last strategy to use in developing the yearly plan involves the consideration of values inherent in a particular content area. Again, using history as an example, freedom of action, human individuality, and humanism help to explain how a relativist views history. For the relativist, personal values and beliefs tend to influence the interpretation of history. As students study history, they can become aware of the values inherent in each discipline they are studying. Using these strategies, there is continuity in purpose and a greater appreciation of what is being studied.

In the multitiered planning process, there are basic components that must be considered. Table 9.3 is a planning chart that illustrates the essential components involved throughout the process. From Table 9.3, it is evident that there is a greater degree of specificity as the planning process moves from the yearly outline to the classroom level. Therefore, more components are included in the daily lesson plan than in the yearly plan. The level of specificity for describing basic skills, for example, is greater for the unit and daily plans than it is for the yearly or semester plan. The planning chart graphically shows that the lesson plan for each day is the foundation of the planning process upon which effective instruction is built.

Figure 9.2 represents various stages of the planning process, which first begins with the big picture of the year, then moves to reporting periods of two semesters, then moves to reporting periods of three 6-week intervals within each semester, next to the various units that comprise the course of study for each six weeks, and finally to the daily lesson plan. The significance of Figure 9.2 is that planning can be viewed as a spiral which is somewhat general and inclusive at the yearly plan level, but continues to narrow and become more focused, detailed, and specific as the planning gets closer to the students and the subjects that they are taught daily.

Unit Planning

Once the yearly or semester plan, which includes concepts, skills, and values, has been established and sequenced, the unit plans are developed. Unit plans are developed around a concept, topic, or theme and extend over several class periods, normally one to three weeks. To better organize the content, concepts, and skills in blocks of time according to reporting periods (normally six weeks in length), teachers review the yearly scope and sequence and then develop unit plans accordingly.

Although not as complete as lesson plans, the unit plan is the first step in the curriculum development process which are directly related to the daily

Table 9.3 ESSENTIAL COMPONENTS FOR LESSON PLANNING

Plans (levels)	Concepts	Basic skills	Values	Goals	Activities	Resources/ materials	Objectives (3 domains)	Student behaviors	Teacher behaviors	Evaluation
Yearly	X	X	X	X						
Unit	X	X	X	X	X	X	X			
Daily	X	X	X	X	X	X	X	X	X	X

Generated from Task Analysis Process

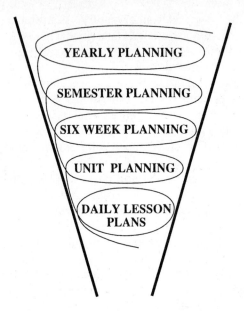

Figure 9.2 Curriculum planning spiral

plans. In some districts, as a part of curriculum development, unit plans are developed through a centralized, district-wide process. In most schools however, the unit plan is prepared by a single teacher or groups of teachers at the building level. The unit plan, although not complete with details, is the first curriculum document that could be used for classroom instruction. In using the unit plan as the basis for instructional planning, it is important to identify the essential components. Unit plans have five main components, including: (1) goals and objectives; (2) content, concepts, and/or skills; (3) procedures or activities; (4) materials and/or resources; and (5) evaluation procedures.

The instructional objectives are stated in ways which describe the expected learner behaviors. The first step in the unit planning process is to focus on the student behaviors, and the verbs that are used provide some direction for planning the rest of the lesson. At this point, the teacher examines the scope and sequence that the lesson is based on as identified in the yearly (or semester) plan. The scope expands as the teacher develops the unit and begins by adding details to flesh out the skeletal framework provided by the scope and sequence chart. In secondary schools, the content normally provides the theme for the unit, and the skills and values help embellish the information and give it meaning.

In developing units, the content or concepts to be taught are important as they relate to the instructional objectives. Consideration of cognitive, psychomotor, and affective skills also become part of process. Skills may be subject-specific, but they can also be general academic skills that should and can be incorporated in any of the secondary subjects, including skills such as critical thinking, reading, writing, speaking, listening, and problem solving.

In addition to content and skills, there are learning activities or procedures which are the outgrowth of the objectives, the content, concepts, and skills as well as the needs and interests of the students. These activities or procedures may range from taking notes and reading assigned material to hands-on, laboratory-oriented experiences, games, field trips, studio productions, art projects, and/or musical recitals.

Also identified in the unit plans are the materials and resources that will be needed to teach the unit. These materials are those in addition to the text and would include items such as supplemental readings, films, videotapes, audiotapes, filmstrips, computer programs, or field trips (see Table 9.2).

The last component of the unit plan, evaluation, incorporates both formative and summative procedures. These procedures should clearly be mapped out and the criteria established for grading and assessing quizzes, exams, projects, laboratory experiments, individual and group work, and so on. Figure 9.3 is an example of a unit plan on Heredity which has been fleshed out and has many specifics for daily use.

Each of the major components of the unit plan are represented in Figure 9.3: objectives, content, or concepts, and skills, activities, resources and materials, and evaluation procedures. The unit plan, as described here, prepares the curriculum for the classroom. The year's curriculum is broken into manageable units to be used by the teachers as they prepare their daily lesson plans.

Daily Lesson Plans

Daily lesson planning brings the curriculum to the classroom level, where the students are the direct recipients of the teaching-learning process. The daily lesson plan is a plan of instruction for a single class period for a given group of students and is fashioned from the unit plan. For example, a biology teacher would develop a lesson plan for fifth period biology for Monday. As previously identified in Table 9.3, the task analysis phase helps provide the needed details, examples, and resources/materials that will be used to supplement the textbook in this planning process. According to Funkhouser, Beach, Ryan, and Fifer (1981), the daily lesson plan is "the precise script for what is to occur in the classroom . . . [and the] ability to state exactly what should occur in the classroom will lead to consistency . . . and aid any teacher in conducting the lesson" (p. 59).

As Manatt (1981) and others (Arends, 1988; McCutcheon, 1980) have noted, detailed classroom planning is the key to effective teaching. The level of specificity and the degree of detail advocated here are more than is normally required in school districts. Ultimately, it is the teacher's own preference and priorities that determine the amount of planning that is done. It should be noted, however, that once the detailed lessons have been developed for a unit, they can be modified for future classes, which reduces the amount of work in future planning.

Curriculum development at this level requires a fairly large investment of

Number of

Subject ___Biology___ Grades 9–10 _____ Period(s) ____9____

Unit Title ___Heredity_____

General Objective(s):

Student will be able to describe the mechanisms involved in the transmission of hereditary informa-tion. The student will be able to discuss the principle of dominance and will be able to distinguish between genotype and phenotype. The student will be able to predict possible genetic makeup of offspring based on the completion of a Punnett Square. Students will be able to discuss the nature of human heredity by identifying inherited characteristics and genetic disorders. The student will have a better understanding of the genetic technologies involved in medicine.

Day: Specific Objectives	Activities
Day 1 a. Students will be able to describe the experiments of Mendel. b. Students will be able to define the terms *dominant, recessive, homozygous, heterozygous, purebred,* and *hybrid.*	Begin unit by showing filmstrip "Understanding Mendel's Crosses." Distribute handout of terms and questions for discussion after filmstrip. Describe Mendel's experiments and lead discussion using handout and overhead transparency of handout as a guide. Have students read sections 10.7–10.11 in textbook and at least one newspaper and a magazine article dealing with the topic of genetics.
Day 2 a. Students will be able to define *genotype, phenotype,* and *allele.* b. When given genetic combinations, students will identify possible genotypes and phenotypes. c. Students will be able to predict possible genetic compositions based on the completion of a Punnett Square.	Have students summarize their reading and the previous day's lesson in one paragraph. Discuss student questions from handout and homework assignment. Have a veterinarian make a short presentation and be available for questions. Using overhead transparencies, introduce the use of Punnett Squares to predict possible genetic combinations based on genetic crosses and dominant and recessive genes. Show possible genotypic and phenotypic ratios for monohybrid and dihybrid crosses. Work sample crosses on overhead and have students supply answers. Have students work Punnett Square problems (handout) and read sections 13.1, 13.4, and 13.9–13.11 in textbook.

Figure 9.3 Unit plan form (*Modified from:* Quina, J. (1989). *Effective secondary teaching.* New York: Harper & Row, pp. 104–109.)

Day: Specific Objectives	Activities
Day 3 a. Students will be able to demonstrate and explain monohybrid and dihybrid crosses using a Punnett Square.	Review homework assignment by having students work Punnett Square problems on the blackboard when called on. Students will explain in their own words what the crosses represent. Give students 3 problems to work in class and turn in.
Day 4 a. Students will be able to identify several human genetic traits based on physical characteristics. b. Students will be able to calculate the percentages of each trait and establish ratios.	Begin study of human genetics by having students do the Laboratory Investigation 13: Human Inheritance. Announce group activity for Monday and divide class into groups of 4 and distribute articles to each group to be read for homework.
Day 5 a. Students will be able to describe several (at least 3) inherited characteristics. b. Students will be able to identify possible genetic disorders.	Collect lab reports. Lead follow-up discussion on the laboratory investigation. Lecture on human genetic disorders and detection techniques. During lecture show slides of examples of genetic disorders. Allow 15–20 minutes for small group discussions in preparation for Monday's presentations.
Day 6 a. Students working in groups will be able to describe in vitro fertilization versus in utero fertilization. b. Students will be able to discuss the impact of alcohol, tobacco, and drugs on prenatal development. c. Students will be able to discuss the need for prenatal care.	After working in their groups, one student will present the group report to the class based on the articles distributed, which discuss in vitro and in utero fertilization; effects of alcohol, tobacco, and drugs on prenatal development; and the need for prenatal care. Each student will provide a 1-page summary of their group's report.
Day 7 a. Students will be able to discuss the importance of genetic counseling when problems might arise.	Show videotape special "In Search of the Perfect Baby." Lead discussion of major points in the tape and have students write a summary statement about videotape.

Figure 9.3 *Continued*

continued

Day: Specific Objectives	Activities
Day 8 a. Students will be able to explain the principles of segregation, independent assortment, and blending in genetic characteristics.	Lecture on principles of segregation, independent assortment, and blending. During the last 15 minutes of the class, provide writing prompts to the students to get them to think about the effects of substances on prenatal development, etc.
Day 9 None	Give major unit test on patterns of heredity.

Vocabulary: Dominant and recessive trait, homozygous, heterozygous, segregation, independent assortment, allele, genotype, phenotype, monohybrid, dihybrid, Punnett Square, blending, in vitro and in utero fertilization.
Resources/Materials: Text: Biology (Harcourt Brace Jovanovich), chalkboard, chalk, pens, pencils, paper, overhead projector, transparencies, handouts, filmstrip, videotape, writing prompts, VCR player, guest speaker.
Evaluation: Students receive daily grades for terms and questions and Punnett Square problems, a laboratory grade, a group grade, and a major unit test grade.

Figure 9.3 *Continued*

time initially, yet it will yield large dividends when future preparation and planning is reduced. As Funkhouser, Beach, Ryan, and Fifer (1981) suggest, "The best recommendation is to plan in the greatest amount of detail possible, until planning becomes aversive, then stop" (p. 60). We believe that all secondary teachers, especially beginning teachers, need to plan detailed lessons to build the confidence needed in the classroom and to deliver the content as they interact successfully with the students.

Daily lesson planning brings specificity to the teaching-learning scope and sequence. When teachers make decisions about what content, concepts, or skills to teach based on the specific instructional objectives, as well as the activities and procedures and evaluation measures, it requires their best judgment. Often, teachers need to be flexible to self-correct the pace and the difficulty level of the lesson if it becomes necessary. In planning for instruction at the classroom level, to avoid major adjustments in the lesson it is helpful to conduct a task analysis as a part of the lesson planning process and prior to teaching the lesson.

TASK ANALYSIS PROCESS

Task analysis is a planning tool that is helpful in adding the necessary details and elaborating on the concepts or contents in order to make the unit plans meaningful. Task analysis or task detailing includes several steps. Figure 9.4 depicts the task analysis process (TAP). TAP includes five major steps with several substeps to follow.

Student Assessment

The first step in the task analysis process is to assess student knowledge, abilities, and/or attitudes. This assessment can be done in a variety of ways and does not have to be complicated or lengthy. One way is to refer to the unit objectives to see if they are appropriate for the students in a particular class. If they are not, the objectives should be modified to accommodate secondary students in the class. Second, it is helpful to consider the prerequisite knowledge that is required for a specific lesson or the experience and/or skills the students should have to be successful. For more information about meeting students' interests and learning needs at the appropriate physiological, psychological, and cognitive levels, consult Chapters 5 and 6.

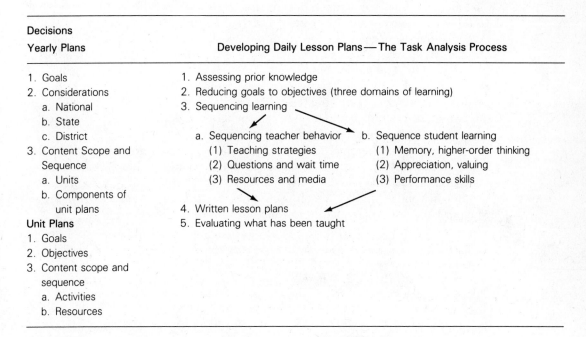

Decisions

Yearly Plans	Developing Daily Lesson Plans — The Task Analysis Process
1. Goals	1. Assessing prior knowledge
2. Considerations	2. Reducing goals to objectives (three domains of learning)
a. National	3. Sequencing learning
b. State	
c. District	a. Sequencing teacher behavior b. Sequence student learning
3. Content Scope and	(1) Teaching strategies (1) Memory, higher-order thinking
Sequence	(2) Questions and wait time (2) Appreciation, valuing
a. Units	(3) Resources and media (3) Performance skills
b. Components of	
unit plans	4. Written lesson plans
Unit Plans	5. Evaluating what has been taught
1. Goals	
2. Objectives	
3. Content scope and	
sequence	
a. Activities	
b. Resources	

Figure 9.4 Task analysis process (TAP) for planning daily lesson plans

Reducing Goals to Objectives

The second major step in **TAP** is reducing goals to instructional objectives as depicted in Figure 9.4. Writing and selecting instructional objectives, as discussed in Chapter 8, is the final step in the Tyler model of curriculum development. Specific objectives, often referred to as instructional or behavioral objectives, provide direction for planning and teaching, and often clarify the general goals of education. The general goals are translated into specific learning outcomes, which provide the central focus of daily lesson planning. Along with instructional objectives, strategies and activities are selected as well as assessment or evaluation procedures. It is during the lesson planning stage that all teachers are involved directly in curriculum development as they write and evaluate the instructional objectives related to their unit of instruction. By using the goals and instructional objectives listed in the unit plan, teachers conduct the goal reduction procedure at the daily lesson plan level.

Reducing goals to meaningful instructional objectives is complex and requires knowledge of the subject matter as well as knowledge of the learners. Box 9-2 is an example of the goal reduction process using the general goals established as the *Seven Cardinal Principles of Education* (1918). The goal as identified by the principles related to good health habits is reduced to an instructional objective in the illustration that follows.

Instructional Objectives

The first decision that is made in reducing goals to instructional objectives has to do with exactly what the student is expected to learn each day of the unit. The key question each teacher attempts to answer is, "What do I want the students to know or be able to do following instruction?" (Beach and Reinhartz, 1989, p. 110). The response to this question is made a little easier because of the scope and sequence charts that have been established earlier. It is the responsibility of the classroom teacher to write instructional objectives in such a way that the specific behaviors students will be expected to exhibit or demonstrate will be clearly articulated.

According to Mager (1962), instructional objectives are designed to describe observable or measurable student behaviors and should be clearly articulated and explicated. The objectives become the instructional road map for the teacher in conducting the lesson. To emphasize the importance of objectives, Mager (1962) provides a fable to illustrate the point.

> Once upon a time a Sea Horse gathered up his seven pieces of eight and cantered out to find his fortune. Before he traveled very far he met an Eel who said,
> "Psst. Hey bud. Where 'ya going?"
> "I'm going out to find my fortune," replied the Sea Horse proudly.
> "You're in luck," said the Eel. "For four pieces of eight you can have this speedy flipper, and then you'll be able to get out of here a lot faster."
> "Gee, that's swell," said the Sea Horse, and paid the money and put on the flipper and slithered off at twice the speed. Soon he came upon a Sponge, who said,

Box 9-2 Reducing Goals to Instructional Objectives

1. *Health* Good health habits need to be taught and encouraged by the school. The community and school should cooperate in fulfilling the health needs of all youngsters and adults.

2. *Command of Fundamental Processes* The secondary school should accept responsibility for continuing to teach and polish the basic tools of learning, such as arithmetical computation, reading, and writing, that were begun in the elementary school.

3. *Worthy Home Membership* Students' understanding of the interrelationships of the family, in order for the give-and-take to be a healthy, happy affair, should be advocated by the school. Proper adjustment as a family member will lead to proper acceptance of responsibility as a family leader in later life.

4. *Vocation* The secondary school should foster an attitude in students that will lead to an appreciation for all vocations. The basic skills of a variety of vocations should be made available to students who have the need and/or desire for them.

5. *Citizenship* A basic commitment to proper citizenship on the part of students needs to be fostered and strengthened during the adolescent years. The secondary school needs to assume this responsibility not only in the social sciences, where one would ordinarily assume it would be handled, but in all subjects.

6. *Proper Use of Leisure Time* The student should be provided opportunities while in secondary school to expand the available possibilities for leisure time. The commission felt that leisure time properly used would enrich the total personality.

7. *Ethical Character* The secondary school should organize its activities and personal relationships to reflect good ethical character, both to serve as an exemplar and to involve the student in a series of activities that will provide opportunities to make ethically correct decisions.

Example of reducing goals for good health habits:

1. *State the Goal* Cardinal principle: Health. Health education should develop in the individual those qualities whereby he/she will be able to exhibit good health habits in order to lead a productive life.

2. *State the Subject Responsible* Various health education organizations claim that skill in the use of rational decision making as a means of approaching the solution of personal health problems is a responsibility of health classes.

3. *State the Course Responsible* One of the objectives of Health I is to enable students to recognize good health habits and apply accurate information relative to communicable diseases.

4. *State the Instructional Objective* When given a dialogue between two students concerning the transmission and treatment of AIDS, the student will underline the statements which are factual and circle those which are generalizations not supported by medical research.

"Psst. Hey, bud. Where 'ya going?"

"I'm going out to find my fortune," replied the Sea Horse.

"You're in luck," said the Sponge. "For a small fee I will let you have this jet-propelled scooter so that you will be able to travel a lot faster."

So the Sea Horse bought the scooter with his remaining money and went zooming through the sea five times as fast. Soon he came upon a Shark, who said,

"Psst. Hey, bud. Where 'ya going?"

"I'm going out to find my fortune," replied the Sea Horse.

"You're in luck. If you'll take this short cut," said the Shark, pointing to his open mouth, "you'll save yourself a lot of time."

"Gee, thanks," said the Sea Horse, and zoomed off into the interior of the Shark, there to be devoured.

The moral of this fable is that if you're not sure where you are going, you're liable to end up someplace else—and not even know it (p. 3).

As illustrated in the fable, Mager (1962) saw objectives as critical in helping educators not only map out where they are going, but also in knowing when they have arrived. He says, "if you are teaching things that cannot be evaluated, you are in the awkward position of being unable to demonstrate that you are teaching anything at all . . ." (p. 73). Thus, according to this perspective, instructional objectives form the building blocks not only for instruction but evaluation as well.

Instructional objectives include the condition under which the measurable behavior will take place. The condition sets the stage for the student to perform the task. A third criterion of an instructional objective is the minimal level or degree of performance. This third criterion establishes the basis for evaluating the acceptable level of student performance. For example, an objective might say: after examining three different animal habitats, the student will be able to name and describe an animal that lives there and describe how the habitats differ from each other. When this activity is taking place, the teacher will be able to evaluate the students on their ability to match animals with each habitat correctly, but also evaluate their responses on how the habitats differ.

Using Mager's technique of writing instructional objectives, which includes the condition along with the acceptable level of performance, the teacher has a precise picture of what students are expected to accomplish and what the teacher needs to do to successfully execute the objective. Bluestein (1989) suggests that teachers use a planning sheet for each objective. The planning sheet would include space for:

1. Instructional objective (in one of the three domains of learning)
   a) Condition
   b) Precise verb
   c) Level of performance
2. Type of presentation
3. Materials needed

These three categories from the planning sheet provide enough detail for the teacher to successfully teach the objective.

Domains of Learning

Once the instructional objectives have been written, they are classified according to specific levels and domains of learning. The domains of learning include cognitive, affective, and psychomotor. The classification system or taxonomy for each domain helps to categorize and evaluate the instructional objectives.

The cognitive domain includes those objectives which involve intellectual skills. These skills range from knowing content to making decisions by judging information and providing reasons for making specific choices. According to Bloom et al. (1956), cognitive objectives can be assessed by moving from simple intellectual behaviors to more complex behaviors. The levels of the cognitive domain and the characteristics of each are:

1. *Knowledge:* recalling information (factual) that has been previously learned (naming the five major causes of World War II)
2. *Comprehension:* interpreting or translating information from one form to another without fully understanding all aspects or implications (interpreting the wedges of a pie chart)
3. *Application:* using rules, laws, principles, or theories (information and abstractions) in new or different situations (using the associative property in math to solve a problem)
4. *Analysis:* taking apart or breaking down information or material into smaller components or parts to observe relationships or structure (explaining each part of the Declaration of Independence)
5. *Synthesis:* combining elements or components to create something new (creating an original piece of art)
6. *Evaluation:* making judgments or decisions about information or materials using criteria from someone else or developing personal criteria (when given three options, deciding which would be the best possible ending to a short story)

Table 9.4 provides additional information relative to each of the levels of the cognitive domain, including definitions, student and teacher behaviors, and verbs that can be used for the specific level of behavior.

The second domain of learning is the affective domain. It emphasizes the values, feelings, and attitudes of students within a curriculum area. The affective behaviors range from paying attention to personal behavior consistent within a value system. According to Krathwohl et al. (1964), the affective domain has five levels, which include:

1. *Receiving:* being sensitive to external stimuli and paying attention
2. *Responding:* reacting or responding to the stimuli or being involved as a result of the stimuli
3. *Valuing:* appreciating or valuing someone or something, an event or behavior
4. *Organizing:* internalizing values and developing a set of values (value system) that helps guide and shape behavior
5. *Characterization by value complex:* constantly behaving in ways that are consistent with a value system

Table 9.4   MAJOR CATEGORIES IN THE COGNITIVE DOMAIN

Level of taxonomy	Definition of term	Student behaviors	Teacher behaviors	Behavioral verbs
Knowledge	Recalls specific facts and other information	Remembers Recalls information	Lectures Shows Directs Tells	List, state, name, define, label, match, select
Comprehension	Understands the meaning of information and communicates it	Describes Explains Demonstrates	Questions Explains similarities and differences	Paraphrase, summarize, describe, give examples, compare, interpret
Application	Uses information, rules, concepts, data	Uses information to solve problems, dilemmas, situations; demonstrates can use information	Critiques Facilitates	Apply, illustrate, solve, practice, classify, compute, manipulate
Analysis	Breaks down, takes something apart into its basic components	Analyzes situations Uncovers Dissects	Challenges Guides Serves as a resource	Analyze, distinguish, compare, contrast, group, differentiate
Synthesis	Creates something new; puts together ideas in a new way or plan	Generalizes Conceptualizes	Reflects Enriches	Invent, compose, rewrite, create, design, diagram, propose, combine, revise
Evaluation	Judge the value of situations, ideas, art based on standards	Expresses opinion	Agrees Disagrees Asks for support/criteria	Judge, decide, debate, appraise, criticize, justify, assess, support

The last domain of learning is the psychomotor domain. This domain stresses neuromuscular coordination or motor skill learning. Bloom, Krathwohl, and their associates developed three levels for this domain, but never published a hierarchy. Harrow (1972) revised the earlier work and established six levels, which include:

1. *Reflex movements:* exhibiting involuntary movements, such as flinching, that are present at birth and continue until neuromuscular maturation

2. *Fundamental movements:* basic movement patterns, such as crawling or twisting, that develop and form the basis for specialized, complex movements

3. *Perceptual abilities:* integrating the physical skills with mental abilities,

such as hitting a ball with a bat; the brain receives a sensory stimulus and makes a physical response

4. *Physical abilities:* developing a sound, efficient body with behaviors, such as strengths, endurance, and agility, that form the building blocks for skilled movements
5. *Skilled movements:* developing complex movements, such as dance steps or gymnastic exercises, that require learning through practice
6. *Nondiscursive communication:* communicating using behaviors that incorporate previously learned behaviors, from facial expressions to dance choreographies

These domains of learning and the levels within each give teachers a framework for examining instructional objectives for each lesson. For Smith (1975), each topic should have objectives in each of the three domains, and these objectives should be written at different levels of each domain. Educators are encouraged to incorporate within the curriculum development process, multiple levels of the domains.

Sequencing Teaching-Learning Activities

The third step in the task analysis process is sequencing learning into manageable steps. This is a two-pronged process: one is sequencing the learning for the students and the second is sequencing the teacher's instructional behaviors. The first prong, sequencing student behaviors, has been discussed to a large degree under instructional objectives and learning domains. Once the condition and acceptable level of performance have been decided, the student behaviors are determined and then these behaviors have to be prioritized and put in some order to be performed. Reducing goals to objectives is the key to identifying and sequencing these behaviors.

The second prong deals with teacher instructional behavior, such as identifying and determining specific activities, games, printed and nonprinted media/resources to use each day. In the task analysis process, precise instructional strategies are identified and written down in great detail. If direct instruction is selected as a teaching strategy, for example, then the lecture/presentation has to be outlined with key questions, motivational techniques, relevant examples, explanations, facts, definitions, and so forth to be presented during the "teach" part of the lesson. If, on the other hand, an inquiry lesson is planned, the teacher writes different types of questions, the tasks to be accomplished, the directions, the materials, and so on. There is no single best instructional strategy to use during the course of a lesson, but variety seems essential to maintain interest and involvement (Joyce and Weil, 1986). Reinhartz and Beach (1983) have identified a continuum of teaching strategies from which teachers can select that range from pure telling to pure discovery.

For example, if the teacher is teaching the first year of a foreign language (Russian) and selects cooperative learning as the teaching strategy to use, students might do the following. Students in their groups would be asked to write simple plays to be presented at the "Grand Festival of Russian Drama" at the end of the first semester. Students would be expected to work in teams and write a play using correct word usage and authenticity of the time period, as well as the correct punctuation, accent, and expression. The plays would then be presented to the rest of the class(es) or students in school (Reinhartz and Reinhartz, 1988).

In addition to selecting teaching strategies, the questions to be asked should be written down to help prompt students to think about the concepts, themes, and skills that are being presented. The types of questions planned can serve as one way to assess student understanding of the topic. Also, consideration should be given to the amount of "wait time" that is used. Any less than 3–5 seconds tends to discourage students from thinking about and analyzing the situation, event, and/or dilemma.

Written Lesson Plans

The fourth step in the task analysis process is to put in writing all of the previous steps. This product is called the written lesson plan. Experienced teachers may find completing a matrix easier when planning daily lessons. Figure 9.5 is a form that can be used to write a lesson plan. There is room to describe concepts, objectives, teaching-learning activities, questions, resources needed, and evaluation to accurately assess student performance as the lesson progresses.

Beginning teachers may need to have lesson plans that are written out and followed to ensure that nothing is omitted. Also, by detailing all the steps in the task analysis process (TAP), teachers have the opportunity to rehearse on a piece of paper what they will be expected to do during the lesson (Eisner, 1983).

Writing out the lesson in a form with which a teacher is comfortable is the key. There is no best format, but the format that is selected must be well organized and easy to follow to be helpful. There should be a starting point for the lesson, and then a sequential listing of the teaching-learning events in the lesson. Grouping the materials and resources where and when they are needed during the lesson is also helpful.

When the lesson plans are ready, a brief outline with key points can be prepared to guide the teacher as well as the students in what will take place during the class period. The Daily Lesson Plan Form featured in Figure 9.6 may prove helpful. The form identifies the important information from the outline. The main headings guide the teacher when preparing to teach. The material for this form can be found in the detailed plans that were previously prepared.

Assessment of Teaching and Learning

The final step in the task analysis process (TAP) is to assess what has been taught and what the students have learned. The evaluation procedures should be cited or referred to in the instructional objectives. The assessment can be

Day	Content/concepts	Instructional objectives	Teaching strategies	Learning activities	Questions	Resources	Evaluation	Special notes

Figure 9.5 Lesson planning matrix

Teacher's Name _____   Date _____

Subject _____   Period(s) _____

Unit Title _____   Lesson No. _____

Instructional objectives

Content (concepts, facts, vocabulary)

Teacher activities

Student activities

Materials/resources

Figure 9.6 Daily lesson plan form

Preassessment to determine what students already know

Motivation

Class assignment   Homework assignment

Evaluation (questions, test items, performance)

Figure 9.6 *Continued*

based on student performance when doing group work and laboratory activities, completing hands-on projects, writing research papers, and/or taking tests and quizzes.

Teachers, as part of the assessment phase, would have the students

. . . summarize the main points of the lesson by writing a single paragraph . . . play a game in which students, either individually or in teams, are asked to identify key materials from the lesson, or . . . call on students randomly and ask questions related to the lesson of the day (Beach and Reinhartz, 1989, pp. 113–114).

An important part of the planning process is to have a product, the lesson plans, which can be followed as a guide and help the teacher in instruction. Once the lesson plans have been written, the next step is to implement them. How can secondary teachers know if they have planned effective lessons for their students? How can teachers monitor what they have produced? A system has been developed by Maglaras and Lynch (1988) in Aurora, Colorado, to monitor written plans. The system involves identifying classroom events as either green or red flags. The green flags indicate that the teacher has planned an appropriate lesson for the class and according to this procedure would include:

1. Heterogeneous classes with groups within
2. Student interest and teacher enthusiasm . . .
3. Recognizing that students may change in . . . skill[s]
4. Integration of problem solving
5. Students apply [content] to real-life situations
6. Use of manipulatives
7. Enrichment activities available to students (p. 59)

If these flags are present, then the lesson is considered a success.

Red flags, on the other hand, signal trouble and the teacher may need to reconsider what has been planned. For example, the red flags include:

1. All students in the class doing the same assignment
2. No or excessive homework
3. Are students grouped homogeneously?
4. Excessive or no purpose for chalkboard work
5. Teacher grading papers while students do homework or students doing homework on own; homework consisting of an excessive number of similar problems [or definitions]
6. Students repeating options they have mastered
7. Class bogged down on 'mastery' of specific operations
8. No diagnostic testing
9. Lack of variety of strategies and class activities at various levels
10. Too much or too little [lecture, demonstration]
11. Students not understanding purpose of their homework
12. Rigidity of [student] groupings, no fluidity of movement to allow for weaknesses, strengths, or ability
13. [Lack of] checking for understanding
14. Overemphasis on 'drill and practice'
15. Never any use of [supplementary materials or media] (p. 59)

This system can help teachers monitor their lesson plans as they are implemented.

Blount and Klausmier (1968) concisely summarize the curriculum development process which emphasizes the importance of planning when they state:

In any planning that seeks to direct action . . . three stages can be identified: (1) An over-all design or plan for action is outlined. This plan is a clearly defined statement that delimits the total structure . . . and indicates the activities and materials necessary for the desired results . . . this over-all design or plan may take the form of a curriculum guide. (2) The over-all plan is then divided into cohesive units that are outlined in more detail . . . (3) Specific details of each unit are outlined . . . and are meant to be readily adaptable to the specific situations and . . . resources that are available when the plan is put into effect. In curriculum planning . . . these detailed plans are incorporated into a . . . unit, finally are developed into a daily lesson plan (p. 186).

The task analysis process may appear complicated. However, if the steps are followed in the suggested sequence, teachers can be somewhat assured that a successful lesson is planned. With experience, the steps in the planning process become a permanent part of the teacher's repertoire and each time the lesson is taught, the teacher makes modifications based on feedback or changes in the students.

SUMMARY

The previous chapters dealt with the broad view of curriculum planning and development. This broader perspective provided the curriculum infrastructure from which classroom planning emerges. Chapter 9 provided a narrower perspective on the curriculum planning and development process which focused on curriculum building at the district, campus, and classroom levels. The chapter brought the curriculum planning and development process to a level of consciousness that should be beneficial to preservice and inservice teachers.

The chapter began with a brief presentation of the resources that teachers have available when planning yearly (or semester) unit and daily lesson plans. Each of these levels of planning was discussed in some detail and attempts were made to link the big picture, the general view of curriculum planning and development, with the classroom level of curriculum implementation. As part of the movement toward classroom implementation, the daily lesson planning process was presented in detail using the task analysis process (TAP).

The task analysis process provides a systematic procedure, which is an outgrowth of the unit as well as the year or semester, for generating curriculum for daily teaching. A part of the task analysis process involves taking the general goals of instruction as identified at the unit level and reducing them to instructional objectives for unit and daily lesson planning. Chapter 9 concluded with a step-by-step approach for generating curriculum for individual secondary classrooms.

YOUR TURN

9.1 As a part of the task analysis process, identifying objectives according to a specific domain of learning was an important part of the daily lesson planning process. Read each of the following objectives and classify each according to one of the three domains: COGNITIVE, AFFECTIVE, PSYCHOMOTOR. The student will be able to:

(a) Select the best of three solutions to an analysis problem using criteria provided by the teacher.

(b) List the names of the scientists and their contributions when given general descriptions.

(c) Demonstrate interest and enthusiasm for music by singing in the school choir.

(d) Dribble a basketball 10 times in a 5-minute time span.

(e) Write in their journals how they feel about a poem.

(f) Write a short story based on facts gained from interviewing a relative or friend.

(g) Anonymously complete a survey designed to determine political party preference of high school students.

9.2 Review each of the following questions and decide what level of the cognitive domain each represents:

(a) What is the difference between direct sunlight and indirect sunlight?

(b) What alternative formula could you use to solve this problem?

(c) How can you use this principle to explain the nature of matter?

(d) How many new ways can you devise which communicate praise and support?

(e) What does the largest portion of the pie graph represent?

(f) How many different kinds of sanding techniques have we studied so far in class? Can you name them?

(g) What do you think is the climax of the story and why?

(h) In what chronological order would you rank each of the following pieces of music?

9.3 If you were going to present a lesson on life in rural America in the Northeast and the South, you would need to make several decisions. You decide to use folk art as one way to express the culture from these two regions of the United States. Using art as the vehicle,

(a) What painters would you select to represent each of these regions?

(b) What content/concepts will you stress or focus on during the lesson?

(c) What primary sources or paintings/illustrations will you show to illustrate your points?

9.4 You have been asked to teach a unit using maps. In planning for the unit, respond to the following items:

(a) Identify 3–5 key goals for this unit and reduce these goals to instructional objectives.

(b) Develop a scope and sequence outline of the content to be presented to the students.

(c) Identify at least two teaching strategies that you will use and match them with the content.

(d) Identify and describe the materials and resources that you will use to teach the unit.

(e) Identify the questions that you will ask to serve as a focus to get the unit started and the questions that you will use throughout to stimulate thinking and close the lesson.

(f) Describe the kind of evaluation process you will use to determine if the objectives have been achieved and if a test is a part of the evaluation process; identify at least 3–5 key questions to be answered correctly.

9.5 If you were presented with the following goal in a unit plan, rewrite it so that it reflects precise language that is characteristic of an instructional objective for your subject area.

(a) Goal: The student will appreciate the diversity of the American society and the various cultures.

(b) Instructional objective:

9.6 Take the goal stated in number 9.5 and, following the steps in the task analysis process, develop a lesson plan for your subject area.

9.7 Assume that you are a faculty member of a particular secondary school. Select a curriculum guide in your content area. Examine the guide in light of the steps involved in the task analysis process. As you review the guide, assume the different roles identified below. Did you view the curriculum guide differently from the various perspectives you assumed in the different roles? How were the views different?

(a) Mr. Johnson, the 48-year-old traditional principal

(b) Ms. Carson, the 35-year-old subject coordinator and career-minded teacher

(c) Mr. Matthews, the 23-year-old progressive-minded new teacher

(d) Mrs. Arnold, the 55-year-old teacher who is president of the local chapter of the Daughters of the American Revolution (DAR)

(e) Ms. Ebert, the 40-year-old counselor, who views kids as the most important part of the school

REFERENCES

Arends, R.I. (1988). *Learning to teach*. New York: Random House.

Beach, D.M. & Reinhartz, J. (1989). *Supervision: Focus on instruction*. New York: Harper & Row.

Bloom, B.S. et al. (1956). *Taxonomy of educational objectives. Handbook I: Cognitive domain*. New York: McKay.

Blount, N.S. & Klausmier, H.J. (1968). *Teaching in the secondary school*. New York: Harper & Row.

Bluestein, J.E. (1989). *Being a successful teacher: A practical guide to instruction and management*. Belmont, Calif.: Lake.

Bruner, J.S. (1960). *The process of education*. Cambridge, Mass.: Harvard University Press.

Commission on the Reorganization of Secondary Education. (1918). *Cardinal principles of secondary education*. Bulletin No. 35. Washington, D.C.: National Education Association.

Cotton, A.B., Sparks-Langer, G.M., Tripp-Apple, R. & Simmons, J.M. (Fall 1989). Collaborative inquiry into developing reflective pedagogical thinking. *Action In Teacher Education, 11*, 3, 47–48.

Eisner, E. (1983). The art and craft of teaching. *Educational Leadership, 40*, 4, 4–14.

Funkhouser, C.W., Beach, D.M., Ryan, G.T., & Fifer, F.L. (1981). *Classroom applications of the curriculum: A systems approach*. Dubuque, Iowa: Kendall Hunt.

Guidelines for science curriculum in Washington schools. (November 1988). Olympia, Wash.: Office of the Superintendent of Public Instruction.

Harrow, A.J. (1972). *Taxonomy of the psychomotor domain: A guide for developing behavioral objectives*. New York: McKay.

Joyce, B. & Weil, M. (1986). *Models of teaching* (3rd ed.). Englewood Cliffs, N.J.: Prentice Hall.

Krathwohl, D.R. et al. (1964). *Taxonomy of educational objectives. Handbook II: Affective domain.* New York: McKay.

Mager, R.F. (1962). *Preparing instructional objectives.* Palo Alto, Calif.: Fearon.

Maglaras, T. & Lynch, D. (October 1988). Monitoring the curriculum: From plan to action. *Educational Leadership, 46,* 2, 58–60.

Manatt, R.P. (1981). *Manatt's exercise in selecting teacher performance evaluation criteria based on effective teaching research.* Albuquerque, N.M.: National Symposium for Professionals in Evaluation and Research. (Mimeographed)

The mathematics program of the Decatur County Community School Corporation. (August 1986). Greensburg, Ind.: Decatur County Community School Corporation.

McCutcheon, G. (September 1980). How do elementary school teachers plan? The nature of planning and influences on it. *Elementary School Journal, 81,* 1, 4–23.

Nicholls, A. & Nicholls, S.H. (1978). *Developing a curriculum: A practical guide.* London: Allen and Unwin.

Ornstein, A.C. (1990). *Strategies for effective teaching.* New York: Harper & Row.

Quina, J. (1989). *Effective secondary teaching.* New York: Harper & Row.

Reinhartz, J. & Beach, D.M. (1983). *Improving middle school instruction: A research-based self-assessment system.* Washington, D.C.: National Education Association.

Reinhartz, J. & Reinhartz, D. (1988). *Teach-practice-apply: The TPA instructional model 7–12.* Washington, D.C.: National Education Association.

Saylor, J.G. & Alexander, W.M. (1954). *Curriculum planning for better teaching and learning.* New York: Holt, Rinehart & Winston.

Smith, M.D. (1975). *Educational psychology and its classroom applications.* Boston: Allyn & Bacon.

Stearns, P.N., Schwartz, D.R. & Beyer, B.K. (1990). *World history: Traditions and new directions.* Teacher's edition. Menlo Park, Calif.: Addison-Wesley.

World history: Traditions and new directions. (1990). Teacher's edition. Menlo Park, Calif.: Addison-Wesley.

Yinger, R.J. (1980). A study of teacher planning. *Elementary School Journal, 80,* 3, 107–127.

Zahorik, J.A. (1970). The effect of planning on teaching. *Elementary School Journal, 71,* 143–151.

Chapter
10

Curriculum Evaluation

*T*he previous chapters described in detail the curriculum development process from the perspective of what happens prior to and during instruction. The process of developing educational goals and then reducing them to instructional objectives provided the focus for assessing educational outcomes. Although educators use goals and objectives as criteria for determining content and procedures in instruction, the ultimate measure of effectiveness is in the achievement ends, not the procedural means.

Evaluation, then, follows planning and implementation and examines the results of the total teaching-learning process. As Funkhouser, Beach, Ryan, and Fifer (1981) note, "Curriculum evaluation . . . seeks to answer the question, 'Did the students learn the knowledge, skills, and attitudes they were supposed to learn?'" (p. 112). For them, the acid test when planning and implementing the curriculum is whether the students have achieved or learned.

Curriculum evaluation provides the proof, the necessary documentation, the data or evidence that the curriculum as designed and implemented produced results: learning. For Caswell (1978), the ultimate criterion for evaluating all curriculum work is to look at the success of the students. Regardless of how elaborate the instructional program is or how dedicated and enthusiastic the staff, unless student performance is changed so that educational outcomes are better than before, the curriculum development process cannot be considered a success.

When done properly, curriculum evaluation is comprehensive and sometimes one of the most difficult tasks of curriculum development. As Saylor and Alexander (1954) have noted, evaluation is just one part of the total curriculum planning and development process:

> Evaluation and planning are really complementary processes. . . . We plan on the basis of evaluation and we evaluate on the basis of planning: evaluation without planning or planning without evaluation is incomplete and hence unwise (p. 579).

In spite of the obvious importance of curriculum evaluation, Ornstein and Hunkins (1988) point out that words do not match actions. While evaluation is considered crucial to all phases of curriculum development and implementation, in practice the opposite is often the case because evaluation results are ignored in the educational decision-making process. Part of the discrepancy between what is said and what is done may be due to the confusing nature of the term *evaluation*. One of the earliest and most comprehensive definitions of curriculum evaluation, presented by Stake (1967), says evaluation is expository because it results in a story that is supported with data and profiles that tell what happened, what perceptions and judgments individuals and groups hold, and what the merits and shortcomings are as well as offering guidance for future programs. Stake (1967) elaborates by saying that the curriculum evaluation process "requires collection, processing, and interpretation of data pertaining to an educational program . . . [which] should lead to better decision making, to better development, better selection, and better use of curricula" (p. 5).

Others view the curriculum evaluation process a bit differently. For Scriven (1967), curriculum evaluation is a judgmental process, and for Armstrong (1989), it is an interpretative opinion based on measurements gathered, which go beyond the givens. Perhaps Ornstein and Hunkins (1988) provide one of the most comprehensive definitions when they say that curriculum evaluation

> is a process or cluster of processes that people perform in order to gather data that will enable them to decide whether to accept, change, or eliminate something—the curriculum in general or an educational textbook in particular. In evaluation people are concerned with . . . relative values . . . [and] make statements of worth regarding the focus of the evaluation (p. 250).

It should be noted that evaluation is different from measurement, a term that is often used interchangeably, but which has a different meaning. Measurement is defined as "the description of a situation or a behavior using numerical terms . . . [which] enables educators to record students' degrees of achieving particular competencies" (Ornstein and Hunkins, 1988, p. 252). Measurement provides the score to establish the level of proficiency. For example, a score of 75 percent on a test has no inherent meaning until the standard for passing is established. A score of 75 percent could be failing if the degree of competence is established as 80 percent. Educators, therefore, give meaning to data by making value judgments. As opposed to measurement, evaluation seeks to answer the question: if 80 percent is passing, how many students demonstrated mastery of the content at this level and how effective was the curricular program in preparing students for this level of achievement?

Adding to the complexity and difficulty in understanding curriculum evaluation is the fact that many aspects of the curriculum development process can be evaluated: the product or student performance, the process or instructional process, the objectives, and the materials. When these factors are coupled with the various levels, such as national versus state, or state versus classroom, the complexity of the process increases significantly.

Curriculum evaluation in recent years has become increasingly important as schools have sought to validate the effectiveness of educational programs. Yet curriculum evaluation is not perfect because it is a complex process that examines many different factors at various levels of the instructional process. Curriculum evaluation occurs at the national, state, district, and classroom levels, and when evaluation occurs, it does not always produce a clear "bottom line." Trump and Miller (1968) describe the complexity of this process by saying

> Knowing whether a school is a good school, . . . whether students are learning what they should be learning, and whether a curriculum change is better than what it replaced are . . . fundamental factors in good curriculum development. . . . Yet, finding imaginative and comprehensive answers to these questions has plagued curriculum planners for generations (p. 339).

This statement by Trump and Miller (1968) clearly describes how important the curriculum evaluation process is and how critical its role is in improving instruction. It is also evident that curriculum evaluation, curriculum change, and curriculum improvement go together hand-in-hand. It is also evident from these definitions and descriptions that curriculum evaluation is multifaceted and complex and can be studied in many different ways and at various levels (classroom, school, state, etc.) of the curriculum planning and development process. An equally important dimension of evaluation involves the implementation of the curriculum.

This chapter describes the last and, for some, the most important part of the curriculum planning and development process. The formative and summative evaluation procedures used in curriculum development are discussed. Several methods and models of curriculum evaluation are presented and examined and the continuous nature of the evaluation process as it relates to school improvement and student achievement is described.

FORMATIVE AND SUMMATIVE EVALUATION

There are generally two types of evaluation used to assess curriculum. The first is formative, which is used to evaluate programs or treatments, such as writing across the curriculum, that are in progress. Formative evaluation seeks data regarding the current instructional program that is being implemented and the curricular dimensions associated with that instruction. For Zais (1976), formative evaluation "is conducted during the curriculum development process for the additional purpose of providing data that can be used to 'form' a better finished product . . . [and] takes place at a number of intermediate points during the development of curriculum" (p. 381). Cronbach (1963) suggests the following uses for formative evaluation: (1) obtaining data regarding changes produced in students by a course; (2) identifying multidimensional outcomes and separating the effects of instruction according to the dimensions; (3) looking for aspects of a course in which revisions are needed; (4) collecting information while a course is being developed and/or taught; (5) identifying aspects of the curriculum which produce an effect and looking for what produces the effectiveness; (6) conducting systematic observations to identify desired pupil behaviors; and (7) identifying outcomes beyond the content of the curriculum, such as attitudes, aptitude for future learning, or general understanding. Box 10-1 provides a set of questions that can be used to guide formative curriculum evaluation procedures.

The intent of such formative data collection procedures is to allow educators to make adjustments in the curriculum during the instructional process. This type of evaluation allows educators to assess the curriculum while it is being implemented. Judgments about the overall effectiveness, the need to continue the instructional program, or similar decisions are made at this point in the process. Other names for the formative evaluation process include *continuous, ongoing,* or *developmental.*

Unlike formative, summative evaluation requires comparative data or information and results in a judgment or decision. Summative evaluation makes comparisons between and among programs as to which one is the best. According to Zais (1976), "Summative evaluation . . . is conducted in order to obtain a comprehensive assessment of the quality of a completed curriculum . . . [which] takes place at the completion of the curriculum development process and provides a . . . judgment on the completed product" (p. 381). As a result of this evaluation process, educators arrive at a decision regarding the instructional effectiveness of a curriculum or instructional program. Educators can then determine which curriculum or instructional program should be selected over another based on the kinds of results that are produced.

Clearly, student performance data are an important aspect of the summative evaluation process. In summative evaluation, the question becomes "Did the curriculum or instructional program produce the kinds of results desired?" rather than the formative question of "Is the curriculum producing the kinds of learning outcomes desired?" One thing that educators can do is to examine student achievement data as a part of the summative decision. For example, at the classroom level, the teacher might track six-week grades or scores on publisher-made tests to determine the level of student learning. If students are not successful after the teacher has taught several periods and/or groups of students, the decision will have to be made concerning the continued use of the curricular materials. At the building level, teachers and administrators might

Box 10-1 **Formative Evaluation of Curriculum Development Process**

	Yes	No
1. Was the curriculum/instructional program implemented with minimal difficulty?	___	___
2. Were teachers initially successful with the curriculum/instructional program?	___	___
3. Has student response to the curriculum/instructional program been positive?	___	___
4. Has enough time elapsed to obtain valid or accurate data?	___	___
5. Given the nature of the curriculum/instructional program, have the costs been within the budgeted amount?	___	___
6. Have there been unexpected difficulties? What? _____ _____	___	___
7. Were training and staff support services sufficient to ensure successful implementation of the curriculum/instructional program?	___	___

analyze achievement data from state or national tests to determine trends by grade level. If the majority of juniors (eleventh graders) who have successfully completed English I, II, and III are not successful on English language arts achievement tests, summative evaluation decisions will need to be made concerning the instructional program. In one school, it was determined that the textbook adopted did not match the state achievement tests, so the curriculum was changed. Box 10-2 provides a set of questions that can be used to guide summative curriculum evaluation decisions.

Other names for summative evaluation have been *outcome-based, terminal,* or *product.* Horst and colleagues (1975) identified several hazards of evaluation and warn against using inappropriate data for making summative curriculum decisions. These practices are hazards because, in using these data, it is difficult to determine if students perform better in a particular curriculum program than they would have without it. Among the hazards are the following practices:

1. Using raw gain scores (posttest minus pretest scores) for comparison purposes
2. Using norm-group comparisons with wide variances in test dates
3. Using noncomparable treatment and comparison groups

Box 10-2 **Summative Evaluation of Curriculum Development Process**

	Yes	No
1. Is the curriculum/instructional program effective based on student success on achievement measures?	___	___
2. Have all teachers adopted and implemented the curriculum/instructional program?	___	___
3. Is the curriculum/instructional program cost-effective?	___	___
4. Is the data regarding student performance accurate and valid?	___	___
5. Has the curriculum/instructional program produced the desired results?	___	___
6. Will you maintain this curriculum/instructional program? Why? Why not? _____ _____ _____	___	___

4. Using pretest scores (especially low scores) to select program participants
5. Using results from tests that have been administered carelessly
6. Assuming that achievement gain is solely due to treatment and not recognizing other variables or plausible explanations for the gains

In addition to using inappropriate data to make decisions regarding the curriculum, Zais (1976) cautions that summative evaluation should not be thought of as strictly a one-time only procedure that occurs exclusively "at the end." In fact, summative evaluation can and should occur infrequently at specific strategic points during the curriculum development process. As educators use summative data to guide the curriculum development process, they might develop a continuous evaluation system to track six weeks and semester grades with grade level and subject achievement tests. For example, if a school is evaluating the effectiveness of the writing curriculum in English, it would track the number of failures by grade level for each six weeks reporting period and for each semester. The school would also chart achievement test results by grade level, where given, and would then look at the percent of students mastering concepts on standardized achievement tests such as presented in Figure 10.1.

SAMPLE PRINTOUT OF ACADEMIC PERFORMANCE OF STATE MANDATED TESTS

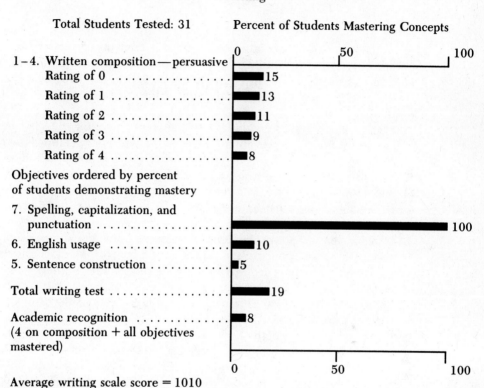

Grade: 11–Exit Level
District: 999–001 Example ISD

Report Date: December 1990
Date of Testing: October 1990

Writing

Total Students Tested: 31

Percent of Students Mastering Concepts

1–4. Written composition—persuasive
    Rating of 0 15
    Rating of 1 13
    Rating of 2 11
    Rating of 3 9
    Rating of 4 8

Objectives ordered by percent
of students demonstrating mastery

7. Spelling, capitalization, and
   punctuation 100

6. English usage 10

5. Sentence construction 5

Total writing test 19

Academic recognition 8
(4 on composition + all objectives
mastered)

Average writing scale score = 1010

Figure 10.1 Sample printout of academic performance of state mandated tests (*Source:* Texas Education Agency. Austin, Tex.: TEA.)

Figure 10.1 shows the kind of database the school would build as a continuous summative profile is developed. This profile would provide information at various points in time and from a variety of perspectives that would reflect the success of the English curriculum in developing writing skills.

Curriculum developers and other educators have available two evaluation procedures that are helpful in making decisions about the curriculum planning and development process. Formative evaluation collects information during the implementation of curricular programs so that modifications can occur along the way. Summative evaluation collects information, especially student achievement data, that is used to make comparisons and, ultimately, judgments regarding the instructional effectiveness of a curricular program or treatment.

MODELS OF CURRICULUM EVALUATION

At the root of the evaluation process is the measurement of human change, which educators associate with learning. That measurement, however, takes different forms depending upon the approach or model used or the changes desired in instruction. A part of the change process involves making decisions —decisions based on accurate data or information. According to Beach and Reinhartz (1989), "decisions made in schools about . . . instruction are not routine [and] should involve careful analysis" (p. 264). Decisions about what model of curriculum evaluation to use or what curriculum is more effective rests upon what will, what is, and what has happened. Decision making is complex and requires time and careful thought. As curriculum developers make decisions about programs and people, they need to consider ". . . the personal variables that influence the actions of the decision maker" (Beach and Reinhartz, 1989, p. 266). These variables, according to Gorton (1987), are concern for risk, attitude toward people, educational philosophy, concern about status, and concern for authority and control. Many curricular programs fail because teachers are fearful of losing their status, authority, and/or control in the classroom or because the curriculum violates their basic educational philosophy. Taking these variables into account and the process of decision making into consideration, an instructional program or a curriculum can be evaluated more objectively.

There are several models in the literature that examine the effectiveness of educational programs in producing results or in promoting change. In this section, six models of curriculum or program evaluation will be described. These include: Tyler's Goals and Objectives Model, Stake's Countenance Model, Stufflebeam's CIPP Model, Provus's Discrepancy Model, English's Curriculum Management Model, and the School Accreditation Model.

The Goals and Objectives Model

As indicated earlier in the text, Tyler has had a profound effect on understanding of the curriculum development process, and modern educational evaluation is attributed to him (Stufflebeam and Shinkfield, 1985). For Tyler (1949), evaluation begins with the objectives of the instructional program because the evaluation process should seek to ascertain the degree to which instructional objectives are attained or accomplished.

Tyler's model is most accurately seen in "The Eight Year Study," which he conducted for the Progressive Education Association from 1933 to 1941. This large-scale, longitudinal study examined the total process of curriculum development and used a variety of tests, scales, inventories, checklists, questionnaires, and logs to obtain data (Ornstein and Hunkins, 1988). In this model, the emphasis is on instructional objectives, and Tyler (1942) provided the following guidelines for the process:

1. Establish general program goals and objectives.
2. Reduce general goals and objectives to specific instructional objectives stated in behavioral terms.
3. Classify objectives according to domains of learning and levels.
4. Obtain data or find other evidence where achievement of objectives can be shown.
5. Construct or select measurement techniques.
6. Collect data concerning student performance on objectives.
7. Compare the results of student performance data with behaviorally stated objectives to determine degree of mastery.

Metfessel and Michael (1967) have elaborated on the Tyler Model and established a variation, which is an eight-step process for curriculum evaluation that includes:

1. Involve members of the total educational community: teachers, professional organizations, students, parents, citizens.
2. Develop a framework of goals and objectives and arrange them in a hierarchical order from general to specific outcomes.
3. Translate and communicate the specific instructional objectives to the curricular program.
4. Establish criterion measures that can be used to measure program effectiveness relative to the objectives.
5. Conduct periodic assessments and observations during program implementation using appropriate instruments.
6. Analyze data collected using appropriate statistical procedures.
7. Interpret the data relative to values and standards and make judgments about learners' growth and progress toward instructional objectives.
8. Generate recommendations based on information collected and judgments made that will serve to modify the appropriate elements in the curricular design.

A diagram representing one cycle of the eight-step expanded Tyler model as proposed by Metfessel and Michael (1967) is shown in Figure 10.2.

This model and subsequent variations are often referred to as technical, behavioral objectives models because of the emphasis on measuring the degree to which behavioral changes have occurred with little or no regard for why the behaviors are important or desirable. The focus of such evaluation models is to measure or determine if behavioral changes resulted and to what degree.

The Countenance Model

Stake (1967) was among the first in the field of curriculum evaluation to propose a pluralistic view of the process. The Countenance Model differs from the earlier more technical models in that it requires more extensive data

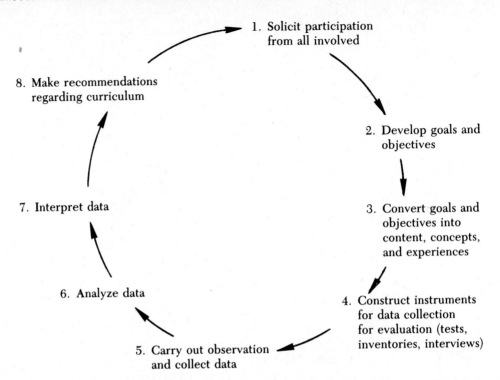

Figure 10.2 The Tyler-Metfessel-Michael model of curriculum evaluation (*Modified from:* Ornstein, A.C. & Hunkins, F.P. (1988). *Curriculum foundations, principles and issues.* Englewood Cliffs, N.J.: Prentice Hall.)

collection from a variety of sources. It is also more sensitive to the different values of program participants (McNeil, 1985). Stake (1967) was concerned based on evaluation. He recognized the possibility of discrepancy between the perceptions and expectations of a school staff and outside evaluators. According to Stake (1967),

> The countenance of evaluation beheld by the educator is not the same one beheld by the specialist in evaluation. The specialist sees himself [or herself] as a describer. . . . The teacher and . . . administrator . . . expect an evaluator to grade something . . . against external standards, or criteria perhaps little related to the local school's resources and goals (p. 374).

The intent of the model, then, is to collect appropriate data that will assist in providing accurate, relevant information to the recipients.

The Countenance Model examines three phases of the educational program, which Stake (1967) calls antecedent, transaction, and outcomes. Antecedents are those conditions in the educational environment that existed prior to instruction and may impact or relate to outcomes. Transactions are described as the teaching-learning behaviors associated with the process of instruction. Outcomes are the effects or results of the educational program. Figure 10.3 provides a description of the data needed in the evaluative process for each of the three phases.

As seen in the figure, the model has two operations associated with each phase. These are descriptions and judgments. The description matrix relates to what was intended and what was actually observed and serves as a formative evaluation component. Judgments about aspects of the program are divided into those decisions relative to standards used to make the judgments which serve as a summative component. McNeil (1990) describes the evaluator's main task in this model as "discovering what those concerned want to know, making observations, and gathering multiple judgments about the antecedents, transactions and outcomes" (p. 243). In generating the data for the matrix, a variety of individuals may participate—teachers, students, psychologists, as well as outside experts.

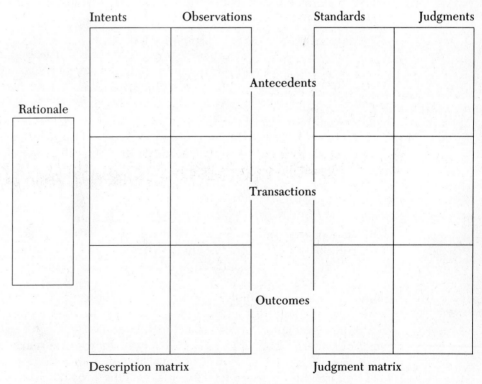

Figure 10.3 Stake's antecedents, transactions, and outcomes framework (*Source:* Stake, R.E. (April 1967). The countenance of educational evaluation *Teachers College Record, 68*, 2, p. 529. Used with permission.)

The Context-Input-Process-Product (CIPP) Model

The CIPP model is the result of the work of Stufflebeam and his colleagues on the Study Committee on Evaluation, which was supported by Phi Delta Kappa. The basic premise of the model is that program evaluation should assist in the improvement of the school curriculum. Often described as a comprehensive, decision-management-oriented approach, this model considers evaluation to be a continuous process. The CIPP Model has four components: context, input, process, and product. Context evaluations focus on the environments in which educational programs operate. In examining context, evaluators seek to define the relevant environment and conduct a situation analysis. According to Armstrong (1989), context evaluation recognizes that planning decisions that precede implementation have an effect on educational programs. Therefore, context evaluations should seek information about prior events and look carefully at the nature of the population served by the educational program.

Input evaluation is designed to provide information relative to the use of materials and resources to attain program goals. Input evaluation examines the means by which goals will be implemented. This process involves examining strategies, designs, alternatives, and general capabilities to be successful. According to Ornstein and Hunkins (1988), input evaluation looks at specific aspects and components of the curriculum plan and asks questions such as:

1. Are the objectives stated appropriately?
2. Are the objectives congruent with the stated aims and goals of the school?
3. Is the content congruent with the aims, goals, and objectives of the program?
4. Are the instructional strategies appropriate?
5. Do other strategies exist that can help meet the objectives? (p. 263)

In answering these questions, the evaluation process can move from simple to complex depending upon the magnitude of the program and the nature of the evaluation process. Armstrong (1989) notes that "input evaluation attempts to validate the adequacy of the instructional design with the goal of helping program developers make the best possible plans before instruction commences" (p. 241).

Process evaluation examines the decisions that control the curriculum implementation process and occurs as instructional programs are put in place. Process evaluation monitors instruction during delivery to determine the congruency between planned and delivered, and requires frequent feedback to the instructional staff. Process evaluation also provides information relative to the abilities of the persons delivering instruction and serves to provide direction for staff development activities.

Product evaluation occurs after instruction and seeks to assess the outcomes of the instructional program. This evaluation phase seeks to determine the degree of success of an instructional program and the attainment of the goals. Information gathered in this stage helps provide a basis for making judgments about the need to maintain, modify, or eliminate aspects of an educational program.

Table 10.1 provides an overview of the CIPP Model, with a description of objectives, methods, and decisions relative to each of the four components.

Table 10.1   FOUR TYPES OF EVALUATION: CONTEXT, INPUT, PROCESS, AND PRODUCT

	Context evaluation	Input evaluation	Process evaluation	Product evaluation
Objective	To define the existing context, to determine the needs and opportunities present, and to diagnose the problems underlying the needs	To identify and assess the school system's capabilities, the presence of input strategies, and the various designs for implementing strategies	To identify or predict, in process, defects in the procedural design or in the implementation plan; to maintain account of actions taken	To gather and communicate information regarding outcome, information about objectives achieved and content covered; to relate findings to the previous three stages of evaluation
Method	Describing the context, comparing the actual and intended inputs and outputs, gathering data to compare probable and possible system performance, and determining why certain deficiencies exist	Describing and analyzing available human and material resources, solution strategies, and systems designs in light of the course of action being suggested	Monitoring the actual implementation of the plan with its related activities to determine potential procedural barriers; gathering information to describe the actual procedures employed	Defining operationally and measuring criteria associated with the objectives; comparing the results exhibited with pre-determined standards; interpreting the overall results relative to the previous three evaluations
Relation to Decision Making	Used to decide the setting to be served, the goals to be addressed, and the particular objectives to be considered	Used to decide what sources of support are required, what solution strategies are appropriate, and what procedural designs can be employed to initiate the program change desired	Used to make decisions regarding implementing and refining the program	Used to gather information to determine whether to continue, terminate, or modify the program

Source: Stufflebeam, D.L. (1982). The CIPP model. In G.D. Borich and R.P. Jamelka. (Eds.) *Programs and systems: An evaluation perspective.* Orlando, Fla.: Academic Press, p. 11. Used with permission.

The CIPP Model as presented in the figure demonstrates the broad view of evaluation by involving evaluators early in the initial planning stages. While summative or product evaluation is important in many areas today, it is only one factor in the total evaluation process. Evaluation, as viewed within this model, is primarily for program improvement.

The Discrepancy Model

Provus (1971) developed a model of evaluation which analyzes or compares the difference or discrepancy "between reality and some standard or standards" (p. 46). The Discrepancy Model combines evaluation with systems-management and consists of five stages: design, installation, process, product, and cost. In the design stage, evaluators work closely with curriculum developers to determine what they wish to accomplish. The standard that is applied in this stage is called design criteria, which determines the degree of fit between the desired ends and the adequacy of personnel, space, materials, and other resources to accomplish the goals. The design stage specifies what is to be done instructionally and evaluators try to determine in advance if the design of the program is internally sound and they try to identify any potential problems.

In the installation stage, evaluators try to determine the extent to which the planned program is being implemented. This standard is called the fidelity criterion and seeks to establish the degree to which the agreed upon instructional design or program is being implemented and determine how true teachers are to the agreed upon plan. If there are discrepancies in staff abilities, student abilities, program resources, or facilities there is a likelihood that teachers are modifying the agreed upon plan to meet the situation.

In the process stage, evaluators examine the short-term or interim results of the instructional program. To what degree are students meeting the standard of performance? Is the program obtaining the desired results? These are the questions that must be answered in this stage. If the processes for instruction are inadequate and therefore the desired results have not been attained, modifications will need to be made in the instructional program. As Armstrong (1989) notes, "Corrective action could involve, among other things, tinkering with the program design or checking on the adequacy of implementation" (p. 248).

The product stage involves an analysis of the whole program in terms of the original goals and seeks to determine if program standards have been met. Products involve not only students and staff, but the community as well. Information gathered in this stage helps to determine if the program is worthwhile. Finally, when all the data are in, the cost analysis stage seeks to determine the degree of cost-effectiveness or cost-benefit. While some programs may produce spectacular results, their costs make them unrealistic to adopt on a district-wide basis. In this stage, the question may be asked, "Could we have obtained the same or similar results with a less expensive program?"

In each stage of the Discrepancy Model, evaluators are confronted with several decisions. As they compare the desired performance with the actual

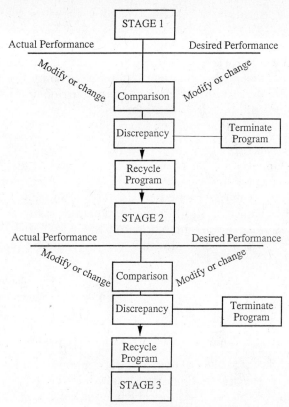

Figure 10.4 Provus's Discrepancy Model (*Modified from:* Provus, M. (1972). The discrepancy evaluation model, In P. Taylor and D.N. Cowley (Eds.). *Readings in curriculum evaluation*. Dubuque, Iowa: Brown, 1972.)

performance they determine the discrepancy and the decision is made to terminate, modify or recycle the program. If the program is recycled, the evaluation process moves to the next stage and the same decisions are repeated. The components of the decision-making process within the first two stages of the Discrepancy Model are presented in Figure 10.4. The Discrepancy Model is designed to be used to evaluate programs in any stage of development, from planning to implementation. It has also been used not only at the school level, but at the district and state level as well.

The Curriculum Management Model

Recently, English and Steffy (1989) described a curriculum management model that evaluates the overall curriculum design. English (1988) refers to this curriculum evaluation process as an audit, which is "an objective, external review of a record, event, process, product, act, belief, or motivation to commit an act" (p. 1). Within this model, the evaluator surveys documents as well as practices and seeks to determine the degree of fit between and among the planned curriculum, the taught curriculum, and the tested curriculum. The degree to which these three components are congruent determines the quality control that is present within the instructional program.

The planned curriculum is reflected in the curriculum documents of the district and school and most frequently takes the form of a curriculum guide. English and Steffy (1989) advocate a "lean and mean" curriculum guide that would meet the following criteria:

1. Clarity and validity of objectives by indicating the what, when, and how performed and the amount of time spent learning the objective
2. Congruence of the curriculum to testing and evaluation by having objectives keyed to performance evaluation and tests in use
3. Delineation by grade and subject of the essential skills, content, and attitudes with specific documented prerequisite or discrete skills required
4. Delineation of major instructional tools, resources, or materials so that there is a match between the textbook and other instructional resources objective by objective
5. Linkage for classroom utilization showing specific examples of how to approach key concepts and skills in the classroom

For English and Steffy (1989) the written curriculum should contain the goals and objectives of the instructional program and should be understood and guide instruction. As a result of the curriculum documents, teachers should have high expectations for their students and operate within a more structured educational program. The process for developing the written curriculum should be fast, simple, and inexpensive; focus on student mastery; reflect a thorough knowledge of the subject; and not dictate a particular teaching style.

The taught curriculum should be based on the planning contained in the curriculum documents (curriculum guides and lesson plans). The taught curriculum should involve learners in the instructional process with the activities directed and chosen by the teacher. In implementing the curriculum, schools should provide opportunities for teachers to (1) meet regularly and discuss problems; (2) share successful ideas and techniques; (3) review the written curriculum to make changes; and (4) build supportive resource groups.

The tested curriculum should assess student mastery of the planned and taught curriculum. Results of the tested curriculum should provide data relative to program effectiveness and can suggest areas for possible modification. The testing and evaluation process should cover all formal goals of the instructional program, facilitate learning, and provide information for ongoing modifications of curriculum and policy.

Figure 10.5 provides an overview of the relationship of the Curriculum Management Model and the planned, taught, and tested curriculum to the total process.

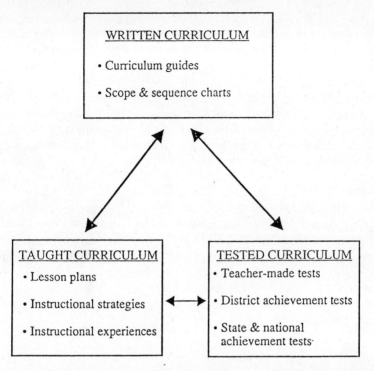

Figure 10.5 Components of the curriculum evaluation process (*Modified from:* English, F. W. (1988). *Curriculum auditing.* Lancaster, PA.: Technomic Publishing Co.)

Although the Curriculum Management model is different from some of the other models presented, it does emphasize the evaluation process by focusing on the three main components of the teaching-learning process: planning, teaching-learning, and testing. The greater the degree to which curriculum developers can align these three components, the greater the degree of fit in the instructional process.

The School Accreditation Model

This model of curriculum evaluation involves self-analysis or self-study and the collection of data that support a critical self-analysis. This evaluation process may involve regional accrediting agencies or state accrediting procedures. Schools are asked to consider the standard and then respond on the basis of self-evaluation by providing supporting documentation. Areas that are most often examined in regard to the school program include financial support and governance, curriculum development and alignment, delivery of instruction, facilities and resources, and student services. One of these standards is applied to the operations of the programs of the school or district, and the entity seeks to collect information internally that will support compliance with the standard. Outside evaluators or team members come to the school district or campus and, after reviewing the documentation provided in the self-study, make recommendations regarding the degree to which the standard has been met based on the information provided by the school, the interviews conducted at the site, and any additional information provided.

Recently, schools have had to assess their institutional effectiveness. They have had to answer the question, "Did the instructional program make a difference educationally in the lives of our students?" Schools have had to examine their results and compare them with the client with whom they had to work. This evaluation process seeks to assess the impact of the educational program on the educational development and advancement of the student.

Regardless of the model selected, the curriculum evaluation process is a complex, multifaceted endeavor with many variables to consider. Individuals are being overly simplistic if they think that the instructional process can be accurately assessed with a product-only evaluation strategy. Too often there is a temptation to measure learning in all of its many different forms by simply administering a standardized test. If these models demonstrate one thing it is that curriculum evaluation cannot be accurately expressed using a test score, or a single product.

SUMMARY

Chapter 10 presented a discussion of curriculum evaluation, the final phase of the curriculum planning and development process. On the surface it appears that curriculum evaluation is a process of looking back only; upon closer examination, looking back is certainly an important part of this process, but evaluation of the curriculum begins when the curriculum planners start to design the instructional program. As they look ahead into the future and put in writing their desired outcomes, curriculum evaluation attempts to determine to what extent these outcomes have been achieved. In effect, curriculum evaluation asks the question, "Did the curriculum produce the kinds of results desired?" This question is tied inextricably to the beginning of the process when the curriculum developers ask, "What kinds of results do we want to produce in students?"

The chapter began with a discussion of the evaluation process, both formative and summative, with some attention given to the role of change and decision making in the endeavor. In the remaining part of the chapter, six specific models of curriculum evaluation were discussed. First, a general description of each model was provided, followed by a diagram of the components to illustrate how each model operates. In addition, the models were compared according to their purpose, strengths, and weaknesses.

These models should be selected on the basis of the type of curriculum that is being examined. Thus, a match is needed between the type of curriculum produced and the means by which it will be evaluated. Since evaluation is the final task to be conducted, this chapter brought the curriculum development process to a close.

YOUR TURN

10.1 Review several curriculum documents, particularly those developed by new or innovative programs in a school district.

(a) After identifying the curriculum documents, describe the evaluation procedures that have been planned to assess the effectiveness of the instructional program.

(b) Select one of the evaluation models presented in this chapter and develop an evaluation system for one of the curricular programs.

10.2 After reviewing several curriculum documents (guides), record the statements that would indicate that the document has included ways to evaluate student performance in the program and the program itself. For example, cite the specific ways to measure change in reaching the desired ends. A statement such as "The curriculum will change pupil performance; students will feel more comfortable in higher mathematics" exemplifies such statements.

10.3 There is a lot in the professional literature about empowering teachers. If you were given the responsibility to do so, what efforts would you make to involve teachers in the curriculum evaluation process in a specific school district. Consider doing the following:

(a) Survey various districts for new instructional programs being implemented (whole language, Writing Across the Curriculum, global education, interactive video instruction in the sciences, etc.).

(b) Determine the number of teachers who would participate in the curriculum evaluation process (have a willingness to be a part).

(c) Decide on the roles and responsibilities each will play and the recommendations that can or should be made (e.g., a case study approach).

10.4 What if you were presented with the following dilemma: you have statistical results that the students did not score significantly higher on the posttest than on the pretest. However, the data concerning the affective changes brought about by the new program are glowing. Students love it and so do the parents. What would you do? Consider the following steps and then write your own plan of action.

(a) First, clarify what your role is. Is it to make the decision to keep the program or not, or are you simply fact finding?

(b) If your role is to make a decision or recommendation at the policy level, consider the following questions: (1) Do you need more data? (2) Are the academic data appropriate in helping to answer the question related to program effectiveness? (3) Have you looked at several sources of summative data? and (4) Should student opinions be considered?

(c) What evaluation model will you use to help you make these decisions? Justify your answer.

10.5 In the next part of the textbook, each curriculum area is presented. Turn to the chapter in which you have an instructional interest or expertise and review the trends described. If you were given the role to evaluate this curriculum area for a school/district, how would you go about the task? Consider the following:

(a) Make a list of the proposed trends.
(b) Describe the trend and its impact on student learning.
(c) Select an evaluation model and try to complete it based on the information provided in the chapter.
(d) What would you recommend? What would you heartily endorse? Why?

10.6 Take a curriculum document and evaluate it according to the following criteria (Zenger and Zenger, 1973) on a scale of excellent, good, acceptable, poor, not included.
(a) *Format*: arrangement of objectives, content, evaluation
(b) *Design*: organization, direction, structure, or guide
(c) *Content, Materials, and Procedures*: methods suggested, activities, materials
(d) *Evaluation*: matches philosophy and ways to assess student progress

REFERENCES

Armstrong, D.G. (1989). *Developing and documenting the curriculum.* Boston: Allyn & Bacon.

Beach, D.M. & Reinhartz, J. (1989). *Supervision: Focus on instruction.* New York: Harper & Row.

Caswell, H. (November 1978). Persistent curriculum problems. *The Educational Forum, 43,* 1, 99–110.

Cronbach, L.J. (May 1963). Course improvement through evaluation. *Teachers College Record, 64,* 3, 672–683.

English, F.W. (1988). *Curriculum auditing.* Lancaster, Pa.: Technomic Publishing Co.

English, F. & Steffy, B. (March 1989). Curriculum management. Paper presented at the National Curriculum Study Institutes of the Association for Supervision and Curriculum Development, Orlando, Florida. (Mimeographed)

Funkhouser, C.F., Beach, D.M., Ryan, G.T. & Fifer, F.L. (1981). *Classroom applications of the curriculum: A systems approach.* Dubuque, Iowa: Kendall Hunt.

Gorton, R.A. (1987). *School leadership and administration.* Dubuque, Iowa: Brown.

Horst, D. et al. (1975). *A practical guide to measuring project impact on student achievement.* Monograph Series on Education, No. 1. Washington, D.C.: U.S. Office of Education.

McNeil, J.D. (1990) *Curriculum: A comprehensive introduction* (4th ed.). Glenview, Ill.: Scott Foresman.

McNeil, J.D. (1985) *Curriculum: A comprehensive introduction* (3rd ed.). Boston: Little Brown.

Metfessel, N.S. & Michael, W.B. (Winter 1967). A paradigm involving multiple criterion measures for the evaluation of the effectiveness of school programs. *Journal of Educational Research, 27,* 4, 931–943.

Ornstein, A.C. & Hunkins, F.P. (1988). *Curriculum foundations, principles and issues.* Englewood Cliffs, N.J.: Prentice Hall.

Provus, M. (1972). The discrepancy evaluation model. In P. Taylor and D.M. Cowley (Eds). *Readings in curriculum evaluation.* Dubuque, Iowa: Brown.

Provus, M. (1971). *Discrepancy evaluation for educational program improvement and assessment.* Berkeley, Calif.: McCutchan.

Saylor, J.G. & Alexander, W.M. (1954). *Curriculum planning for better teaching and learning.* New York: Holt, Rinehart & Winston.

Scriven, M. (1967). The methodology of evaluation. In R.W. Tyler, R.M. Gange & M. Scriven (Eds.). *Perspectives of curriculum evaluation.* Chicago: Rand McNally.

Stake, R.E. (April 1967). The countenance of educational evaluation. *Teachers College Record, 68,* 2, 523–540.

Stufflebeam, D.L. & Shinkfield, A.J. (1985). *Systematic evaluation.* Boston: Kluwer-Nijhoff.

Texas Education Agency. Sample printout of academic performance or state mandated tests. Texas Education Agency. Austin, Tex: Texas Education Agency.

Trump, J.L. & Miller D.F. (1968). *Secondary school curriculum improvement* (2nd ed.). Boston: Allyn & Bacon.

Tyler, R.W. (1949). *Basic principles of curriculum and instruction.* Chicago: University of Chicago Press.

Tyler, R.W. (1942). General statement on evaluation. *Journal of Educational Research, 35,* 43, 492–501.

Zais, R.S. (1976). *Curriculum principles and foundations.* New York: Harper & Row.

Zenger, W.F. & Zenger, S.R. (1973). *Writing and evaluating curriculum guides.* Belmont, Calif.: Fearon.

PART
FIVE

Content Areas of the Secondary Curriculum

Part five provides an overview of the major content areas offered in secondary schools. Social studies, English language arts, mathematics, and science are discussed in detail because they represent a major part of secondary school curriculum. Health and physical education, foreign languages, fine arts, and other programs are briefly presented as well.

In Chapters 11, 12, 13, and 14, the goals, overview of the 7–12 curriculum, and trends and issues are included along with the general scope and sequences for social studies, English language arts, mathematics, and science. At the end of each chapter, the pertinent trends and issues are presented.

The final chapter in this part represents several diverse subjects, and it is organized somewhat differently. Chapter 15 is designed to explore the nature of each elective curriculum area. Each area is discussed briefly and historical and background information, a general overview, and general trends and issues are discussed. The purpose of this chapter is to provide a general awareness of the value, purpose, and function of each of these elective areas.

Chapter
11

Social Studies in the Curriculum

O f all the disciplines in the secondary curriculum, the ". . . social studies are among the oldest and most respected fields of human study and scholarship . . ." (Beckner and Cornett, 1972, p. 242). For Beard (1938), the social studies curriculum represented the "creation of rich and many-sided personalities, equipped with practical knowledge and inspired by ideals so that they can make their way and fulfill their mission in a changing society which is part of a world complex" (p. 179). Yet, the reputation of the social sciences among secondary students is less than attractive and interesting because students are often required to memorize lists of names, dates, and places. There are several areas of study included in the broad field of the social studies. These areas include history, geography, government, anthropology, economics, sociology, and psychology.

The goals and objectives of the present social studies curriculum in the secondary schools can be traced back to 1916 when the National Education Association Committee on the Reorganization of Secondary Education met. Then, in the 1930s, the Commission on Social Studies attempted to realign the goals and programs of the social studies, but it ". . . made no clear or forceful recommendations on the framework of the curriculum itself, and its impact was thereby dissipated (National Commission on Social Studies, 1989, p. v).

Other attempts to change the social studies were made in the 1950s, 1960s, and the early 1970s, but they were not successful in bringing about significant changes. In the 1960s, the "new" history was to provide students with the conceptual foundation which emphasized methodology, analysis, and interpretations (McNeil, 1990). Over 40 social studies curriculum projects were funded during the 1960s by a variety of governmental agencies, institutions, and private foundations. Although many projects were generated, there was little agreement among the creators as to the academic structure of the social studies (McNeil, 1990). Each project included generalizations, concepts, and/or models of inquiry as a way to define the academic structure, but the agreement ended there. Inductive teaching was recommended as the primary model of instruction. However, without an agreed upon structure for the social studies, the discipline remained in disarray. Parker (1988) uses strong language when he states, "even the innovative social studies programs produced in the 1960s sidestepped history, history opting instead to develop in students the skills of investigating history or inquiry" (p. 86).

It was not until representatives from all major social studies organizations were included on the National Commission on Social Studies (1989) that a ". . . coherent vision of the role of social studies in the general education of our young people" was developed (p. vii). The report of this commission provides a model for the development of the social studies curriculum and gives direction to educators who will be responsible for developing social studies programs for adolescents. The proposed model advocates a social studies curriculum that will help students meet the challenges that lie ahead in the twenty-first century.

Through learning about various disciplines within the social studies — history, geography, government, economics, anthropology, American government, sociology, and psychology — students ". . . comprehend the interrelationships among those subjects and their combined power to explain the past and current human condition, and future possibilities" (National Commission on Social Studies, 1989).

According to this National Commission on Social Studies, the most important problems are becoming international in scope and ". . . in such a world the multidisciplinary study of humankind in its variety, rootedness, and interrelatedness becomes even more essential" (1989). For members of the commission, the social studies convey the essential knowledge that provides a bridge and a context to understand the societal, humanistic, and scientific values and concerns. In addition, the group believes that the social studies provide the realization that knowledge is made by man and not generated by natural phenomena. The study of people through the social studies helps students understand how they go about "the business of governing and conducting the affairs of a dynamic society (Bragaw and Hartoonian, 1988, p. 10).

Until very recently, the social studies curriculum has been relegated to the role of educating students to be tomorrow's American citizens (Hertzberg, 1981). While this remains one of the many goals of the social studies curriculum, McFarland (1990) reminds us that it is not the only one. According to the National Commission on Social Studies (1989), the goals of the social studies curriculum are changing. The social studies curriculum is seen as a way to help students become citizens of the world who are historically, geographically, politically, economically, and socially aware and knowledgeable.

This chapter begins with a discussion of the major goals of the social studies curriculum. This section is followed by an overview of the scope and sequence of the social studies curriculum in grades 7 and 8 and then grades 9–12. The remaining part of the chapter is devoted to the individual disciplines within the social studies. History is presented first because of its link with all of the other subjects. Much of what is presented is based on the work of the Bradley Commission (1988) and the National Commission on Social Studies (1989). These two groups have issued guidelines for restructuring improvement of the social studies curriculum.

GOALS FOR THE SOCIAL STUDIES CURRICULUM

In the 1990s there is renewed interest in history and geography as the world continues to get smaller in terms of travel and communication. The emphasis seems to be in the direction of integration: integrating literature with history, history with geography, and so on. The approach in history is to present concepts in American and world history in a way that provides an in-depth study rather than a quick superficial coverage of the topics (McNeil, 1990). These trends recommended by the Bradley Commission are evident in the California scope and sequence for history. According to the Bradley Commission (1988), the social studies curriculum should enable students to develop:

1. Civic responsibility and active civic participation
2. Perspectives on their own life experiences so they see themselves as part of the larger human adventure in time and place
3. A critical understanding of the history, geography, economics, political and social institutions, traditions, and values of the United States as expressed in both their unity and diversity
4. An understanding of other peoples and the unity and diversity of world history, geography, institutions, traditions, and values
5. Critical attitudes and analytical perspectives appropriate to analysis of the human condition (p. 6)

These goals attempt to chart the future course for the social studies curriculum in the secondary school. The social studies curriculum relies heavily on attitudes and values which, as noted by McNeil (1990), get the students thinking about "ecological and political matters" that will be of interest to world citizens in the twenty-first century (p. 352). For example, in Walnut, California, in the eighth grade social studies curriculum, the "We Care" program emphasizes the environment and the political systems of the world (Haskvitz, 1988).

OVERVIEW OF THE SOCIAL STUDIES CURRICULUM FOR GRADES 7 AND 8

The focus of the curriculum during junior high school years is on the knowledge, skills, and ethical behavior that are needed to be an effective, active citizen (Bradley Commission, 1988). The emphasis should be on the social, economic, and political relationships and patterns that exist on the local and national levels. The curriculum includes two courses, one focusing on the local community and the other on the study of the nation. In most states the former is usually a study of that state's history, sociological makeup, and governing structure.

The National Commission on Social Studies (1989) suggests that local or state history be taught as a way of breaking down barriers that exist between the school and the outside world. By taking such an approach, architectural styles, historical census data, old newspaper articles, photographs, and interviews with older adults help students understand their immediate surroundings as well as the entire state.

United States history is usually found in the course inventory at the eighth grade. It traditionally begins with the pilgrims and follows a chronological approach. As recommended by the National Commission on Social Studies (1989), the study of the United States should help develop an understanding of the Constitution along with the amendments that helped shape our country during the last two centuries. It is the time when students learn about the differences between the various forms of government and economic systems. Through a careful analysis of our nation's past comes a greater appreciation and understanding of diverse groups of people living together in different states within one nation governed by a common document of laws. This appreciation and understanding should prepare them to study other peoples and places of the world with new insights.

OVERVIEW OF THE SOCIAL STUDIES CURRICULUM FOR GRADES 9–12

Students in the secondary schools ". . . should have a good grounding in history and government of their own nation, the culture of Europe, and the culture of several nonwestern areas" (Bragaw and Hartoonian, 1988, p. 22). Students should be exposed to many topics and several disciplines within the social studies curriculum. Attention should be given to a balance among American, European, and non-European issues, concerns, and concepts. In the next section, the components of a high school social studies program are described. The National Commission on Social Studies (1989) suggests three specific courses to be taught in grades 9–11. These courses include:

1. World and American History and Geography to 1750
2. World and American History and Geography from 1750 to 1900
3. World and American History and Geography since 1900

It is evident from the titles that geography plays a key role along with history in these three courses. The members of the National Commission believe that history conveys the essential knowledge and geography provides the bridge and context to understanding people, civilizations, ideas, land formations, and so on. For them, history and geography are twin disciplines around which the social studies curriculum can be organized. Teaching history and geography in a single course helps us understand our historical roots within a global community.

In grade 12, the National Commission recommends that two courses, each a semester in length, be taught. These two courses are government and economics and other options within the social studies curriculum (anthropology, sociology, psychology, etc.). It is at this level that students leaving high school should have a grasp of the principles of American government as it relates to the economy. Viewing these two courses as a combined subject, students would examine both political theory as well as economic theory, which would lead to an examination of political and economic behavior. Such an approach places the United States in a comparative framework which would point to the distinctiveness of America and, at the same time, its interdependence when it comes to politics and economic matters.

The social studies curriculum in the secondary school of the future may appear to be a collection of courses and programs, but the common thread or theme is understanding the role of being a citizen in the United States as well as the world. Through the social studies curriculum, students learn to act their parts as responsible members within their individual communities. The *Foxfire* experience, started by Wigginton (1985) in Rabun Gap-Nacoochee School in Rabun, Georgia, has provided an integrated approach to the social studies, that is becoming an integral part of the community. With an added emphasis on participatory government and global education, the social studies curriculum can make a difference in the quality of life in the twenty-first century if students can apply what they have learned in their everyday lives as future voters and citizens and guardians of the planet earth.

COMPONENTS OF THE SOCIAL STUDIES CURRICULUM

History

Of all the disciplines in the social studies curriculum, history receives by far the most attention. The discipline of history will be discussed in greater detail because it serves as an important link to one or more of the other social studies disciplines. History, like geography, is central to understanding and explaining how and why events occurred and why they happened the way they did.

According to the Bradley Commission (1988), the broad field of social studies expanded to include more disciplines yet, ". . . the number of required [high school] courses has declined" (p. 1). Fifteen percent of high school students do not take American history, while only 50 percent take world history. There has been a call since the early 1980s for an academic core that is more substantial and that can be delivered in more varied and imaginative ways. The Bradley Commission's recommendations include the statement that "all children in a democracy . . . deserve the knowledge and understanding that history imparts" (1988, p. 4). The members of the commission believe that "history provides the only avenue we have to reach an understanding of ourselves and our society, in relation to the human condition over time" (1988, p. 5).

History as a discipline, according to many of the leaders in the field, helps students understand and deal with change as they assume adult roles in society. In addition, history contributes to the basic aims of American education, that of preparing for a private life as a public educated citizen within a democratic society. Lastly, history provides the necessary tapestry in which to study other disciplines: geography, the arts, literature, philosophy, economics, and political issues. According to the Bradley Commission (1988), ". . . historical study develops analytical skills, comparative perspectives, and modes of critical judgment that promote thoughtful work in any field or career" (p. 6). For example, history coupled with geography can provide a context of time and place which helps to form the historical tapestry.

The Bradley Commission (1988) adopted several resolutions that recognize the critical value of historical study as a part of the overall education of all Americans. These resolutions include:

1. The study of history is essential for citizens in a democracy and it should be a subject that all students take.
2. The study of history goes beyond simply acquiring useful information, and focuses on broad, significant themes and questions to develop skills in critical judgment and perspective; the memorization of facts without context is short-lived. Historical study should include facts within a context, along with training in critical judgment which is based upon evidence, including original sources.
3. The curricular time for the study of history should be expanded so that a genuine understanding can take place and time is provided to exercise critical judgment.
4. The elementary grades (K–6) should be history-centered.
5. In grades 7–12, at least four years of history should be required.
6. All students should have an understanding of the western world as well as the nonwestern world, that encompasses the peoples of Africa, Asia, the Americas, and Europe.
7. The study of history should include the roles of all constituencies of society which encompasses the history of women and gender issues, racial and ethnic minorities, and men and women of all classes and conditions.
8. At the university level, those certifying in social studies for teaching grades 7–12 should be required to take a substantial program in history (preferably a major, minimally a minor).
9. At the university level, the departments of history should review the structure and content of programs and their suitability for the needs of

prospective teachers, with special attention to the quality of survey courses (world history, western civilization, American history) which are most often taught in the schools.

In addition, the Bradley Commission (1988) identified six vital themes for world history, history of Western civilization, and American history. These themes include:

1. Civilization, cultural diffusion, and innovation
2. Human interaction with the environment
3. Values, beliefs, political ideas, and institutions
4. Conflicts and cooperation
5. Comparative history of major developments
6. Patterns of social and political interaction (pp. 10–11)

The Bradley Commission (1988) identified topics for the study of each of the major history courses in the social studies. These topics can be seen in Table 11.1 (American history) and Table 11.2 (world history). Each of these tables serves as a scope and sequence chart for the history courses in the social studies curriculum in the secondary grades.

Listed in Table 11.1 are several general topics that American history courses typically include. These topics can be presented at the appropriate junior and senior high school levels to accommodate the needs and interests of preadolescents and adolescents. The topic of the American revolution could be treated differently at each level. For example, the complexity of the study of causation could be introduced at the junior high school level, but could be dealt with in greater depth and complexity with students who are juniors in high school.

Table 11.1 GENERAL TOPICS FOR SECONDARY SOCIAL STUDIES CURRICULUM

Grade Level	Subject	Topics
8 and 11	American History	American political democracy
		American revolution, the Declaration of Independence, and U.S. Constitution
		American economy
		Immigration of Europeans
		Cultures that contributed to America and today's society (cultural diversity)
		Civil War and reconstructionism
		Social, ideological, economic, and political institutions
		Role of America in domestic and foreign policy
		American relations with other nations today and historically
		Physical geography
		Family and local history
		New wave of immigrants
		American education
		Issues of equality, individualism, common welfare

Table 11.2 GENERAL TOPICS FOR SECONDARY SOCIAL STUDIES CURRICULUM

Grade Level	Subject	Topics
9	World History	Legacies of Ancient Greece, Rome, Asia, Africa, and Pre-Columbian cultures
		The connections among civilizations
		Origins and ideas of Judaism, Christianity, Buddhism, Islam, Confucianism
		Medieval society, feudalism
		Renaissance, reformation, exploration, colonization
		English Revolution and practices of government
		Enlightenment, scientific revolution of the 17th century, 18th century intellectual revolution
		Development and technology
		American, French, Russian, and Chinese revolutions
		Industrial revolution
		European ideologies of the 19th and 20th centuries
		Decolonization of the 19th century and acceptance/resistance to colonizers' ideas
		World War I and II, and their global impact
		Interdependent world
		Comparative study of selected themes, societies, cultures, art, literature
		Role of geography in history
		Global perspective to shared concerns (economics, diseases, cultures, global warming)

The topics in world history are shown in Table 11.2. Ninth grade students are introduced to several topics ranging from Greco-Roman, Pre-Columbian cultures to the comparative study of shared global concerns. Greco-Roman cultures have long been an integral part of the world history course, but the area of global studies is gaining a prominent position in world history courses as issues of economics, disease, politics, culture, and geography become global in nature.

Geography

The study of geography has gained popularity within the last decade, especially in recent years. Often we see headlines in newspapers that read "Americans Geographically Illiterate." To deal with this lack of knowledge, Grosvenor (1986) advocates geographic education in all grades. He believes that "knowledge of geography is not just a nice idea; it is essential to our well-being as individuals and to our national strength and survival as a world leader . . ." (p. 2).

Geographic education focuses on five central themes. These themes form a part of the guidelines for teaching geography in the schools. The guidelines were prepared by the Joint Committee on Geographic Education (1984). The five themes are:

1. *Location*: position on the earth's surface. This theme helps answer the question "where?" and provides absolute and relative locations using the grid system of latitude and longitude.

2. *Place*: physical and cultural characteristics of the location. The second theme focuses on the special features that distinguish one geographical location from the next. The physical features relate to the topography, climate, vegetation, and geology of a place on earth. The cultural characteristics of a location have to do with the human uniqueness of the location, its economy, beliefs, language system, and politics.

3. *Human-environment interactions*: changing the face of the earth. This theme dealing with interaction helps the students understand the relationships that exist between a place and its habitants over time. Such interactions help students explain how the environment has been modified by humans and/or how they have adapted to it historically. The physical environment poses certain constraints that can limit human activity and people must adjust to these to survive.

4. *Movement*: humans interacting on earth. This theme focuses on the movement of ideas, people, goods, and services. If ideas, people, goods, and services move, questions are raised regarding how they move, why they move, and what encourages movement. These questions help explain how and why places change.

5. *Regions*: how they form and change. Regions have particular unifying characteristics that distinguish them from other places. These unifying characteristics that help define a region include language, governmental structure, and topography.

Table 11.3 lists the five themes that provide the basic structure of the geography curriculum. Whether the concept to learn is the grid system on a map, the route explorers took to find the new world, or the culture of the Middle East, the five fundamental themes form the cornerstone of the lesson. The themes, according to Salter (1989) help students to ". . . make sense of the landscapes of life" (p. 43) and help students deal with the interrelationships that bring places and people together.

Along with the five themes, students learn about geographic inquiry skills, which help them understand the world in which they live. There are four general inquiry skills that students learn: observation, speculation, analysis, and evaluation. These skills help students use the themes in their everyday lives. The skills provide the tools for understanding the geographic themes.

Of all of the disciplines within the social studies, geography is most closely related to history. According to Reinhartz and Reinhartz (1990), "geography is a major causative factor of historical development" (p. 29). They continue by saying that "history has been defined by geographic determinists as nothing more than 'geography over time'" (p. 29). According to the National Commission (1989), history and geography are twin disciplines around which to orga-

Table 11.3 GENERAL TOPICS FOR SECONDARY SOCIAL STUDIES CURRICULUM

Grade level	Subject	Topics

Junior High
Senior High
	Geography	The fundamental five themes:
		1. *Location* (position of people and places)
		   On earth's surface
		   Absolute and relative location
		   Physical features shape the environment
		2. *Place* (physical and human characteristics)
		   Observed characteristics
		3. *Human-Environment Interactions* (humans and environments)
		   Cultural and physical relationships
		   Advantages and disadvantages for human settlement
		   Population densities, environmental planning and management
		4. *Movement* (humans interacting on the earth)
		   Global interdependence
		   Relationships between and among places
		   Interaction of places
		   Movement of product, information, ideas
		   Linkages by transportation and communication lines
		5. *Regions* (state and regional, how they form and change)
		   Uses of regions
		   Unity based on selected criteria (governmental unit, language
		     group, etc.)

Modified from: Joint Committee on Geographic Education. (1984). *Guidelines for geographic education.* Washington, D.C.: Association of American Geographers.

nize the social studies curriculum. In the final analysis, geography is an integral part of the social studies curriculum because it helps students understand why events occur, where they occur, and why some solutions to problems are not feasible, based on the topography, culture, region, and past history.

Geography provides the connection with other humans as well as other places in the world. If world problems are to be solved, ". . . future generations of students need to be connected with their world, and they must have an understanding of geography—location, place, and human environmental interaction—for through it the unity of complex diversity emerges" (Reinhartz and Reinhartz, 1990, p. 85).

Government or Political Science

According to Brody (1989), political science includes the study of politics, government, policy, authority, and power. Government should be a discipline in which everyone is interested because as citizens we are affected by politics and the political process. Students need to understand that their very existence is affected by politics, yet most students, as well as adults, find the study of government remote, confusing, and uninteresting.

According to political scientists, feeling remote and somewhat detached from the political process seems to be a natural consequence of being too involved with one's own daily activities. Americans do not see the connection between politics and what happens in their daily lives; perhaps they have not been taught to see the connection. One way to develop the connection is to provide knowledge that is based on the realities of political life rather than the idealized version. The idealized version provides unrealistic images of human politics that only help create a cynical view of politics, politicians, and the political process. Table 11.4 provides a topic outline of a government course for secondary curriculum.

American government is a required social studies course, as is history. Table 11.4 briefly lists general political science topics, including public policies, political behavior, processes and systems, and political consciousness. The study of these topics should raise the students' political awareness and foster an interest in and commitment to the American political system.

In addition, the government course should include information about the legal structure and the American political system as well as others. Students need to be taught to think critically and distinguish facts and values from jargon and stereotypes. Thinking critically fosters a level of sophistication that encourages students to conceptualize political phenomena. With such a knowledge base and skills to analyze issues and ideas, students learn to deal with diverse opinions, values, and beliefs in a cooperative and collaborative manner (Brody, 1989).

Anthropology

The study of anthropology is a part of the social studies curriculum. Its main focus is the study of people and why and how they differ from other groups of people. Physical characteristics, language spoken, uses of technology, belief systems, and actions in the group form the central core of concerns in the study of anthropology. In effect, anthropologists attempt to explain how groups live and function in the context of their own perspective (White, 1989). Table 11.5 provides an outline of topics commonly found in anthropology courses at the secondary school level.

Table 11.4   GENERAL TOPICS FOR SECONDARY SOCIAL STUDIES CURRICULUM

Grade level	Subject	Topics
12	American Government	Public policies, political institutions, roles, and processes
		Political behavior, processes, and systems
		Governmental institutions and legal structures
		Similarities and differences in political institutions
		Political decisions and policies
		Politics and the role of purposes, ends, and values in human affairs
		Changes in public policy and distribution of power of group interests
		Political consciousness of participating citizens

Table 11.5 GENERAL TOPICS FOR SECONDARY SOCIAL STUDIES CURRICULUM

Grade level	Subject	Topics
Elective 11 and/or 12	Anthropology	Differences among groups of people (physical characteristics, development of language and technology) The study of the concept of culture, society Physical and social development Rise of early/major civilizations and diverse cultures Development of tool making, spread of agriculture, technology Social behavior, religions Examinations of cultural remains, architecture, social systems Cultural contacts and adaptations Human interactions and institutions Cross-cultural studies

High school students can elect to take an anthropology course if it is part of the district's offerings in the social studies curriculum.

Often a case study approach is used to focus on one particular group of people. The case study provides a model that can be used to study other groups of people. According to White, anthropologists use a case study approach to help them ". . . understand what is common about humanity" (1989, p. 31).

There are several subareas of study in anthropology, which include physical anthropology, archeology, cultural anthropology, and anthropological linguistics. Helping students appreciate and understand the uniqueness of different groups is a fundamental goal of anthropology and perhaps is where it makes its greatest contribution in the secondary curriculum, especially in the area of the social studies. Such understanding and appreciation are invaluable as the world continues to get smaller as technology brings people closer together. For Ellison (1960), the study of anthropology helps students understand today's world by understanding themselves.

Economics

According to Hansen (1989), the objectives of economic education are twofold: one is to teach economic analysis and the other economic policy. The fundamental concepts in economics are with us every day — on the news and in the newspapers — and relate to the savings and loan crisis or the supply and demand of oil. Understanding the economy and the basic economic principles is not only taught in economics courses, but can be integrated into the total secondary curriculum (Hansen, 1989).

It is essential that students be cognizant of the consequences of decisions that are made regarding the economy. Whether military bases are closed, subsidies for crops discontinued, or weather conditions changed are events that have an impact on people, goods, and services. When the economic climate changes, citizens make decisions to deal with them. People behave differently and economic and personal goals shift or change. Students need to be able to apply the fundamental concepts to their lives. Without application, economic principles and concepts are remote and abstract. If the content of economic courses is to have an impact on secondary students, then the students must perceive value or usefulness for today or the future. In addition, students need to know how to use the tools of economics: the tables, charts, graphs, and averages.

Economics, usually an elective course, is offered at the high school level as a part of the social studies curriculum. Sometimes it is paired with American government, and each is offered for a semester. Generally, economics concentrates on microeconomics (market economies) and macroeconomics (national economy) concepts. As a part of the curriculum, students learn and use graphing skills as well as learning to read and interpret tables, charts, and ratios. Along with these skills, students functioning in cooperative groups or teams are placed in decision-making roles to deal with economic issues. Table 11.6 provides a composite list of topics presented in a course in economics.

Table 11.6 GENERAL TOPICS FOR SECONDARY SOCIAL STUDIES CURRICULUM

Grade level	Subject	Topics
11 and 12	Economics	Study of goods and services
		Economic policy (system of production and distribution)
		Economic analysis
		Decision making about economic issues
		Economics concepts
		Scarcity
		Productivity
		Economic systems
		Exchange and money systems
		Interdependence
		Microeconomic concepts—market economies
		Markets and prices
		Supply and demand
		Competition
		Role of government
		Failures in the market
		Distribution of income
		Macroeconomics concepts—national economy
		Gross national product
		Unemployment
		Inflation, deflation
		Monetary policy
		Government taxing and spending
		Global economics
		Skills to understand economic principles
		Tables
		Charts
		Graphs
		Ratios
		Percentages

As seen in the table, general economic concepts include the following: scarcity, productivity, economic systems, exchange and money systems, and interdependence.

Sociology and Psychology

Sociology and psychology are two additional social studies electives that were popular during the 1960s and 1970s. With the emphasis on other curricular offerings, these subjects remain but are less popular with secondary students today. The conceptual framework for sociology looks similar to that of the themes of geography. The major concepts that are stressed include culture, socialization processes, consequences of change, dilemmas of freedom and justice, argumentation, and social problems at the national and international levels (Gray, 1989).

Of all the disciplines in the social studies, sociology is the most encyclopedic (Gray, 1989). Sociology is the study of human groups: how they form, how they function, and the resultant problems that develop. The study includes the family, which can be considered the microlevel of behavior. The macrolevel includes the functioning of a total population. Students learn to identify the theoretical generalizations which help explain human behavior in an effort to improve social conditions at the local, regional, national, and international levels (Gray, 1989).

Sociology has subfields which include:

1. Deviance and social control
2. The family
3. Social stratification
4. Education
5. Gerontology

The concepts presented in sociology coupled with those taught in the other social science disciplines help students understand their world.

Psychology, like sociology, is an elective course. There are many ways to teach psychology, but regardless of the approach, the goals are similar. These goals include learning how psychology helps to solve human problems related to how people learn and develop, the concept of personality, cognition and learning, mental health, behavior disorders, and social relationships. In addition to this knowledge, students learn about the scientific method and how it is used in psychological investigations (Baum and Cohen, 1989).

For some, psychology forms a bridge between the natural sciences and social sciences. Although the American Psychological Association recommends that psychology be taught in the secondary schools, there is not a clearly agreed upon curriculum or scope and sequence chart.

TRENDS AND ISSUES IN THE SOCIAL STUDIES CURRICULUM

As cited in the beginning of this chapter, the social studies curriculum is receiving national attention, not only from the general public, but also from social science specialists. These specialists in the field are advocating changes in the content as well as methodologies used. The suggested changes are included in two recent documents. One document, *Charting a Course: Social Studies for the 21st Century*, was prepared by the National Commission on Social Studies in the Schools (1989). The other document, *Building a History Curriculum*, was directed specifically toward history and is the product of the Bradley Commission (1988). In addition, much has been written of late about including geographic and economics education in the secondary schools. For one member of the National Commission on Social Studies the ideal social studies curriculum would follow these general guidelines:

1. The curriculum must be coherent and continuous through the grades.
2. The curriculum must be global in nature to include Western as well as Non-Western cultures and perspectives.
3. The curriculum must include knowledge that instills a love for American institutions.
4. The curriculum must acquaint students with their community as a means of understanding the world (*Education USA*, 1989, p. 66).

Regarding suggested improvements, there are recurring trends that all of the reports and recommendations have in common. These recurring trends include applying social studies content and skills to contemporary society to establish relevancy for students studying particular concepts and topics. If students do not see how it fits into their daily lives, social studies instruction remains remote and esoteric. Just "covering the subject" will no longer meet students' needs or be meaningful in the years to come.

The second trend, which appears in many reports, is the need to help students become informed future citizens. Informed citizens are contributing members of their society and participate in the social and political processes. Take for example, the Traskville Town decision-making activity shown in Figure 11.1. This simulation places the students in decision-making roles similar to those that they may occupy as future voting citizens. The decision revolves around where a highway should be built. The students must consider many options and the ramifications for each option.

Traskville is a town with a problem to solve and a decision to make. A highway is going to be built connecting point A, on one side of Traskville, to point B on the other side. This highway will be a controlled access highway which means that individuals cannot cross the controlled access highway. In addition, motorists cannot get on or off the highway except where exits are provided.

The controlled access highway has been completed by the state to point A and to point B. Now it is time for the state to connect point A and point B. Five well known engineers from the state highway department surveyed three possible

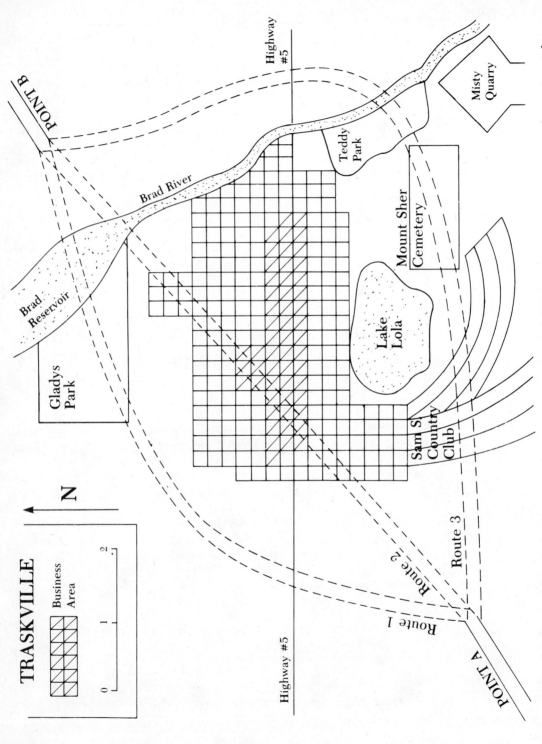

Figure 11.1 The Traskville Town Decision (Source: Trask, J.A. (1990). Arlington, Texas: The University of Texas at Arlington. Mimeographed. Used with permission.)

routes. These are the only possible routes. No other routes may be chosen because these three are the only acceptable routes.

To build the controlled access highway numerous costs must be considered. First, the state has the right to buy any and all property it needs to build the controlled access highway. This is known as Eminent Domain which means that the property owners must sell their land; however, they will receive a fair price. To purchase the property on Route 1 will cost the state $520,000. To purchase the property on Route 2 will cost the state $5,100,000. To purchase the property on Route 3 will cost the state $2,200,000. The previous figures represent the cost to purchase the land on which the highway will be built. To actually build the highway will cost an additional $900,000 per mile. On each route a bridge must be built across the river. The bridge on Route 1 would cost $5,000,000 since it would be built across the reservoir. The bridge on Route 2 would be built across the base of the dam and would cost $1,300,000. The bridge on Route 3 would cost only $900,000. The Route 3 bridge is the least expensive to build; however, if Route 3 is chosen then Mount Sher Cemetery must be moved. This move would cost about $500,000.

Additional cost considerations must be analyzed in order to make a route decision. If a particular route is going to have an exit then it will cost an additional $650,000 per exit. Each exit will provide an on and off ramp on each side of the highway. The state highway department has allocated an absolute maximum amount that they will contribute to the building of this highway. That amount is $9,400,000, which includes the exit and all other costs.

Financial costs are not the only consideration in the route decision. Every route has problems, other than financial, associated with its construction. Route 1 would take up farm land and farmers may not want to sell their land; however, they would have to sell due to Eminent Domain. The location of Route 1 would go through and destroy most of Gladys Park. This is the most popular entertainment area in the town of Traskville. A large town fair is held annually in Gladys Park and the only baseball diamond in town is located here. Gladys Park also represents one of the few picnic areas in Traskville. Therefore, Gladys Park is an extremely important recreation spot for the town of Traskville.

Route 2 will cut through the center of town. About twelve blocks of the main business area will have to be torn down and relocated in some other part of the town. Route 2 will also go through part of the slum area of Traskville. The slum area contains a lot of old, low rent apartments and some old, small homes. The people who live in this area of town are poor and cannot afford to live in any other part of Traskville. If Route 2 is chosen then a decision must be made about what to do with these people.

Route 3 will go through the Sam S. Country Club area and totally destroy the golf course. This entire area is relatively new and very pretty. Only the wealthy, influential people of Traskville live in the country club area. Another large concern of Route 3 is that it will go through Mount Sher Cemetery which means the cemetery would have to be moved if this route is chosen. About 70 percent of the people of Traskville are Catholic, and Mount Sher Cemetery is a Catholic cemetery. The rest of the residents of Traskville come from various different religious backgrounds and use a cemetery on the far south side of the city. The Catholics of Traskville are extremely upset about the prospect of the cemetery being relocated. They do not think that it is right or proper for the cemetery to be moved. Most of the other 30 percent of the Traskville citizens do not care about this one way or other; however, it has made the Catholics very rebellious and angry. In addition to the cemetery issue Route 3 will also go through Teddy Park, a nice little park along the river where many citizens of Traskville go for picnics.

Traskville has one claim to fame which is their tourist attraction called Settler's Village. It is located just to the north of Lake Lola and is a very popular attraction. People come from all over the country to see this re-creation of a settler's village from the 1860s. The businesses that profit most from Settler's Village are the motel, hotel, and restaurant owners; however, many other businesses profit from its existence. The business owners of Traskville believe that the new highway will bring more tourists and visitors than ever before. They argue, however, that it is necessary, regardless of the route chosen, that an exit be placed in Traskville so that tourists and visitors will stop at Settler's Village. If no exit is built in Traskville then visitors would have to leave the highway 18 miles down the road and then come into Traskville on old highway number 5. Once they reached Traskville, they would have to go another 18 miles on the other side of town to get back on the highway. In addition, old highway 5 is in relatively poor condition.

All possible routes have problems associated with their selection. You need to weigh all of the opportunity costs and choose one of the routes. There is no correct answer and if you go over the budget allocated by the government you will need to propose how you would raise the additional needed funds.

As the simulation illustrates, students are capable of making decisions on critical issues by using critical thinking skills and the data presented. The need to have students begin early to become involved in their communities in the various social processes is critical to their development as responsible, informed citizens.

The third trend that emerges in the social studies curriculum is helping students view their world in a global context. Some schools are including the study of world history as a component within American history. Current affairs from around the world also are included as reinforcement for topics under consideration. Passow (1989) proposes a global curriculum that will nurture commitment to a world society and believes that topics such as peace education, intercultural studies, thinking and valuing skills, world problems, as well as moral and ethical dimensions should be included in such a curriculum. Bebensee and Evans (1990) suggest that history should move beyond the classroom and into the world and describes a project that immerses students in a conflict simulation that demonstrates the complex dynamics of international reality. Kniep (1989) presents a scope and sequence for social studies grounded in global education. It includes: (1) the study of systems, (2) the study of human values, (3) the study of persistent global issues, and (4) the study of global history. Infusing a global perspective into the social studies curriculum will help future citizens feel a part of the greater whole, the entire world.

The fourth trend that is mentioned in the reports focuses on instructional methods or approaches that teachers should use when teaching history, geography, government, or anthropology. For example, to learn more about monastic life during the Middle Ages in western Europe, the students can read all or parts of *The Name of the Rose* by Umberto Eco. Students can then assume the role of a guide, adventurer, or newspaper reporter and describe their travels. These roles help students use critical thinking, and analytical and evaluation skills. In addition to role playing and simulations, other trends involve the recording of history, especially through the oral tradition, by having students interview people regarding events and issues. These approaches, along with fresh ideas, will excite students and encourage them to want to learn about their economy, government, society, and world.

Developing skills of inquiry, analysis, and evaluation has become a cornerstone for studying all of the social studies disciplines. This final trend encourages students to be active participants in the learning process; when using these skills students learn and practice the art of decision making, drawing conclusions, framing generalizations, and making comparisons. These skills help students cover social studies content in greater depth and from many different disciplinary vantage points. Such skills are invaluable to students as they assume adult roles. As future citizens they will be called upon to vote on an issue that may affect millions of people in the United States and perhaps the world.

These trends of relevancy, becoming an informed citizen, infusion of a global perspective, exposure to varied ideas and approaches, and the development of skills and processes should distinguish the social studies curriculum of the 1990s. The various members of the two commissions recognized the need to have students keep pace with the development of technology. Since technology allows people to be closer in time and space, students need to understand different opinions held by others who live thousands of miles away and who have different beliefs, value systems, culture, religion, language, and economic and political structure. Students, for example, even if they are living in Florida, cannot ignore the needs and concerns of their fellow students in Oregon because of what is found in a newspaper or on a news program. This principle holds true for those living in Germany or Jordan.

Using technology in the classroom can help students understand and appreciate the role of inflation in today's economy and the impact of a natural disaster in any part of the world. In addition, technology helps the students to gain a broader understanding of their world as well as understand the cultural, political, and environmental challenges on a daily basis (Grosvenor, 1989). In addition, computer simulations, such as *USA Geograph* and *World Geograph*, provide ". . . versatile, easy-to-use visual geographic data bases, consisting of map projections . . . and comparisons can be made between states, countries, and regions by manipulating the data graphically (Reinhartz and Reinhartz, 1990, p. 80). Other computer simulations include the famous *The Oregon Trail* from Minnesota Educational Computing Consortium, the *Rivers and Ancient Cultures* from the Teach Yourself series by Computer Software, and *Malthus* from Albion. These programs introduce the students to demography, the linkage with population growth, food supplies, and nonrenewable resources.

Mocium (1989) provides another example of how technology helps students learn about another part of the world. Using telecommunications, these students tracked a cargo ship bound for Japan. Students located in California received daily weather reports from the ship along with its position using the coordinates given. In addition, these students had an opportunity to talk to their peers in Japan. From this experience, students learned first hand where Japan is located, and they could decide for themselves what it would be like traveling across the Pacific Ocean in a cargo ship.

Taken together, these trends and the use of technology provide a social studies curriculum that is timely and meaningful. The materials may include historical census data, old newspaper articles, and/or photographs. The approaches might include role playing, simulations, computer and board games, as well as reading short stories about different cultural or ethnic groups, and participating in meetings to discuss local, state, national, and international issues. Varying the instruction when teaching social studies creates enthusiasm and interest when studying history, geography, economics, and so on.

These experiences help students to develop a sense of citizenship. If hands-on, minds-on approaches are used, the time honored social studies curriculum focusing on names, dates, and places will give way to a curriculum that is driven by content and which is integrative in nature, and that emphasizes skills that are needed for an enriched life. Becker (1990) reports that in a recent survey, 80 percent of the school principals reported weekly or daily use of fact drills while discussion was used less frequently, only 68 percent of the time. If the trends focus on broader, more interdisciplinary content and process skills, then special attention needs to be given to how to evaluate these end products. Drills and low level cognitive questions will no longer accurately measure what has been taught and learned.

If students are to live satisfying and productive lives as future citizens, then fresh ideas and approaches are needed. In light of recent efforts, the social studies curriculum for the secondary grades in the 1990s will be more interdisciplinary, more coherent, and more cohesive, with history and geography forming the core. In the final analysis, the major objective of the social studies curriculum in the secondary schools will be to help students gain a sense of today's world for tomorrow's living. The curriculum as described will encourage teachers to think in broader terms and to overcome a curriculum being criticized for being too general. With the help of these reports there is great hope that by the year 2000 a different social studies curriculum will be taught in the secondary schools.

SUMMARY

Chapter 11 began with an overview of the social studies curriculum in the secondary schools. The social studies curriculum includes several disciplines: history, geography, government, anthropology, economics, sociology, and psychology. The overview provided a brief historical account of the social studies curriculum during the past 70 years, beginning with the work of the National Education Association's Committee in the 1930s and ending with the work of two national commissions in the late 1980s. It is evident from the brief historical account that attempts to reform the social studies curriculum have not yet been accomplished. In fact, these attempts have failed because previous goals for reform were unclear and the vision of what should be was not coherent.

However, the work done recently by the National Commission on Social Studies in the Schools and the Bradley Commission has charted a course for the future. These commissions advocate a social studies curriculum that will help students meet the challenges of the next century as citizens of both the United States and the world.

In addition, the chapter described the recommendations found in each report. The specific recommendations generated by each commission regarding the content to be taught and the skills to be developed are included. The Bradley Commission focuses almost exclusively on history, viewing it as the kingpin discipline within the social studies curriculum. The National Commission deals with all the disciplines within the social studies, first collectively and then individually. These documents are mentioned several times throughout the chapter.

The next section of the chapter described the social studies curriculum in the junior and senior high schools. After a general overview, the goals of the social studies curriculum were presented along with the major concepts. The components of the social studies curriculum section provided a general outline for each of the content areas. The chapter concluded with a discussion of the major trends that are influencing the development of the social studies curriculum for the 1990s. These trends include relevancy, being an informed citizen, infusing a global perspective, and using a variety of materials and approaches in instruction. These trends should produce a social studies curriculum that looks different from the emphasis on memorization of people, places, and dates.

YOUR TURN

11.1 Obtain a copy of a recent history textbook (or any other discipline in the social studies curriculum) and review the organization of concepts. For example, what are the general patterns:
   (a) Chronological order: How is it sequenced? By time? By topic?
   (b) Cause and effect: Are relationships stressed? What viewpoints are included? Are students encouraged to make decisions?
   (c) Compare and contrast: Are there opportunities to compare and contrast and to validate for accuracy and/or bias?
   (d) Higher order skills: Are students encouraged to make inferences, draw conclusions, use evaluative thinking?

11.2 Take the topic of prehistoric cultures (or any other topic in the social studies curriculum mentioned in the chapter) and develop a matrix to help students organize what they already know and what they still need to know.
   Step 1: Begin with a semantic map and record all of the information that you know about this concept. Put the major concept in the center of a sheet of paper (e.g., prehistoric cultures) and draw lines out with ideas that come to mind. See the example that follows.

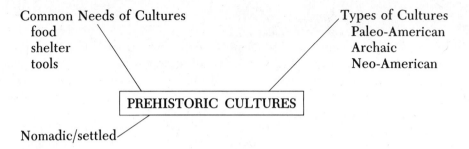

Common Needs of Cultures
   food
   shelter
   tools

Types of Cultures
   Paleo-American
   Archaic
   Neo-American

PREHISTORIC CULTURES

Nomadic/settled

Step 2: Research the topics and add more information to your semantic map (or correct items that are incorrect).

Step 3: Organize the information in your map into a matrix or grid; now it is your turn to determine what is needed.

11.3 You want students to develop analytical and group skills. You pose a dilemma, such as "Are wars inevitable?" and have the students develop an argument for their positions. Use the following t-chart as a way to focus on their argument.

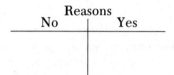

Reasons

No | Yes

References

Baum, C.G. & Cohen, I.S. (1989). Psychology and the social science curriculum. In *Charting a course: Social studies for the 21st century*. National Commission on Social Studies in the Schools. Washington, D.C.: National Council for the Social Studies, 65–69.

Beard, C. (1938). *The nature of the social sciences*. New York: Scribner's Sons.

Bebensee, L. & Evans, M. (Winter 1990). Interacting with the world: Moving history beyond the classroom. *History and Social Science Teacher*, 25, 2, 71–77.

Becker, H.J. (February 1990). Curriculum and instruction in middle grade schools. *Phi Delta Kappan*, 71, 8, 450–453.

Beckner, W. & Cornett, J.D. (1972). *The secondary school curriculum: Content and structure*. Scranton, Pa.: Intext Educational Publishers.

Bradley Commission on History in Schools. (1988). *Building a history curriculum: Guidelines for teaching history in schools*. Washington, D.C.: Educational Excellence Network.

Bragaw, D.H. & Hartoonian, H.M. (1988). *Content of the curriculum: 1988 ASCD yearbook*. Alexandria, Va.: Association for Supervision and Curriculum Development.

Brody, R.A. (1989). Why study politics? In *Charting a course: Social studies for the 21st century*. National Commission on Social Studies in the Schools. Washington, D.C.: National Council for the Social Studies, 59–63.

Education USA. (October 30, 1989). Social studies must stress global ed., 32, 9, 66.

Ellison, J. (1960). Anthropology brings human nature into the classroom. *Social Education, 24*, 327–328.

Gray, P.S. (1989). Sociology. In *Charting a course: Social studies for the 21st century*. National Commission on Social Studies in the Schools. Washington, D.C.: National Council for the Social Studies, 71–75.

Grosvenor, G.M. (November 1989). The call for geography education. *Educational Leadership, 47*, 3, 29–32.

Grosvenor, G.M. (September 1986). Geographic education and global understanding. *NASSP Curriculum Report*. Reston, Va.: National Association of Secondary School Principals.

Hansen, W.L. (1989). Economics. In *Charting a course: Social studies for the 21st century*. National Commission on Social Studies in the Schools. Washington, D.C.: National Council for the Social Studies, 37–41.

Haskvitz, A. (1988). A middle school program that can change society. *Phi Delta Kappan, 70*, 2, 175–178.

Hertzberg, H.W. (1981). Social Studies reform—1880–1980. *A report of project SPAN*. Boulder, Colo.: Social Science Education Consortium.

Joint Committee on Geographic Education (1984). *Guidelines for geographic education*. Washington, D.C.: Association of American Geographers.

Kniep, W.M. (October 1989). Social studies within a global education. *Social Education, 53*, 6, 399–403.

McFarland, M. (February 1990). Quoted in Who needs the social studies? The case for the social studies in the elementary school curriculum. *Instructor, 99*, 6, 37–44.

McNeil, J. (1990). *Curriculum: A comprehensive introduction*. New York: Scott Foresman.

Mocium, T. (November 1989). Geography by cargo ship. *Educational Leadership, 47*, 3, 34–36.

National Commission on Social Studies in the Schools. (1989). *Charting a course: Social studies for the 21st century*. Washington, D.C.: National Council for the Social Studies.

Parker, W.C. (April 1988). Restoring history to social studies—had it ever left? *Educational Leadership, 47*, 7, 86–87.

Passow, A.H. (1989). Designing a global curriculum. *Gifted Education International, 6*, 2, 68–70.

Reinhartz, D. & Reinhartz, J. (1990). Geography across the curriculum. Washington, D.C.: National Education Association.

Salter, C. (1989). Geography. In *Charting a course: Social studies for the 21st century*. National Commission on Social Studies in the Schools. Washington, D.C.: National Council for the Social Studies, 43–47.

Trask, J.A. (1990). The traskville town decision. Arlington, TX.: The University of Texas at Arlington. Mimeographed.

White, J.J. (1989). Anthropology. In *Charting a course: Social studies for the 21st century*. National Commission on Social Studies in the Schools. Washington, D.C.: National Council for the Social Studies, 31–36.

Wigginton, E. (1985). *Sometimes a shining moment: The foxfire experience*. New York: Doubleday.

Chapter
12

The English Language Arts Curriculum

*T*he English language arts curriculum continues to be one of the most important subject areas in the secondary curriculum and receives a lot of attention from the general public and citizens as well as Boyer (1983) notes, "The first curriculum priority is language. . . . Language provides the connecting tissue that binds society together, allowing us to express feelings and ideas and powerfully influence the attitudes of others" (p. 85). In the English language arts area, students explore the values and events reflected in the literature and history of the past and learn how to write the future. Whether students approach the study of this curricular area through (1) usage and/or semantics, (2) reading of traditional and contemporary literature, (3) production of media (films and videotapes), (4) speaking, listening, and/or writing of language, (5) in other content areas, or (6) as a way of perceiving, knowing, learning, and becoming, they acquire knowledge, skills, values, attitudes, and habits that will help them be successful adults and contributing members of society (Tchudi and Mitchell, 1989; Hipple, 1973).

Although English language arts is a relatively young curriculum area, just over 100 years old (McNeil, 1990), its importance can be seen in the fact that it is the only content area that is normally required of secondary students from grade 7 through grade 12. Perhaps as a result of this emphasis, no other area of the curriculum receives as much criticism or blame. It becomes a media story when test scores reveal that students cannot read and write. As Trump and Miller (1973) note,

> College teachers complain of poor preparation . . . in secondary schools. High school teachers contend they . . . spend too much time teaching things that ought to have been mastered in the elementary grades. This leaves only the parents and elementary teachers to blame when some [students] use their native tongue improperly (p. 62).

In spite of the criticism, the importance of this curriculum area cannot be overstated. Beckner and Cornett (1972) have observed that the English language arts area will, as it has in the past, shape the future of mankind through its effect on human thought and behavior; language largely determines our ability to live with ourselves and with each other. It is through spoken and written language that our cultural roots are recorded and passed from one generation to another.

The English language arts curriculum has become the core of American secondary education. According to the National Council of Teachers of English (1982), "The study of English includes knowledge of the language itself, development of its use as a basic means of communication, and appreciation of its artistry as expressed in literature" (p. 2). The skills of reading, writing, speaking, listening, and observing are integral parts of the English language arts curriculum. As Beckner and Cornett (1972) note, this curriculum area ". . . helps students understand and use the system of symbols, gestures, and sounds . . . to communicate by means of the spoken and written word" (p. 308).

In their brochure *Essentials of English*, the National Council of Teachers of English (1982) identifies the following major areas to be included in the total English language arts curriculum:

1. Language
2. Literature
3. Communication skills
   a. Reading
   b. Writing
   c. Speaking
   d. Listening
   e. Using media
4. Thinking skills
   a. Creative
   b. Logical
   c. Critical

This chapter provides a historical perspective on the English language arts curriculum area and elaborates on each of the areas listed above as integral parts of the curriculum in the secondary school. These skills will be discussed as a part of the goals of the language arts curriculum. In addition, the chapter provides a general overview and scope and sequence for the English language arts curriculum in grades 7 – 12 and ends with a discussion of the current trends and issues related to this content area.

HISTORY OF THE ENGLISH LANGUAGE ARTS CURRICULUM

As indicated earlier in Chapter 2, English first became a part of the secondary school curriculum in the English grammar schools in the 1700s and then was required in the academies that developed in the 1800s. After 1850, during the latter part of the 1800s, English was divided into a number of subjects that included rhetoric, oratory, spelling, reading, composition, and literary history. It was not until decades later, near the turn of the century that these courses were combined into a single course of English language arts (McNeil, 1990).

In the early 1900s, the college preparatory nature of the English curriculum shaped or determined the content for the courses. The core of the curriculum was the reading of classics in literature and the study of grammar. The typical program of studies included reading selections from literature or delivering book reports, spelling and vocabulary drill, composition, and testing (Beckner and Cornett, 1972). By the 1920s, efforts were successful in modifying the English language arts curriculum and the college preparatory aspect was deemphasized. Functional English skills were identified that were shown to be beneficial to people in a variety of situations (social, academic, and work) and as a result, an experience-based curriculum in English was adopted. This curriculum focused on functional instruction in speaking and writing and promoted creative expression as well. This practical aspect of English was carried forward through the 1930s and 1940s, when further modifications were made to meet the changing needs of adolescents. Topics such as family life, international relations, and daily living were a part of the English curriculum (McNeil, 1990).

As noted previously, the launching of the Sputnik in the 1950s created a "back to the basics" movement in the English language arts curriculum. McNeil (1990) observes that there was a reaffirmation of the college preparatory role of English, high schools began to model their courses after colleges, and there was an emphasis on "intensive reading, the Great Books, and literary rather than personal pursuits" (p. 342). In summarizing the trends in the English language arts curriculum of this era, Trump and Miller (1973) have concluded that

> . . . the high school English curriculum has made at least two radical changes in half a century. The "activity" or "experience-centered" programs of the thirties and forties, and the communication theory of semantics of the early fifties. . . . But basically these changes were superficial, since the teaching of English . . . continued to be patterned after Latin. . . . Even today . . . students begin their study of English . . . by learning an almost identical list of parts of speech (p. 63).

The many social factors that impacted the curriculum during the 1960s and 1970s also had an effect on the English language arts curriculum. In an effort to meet the individual needs and interests of students during this period, the emphasis in the curriculum changed from a college preparatory nature to a more contemporary approach and view of the content. In literature, there was a move away from the traditional approach to topical or themetic units and the inclusion of contemporary and black authors. As McNeil (1990) notes, a theme like justice was addressed by a variety of authors—poets, playwrights, and novelists—and reading literature was more important than reading reviews and critiques of literature.

The English language arts curriculum of today represents a compromise between the contemporary emphasis of the 1960s and 1970s and the traditional college preparatory approach of earlier times. Curriculum specialists in English continue to debate whether the program of studies should emphasize the great works of literature or focus on contemporary topics that are of immediate interest to high school students. The solution has been to include both traditional and contemporary units of study and select themes that reflect the universal aspects of the human situation. English language arts courses, then, use selections from traditional and modern British and American literature, folklore, and mythology to illustrate the theme of the unit (McNeil, 1990).

While the chapter closes with a detailed discussion of current trends and issues, it should be noted here that new approaches to language arts instruction which integrate reading, writing, speaking, and listening have been incorporated within this more traditional approach. As Jensen and Roser (1990) note, teachers are finding support in promising research which focuses on connections among the language arts areas and "many teachers are creating literacy-learning environments in which students' uses of reading and writing are inseparable" (p. 7). The connection between the language arts and other subjects can be seen in the writing across the curriculum movement, which emphasizes the writing process in all subject areas and is discussed in more detail later in the chapter. If the current trend continues, the English language arts classrooms of the next decade, indeed the next century, will be characterized by an integrated or unified curriculum that builds not only on reading and writing skills simultaneously, but incorporates other dimensions, such as speaking, listening, and thinking critically as well.

GOALS OF THE ENGLISH LANGUAGE ARTS CURRICULUM

The English language arts curriculum focuses on the study of language itself, the development of the use of language as a way of communicating, and the appreciation of the artistry expressed in literature. Skills essential to success in the English language arts area include: (1) reading, (2) writing, (3) speaking, (4) listening, and (5) observing. While the development of these skills occurs over a lifetime, they are a central part of secondary school instruction. The National Council of Teachers of English (1982) has identified goals and general objectives for students in each of the skill areas. These goals are presented below. Regardless of the specific course, these skill areas should be an integral part of the secondary school language arts curriculum.

Language By studying language, students should be able to:

1. Describe how the English language has evolved and how it continues to change and develop
2. Explain how differences in English usage are influenced by social, cultural, and geographical factors
3. Describe how language can be used as a powerful tool for thinking and learning
4. Explain how grammar makes meaningful communication possible through structure and orderliness
5. Identify ways that context (topic, purpose, and audience) affects the structure and use of language
6. Describe the role of language as a unifying force in society

Literature Students, through their study and enjoyment of literature, should be able to:

1. Identify and describe how literature serves as a mirror of human experience, reflecting values, motives, conflicts, and behaviors
2. Identify with fictional characters as a way of relating to others and, in doing so, gain understanding and insights about people through literature
3. Recognize a variety of important writers from diverse backgrounds and identify masterpieces of literature, both past and present
4. Discuss, both orally and in writing, the unique features of various forms of literature
5. Identify the rhythms and aesthetic dimensions of language expressed in various forms of literature
6. Develop reading habits that sustain a lifelong love of reading

Reading Students, through reading, should be able to:

1. Describe how reading serves as an academic function (acquisition of knowledge) as well as an aesthetic function
2. Develop the ability to search for meaning and use the appropriate reading skills, when reading a variety of forms of literature, to comprehend the meaning presented
3. Read accurately and make inferences while also judging literature critically based on personal response and literary quality

Writing   Through the study and expression of writing students should be able to:

1. Write clearly and honestly
2. Describe the ways that writing provides opportunities to develop personally as well as communicate with others
3. Generate ideas for writing, select and arrange them, determine the best or most appropriate way to express the ideas, and evaluate, edit, and revise what is written
4. Modify or adapt written expression for various audiences
5. Develop writing techniques and skills that will allow students to appeal to others and persuade them to a point of view
6. Use writing as an outlet for imaginative and creative expression
7. Develop skills and precision in the use of punctuation, capitalization, spelling, and other elements of manuscript form as a part of being an effective writer

Speaking   By being involved in the expression of ideas by speaking to others, students should be able to:

1. Speak clearly and expressively about ideas and concerns
2. Adapt words and strategies according to the audience and the situation (one-on-one versus a large group)
3. Participate productively and effectively in large and small group discussions
4. Present arguments in a rational, orderly, and convincing way and interpret and assess various kinds of communication (intonation, pause, gesture, and body language)

Listening   Students, while demonstrating good listening skills during instruction, should be able to:

1. Listen with the intent to determine the speaker's purpose
2. Attend to details and describe their function in the overall communication process
3. Evaluate the messages and effects of mass communication

Use of Media   Students should use media in such a way that they will be able to:

1. Describe the impact of technology on the communication process and identify ways that electronic communication modes (recordings, film, television, videotape, and computers) require special skills to understand
2. Describe ways that new modes of communication require new kinds of literacy

Creative, Logical, and Critical Thinking Skills   Students, by using thinking skills, should be able to:

1. Recognize and describe elements of originality and inventiveness
2. Describe critical characteristics of creative thinking (i.e., being able not only to look, but to see; not only to hear, but to listen)
3. Think logically by creating hypotheses and predictions
4. Test the validity of an assertion by generating and testing the data or evidence
5. Construct logical sequences and recognize the conclusions that are evident
6. Detect fallacies in reasoning
7. Ask questions that will assist in discovering meaning
8. Differentiate between subjective and objective viewpoints, and separate fact from opinion
9. Evaluate intentions and analyze the message to determine attempts to manipulate the language in order to deceive
10. Make judgments based on criteria that are supported with facts and data and can be explained

An example of the integration of these skills in a language arts curriculum can be seen in the program developed at the Oyster River Middle School in Durham, New Hampshire. According to Rief (1990), by using a portfolio approach in the development and assessment of language skills, teachers get to know their students not only as readers and writers, but as thinkers and human beings. Students, in developing their language arts portfolios ". . . choose what they write, what they read, and what they need to work on in order to get better at both" (p. 27). As teachers interact with them, students develop speaking and listening skills in the conferencing process. As students read, write, and edit, they develop their basic English language arts skills. Historically, the development of creative, logical, and critical thinking skills has not been a stated goal of the language arts curriculum. However, in this middle school program, as students read and critique their own work, they are called upon not only to create, but to logically and critically analyze their efforts and make recommendations for areas of improvement.

This program at the middle school illustrates how the goals and objectives of the National Council of Teachers of English, as described in the skill areas, can be integrated and implemented at the classroom level and how the goals can serve as the primary focus of the secondary English language arts curriculum. As noted by the National Council of Teachers of English (1982), "Language is . . . basic to learning in all disciplines. Skillful use of language may be the single most important means of realizing the overarching goal of education to develop informed, thinking citizens" (p. 1).

OVERVIEW OF THE ENGLISH LANGUAGE ARTS CURRICULUM FOR GRADES 7–12

For students to be successful in and out of the classroom, they must be competent users of the language. The spiral curriculum of the English language arts area attempts to integrate all of the skills previously discussed into a total instructional program. In order to do this, the English language arts curriculum deals with language in all of its manifestations: literature, grammar, composition, speaking, listening, reading, and visual communications. The curriculum overview for the English language arts area reflects this integrated approach and all of the various components.

English language arts courses, which are offered at the high school level, are varied and cover many topics. The courses listed below are representative of the different kinds of language arts courses that high schools sometimes offer, usually on a semester basis, with the exception of English I–IV.

English I–IV   This is the traditional sequence of English courses intended for students preparing for college or work after graduation. This is the most typical course structure that incorporates many of the skills previously identified in the goals and objectives section.

Reading Improvement   This course is designed to assist secondary students who have limited reading ability. The emphasis is to develop competency in reading skills and apply these reading skills to a variety of situations, such as catalogs, encyclopedias or other reference books; popular novels and writing; newspapers and magazines; and tables, charts, and graphs within a printed context.

Research and Technical Writing   This course is designed to prepare students to write research papers and technical reports. The course emphasizes the fundamentals of research, locating sources of information, note taking, and organizing and structuring information and materials. Students then practice putting their results into appropriate formats, such as outlines, footnotes, bibliographies, quotations, papers, and reports.

Creative/Imaginative Writing   This course is designed to help students develop the fundamental principles of creative writing, such as suspense, proportion, structure, contrast, and repetition for emphasis. Students read and analyze examples of each genre of literature and then attempt to develop a personal style in one or more genres. In doing so, students are encouraged to experiment with various literary devices, imagery, and figurative language, as well as writing from different points of view.

Humanities/Human Condition   This course is designed to explore the nature of artistic creativity, the various forms of artistic expression, and the influence of cultural and historical movements on this expression. Students explore themes common in art forms through history and compare and contrast points of view. Although the course emphasizes imaginative literature and its relationship to other fine arts, it also gives students an opportunity for self-expression in an other-than-literary form.

Visual Media   This course is designed to give students information about and tools for analysis of two dimensions of contemporary life: movies and television. The course covers the history of films and television, the purposes and techniques used in film and television, the relationship of this medium to other arts, and criteria for analyzing and evaluating these media. Students examine the way image and sound are used to create an effect similar to that which language (oral and written) creates.

Speech Communication   This course focuses on skill development that begins with an understanding of the communication process in general and continues through interpersonal communication within small-group interactions to public speaking. The course develops competencies and skills that make students effective and responsible senders and receivers of messages on various levels of communication.

Debate   This course stresses the development of competencies and skills in research, analysis of public issues, formulation of various logical positions on issues, construction of logical arguments to support positions, and refutation and defense of an argument. Students examine a variety of debate formats and styles used in a public forum, focusing on the ethical considerations and constraints of the presentation of the argument.

Journalism   This course is designed for students interested in journalistic writing. After reviewing significant historical events in American print journalism, students examine all aspects of publications production, from fact-gathering to graphic design. The course helps students to recognize and use journalistic style in the writing of news, features, and editorials. They also practice techniques of copy editing, proofreading, and headline writing.

These specialized courses represent the variety of English language arts curriculum opportunities for secondary students. Some schools require that students take at least two years of traditional English and then allow them to choose courses like those listed above from a list of offerings. Generally speaking, most schools deliver the curriculum in a traditional, integrated fashion (English I–IV) rather than a specialized segmented approach. The content for this approach focuses on four different areas, which include: (1) purpose and form of language; (2) art of language in speaking, listening, and writing; (3)

grammar and semantics as an organizational structure; and (4) conventions or mechanics of language, such as usage, handwriting, and spelling. At the junior high or middle school level, students seldom have options regarding the English language arts curriculum. Students in the seventh and eighth grades follow the traditional course format. The scope and sequence outline for the traditional, integrated English language arts curriculum for grades 7–12 is presented in Table 12.1.

As seen in Table 12.1, the essential elements or key concepts for the English language arts area include: writing concepts and skills, language concepts and skills, literature concepts and skills, reading concepts and skills, and speaking and listening concepts and skills. The scope and sequence of the English language arts curriculum allow students to progress at rates parallel to their cognitive and affective development. As they progress through each sequence, they build on previously learned skills and experiences.

TRENDS AND ISSUES IN THE ENGLISH LANGUAGE ARTS CURRICULUM

One of the dominant trends in the English language arts curriculum in recent years has been the use of computers to promote writing. Because of the emphasis that society is placing on the use of technology, especially computers, this approach to writing instruction seems appropriate. Research, however, has produced some mixed data regarding the value of computers in the classroom. Some data suggest that the computers produce little difference in writing quality when compared with conventional means, while other data suggest a marked improvement in the quality of work done using the word processing capabilities of the personal computer. Perhaps the greatest benefits derived from the use of the computer are the increased motivation and the capability of students to go back and edit their work in a less painful way. Not only are students more willing to attempt a writing assignment, they are also more willing to correct and improve their work (Hawisher, 1989).

According to Cronin, Meadows, and Sinatra (1990), the integration of computers, reading, and writing has "provided an avenue to improve students' reading comprehension, writing proficiency, and computer application" (p. 57). In the Moss Point, Mississippi schools, students learn, through the use of structured computer programs, how to embed information within a meaningful whole and how to use the computer and writing skills as important tools in all subjects. While the outcome cannot be predicted with certainty regarding the effectiveness of computers in improving students' writing because of the mixed research data, the word processing capability does seem to make a difference in the motivational and editing level of students in the classroom.

Another trend in the English language arts curriculum involves the teaching of writing in combination with reading to prompt more critical thinking which writing or reading alone cannot produce. Critical thinking skills are

Table 12.1 SCOPE AND SEQUENCE CHART
English Language Arts

Essential Elements	Grade 7	Grade 8	English I	English II	English III	English IV
Writing concepts and skills	Use the composing process to plan and generate writing		Use the composing process to plan and generate writing			
	Synthesize information from several sources	Demonstrate clear and logical thinking in support and development of a central idea	Write multiple-paragraph compositions incorporating information from sources other than personal experience	Write multiple-paragraph compositions incorporating outside information with documentation	Write longer compositions Incorporating outside information with documentation	→
	Write for a variety of purposes and audiences	→	Write descriptive, narrative, and expository paragraphs	Write descriptive, narrative, and expository paragraphs of increasing length and complexity	Write a variety of forms of Informative and persuasive discourse	→
			Write informative discourse of a variety of types	↑		
			Write persuasive discourse of a variety of types	↑		
				Write literary discourse of a variety of types including character sketches, stories	Write at least one form of literary discourse	→
	Use formal and informal language appropriately	Edit for clarity of language, appropriate word choice, and effective sentences	Evaluate content organization, topic development, appropriate transition, clarity of language, and appropriate word and sentence choice accord-		Revise written work for content, organization, topic development, appropriate transition, clarity of language, and appropriate word and sen-	→
	Substitute specific words for general words					

258

Use direct quotations from written and oral sources

Avoid cliches and trite expressions

Evaluate the content and organization of one's own writing as well as that of others

ing to the purpose and audience for which the piece is intended

tence choice according to the purpose and audience for which a piece is written

Refine sentences and paragraphs into compositions exhibiting unity, clarity, and coherence

Evaluate one's own writing as well as that of others

Proofread for punctuation, capitalization, spelling, and syntax

Use punctuation and capitalization appropriately in writing

Proofread written work for punctuation, spelling, grammatical and syntactical errors, paragraph indentation, margins, and legibility of writing

Proofread written work for internal punctuation, spelling, grammatical and syntactical errors, paragraph indentation, margins, and legibility of writing

Omit sentence fragments, run-on sentences, nonagreement, and faulty tense changes

Use the forms and conventions of written language appropriately

Apply common generalizations about spelling

Use the dictionary to check spelling

Use a variety of sentence structures including simple, compound, and complex

continued

Table 12.1 Continued

Essential Elements	Grade 7	Grade 8	English I	English II	English III	English IV
					Make rhetorical choices based on audience, purpose, and form	Achieve precision in meaning through sophisticated language and rhetorical choices
						Use each of the commonly recognized patterns of organization
						Analyze the presentation of ideas in written discourse, including forms of logical reasoning, common fallacies of reasoning, and techniques of persuasive language
Language concepts and skills	Use objects, complements, phrases, and clauses to produce a variety of simple, compound, and complex sentences		Produce well-formed simple, compound, and complex sentences ⟶		Produce well-formed simple, compound, complex, and compound-complex sentences	
	Use all parts of speech correctly, including nouns, pronouns, verbs, adjectives, adverbs, prepositions, conjunctions, and interjections, in written and oral communication		Use all parts of speech effectively in sentences ⟶		Analyze the grammatical structure of sentences	

Use oral language effectively for a variety of purposes and audiences

Use oral language effectively in a variety of situations

Use the fundamentals of grammar, punctuation, and spelling

Use correct agreement between subjects and verbs and between pronouns and antecedents

Use correct subject-verb agreement with personal pronouns, indefinite pronouns, and compound subjects

Use common affixes to change words from one part of speech to the other

Choose appropriate words to convey intended meaning

Exhibit sophisticated and precise word choice to convey meaning

Recognize the meanings and uses of colloquialism, slang, idioms, and jargon

Describe the history and major features of American dialects

Describe the major features of the origins and development of the English language

Vary word and sentence choice for purpose and audience Produce sentences that convey, coordinate, and subordinate ideas appropriately

Table 12.1 *Continued*

Essential Elements	Grade 7	Grade 8	English I	English II	English III	English IV
					Recognize the sociological functions of language	→
					Demonstrate facility with word analogies and other forms of advanced vocabulary development	→
Literature concepts and skills	Recognize folk literature, legends, and myths	Recognize different types of literature: short stories, novels, poems, and plays	Recognize the major differences among poems, short stories, plays, and nonfiction	Recognize the major differences among poems, short stories, novels, plays, and nonfiction	Recognize the major authors, periods, forms, and works in American literature	Recognize the major authors, periods, forms, and works in British literature
		Recognize the basic types and characteristics of nonfiction				
	Recognize figurative language	Recognize the ways in which figurative language and sound devices contribute to meaning	Identify basic sound devices and figurative language →		Recognize the major types of figurative language and sound devices	
	Follow plot and character development in stories	Follow more complex plot and character development in stories				
		Describe plot, setting, character, and mood in more complex literary selections				
		Use basic literary terminology	Use basic literary terminology →		Use literary terminology appropriately →	
	Recognize literary traditions of cultural groups	Recognize cultural attitudes and customs in literary selections	Recognize cultural attitudes and customs in literary selections			
		Recognize point of view in literary selections	Recognize point of view in literary selections →			

Reading concepts and skills

(Scope-and-sequence chart; arrows indicate continuation of a skill strand across levels.)

Level 1
- Choose the appropriate meaning of multi-meaning words →
- Identify and evaluate main idea statements →
- Perceive cause and effect relationships
- Distinguish between fact and nonfact →
- Arrange details in sequential order →

Level 2
- Expand vocabulary; Determine word meanings by contextual clues →
- Recognize relevant details →
- Identify the stated or implied main ideas of a selection →
- Identify implied main ideas and related details
- Distinguish between fact and nonfact
- Distinguish between and evaluate fact and nonfact →
- Identify the sequential order of events →

Level 3
- Recognize the development of an overall theme in a literary work →
- Identify use of basic symbols in literary selections →
- Select main ideas of a selection →
- Express main idea in one sentence →
- Differentiate between fact and nonfact →
- Distinguish between fact and opinion, grounded belief, and ungrounded belief, and rational thought and rationalization →
- Arrange events in sequential order →

Level 4
- Recognize recurring themes in literary selections →
- Identify irony, tone, mood, allusion, and symbolism in literary selections
- Distinguish between language used denotatively and connotatively in literary selections
- Recognize characteristics of various literary genres →
- Recognize characteristics of literary selections
- Identify main idea and supporting details →
- Distinguish between fact and opinion, grounded belief, and ungrounded belief, and rational thought and rationalization
- Recognize the devices of propaganda

continued

Table 12.1 *Continued*

Essential Elements	Grade 7	Grade 8	English I	English II	English III	English IV
	Summarize and make generalizations	Arrive at a generalization from a given set of details and/or assumptions	Draw conclusions and make inferences	Make inferences and draw conclusions; Evaluate and make judgments		Make generalizations from a given set of assumptions
	Predict probable future actions	Predict probable future actions and outcomes	Predict outcomes and future actions			Predict probable future outcomes
			Vary rate of reading according to purpose	Adjust reading rate according to purpose	Adjust reading procedures, techniques, and rate according to purpose	Adjust rate and purpose for type of reading
	Identify the author's point of view and purpose →				Evaluate the author's point of view	Determine the author's point of view, purpose, and qualifications
	Follow written directions including substeps	↑	Follow directions involving substeps	Follow complex directions	↑	
		Use parts of book	Use format and organization of a book	Use parts of a book including footnotes, appendices, cross references	Use parts of a book appropriately	

Use advanced and special dictionaries

Use advanced dictionaries in determining pronunciations and meanings of words

Interpret complex maps, charts, and tables

Use specialized references independently

Use various reference materials

Use advanced dictionaries for determining word meaning

Use selected sections of advanced and special dictionaries

Read complex maps, charts, and tables

Use reference materials such as atlas, encyclopedia, almanac, and bibliography

Interpret diagrams, graphs, and statistical illustrations

Use the card catalog and standard references

Use the card catalog and standard library references

Speaking and listening concepts and skills

Participate in group discussions

Present information in a variety of oral situations

Follow ways a speaker signals important ideas and examples

Respond appropriately to a presenter

Take notes from an oral presentation

promoted significantly when reading and writing are combined with other types of activities. Tierney and colleagues (1989) suggest that there is a positive correlation between the development of critical thinking, reading, and writing, when done in conjunction with each other. Their research showed that students who were engaged in both reading and writing produced more revisions and were more willing to revise than those who only did one activity (read or write) independently. Tierney (1990) notes that the reader as a writer concept has influenced the definition and understanding of reading, not as a mechanical operation, but as a creative endeavor. Students who both read and write are more critical of their own writing and their own thinking. This trend is evident in the English language arts curriculum of today, where in many secondary classrooms the majority of the writing tasks are done in conjunction with reading assignments. This integration of reading and writing is emphasized in the goals and objectives of language arts instruction and is seen when students make analyses and evaluations based on specific stories or areas.

Other ways that critical thinking is emphasized in the English language arts curriculum is by teaching literature as experience. Martin (1989) says that the current trend in teaching literature is to cast off the "Neo-Aristotelianism" methods that many of today's English teachers learned in college, and develop a nonauthoritarian methodology. If students are *told* what a story means, they seldom do more than repeat what the teacher has told them. Students do not develop thinking skills, nor do they develop critical reading skills. They are only reading words and repeating the observations of someone else. Martin (1989) feels that by becoming less authoritative in the teaching of literature, students will make interpretations on their own, drawing on their rich variety of experiences in life. Wells (1990) notes that students must become more involved in the learning process because they "learn most effectively through participation in meaningful joint activities" (p. 16). The involvement of students in the experience of literature helps to develop critical thinking skills which are central to the study of language and literature (Martin, 1989). This trend in the English language arts curriculum encourages teachers to develop techniques to prompt students to develop their own assumptions about what a particular story means and how it relates to their individual lives.

A third trend or issue in the English language arts curriculum is the move toward gender balance in literature. This trend is directed mainly at highlighting the role of women in literature and how they are perceived by both men and women. Carlson (1989) states that since books help us form our social selves and affect "what we value, how we see, and perhaps even how we act," it is important that literature reflect a gender balance. Because women in society in the 1990s function as single mothers and career persons and often are the sole wage earners in the family, students need role models from literature that reflect this reality. These role models help students to assimilate appropriate roles and function in the larger society.

Support for this trend can be seen in the literature textbooks. More women authors are being included in the latest adoptions and more stories concerning the roles of women are being included. Consequently, women are being portrayed in numerous nontraditional roles, and as Carlson (1989) points out, this is also advantageous to males because it allows them to understand women in ways that had previously been ignored. Society will benefit from this move toward gender balance in the English language arts curriculum because it will negate some of the misplaced prejudices.

Closely associated with the issue of gender is the aspect of cultural background. Recognizing the multicultural nature of school populations, the English language arts curriculum also reflects this diversity. As Tchudi and Mitchell (1989) note, "in the course of a literature program that focuses on meaning, students will be given a great deal of cultural background. Over time, many students will read and delight in a wide range of works . . . and they will enjoy gaining insights into periods of history and cultures other than their own" (p. 135). Through the English language arts curriculum students are exposed to the ideas of other cultures through poems, essays, novels, and dramas.

Another trend that is currently advocated is writing across the curriculum. There is frequently a misunderstanding about what is actually meant by this process. According to Shuman (1990), this approach recognizes that each subject area has its own system of words or symbols and an effective way for students to make connections within the specific subject area is to write regularly on that subject. In this sense, writing becomes the responsibility of everyone in school. There are some problems with this approach. Not all teachers, even English teachers, write well, and even if they do, they may not be confident enough to support others, especially students, in their attempts. Kirsch, Finkel, France, and Blair (1989) note that for the program to be successful, a tremendous amount of collaborative goal setting is required along with specific funds for training teachers in the process. The success or failure of the program should not rest entirely on the shoulders of the English language arts department. To help teachers with this process, Shuman (1990) offers five suggestions for implementing writing across the curriculum:

1. Begin every class by having students spend five minutes writing a summary of the last class or their reading assignment
2. End every class by having students spend five minutes writing a summary of that class (use 1 or 2, not 1 and 2)
3. Before in-class discussion, allow students five minutes to jot down their thoughts about the topic under discussion
4. After the presentation in class of any particularly complex material, give students a couple of minutes to write down questions they have about it, then collect the questions and address . . . them
5. When students work in groups, have each member of the group write a brief evaluative summary of the group activity (p. 90)

This trend is becoming more evident in the curriculum as many of the goals and objectives of the English language arts curriculum address the need to be knowledgeable of specific terminology and the words and symbols of different subject areas. The writing across the curriculum concept is particularly helpful as teachers work with students to generate many ideas to write about and then help them select one and develop it.

A final trend in the English language arts curriculum involves the concept of "whole language" as a process of instruction for language development. Although predominantly used at the elementary level now, the movement of this approach to the secondary classroom is inevitable. According to the Association for Supervision and Curriculum Development (1990), "The 'whole language' approach, which treats reading as a holistic process and de-emphasizes instruction in separate skills, is influencing an increasing number of school programs" (p. 7). The whole language approach integrates the areas of reading, speaking, listening, and writing. The whole language or integrated language arts approach starts with the student's own language skills and interests rather than with a predetermined curriculum. As Goodman (1986) describes this process, it is not just an hour or two, it involves everything that students do and involves "kid watching," because knowledge of the individual student's interests is critical to the process. Butler (1987) and Robbins (1990) suggest a complex process which incorporates ten elements. These elements are:

1. The teacher reads to the students to model and promote reading
2. Students and teacher share books together
3. Everyone, including the teacher, engages in silent sustained reading for an extended period of time
4. Based on student ability and interests, the teacher involves students in guided reading by assigning books to groups of students to read independently, and then follows up with a conference
5. Students are engaged in individualized reading, which provides an organized alternative to guided reading
6. Students are involved in a language experience that transcribes oral language to written form, and firsthand or vicarious experience is translated into written language
7. The writing process involves the elements of rehersal, drafting, revision, editing, publishing, and response
8. The teacher also models the writing process and behaviors identified in the elements
9. Students share their finished work with an audience
10. Students see different kinds of reading and writing based on subject area texts and learn to vary speed and look for context clues

To better understand the process, Espe, Worner, and Hotkovich (1990) describe a whole language junior high school language arts classroom. Students' outside interests can be tapped and shared with their peers. For example, in Worner's classroom a student indicated an interest in the *Titanic*. When the teacher heard that the student had constructed a model, she asked him if he would share it with the class. When the student brought the model to school, he immediately became the "expert." Because of the student's enthusiasm and interest, other students became interested. The teacher directed them to reading and writing about the catastrophe, and students began to generate factual and fictional accounts. The class viewed a videotape which depicted the recent discovery of the Titanic on the ocean floor and were exposed to historical and scientific information while becoming knowledgeable about recent scientific discoveries. For Espe, Worner, and Hotkevich, the "possibilities for launching reading and writing projects are limitless" (p. 45). They encourage teachers to listen to and watch their students to find out what they want to know; then let them use their "expert" knowledge in a cooperative manner as they share in both the teaching and the learning process.

The English language arts curriculum continues to examine the key components of effective instruction and question not only what is taught, but how it is taught. This chapter presented the curriculum framework for the English language arts curriculum for secondary schools and identified several trends and issues related to English instruction. Suhor (1988) summarizes the state of affairs in this curriculum area by cautioning educators against "factmongering" in secondary English programs and noting that "teachers and curriculum developers should indeed guard against the persisting tendency to consider English as a conglomerate of facts about literature, grammar, and composition" (p. 48). The English language arts curriculum must be conceived of in an integrative manner where reading, writing, speaking, listening, and observing come together in a coherent manner.

SUMMARY

Chapter 12 provided an overview of the English language arts curriculum for the secondary school. This curriculum area is concerned with grammar and usage; semantics; literature; speaking, listening, and/or writing language; and print and visual media. The English language arts curriculum area includes the skills of reading, writing, speaking, listening, and observing, which are critical to students' ability to communicate by means of the spoken and written word. The importance of this curriculum area in the secondary school is emphasized; normally it is required each year during junior and senior high school.

This chapter provided a historical perspective on the English language arts curriculum by tracing the development of the subject area from colonial times to the present day. In describing the importance of the curriculum area, the chapter noted that it has been an integral part of the secondary curriculum since the days of the academies during the 1800s.

The chapter also provided an overview of the goals of the English language arts curriculum. These goals are broken down by categories, which include language, literature, reading, writing, speaking, listening, use of media, and creative, logical, and critical thinking skills. The general courses for each grade level were then briefly described, with English and reading being required for most junior high school students and a variety of options offered for senior high students. Courses such as creative writing, visual media, and journalism are some of the specialized areas of the English language arts curriculum designed to meet the needs and interests of secondary students.

The chapter ended with a discussion of current trends and issues. Of particular interest is the development of the "whole language" or integrated language arts curriculum. In this curriculum, students do not experience reading, writing, literature, and spelling as separate entities, but approach the study of the language arts in combination. Also of interest in the teaching of the language arts is the use of computers, which allows students to compose and edit as they are engaged in the writing process. A final trend involves the concept of writing across the curriculum, where students participate in writing activities in all subjects. Clearly the English language arts curriculum is in a state of transition, with the intent to provide a more integrated, comprehensive approach to the study of the subject.

YOUR TURN

12.1 Visit a junior high school and interview two or three English language arts teachers. Try to determine the curricular approach they are using in their English language arts class. Questions that might prove helpful in the interview process include:

(a) Do you have separate classes for reading, spelling, and English?

(b) Do you use a grammar book to teach parts of speech?

(c) How do students select topics for writing in this class? Do you assign them or do students choose from a list that they have generated?

(d) What is the relationship of literature, composition, and grammar in this class? Are they taught separately?

Based on the responses to these and other questions that you develop, can you assess the curriculum as being whole language or integrated in its approach?

12.2 Consult several educational supply catalogs and review them for computer software that would be appropriate for secondary classrooms. Complete the chart below using the titles you have selected.

Program (Grade level)	English Language Arts Goal/Skill	Cost
1.		
2.		
3.		
4.		
5.		
6.		

12.3 Obtain a copy of a curriculum guide for secondary English language arts. Review the guide to determine the approach that the district is using in the teaching of this content area. Do the goals closely match the general goals described in the chapter? What specific skills are required? What evaluation techniques are used? Is the approach integrated, or are the skills and concepts taught as separate, discrete facts? How guilty is the district of "factmongering"?

12.4 Randomly survey teachers to determine if they write. If so, do you write on a regular basis to serve as a role model for your students? Why? Why not? Even if they do not write on a regular basis for your students, are they convinced of the importance of writing in every subject area, even mathematics? Develop a position paper on why "Teachers Should Be Writers Too!" This paper should provide the rationale for convincing the faculty to establish a writing across the curriculum program. As you prepare the paper, consider the following items:

(a) Reasons pro and con for writing across the curriculum
(b) The sequence of activities which would encourage students to write
(c) A list of possible outlets for your writing as well as for your students
(d) Ways to support and encourage writing throughout your school

12.5 Use the following language experience to get students to anticipate what they will be reading in their texts through graphic representations. For example, students are studying the plant and animal life in the marshlands of Florida. One particular animal is the crocodile. Ask the students what comes to mind when they hear the words "marshlands" and "crocodile." Students will use concepts that might range from wet, soggy, and mosquitoes, for marshlands to rough skin, big mouth, and dangerous, for the crocodile. As the students respond, categorize the responses into habitat, behavior, uses, and physical features. Step three is to have the students write a poem, limerick, short story, travel monologue, or prose narrative using the term(s).

REFERENCES

Association for Supervision and Curriculum Development. (February 1990). Issue. *Update, 32,* 2, 7.

Beckner, W. & Cornett, J.D. (1972). *The secondary school curriculum: Content and structure.* Scranton, Pa.: Intext Educational Publishers.

Boyer, E.L. (1983). *High school: A report on secondary education in America.* New York: Harper & Row.

Butler, A. (1987). *The elements of whole language.* Crystal Lake, Ill.: Rigby.

Carlson, M. (October 1989). Guidelines for a gender-balanced curriculum in English, grades 7–12. *English Journal, 78,* 6, 30–33.

Cronin, H., Meadows, D. & Sinatra, R. (September 1990). Integrating computers, reading, and writing across the curriculum. *Educational Leadership, 48,* 1, 57–62.

Espe, C., Worner, C.C. & Hotkovich, M.M. (March 1990). Whole language—What a bargain. *Educational Leadership, 47,* 6, 45.

Goodman, K. (1986). *What's whole in whole language?* Portsmouth, N.H.: Heinemann.

Hawisher, G. (January 1989). Computers and writing: Where's the research? *English Journal 78,* 1, 89–91.

Hipple, T.W. (1973). *Teaching English in secondary schools.* New York: Macmillan.

Jensen, J.M. & Roser, N.L. (March 1990). Are there really 3 r's? *Educational Leadership, 47,* 6, 7–12.

Kirsch, G., Finkel, D., France, A. & Blair, C. (January 1989). Three comments on "Only one of the voices": Dialogic writing across the curriculum. *College English, 51,* 1, 99–106.

Martin, B.K. (April 1989). Teaching literature as experience. *College English, 51,* 4, 377–385.

McNeil, J.D. (1990). *Curriculum: A comprehensive introduction* (4th ed.). Glenview, Ill.: Scott Foresman.

National Council of Teachers of English. (1982). *Essentials of English*. Urbana, Ill.: NCTE.

Rief, L. (March 1990). Finding the value in evaluation: Self-assessment in a middle school classroom. *Educational Leadership, 47*, 6, 24–29.

Robbins, P.A. (March 1990). Implementing whole language: Bridging children and books. *Educational Leadership, 47*, 6, 50–54.

Shuman, R.B. (May 1990). Trends; English. *Educational Leadership, 47*, 8, 90.

Suhor, C. (1988). Content and process in the English curriculum. In R.S. Brandt (Ed.), *Content of the curriculum*. Alexandria, Va.: Association for Supervision and Curriculum Development.

Tchudi, S. & Mitchell, D. (1989). *Explorations in the teaching of English*. New York: Harper & Row.

Tierney, R.J. (March 1990). Redefining reading comprehension. *Educational Leadership, 47*, 6, 37–41.

Tierney, R.J. et al. (1989). The effects of reading and writing upon thinking critically. *Reading Research Quarterly, 24*, 2, 134–137 and 166–168.

Trump, J.L. & Miller, D.F. (1973). Secondary school curriculum improvement (2nd ed.). Boston: Allyn & Bacon.

Wells, G. (March 1990). Creating the conditions to encourage literate thinking. *Educational Leadership, 47*, 6, 13–17.

Chapter
13

Mathematics in the Secondary School Curriculum

Mathematics has earned and enjoyed an important place in the secondary curriculum, yet over its long history it has received criticism as well as attention (Campbell and Fey, 1988). Much of the attention this subject has received in recent years has been more negative than positive. It is not unusual to see news headlines emphasize that there is a ". . . discouraging pattern of mathematics achievement, particularly in . . . problem solving and higher order thinking skills (Campbell and Fey, 1988, p. 53). This discouraging pattern extends into the international arena as well, with students in the United States lagging far behind their counterparts in highly developed countries (McKnight et al., 1987).

Over the past several decades, mathematics has earned a reputation among secondary students as being difficult, boring, and/or often irrelevant. Too often, mathematics is viewed as a series of special procedures ". . . which, by some magic, can be used to get the answer in the book" (Beckner and Cornett, 1972, p. 169). Others recall the theorems that are memorized and the tricks that are used to arrive at the "truth" in geometry. Burke is reported as saying that "requiring unnecessary math does not create future scientists . . . it creates dropouts and hatred for math and for school" (Southwest Educational Development Laboratory, 1989, p. 4). This view is supported by recent findings of the National Assessment of Educational Progress (Education Commission of the States, 1983). According to the results, nearly 50 percent of 17-year-olds agreed that "learning mathematics is mostly memorizing" and 90 percent agreed that "there is always a rule to follow in solving mathematics problems"; in fact, ". . . most students come to expect one solution and one solution process for each problem and . . . see little sense in looking further" (Driscoll, 1987, pp. 63, 64).

Consequently, for most secondary students, mathematics is viewed as a foreign language that can only be learned through memorization and repeated rehearsal (Schoenfeld, 1983). With such attitudes and perceptions about mathematics, students do not experience the excitement that can come from studying math. Students do not learn the symbol systems of math which provide ways of expressing mathematical concepts. The language along with the methods of reasoning equip secondary students with tools to decipher information from problem situations. In other words, the language of mathematics is one tool that students can use to translate abstract concepts into useable concrete concepts.

As is the case with the English language, the use of descriptive words, short sentences, and adjectives can help students to understand abstract concepts. In addition, language helps students decipher written text; it is during this decoding phase that abstract concepts are processed and accommodated mentally. So too in mathematics, language is a tool. Symbols and numerals, not letters, are the basic building blocks of the mathematical language. When strung together these symbols form mathematical sentences and express mathematical thoughts, which in turn can be deciphered or decoded into ideas that can be understood and applied.

In examining the mathematics curriculum for the secondary school, it seems appropriate to present a brief history of how the curriculum evolved in the United States. Such an overview will help provide a rationale for the current movement to reform the mathematics education program in the United States, not only at the secondary level, but in elementary schools as well.

HISTORY OF THE MATHEMATICS CURRICULUM

Prior to the eighteenth century, the curriculum of the secondary school was dominated by classical language study and little, if any, attention was given to mathematical concepts and skills. It was not until the eighteenth century that mathematics received any attention in the schools, and even then the emphasis was on the simplest mathematical computations. A change occurred at the beginning of the nineteenth century when mathematics became a permanent part of the schools in America as commercial interests increased and mathematics had a practical role to play in education. At this time, as during the recent past, rote memorization of rules and not comprehension of mathematical concepts was the primary goal of mathematics education.

In 1894, the Report of the Committee of Ten on Secondary School Subjects made several specific recommendations for improving the mathematics curriculum in the schools. This committee recommended that concrete geometry be offered at the junior high school level (seventh or eighth grades), that algebra be offered in the ninth grade and continued into the tenth grade, followed by continued study of algebra and geometry at the eleventh grade. Trigonometry and advanced algebra (algebra II) would be taught for those (especially boys) going on to technical or engineering colleges (Beckner and Cornett, 1972). As it turned out, these recommendations became the blueprint for the mathematics curriculum when the twentieth century started and remained fairly constant throughout the early 1900s.

Before the 1950s the common theme for the mathematics curriculum was mastery of basic computational skills. The typical mathematics curriculum at this time included the following courses:

> *Junior High School:* general mathematics and arithmetic for grades 7 and 8; algebra for grades 8 and 9

> *High School:* introduction to algebra for grade 9; plane geometry (elective), grade 10; intermediate algebra (elective), grade 11; solid geometry and trigonometry (elective), grade 12

The back to the basics movement which characterized this time period ". . . produced improvement in precisely those mathematical abilities that are least important in a rapidly changing technological society" (McNeil, 1990, p. 330). Students were able to compute, but they did not know how to solve problems (McKnight et al., 1987).

During the early 1950s, especially after the launching of the Sputnik, the criticism leveled against the mathematics curriculum was fierce and the move toward the "new math" and accelerated curriculum commenced. The following is a composite list of forces which came together and put pressure on the schools to modify the mathematics curriculum during the period of 1950 to 1975 (Beckner and Cornett, 1972).

1. Math concepts and content had grown considerably during the previous 100 years
2. The development of science and technology created a demand for mathematics support
3. Academically talented students had been neglected, especially in the fields of mathematics and science
4. Technological advances made by the USSR and other countries challenged the security of the United States
5. The federal government provided financial assistance for mathematical training through the National Defense Education Act of 1958 and 1965, and private business also supported mathematics education
6. Those involved in mathematics education and professional organizations took a more active role in developing the mathematics curriculum
7. New knowledge from the field of psychology concerning how children

learn mathematics became available and was incorporated as a part of the mathematics teaching process

8. Poor results by students on math evaluation measures and the declining enrollment in advanced mathematics courses by grade 12 (Kinsella, 1965) resulted in only 5 percent of the students enrolled in a mathematics class in the twelfth grade

During the 1960s new trends in mathematics instruction emerged and culminated in the "new math" movement. As one might expect, the "new math" approach was short lived, with the final blow coming from Kline (1973) in his book, *Why Johnny Can't Add*. Kline enumerated many of the problems of the "new math" and the following were among the most often cited:

1. A lack of practical applications of mathematics which made it boring
2. Heavy emphasis on mastering paper and pencil procedures with little attention to comprehension
3. Little consideration of the interests of the students
4. A lack of attention to the noncollege bound, culturally diverse students

Although efforts were made in the last half of the 1970s to address these shortcomings, it has taken another decade to rectify them adequately. Despite all of the reform reports issued during the 1980s, most focused on the total curriculum of secondary schools. However, many of the reports included recommendations concerning the quality of mathematics education in this country.

With this historical perspective as a backdrop, it is not surprising to note that advice for revising the mathematics curriculum in the secondary school has not been in short supply. The National Council of Teachers of Mathematics (NCTM) has published several documents from 1975–1985 which deal with suggestions for changing the direction of mathematics education in the United States. The most recent report, called the *Curriculum and Evaluation Standards for School Mathematics* (1989), attempts to set the course for reforming the K–12 mathematics curriculum and is referred to throughout this chapter as the *Standards*. Not since the curriculum reform movements of the 1960s have there been major efforts to radically change the math content along with the approaches to teaching. The reform movement is calling for new priorities in math content and for improved teacher performance as well as student achievement. One significant emphasis in the mathematics curriculum is problem solving. According to the *Standards* (1989), problem solving is the cornerstone of the new mathematics curriculum because it requires students to develop higher-order thinking. The classic "show and drill" and the passive absorption of concepts must give way to more hands-on, participatory instructional practices that, according to Schoenfield (1983), ". . . provide [students] with thinking skills that they can use after they take . . . final exams" (p. 7).

A recent and important document concerning the mathematics curriculum, which has been widely read, is *Everybody Counts: A Report to the Nation on the Future of Mathematics Education* (National Research Council, 1989). According to this report, the traditional approach of helping students ". . . do well on standardized tests and [learning] lower-order skills . . ." (p. 57) for short-term gains will no longer be acceptable. These ineffective teaching strategies should be modified so that students learn higher-order thinking skills for the long term.

Under the current conditions described in these reports, students are not gaining a sense of mathematics. Such a sense of mathematics helps students to understand that math is more than a set of arbitrary rules to memorize (*Standards*, 1989). Students should also realize that mathematics can be verbalized, written down, and read by all (Lochhead, 1981).

It is important now to examine the goals for secondary mathematics. Although new goals are proposed, the array of choices among the college strands of courses (college preparatory and general) remains remarkably similar to those courses offered 20 to 30 years ago or more. The section on goals is followed by an overview of the curriculum of the junior and senior high school mathematics courses. Each of the major mathematics courses is discussed and key concepts and skills are identified. The chapter concludes with a brief discussion of the trends and issues, as well as new challenges, that confront mathematics educators.

GOALS FOR THE MATHEMATICS CURRICULUM

Mathematics can be described in a variety of ways. We agree with Beckner and Cornett (1972) that mathematics is a ". . . science of numbers and computation (arithmetic) . . ."; a language system with relationships (algebra); a study of shapes and space (geometry); and a system of measuring great distances in space and analyzing oscillations (trigonometry); and further, it is a study of data and graphs (statistics), as well as the "study of change, infinity, and limits (calculus) . . ." (p. 169). With this comprehensive definition, along with new knowledge that has been provided in mathematics as well as in how students learn math, the mathematics curriculum in the secondary schools of the twenty-first century will, in all likelihood, be different from descriptions of the past. The goals of mathematics education will still be rooted in the past with its emphasis on developing "mental powers," but should also be a continuing, spiral experience. The attitude that students develop toward mathematics is the key to whether it is learned or not and whether the memories will be positive or negative (Schoenfeld, 1989).

As discussed in Chapter 4, the goals of the school curriculum are intertwined with societal needs and student interests. The goals in mathematics are no exception. To illustrate this point, *Everybody Counts* (National Research Council, 1989) says,

> . . . mathematics . . . contributes in direct and fundamental ways to business, finance, health, and defense. For students, it opens doors to careers. For citizens, it enables informed decisions. For nations, it provides knowledge to compete in a technological economy. To participate fully in the world of the future, America must tap the power of mathematics (p. 1).

The contributors to the report *Everybody Counts* note that the quality of mathematics education is intrinsically tied to a healthy economy. The recognition that the needs of society play a role in the formulation of mathematics goals is clear. Mathematics is becoming increasingly important to society because it ". . . provides a powerful instrument for understanding the world in which we live" (National Research Council, 1989, p. 4).

The following goals, as identified in *Everybody Counts*, are suggested for tomorrow's mathematics education:

1. To develop mathematics literacy as an integral part of communication
2. To expect students to perform well in mathematics and to develop mathematical powers which require discerning relationships, reasoning logically, and using a broad spectrum of methods to solve problems
3. To help students develop an attitude of appreciation for mathematics as both a science which involves pattern and order and a unique mode of thought that involves modeling, logical analysis, inference from data, and the use of symbols
4. To actively involve students in learning mathematics so that they become excited and challenged by this learning
5. To build confidence in all students so that they learn and experience the importance of mathematical reasoning
6. To develop broad-based mathematical powers that involve the ability to:
   - Perform mental calculations
   - Estimate
   - Identify appropriate mathematical operations and match them to a particular context
   - Use a calculator
   - Use graphs, tables, and spreadsheets to interpret and present numerical information
   - Use computer software
   - Formulate questions
   - Identify and use effective problem-solving strategies
   - Build models to organize and facilitate systematic thinking

With the proposed new focus, the study of mathematics can become useful, exciting, and creative. Mathematics cannot only help secondary students solve problems and think logically, but it can also help students explore and make sense out of their world. Finally the study of mathematics is for *all* students who can experience ". . . mathematical processing, problem solving, and mathematical thinking" skills (NCTM, 1989, p. 130). The goal of the mathematics curriculum at the secondary level is to provide all students with the opportunity to develop mathematical literacy.

OVERVIEW OF THE MATHEMATICS CURRICULUM FOR GRADES 7 AND 8

At the junior high school level, the focus of mathematics has been on topics which would benefit those students going on to college. However, with the revisions called for in the *Standards* (NCTM, 1989), the emphasis at this level is on offering a broad range of topics so that all students experience the study of mathematics regardless of their decision to attend college.

At this level the students are curious and energetic and need to have opportunities to expand their ". . . knowledge of numbers, computation, estimation, measurement, geometry, statistics, probability, patterns and functions, and the fundamental concepts of algebra" (NCTM, 1989, pp. 65–66). The broad-based mathematics curriculum at this level helps meet the diverse nature and developmental abilities of the junior high school students. The proposed mathematics curriculum is "concept driven," and includes a series of relevant mathematics experiences which relate to technology.

The following list from the *Standards* (NCTM, 1989) includes the suggested topics and subtopics recommended for grades 7 and 8, overlapping with grades 5 and 6 as well.

1. Problem solving
   - Investigate and formulate questions when given problem situations
   - Solve problems using different skills (verbal-numerical graphing, geometrically and/or symbolically)
2. Communicating
   - Discuss, read, write, and listen for ideas in math
3. Reasoning
   - In special situations
   - Using graphs
   - Using inductive and deductive thinking
4. Operations and computations
   - Develop number sense
   - Develop operation sense
   - Create procedures for algorithms
   - Use estimating skills when solving problems and checking reasonableness of answers
   - Explore relationships among whole numbers, fractions, decimals, integers, and rational number operations
   - Develop understanding of relationships of ratio, proportion, and percent
5. Patterns and functions
   - Identify and use relationships
   - Develop and use graphs, tables, and rules as a way to describe situations
   - Interpret mathematical representations

6. Algebra
   - Develop an understanding of variables, equations, and expressions
   - Use different approaches to solve linear equations
   - Investigate inequalities and nonlinear equations
7. Statistics and probability
   - Use statistical procedures as a way of describing, analyzing, and evaluating and making decisions
8. Create models of situations involving probability, geometry
   - Develop an understanding of geometric shapes, objects, and relationships
   - Use geometry to solve problems
9. Measurement
   - Estimate and use measurement to solve problems

OVERVIEW OF THE MATHEMATICS CURRICULUM FOR GRADES 9–12

The goal of high school mathematics is to provide students with ways to learn concepts, skills, and methods of thought. This knowledge of mathematics concepts and skills forms the foundation for future roles as citizens and serves to prepare students for specific occupations or postsecondary educational opportunities. With the acceleration in technological advances, secondary students need to gain an appreciation for and confidence in their ability to deal with the "mathematical demands of adult life" (National Research Council, 1989, p. 7).

In the following section, the mathematics curriculum for grades 9–12 is presented. The curricular offerings are sufficiently broad, with an emphasis on the use of calculators and computers, to accommodate the diverse high school student population.

The courses in mathematics for students in grades 9–12 depend upon the focus that they elect to take — college preparatory or general education. Math courses that are a part of the college preparatory mathematics curriculum include algebra I, algebra II (usually ninth and eleventh grades), geometry, and one semester of precalculus, calculus, or trigonometry (Campbell and Fey, 1988). In the general education program of studies, the emphasis is on continuation of topics presented in junior high school, with a special concentration on consumer applications, problem solving, technology (use of calculators and computers), math as communication, mathematical reasoning, and mathematical connections. After a survey was conducted to determine the status of mathematics in the secondary schools, the results revealed that ". . . the traditional mathematics courses — courses that feature drill and practice, computation, and memorization — are taken by slower students and students not planning on college . . ." (McNeil, 1990, p. 328).

The courses identified in this section are the ones most often associated with a college preparation curriculum. The following is a summary of the suggested content in algebra, geometry, trigonometry, and calculus, along with other topics.

Algebra

Courses in algebra focus on a variety of steps in which students are required to manipulate ". . . symbolic expressions to solve equations and inequalities" (Campbell and Fey, 1988, p. 63). In algebra, the concept of equivalence is emphasized and students learn that "you can make the same change to each side of the equal sign, and the equivalence does not change" (McNeil, 1990, p. 332). The concept of equivalence is a departure from what students have been taught up to this point. They were taught to perform the operations to each side in a mechanical fashion without understanding the process. Algebraic operations often pose a challenge that some students, because of their previous training in the mechanics of mathematical operations, find hard to overcome.

The importance of algebra to the study of mathematics is stated in the *Standards* (NCTM, 1989) which says,

> Algebra is the language through which most of mathematics is communicated [and] it provides a means of operating with concepts at an abstract level and then applying them, a process that often fosters generalizations and insights beyond the original context (p. 150).

Recently, courses in mathematics, and in particular algebra, have come under heavy criticism because students learn mostly through rote memorization and have difficulty in applying algebraic concepts and skills to realistic situations. Students lack the ability to use the information and skills obtained in algebra classes to solve real problems. Listed below are the general topics for the study of algebra as identified by the National Council of Teachers of Mathematics in the *Standards* (1989).

1. Represent situations that involve variable quantities with expressions, equations, inequalities, and matrices
2. Use tables and graphs as tools to interpret expressions, equations, and inequalities
3. Operate on expressions and matrices, and solve equations and inequalities
4. Appreciate the power of mathematical abstraction and symbolism
5. Use matrices to solve linear systems
6. Demonstrate technical facility with algebraic transformations, including techniques based on the theory of equations (p. 150)

In addition to these basic algebraic concepts, the following recommendations have been made concerning the teaching of algebra to ninth and eleventh grade students.

1. Use real-world situations and problems as a means of motivating students and applying theory
2. Use computer-assisted instruction (software and problems) to develop conceptual understanding

3. Use computer-based methods which emphasize skills in approximation and graphing to solve equations and inequalities
4. Emphasize the structure of the number systems
5. Use matrices with real-life information and applications

Geometry

For many high school students, geometry remains a mystery. Yet this subject is justified in the mathematics curriculum on the basis that it helps students learn logical and hypothetical reasoning skills. Campbell and Fey (1988) suggest, however, that there is evidence to suggest that this goal is not realized because practical, real-life examples are infrequently presented and the geometric concepts are taught using an abstract approach without any practical applications. According to the *Standards* (NCTM, 1989), geometry

> . . . should deepen students' understanding of shapes and their properties, with an emphasis on their wide applicability in human activit[ies]. The curriculum should be infused with examples of how geometry is used in recreations (billiards or sailing); in practical tasks (purchasing paint for a room); in the sciences (description and analysis of mineral crystals); and in the arts (perspective in drawing) (p. 157).

It is also important to study the connections between algebra and geometry. The geometric ideas of the past can be expressed in the language of coordinate geometry, and this provides new tools for solving a wide range of problems. According to the *Standards* (NCTM, 1989), "The interplay between algebra and geometry strengthens students' ability to formulate and analyze problems from situations both within and outside mathematics" (p. 161).

The following is a list of concepts from an algebraic and synthetic perspective that are recommended for inclusion in a high school geometry course:

1. Translate between synthetic and coordinate [algebraic] representations
2. Deduce properties of figures using transformations and using coordinates
3. Identify congruent and similar figures using transformations
4. Analyze properties of Euclidean transformations and relate translations to vectors
5. Deduce properties of figures using vectors
6. Apply transformations, coordinates, and vectors in problem solving
7. Interpret and draw three dimensional objects
8. Represent problem situations with geometric models and apply properties of figures
9. Classify figures in terms of congruence and similarity and apply these relationships
10. Deduce properties of, and relationships between, figures from given assumptions
11. Develop an understanding of an axiomatic system through investigating and comparing various geometries (NCTM, pp. 157, 161)

In addition to these concepts of geometry, the following procedures are recommended for the teaching of geometry:

1. Integrate geometry concepts into all grade levels of the mathematics curriculum
2. Develop short sequences of theorems for study
3. Create deductive oral arguments, as well as written in sentence and paragraph form
4. Use computer-aided explorations of two-dimensional and three-dimensional figures
5. Include the study of three-dimensional geometry
6. Use real-world applications and modeling to establish the relevancy of geometry to everyday activities

Trigonometry

The focus in trigonometry is on real-world problems. Since trigonometry historically has been based on the study of triangle measurement, the topics of ". . . matrix representations of rotations, direction angles of vectors, polar coordinates, and trigonometric representations of complex numbers . . ." form the core of this math area (NCTM, 1989, p. 183). The following list contains the suggested content for the trigonometry curriculum as identified in the *Standards* (NCTM, 1989):

1. Apply trigonometry to problem situations involving triangles
2. Explore periodic real-world phenomena using sine and cosine functions
3. Understand the connection between trigonometric and circular functions
4. Use circular functions to model periodic real-world phenomena
5. Apply general graphing techniques to trigonometric functions
6. Solve trigonometric equations and verify trigonometric identities
7. Understand the connections between trigonometric functions and polar coordinates, complex numbers, and series (p. 183)

In addition to these concepts or topics that are recommended for trigonometry, the following suggestions relate to the teaching of this mathematics curriculum area:

1. Use scientific calculators to facilitate understanding
2. Include realistic applications of trigonometric functions and model them for students
3. Use graphing utilities to solve equations and inequalities
4. Use computers to provide visual representations of triangle rotations, and other circular and trigonometric functions

Advanced Mathematics

Mathematics beyond algebra I and II, geometry, and trigonometry is essential for the growing technological needs that our society will have in the next decade and beyond. The study of functions is particularly important in developing advanced mathematics skills. According to the *Standards* (NCTM, 1989), "The concept of function is an important unifying idea in mathematics

[and] . . . is a mathematical representation of many input-output situations found in the real world, including those that recently have arisen as a result of technological advances" (p. 154). Students should be able to connect a problem situation with its model as a function in symbolic form and to graph that function. Students should also be able to express function equations in standardized form to check the reasonableness of graphs produced by graphing utilities.

The development of advanced mathematical concepts is critical to the mathematics curriculum, yet the number of secondary students opting to take advanced courses is very limited. Those students who do take advanced courses lack the necessary problem solving skills (Campbell and Fey, 1988). In reporting the results of the academic performance of students over the last two decades, as measured by the National Assessment of Educational Progress, a recent newspaper headline declared "U.S. Students Found Lagging" and indicated that advanced math skills ". . . are so neglected that fewer than half of the nation's high school seniors can handle moderately difficult problems" (U.S. Students, 1990, p. 6A).

Proposals abound concerning how to alter the traditional concepts and skills taught in all math classes, especially in algebra, geometry, calculus, and trigonometry. Fey (1983) recommends that statistics and discrete mathematics replace the concepts and skills. To capture the spirit of the reform movement, the following lesson on continuity (examples of continuous and discontinuous functions in precalculus and calculus) is presented. This lesson explains basic concepts, but it presents the information using a different teaching strategy called *concept attainment*. Concept attainment is a teaching model that encourages students to work independently and to compare and contrast examples and nonexamples. As students look for examples and nonexample, they practice categorizing ideas, objects, or events and differentiate characteristics.

In the first step of the strategy, the teacher presents examples labeled "yes" and "no" and the students try to identify the critical attributes or characteristics of the concept presented. Students are asked to "hypothesize" about the important characteristics of the concept, but not share this with classmates. Next, the teacher has the students test their hypotheses by using unlabeled examples. When the concept is reached or "attained" the students write a definition or description of the concept. In the final step, students are asked to reflect on their thought processes as they made decisions regarding examples and nonexamples. For evaluation, the teacher may present more unlabeled examples and have the students classify them as examples or nonexamples of the concept. Anderson (1990) created and used this lesson with students in advanced placement calculus. Box 13-1 presents a complete description of the lesson, the procedures, and the visuals used in the lesson.

By using this strategy, students were able to recognize the concept of continuity and were able to formalize a definition. This lesson on continuity had the students analyzing where maximum and minimum continuous values occur. Lastly, students constructed the rules for algebraic combinations.

Box 13-1 **Lesson Plan**

DESCRIPTIVE DATA

Grade Level: 11 – 12

Course: Advanced Placement Calculus

Time frame: Two days of fourth week of course

Student level: Honors students

Model: Attaining Concepts

INSTRUCTIONAL OBJECTIVES

1. The student will be able to state an informal definition of continuity in his [or her] own words with 100% accuracy. (knowledge)

2. The student will be able to state the formal definition of continuity with 100% accuracy. (knowledge)

3. The student will be able to distinguish between examples of continuous and discontinuous functions by answering "yes" or "no" with 100% accuracy. (comprehension)

4. The student will be able to produce two examples of continuous functions and two examples of discontinuous functions with 100% accuracy. (application/synthesis)

5. The student will be able to explain why an example of a function is continuous or not according to the formal definition with 80% accuracy. (application)

6. Using a map of the state of Texas, the student will be able to find and to draw a continuous route from Arlington to the university of his or her choice. (application)

METHODS AND TECHNIQUES

Phase One — Presentation of Data, Identifying Concepts (10 min.)

1. Present labeled examples

2. Ask students to compare attributes in positive and negative examples silently on index cards

3. Have students suggest attributes of examples and generate a hypothesis

4. Ask each student to write an informal definition according to the essential attributes on an index card

continued

Box 13-1 **Lesson Plan — Continued**

Phase Two — Testing the Attainment of the Concept (15 min.)

1. Have students mark "yes" or "no" on their index card for each labeled example
2. Teacher confirms the hypothesis by asking several students to state their conclusion and places the unlabeled examples with the appropriate group
3. Teacher names the concept
4. Teacher restates the definitions according to essential attributes both informally and formally
5. Various students are asked to draw examples of continuous and discontinuous functions on the board
6. Students are assigned homework for evaluation purposes as follows.
   a. Students are asked to classify as to continuity nonlabeled examples on a sheet for homework. They must use the formal definition to verify in writing their conclusions
   b. Students are asked to generate two examples of continuous and two examples of discontinuous functions. For each example, students must use the formal definition to verify their conclusions in writing
   c. Students are asked to find a continuous route on a map

Phase Three — Analysis of Thinking Strategies

1. Students would be asked to describe their thoughts as they looked at the examples and at the nonexamples. Did they look at the picture as a whole or at the pieces?
2. Students would discuss the role of hypothesis and attributes.
3. Students would discuss the type and number of hypotheses. How many did they reach? Was each one formed by looking at the whole or at the parts? What caused a student to change or to accept his [or her] own hypothesis or that of another student?

Resources/Supplies/Space

Labeled examples
Unlabeled examples
Pointer
Index cards
Homework sheet
Chalk and chalkboard
Stick-um

EVALUATION

1. Students will be evaluated for participation only during phase one and parts 1–4 of phase two. The students will be asked to orally state informal and formal definitions of continuity.

Box 13-1 **Lesson Plan — Continued**

2. The homework sheet will be graded the next day in class with points being awarded for correctly identifying the examples as to continuity. Points will also be awarded for verification of the identification by use of the formal definition of continuity. The students will earn the other 40 points from their own creations of continuous or discontinuous functions. Selected students will be asked to draw theirs on the board. Of the 100 possible points, students are expected to earn at least 80.

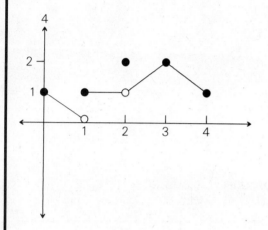

I. Is the function $y = f(x)$ continuous at each of the following places?

    1.) At $x = 1$? _____

        Is $f(x)$ defined? _____

        Does limit exist? _____
           $x \rightarrow 1$

        Does limit $f(x) = f(x)$? _____
           $x \rightarrow 1$

    2.) At $x = 2$? _____

        Is $f(x)$ defined? _____

        Does limit exist? _____
           $x \rightarrow 2$

        Does limit $(x) = f(x)$? _____
           $x \rightarrow 2$

    3.) At $x = 3$? _____

        Is $f(x)$ defined? _____

        Does limit exist? _____
           $x \rightarrow 3$

        Does limit $f(x) = f(x)$? _____
           $x \rightarrow 3$

II. Draw 2 examples of continuous functions.

continued

Box 13-1 **Lesson Plan—Continued**

III. Draw 2 examples of noncontinuous functions. Explain where and why they are not continuous.

IV. Using a map of the state of Texas, draw a continuous route from Arlington to the university of your choice.

ATTAINING CONCEPTS MODEL (CALCULUS)
POSITIVE AND NEGATIVE EXEMPLARS

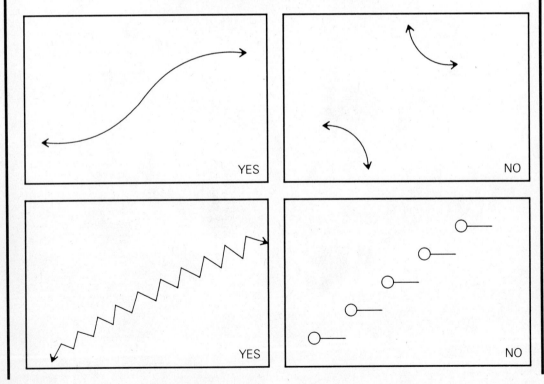

Box 13-1 **Lesson Plan — Continued**

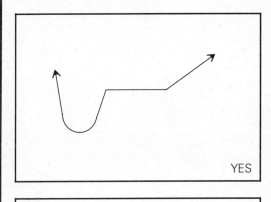

YES

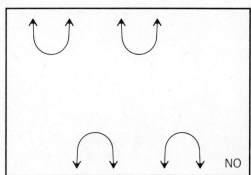

NO

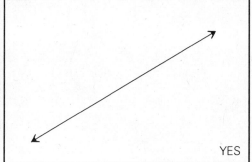

YES

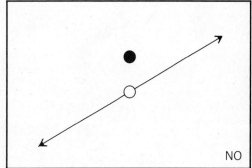

NO

ATTAINING CONCEPTS MODEL (PRECALCULUS)
POSITIVE AND NEGATIVE EXEMPLARS

YES

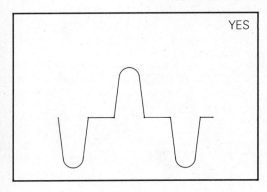

NO

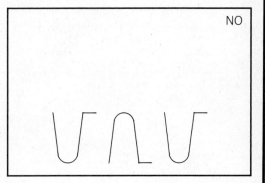

continued

Box 13-1 **Lesson Plan — Continued**

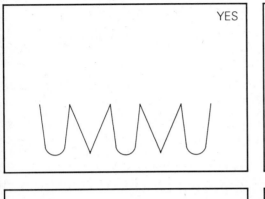
YES

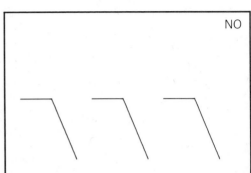
NO

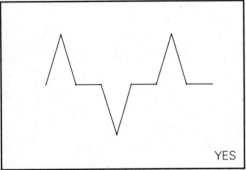
YES

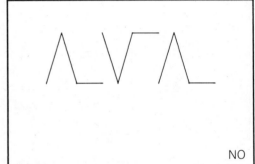
NO

ATTAINING CONCEPTS MODEL
UNLABELED EXEMPLARS

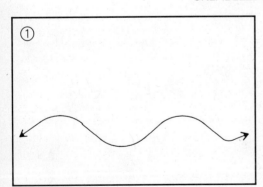
①

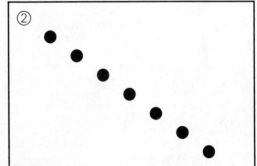
②

Box 13-1 **Lesson Plan — Continued**

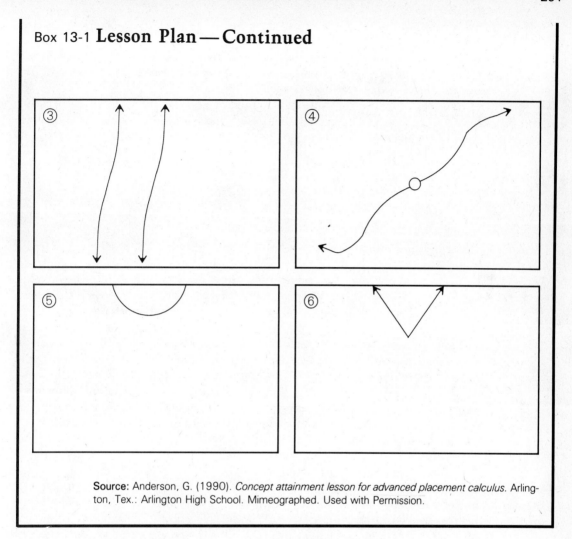

Source: Anderson, G. (1990). *Concept attainment lesson for advanced placement calculus.* Arlington, Tex.: Arlington High School. Mimeographed. Used with Permission.

TRENDS AND ISSUES IN THE MATHEMATICS CURRICULUM

As with the case of the social studies curriculum, the mathematics curriculum is receiving attention from many sectors of society, including those in industry and business as well as math specialists. These groups and individuals are calling for a better way to learn and teach mathematics in grades 7–12. The impetus for change has come from the National Council of Teachers of Mathematics (NCTM) and the National Research Council. The NCTM has called for ". . . sweeping reevaluation of the objectives in math education" (Southwest Educational Development Laboratory, 1989, p. 4). Each has put their recommendations in writing in the *Curriculum and Evaluation Standards for School*

Mathematics and *Everybody Counts: A Report to the Nation on the Future of Mathematics Education*, respectively. These two groups are recommending radical changes for secondary mathematics. These changes would revitalize the curriculum and students would experience the excitement, meaning, and understanding of what mathematics is.

The *Standards* of the National Council of Teachers of Mathematics (1989) have five general goals for mathematics education, which include the following student behaviors:

1. Be mathematical problem solvers
2. Communicate mathematically
3. Develop confidence when doing mathematics
4. Value mathematics
5. Reason mathematically

Currently, not only do many students leave high school believing that mathematics is not for them, they believe that mathematics is beyond their comprehension. In *Everybody Counts* (National Research Council, 1989), the conclusion is that students' poor performance in mathematics has become the norm and even socially acceptable. There is the belief that most people are not supposed to do well in math. What is worse, parents accept this attitude in the students, accept the level of performance, and have even come to expect a poor mathematical ability. If students are to become effective as adults, they will have to use numbers and know what the numbers mean. For those in business and industry, mathematics is the lifeline of our economy, our nation. Reformers believe that the United States must have mathematically literate citizens if our economy, our way of life, is to survive and continue to grow and flourish.

The National Council of Teachers of Mathematics and the National Research Council documents have many similarities and reflect common trends. The first trend that is discussed at length is the role of technology in the mathematics curriculum. The use of technology in the math program helps to make math more relevant. In addition, the use of calculators and computers brings the world of business and industry a little closer to secondary classrooms. Students need to be aware of all of the changes that are occurring in technology and its impact on the mathematics curriculum.

According to the *Standards* (NCTM, 1989), "the new technology not only has made calculations and graphing easier, it has changed the very nature of the problems important to mathematics and the methods that mathematicians use to investigate them" (p. 8). The use of calculators and computers helps students understand decimals, fractions, and algebraic symbols as well as the skill of estimating, scientific notation, exponents, and negative integers (McNeil, 1990; Campbell and Fey, 1988).

One of the newest advances in educational technology for mathematics is the graphing calculator. The use of the graphing calculator is endorsed by the National Council of Teachers of Mathematics in their report. This calculator can be incorporated into the following math courses: fundamentals of mathematics, algebra I, algebra II, geometry, trigonometry, and calculus. Box 13-2

Box 13-2 **How to Graph on the Casio fx-7000G**

Symbol Notation: S - Shift, A - Alpha, G - Graph

BASIC OPERATIONS

Operation	Buttons to Push
1. To clear old graph	$\boxed{S} - \boxed{G \leftrightarrow T} - \boxed{EXE}$
2. To set range of graph	$\boxed{Range}$
3. To trace	$\boxed{S} - \boxed{Graph}$ (use arrow keys to move)
4. To show y = value	$\boxed{S} - \boxed{\downarrow}$
5. To zoom in (changes range)	$\boxed{S} - \boxed{\times}$
6. To zoom out (changes range)	$\boxed{S} - \boxed{+}$
7. To graph Example: $\sqrt{X+1}$	$\boxed{G} - \boxed{\sqrt{}} - \boxed{(} - \boxed{A} - \boxed{+} - \boxed{+} - \boxed{1} - \boxed{)} - \boxed{EXE}$

8. The range can also be changed manually by simply pushing $\boxed{Range}$. To change a number, push $\boxed{EXE}$. This will take you to the next line. When you have changed the part of the range you want changed, push $\boxed{EXE}$. This will take you back to the graph.

9. If you want to see the equation again, push $\boxed{G \rightarrow T}$ key. You don't lose the graph. Just push $\boxed{G \rightarrow T}$ key again.

10. To draw two graphs, use $\boxed{:}$. Then use $\boxed{shift} \rightarrow \boxed{:}$ to draw one graph at a time.

Source: Bargsley, K. (1990). *How to graph on the Casio fx-7000G.* Arlington, Tex.: Sam Houston High School. Mimeographed. Used with permission.

presents a description of the basic steps that are required to do graphing using the Casio fx-7000G calculator. The graphing calculator can help students solve equations using a variety of techniques. These techniques are more general than the algebraic methods previously used. Students can focus on quadratic equations when they have never seen them before.

A second trend that emerges from the various report documents is the role of application when studying mathematics. As mentioned earlier in the chapter, students need opportunities to solve problems and to be able to use the skills of estimating, developing criteria to compare, and summarizing results in mathematical form. It is from these experiences that students learn to construct meanings for specific concepts. When meanings are constructed, the concepts can be used in real life situations. In addition to having students engage in problem solving situations, they learn to value mathematics and develop confidence in their ability to do mathematics.

In middle school mathematics (grades 6–8), application topics include ". . . problem solving, estimation, measurement, graphs and descriptive statistics, and ratio and proportion" (Campbell and Fey, 1988, p. 60). These skills are used in a variety of contexts related to career settings and consumer decisions and involve the interpretation of graphs, tables, and statistics.

In the past, the application exercises have involved the use of paper and pencil — step-by-step procedures in which the students pick a mathematical operation and apply the operation to the numbers provided (Campbell and Fey, 1988). Currently, the emphasis is on having the students think critically and reason logically when given real event situations. According to a middle school teacher, applications of mathematics ". . . make one want to understand and look for 'why' as well as 'how'" (Ames, 1980, p. 10).

The following is an example of how a graphing calculator can serve as a technological tool in the application of mathematical concepts in an algebra class. Barrett and Goebel (1990) pose the problem:

> A travel agency advertises a special deal for group travel to the Super Bowl. Transportation is on a chartered plane that seats 200 passengers. If the group fills the plane, each ticket is $150. The ticket price increases by $1.00 for each empty seat. If the airline charges the travel agency $18,000 for the plane, what is the minimum number of passengers needed for the agency to break even?

In this real life application, the teacher:

1. Conducts a discussion to identify critical data and clarify issues
2. Has students consider specific examples, such as the amount of money the travel agency would get if 190 people paid their money, before considering the abstract relationship
3. Uses small groups of students to develop a table of values with the calculator helping in the process

Related to the trend calling for more application of mathematical skills is the integration of mathematics into other curriculum areas. According to McNeil (1990), "integration of subject matter facilitates the application of mathematical skills in a variety of situations" from homemaking to physics (p. 329). Math helps to translate the quantitative nature of science, social studies, language arts, and other areas as well. The connections between math and other subjects are becoming increasingly important. The connections made between subject areas help to motivate students to want to learn and at the same time reinforce concepts that arise in different contexts (Steen, 1989).

Mathematics can no longer remain isolated from other areas of study nor can it remain fragmented from other subjects within mathematics. For example, when studying leaves in biology or life science, the discussion can focus on the different sets and subsets of leaflets on the stem, the patterns of the leaflets, and the number of leaflets per specific species of plant. In addition, the discussion can focus on where the plants grow by degrees of latitude and longitude. In the social sciences, mathematics can be introduced through the study of timelines. Timelines can function as number lines with movement into the past and future. Parallel events can be studied from the perspective of the arts, politics, economics, and sociology. Table 13.1 provides an example of ways that math concepts can be integrated into the science areas of life science, physical science, and earth science.

A third trend that has been mentioned several times in the literature is the use of a variety of teaching strategies for teaching mathematics in the secondary schools. No longer can teachers of mathematics use direct instruction to the exclusion of other strategies. The key to effective instruction in mathematics is variety, with strategies that foster the direct involvement of students. The recommendation to vary mathematics instruction comes at a time when stu-

Table 13.1   OPPORTUNITIES FOR MATH-SCIENCE INTEGRATION

Math concept	Life science	Physical science	Earth science
Measurement	Metrics	Metrics Temperature	Metrics Map scale Density Specific gravity
Equations	Magnification	Work Speed Temperature conversion Electricity Periodic table	Relative humidity Earthquakes
Probability and statistics	Genetics Environmental sampling		
Ratio/proportion		Balancing equations	
Graphing	Display data	Display data	Display data
Spatial visualization		Lab skills Light	
Geometry/angles		Wave theory Light Sound	Rock/mineral identification
Scientific notation	Growth curves	Electromagnetic spectrum	Radioactive decay Geologic time
Percent		Solutions	
Decimals		Work speed	Specific gravity Density

dents may know basic ideas in algebra and geometry, but they do not understand the underlying concepts (Brown, 1988). There is evidence to suggest that the current instructional practices are not producing results which promote higher-order thinking and problem-solving abilities. One of the major objectives of mathematics education is to help students think clearly and learn concepts in a variety of ways with hands-on experiences. According to *Everybody Counts* (National Research Council, 1989),

> Effective teachers are those who can stimulate students to learn mathematics. Educational research offers compelling evidence that students learn mathematics only when they construct their own mathematical understanding. This happens most readily when students work in groups, engage in discussions, make presentations, and in other ways take charge of their own learning (p. 59).

One teaching strategy that is gaining support is cooperative learning. Cooperative learning can ". . . foster effective mathematical communication, problem solving, logical reasoning, and . . . mathematical connections—all key elements of the NCTM's *Curriculum and Evaluation Standards for School Mathematics*" (Davidson, 1990, p. 52). There is no better way to learn math than to work in groups, to argue about what procedures to use, and to record these procedures in writing (Steen, 1989).

The methods that teachers use should emphasize doing as well as knowing. Math manipulatives have been especially helpful in this endeavor by providing opportunities for students to move objects or rubber bands as they discuss shapes, lines, angles, and proportion and ratio. Methods that teachers use should assist students in learning mathematics through investigation. Some strategies that teachers might consider using when teaching mathematics are advanced organizers, indirect instruction, inquiry/discovery, concept attainment (as presented earlier), alternative questioning strategies and wait time, and the use of technology.

In addition, the incorporation of writing in mathematics classes is gaining momentum. Writing can help students understand mathematics concepts because through the process, they are required to analyze, synthesize, and organize the information that is given. In fact, Steen (1989) says that there is "nothing that helps a student learn a subject better than the discipline of writing about it" (p. 21). Having the students keep a math journal can help them to clarify their misunderstandings, identify abstract concepts, and reflect on their experiences in mathematics classes (Connolly and Vilardi, 1989). By writing about math, students also clarify some of their feelings, which are critical in the development of a positive attitude about learning math.

Students should have the opportunity to write their own definitions, translate symbols, explain formulas, and put problems into words. They should also write out steps as they solve a problem, write their own story problems, and write about math-related current events. It is also helpful to have secondary students write for an audience other than the teacher. Writing can therefore be a useful tool for dealing with mathematical abstractions and for providing students with an opportunity to review and reinforce concepts, and can change the routine of studying math skills through drill and practice.

These trends—the role of technology in the classroom, the application of mathematics to real-life situations, the use of varied instructional strategies, and the integration of math with other content areas, especially writing—are compatible with the other curricular changes identified in this chapter. Reviewing these trends, along with suggested content changes, should bring about change in the overall math curriculum in the secondary schools.

SUMMARY

This chapter discussed the mathematics curriculum in secondary schools. It provided an introduction to the current status of mathematics education in the United States. Because many changes are proposed for mathematics in the coming decade, a brief history of how the curriculum evolved was provided as a background. The chapter continued with a discussion of the general goals for the secondary mathematics curriculum, with attention given to both the junior and senior high school math curriculum.

The objective of mathematics instruction is to have every student explore their world through numbers. Math literacy is the primary goal, getting students to relate what they do in mathematics class with what they do in everyday life. This connection is vital if the next generation of learners is to be successful, productive adults. In addition, mathematically literate citizens are crucial to our economy and the survival of our nation as the world continues to rely on technology.

The chapter concluded with a detailed discussion of the trends that are now occurring in mathematics education. The trends, which include the role of educational technology, the role of application when studying mathematics, and the use of varied teaching strategies, were presented and discussed along with examples. The list is not exhaustive but is significant for the next decade.

YOUR TURN

13.1 Obtain a copy of the *Curriculum and Evaluation Standards for Mathematics* (NCTM, 1989) and review the sections which describe the general goals, the overview for a specific course and grade level, the suggested approaches and use of manipulatives.
   (a) Compare the scope and sequence of the course as it is taught with the recommended topics from the *Standards*.
   (b) Are the topics already included, are concrete examples used, and are examples used that relate to real-life situations? If no, what changes will you make in the future?
   (c) How do you feel about the changes proposed in the *Standards*?

13.2 If in 10 years you are asked to talk to a group of beginning math teachers, what do you think you would say about the teaching of mathematics to adolescents? How would you describe the changes that have occurred in the mathematics curriculum (maybe based on the suggestions from the *Standards*) and the impact of technology on mathematics during the 1990s?

(a) What points would you make specifically to get these new teachers off to a great start?

(b) In your remarks, how would you address or account for the following statement as it relates to mathematics instruction? "Intelligence, cultural background, gender, and motivation 'really' determine if a student will be successful in mathematics."

What are the arguments against this view?

How will you help new teachers overcome these stereotypes?

13.3 How do you feel about mathematics and mathability? Use the following rating scale:

5 — Strongly agree
4 — Agree
3 — Not sure
2 — Disagree
1 — Strongly disagree

1. I am comfortable when someone says solve this math problem.	5 4 3 2 1
2. I am relaxed when given problems to solve.	5 4 3 2 1
3. I get very, very excited when given the opportunity to solve a problem.	5 4 3 2 1
4. I don't feel that people who do math are smarter than anyone else.	5 4 3 2 1
5. I recognize the role of math in everyday life.	5 4 3 2 1
6. I think men are generally better at math than women.	5 4 3 2 1
7. I am good at solving problems.	5 4 3 2 1
8. I freeze when I am told that a situation requires mathematics.	5 4 3 2 1
9. Getting the right answer is my goal when solving math problems.	5 4 3 2 1
10. I encourage students to find several ways to solve the same problem.	5 4 3 2 1
11. I like mathematics.	5 4 3 2 1
12. I am concerned as much about knowing and understanding as getting the answer.	5 4 3 2 1
13. I feel at home using manipulatives to help solve problems.	5 4 3 2 1
14. I view mathematics as a language in which I use symbols (sometimes foreign) rather than letters and words.	5 4 3 2 1
15. The *Standards* provides a coherent plan for secondary school mathematics.	5 4 3 2 1

After responding to each of these items, review your responses. Items 4 and 6 are stereotypes that teachers should try to dispell. Item 8 describes a person who has math anxiety. Item 9 is another example of a stereotype in which many people believe, but education should discourage this process.

13.4 Assume the role of a teacher of mathematics (geometry, algebra I, II, general math, and calculus) how would you get your students to write more (beyond writing problems) in your course (e.g., keep a journal)?

13.5 The use of graphing calculators in teaching and learning mathematics can prove helpful. Review the activity described in Box 13-2 and the steps required to do graphing using the calculator. Develop several activities that you could do to use this tool in algebra, geometry, or trigonometry classes. (Note: For suggestions, consult the article by Barrett and Goebel, 1990).

REFERENCES

Ames, P. (1980). A classroom teacher looks at applications. In D. Bushaw, et al. (Eds.). *A resourcebook of applications of school mathematics.* Reston, Va.: National Council of Teachers of Mathematics.

Anderson, G. (1990). *Concept attainment lesson for advanced placement calculus.* Arlington, Tex.: Arlington High School. Mimeographed.

Bargsley, K. (1990). *How to graph on the Casio fx-7000G.* Arlington, Tex.: Arlington High School, Mimeographed.

Barrett, G. & Goebel, J. (1990). The impact of graphing calculators on teaching and learning of mathematics. In T. Cooney & C. Hirsch (Eds.). *Teaching and learning mathematics in the 1990's: 1990 yearbook.* Reston, Va.: National Council of Teachers of Mathematics.

Beckner, W. & Cornett, J.D. (1972). *Secondary school curriculum: Content and structure.* Scranton, Pa.: Intext. Educational Publishers.

Brown, C. (1988). Secondary school results for the fourth NAEP mathematics assessment. *Mathematics Teacher, 81* 5, 337–347.

Campbell, P.F. & Fey, J.T. (1988). New goals for school mathematics. In R.S. Brandt (Ed.). *Content of the curriculum: 1988 ASCD Yearbook.* Reston, Va.: Association for Supervision and Curriculum Development.

Connolly, P. & Vilardi, T. (1989). *Writing to learn mathematics and science.* New York: Columbia Teachers College Press.

Davidson, N. (1990). Small-group cooperative learning in mathematics. In T. Cooney & C. Hirsch (Eds.). *Teaching and learning mathematics in the 1990's: 1990 Yearbook.* Reston, Va.: National Council of Teachers of Mathematics.

Driscoll, M. (Ed.). (1987). *Research within reach: Secondary school mathematics: A research-guided response to the concerns of educators.* Reston, Va.: National Council of Teachers of Mathematics.

Education Commission of the States. (1983). National assessment of educational progress. *The third national mathematics assessment: Results, trends, and issues.* Report No. 13-MA-01. Denver: Education Commission of the States.

Fey, J.T. (1983). *Computing and mathematics: The impact on secondary school curriculums.* Reston, Va.: National Council of Teachers of Mathematics.

Kinsella, J.J. (1965). *Secondary school mathematics.* New York: Center for Applied Research in Education.

Kline, M. (1973). *Why Johnny can't add.* New York: Vintage Books.

Lochhead, J. (1981). Research synthesis on problem solving. *Educational Leadership, 39,* 68–70.

McKnight, C.C. et al. (1987). *The underachieving curriculum: Assessing U.S. school mathematics from an international perspective.* Champaign, Ill.: Stipes Publishing Co.

McNeil, J.D. (1990). *Curriculum: A comprehensive introduction* (4th ed.). New York: Scott Foresman.

National Council of Teachers of Mathematics. (1989). *Curriculum and evaluation stan-*

dards for school mathematics. Reston, Va.: National Council of Teachers of Mathematics.

National Research Council. (1989). *Everybody counts: A report to the nation on the future of mathematics education*. Washington, D.C.: National Academy Press.

Report of the committee of ten on secondary school subjects. (1894). New York: American Books.

Schoenfeld, A.H. (1989). Teaching mathematical thinking and problem solving. In L.B. Resnick & L.E. Klopfer (Eds.). *Toward the thinking curriculum: Current cognitive research: 1989 ASCD Yearbook*. Reston, Va.: Association for Supervision and Curriculum Development.

Schoenfeld, A.H. (1983). *Problem solving in the mathematics curriculum: A report, recommendations, and an annotated bibliography*. Washington, D.C.: Mathematical Association of America.

Steen, L.A. (1989). Teaching mathematics for tomorrow's world. *Educational Leadership, 47*, 1, 18–22.

Southwest Educational Development Laboratory. (September/October 1989). Working a tough equation: Mathematics educators call for radical overhaul of instructional approaches. *SEDLetter, Vol 2*, No 5.

U.S. students found lagging. (September 27, 1990). *Dallas Morning News*, p. 6A.

Chapter
14

Science in the Secondary School Curriculum

Scientific advancements in medicine, communication, and space have commanded a lot of public attention in the past 25 years. While our nation has relied heavily on science for technological products, our citizens remain scientifically illiterate. Although scientific illiteracy was an issue in the 1960s, it still is a major concern of science educators and those in the business world as we move into the twenty-first century.

One reason students are scientifically illiterate is that they avoid science courses, viewing them as irrelevant and reserved for only those going into science-related occupations. In reality, those entering these occupations are dwindling. Beckner and Cornett (1972) found this was the case over 20 years ago and the 1990s do not seem very different. Champagne (1989) confirms that when she says that the ". . . state of [the] average American's level of scientific literacy" remains deplorably low (p. 85). She reached this conclusion after reviewing over 300 reports that have been written on the status of science education in the United States.

Even though the general public recognizes and acknowledges the need for science and for students to enter the science professions, a dichotomy between desire and action exists (Beckner and Cornett, 1972; Champagne, 1989). Secondary students learn early that scientific knowledge is very technical to really understand and feel that they will never use what they learn in their daily lives now or in the future. Besides, they think, new knowledge is generated at an exponential rate and who can keep up with it.

Even with efforts made during the first wave of reform in the 1960s after Sputnik, the science projects for secondary schools were content-based with little attention paid to process. These projects were aimed at restructuring the content, but not the science curriculum as a whole (Yager, 1988). Although several projects were developed, Introductory Physical Science, Biological Sciences Curriculum Study (which includes Yellow, Blue, and Green versions), and Chemical Bond Approach to name a few, they did little to help bring about lasting change in secondary science education.

Chapter 14 presents a historical overview of the science curriculum during the past 40 years. This account sets the stage for the goals of the science curriculum in grades 7–12 that are presented next. Following the goals, the focus will be on the science taught at the junior and senior high school levels. The chapter concludes with a discussion of the current trends and issues in the 7–12 science curriculum.

HISTORY OF THE SCIENCE CURRICULUM

After the Second World War, the interest in science increased, and in 1950 the National Science Foundation (NSF) was created and funded by Congress as an independent governmental agency (Boyer, 1985; Yager, 1988). In that same year, the first textbook for science teachers was published, and the enthusiasm for science continued to grow.

With the launching of the Sputnik in 1957, legislators at the federal level responded by initiating a war on scientific illiteracy by passing laws that poured millions of dollars into science, mathematics, and foreign language instruction. While $15 million was spent in 1950, $40 million was appropriated in 1959 to revitalize science education, especially in the areas of biology, chemistry, and physics (McCormack and Yager, 1989). Box 14-1 lists several of the science projects developed for junior and senior high school students. As you can see from the list there are projects for earth science, life science, physical science, biology, chemistry, and physics. Scientists played a prominent role in developing and directing these projects (Kyle, no date cited).

Consequently, the science curriculum of the 1960s was shaped by those who believed that the content should be taught by science specialists. The long-term objective of science instruction during the 1960s in grades 7–12 was to train ". . . highly skilled scientists and technicians" for the next decade (McNeil, 1990, p. 333). Therefore, science was not taught with all the secondary students in mind, but rather for those who were academically talented.

During the 1970s, there was an effort to "humanize the sciences" (McNeil, 1990, p. 333). With this new effort came an interest in using a multidisciplinary approach. Science teachers worked in teams with those outside the sciences in an attempt to integrate science into the total secondary curriculum. These

---

Box 14-1 **Representative Science Curricula**

JUNIOR HIGH CURRICULA

Earth Science Curriculum Project (ESCP)

Individualized Science Instructional System (ISIS)

Interaction Science Curriculum Project (ISCP)

Intermediate Science Curriculum Study (ISCS)

Introductory Physical Science (IPS)

HIGH SCHOOL CURRICULA

Biological Sciences Curriculum Study (BSCS)
  Yellow Version
  Blue Version
  Green Version

Chemical Bond Approach (CBA)

Chemical Education Materials Study (CHEM Study)

Harvard Project Physics (HPP)

Physical Science Study Committee (PSSC)

---

teams of "specialists," as they called themselves, focused on the principles of science as they dealt with contemporary issues (McNeil, 1990). One such issue that gained importance during the 1970s was the use of chemicals during the Vietnam War. Questions were raised about the effect these chemicals would have on living things, particularly humans, and the genetic code passed on to future generations. In addition, questions were raised about how to dispose of chemical wastes. It took another twenty years before these questions were dealt with seriously by the general public and state and federal lawmakers.

The attention that science education had received during the previous 15 years had begun to wane in the 1970s when reading and math literacy became the national issues. It was during this time that parents pressed for higher test scores in reading, leaving science behind. Science was no longer occupying center stage, it had been replaced with a new concern. It was during this time that the enrollment in high school science courses began to decline. It became clear by the late 1970s and early 1980s that the "back to the basics" movement and testing were the educational concerns for those at the state and national levels.

While attention was focused on reading, science education continued to decline. According to McNeil (1990), 50 percent of high school students did not take science after the tenth grade. The situation gradually worsened, and by the end of the 1980s science instruction was reduced to rote learning, the text became the major approach used, and the elective offerings were at an all-time low (McCormack and Yager, 1989).

It was evident by the 1980s that science education in the United States was in crisis (McNeil, 1990). During the early part of the decade, science instruction lacked the spark needed to make it an important national agenda item. What made matters worse was that in 1981 science education accounted for only 2 percent of the National Science Foundation budget from an all-time high of 47 percent in 1959 (Yager, 1988).

As early as 1978, science educators were writing papers outlining the many problem areas that were plaguing the science curriculum. The following is a composite list of these concerns and problem areas as contributed by Harms and Yager (1981), Stake and Easley (1978), and Weiss (1978). However, it took another five years for the public and lawmakers to recognize that there was indeed a crisis.

Their concerns focused on

1. *Science instruction:* secondary students did not receive the instruction in science that they needed or wanted
2. *Lack of direct science experiences:* the science text served as the major resource in 95 percent of the classrooms
3. *Purpose of science instruction:* the purpose of science was to prepare students for the next science course they would take rather than helping students become scientifically literate
4. *Lack of a comprehensive scope and sequence:* there was no scope and sequence for science except for what the text provided in each course
5. *Lack of concern about preparing scientifically literate future citizens:* science instruction was not directed toward helping all students become scientifically literate about their immediate environment or the world beyond it

Such concerns prompted state officials to increase science requirements for graduation. As more and more people wrote about the state of science education, the reform movement began to take shape. McCormack and Yager (1989) found that in 1987, 47 states ". . . reported having course credit requirements in science . . . [and] of these, 39 required two courses . . . in science" (p. 3).

If the Sputnik shocked Americans into focusing on science in the late 1950s, the "economic Sputnik" of the early 1980s forced them to reassess the status of science education again. No longer were we competing with the Soviet Union; now our competitor was Japan. At this time, the cry was not for the United States to be number one in the space race, but to become more competitive in the economic world arena. The economic future of the United States was at stake, and the future depended upon students who were scientifically literate and who could enter the job market with problem-solving skills and an understanding of technology and its role in the world community (Hurd, 1988).

By 1988, science education had reached its lowest level when *The Science Report Card: Elements of Risk and Recovery* was written. The data included in *The Science Report Card* are not encouraging and provided the final blow that the reform movement needed to influence the thinking of key citizens and reverse the downward spiral that science education had experienced during the past 25 years. *The Science Report Card* included the following statistics:

1. Science achievement of 17-year-olds in 1986 was far below that of their counterparts in 1969
2. Science achievement for 13-year-olds was below that of their counterparts in 1970
3. Over half of the 17-year-olds were not prepared for the technical jobs waiting for them in industry
4. Only 7 percent of those graduating from high school had the knowledge and skills to be successful in college level science courses
5. Black and Hispanic 13- and 17-year-olds were nearly 4 years behind their white counterparts
6. Only half of the boys and one-third of the girls could analyze using scientific procedures

This document along with many others reported that the goal of an experience-based science curriculum had given way to one that was textbook- and direct-instruction-driven (McCormack and Yager, 1989). Ashworth (1990) puts this statement in perspective when he says that during the last 20 years students have not mastered the science concepts and skills needed to function successfully and productively in society. In addition, he says, they are lagging behind their international counterparts. With these significant shortcomings, the 7–12 science curriculum was destined to change in favor of a more hands-on, inquiry-based approach (Wellington, 1989).

Another dimension of the reform movement was the role of ethics and values associated with scientific discoveries. The ethics related to genetic engineering, chemical warfare, use of pesticides, and so on would be an issue facing citizens of the twenty-first century, who would have to make decisions. Therefore, secondary students not only need the scientific knowledge to understand what is involved in these issues, but also the decision-making skills to make choices.

The history of science education during the past 40 years had an initial boost in the years following the Sputnik, but science experienced a gradual and steady decline in the 1970s that continued into the 1980s. It appears that the reform movement in science education is taking hold, with Project 2061 leading the way. Project 2061 is unlike the projects of the 1960s; its objective is to completely rethink the learning outcomes of the K–12 science curriculum (Rutherford and Ahlgren, 1990, 1988). As a result of building a comprehensive science curriculum, students will graduate from high school with a basic understanding of ". . . the nature of science, mathematics, and technology as human enterprises" (Ahlgren, 1990, p. 84). With such efforts expended by those in the National Science Teachers Association, these goals for science education will be realized.

GOALS FOR THE SCIENCE CURRICULUM

Historically, science educators have advocated a process approach to learning science; in fact as early as 1831 the process approach was mentioned, so a hands-on strategy certainly is not new, or radical. Brook, Drive, and Johnston (1989) go a step further by saying that science learning occurs when students have opportunities to construct and reconstruct their own learning and understanding of the world in which they live. Kirkham (1989) sums up the objective of the science curriculum when he says that science teaching/learning should be based on the dynamic interaction of process skills, scientific attitudes, and knowledge that is acquired through a laboratory approach.

Rothmer (1987) believes science is for *all* students, not just those interested in a career in science. Atkin (1983) concurs, saying that high school science should be broad based, not just a place to prepare for college. Rather than an end in itself, science should be the means of learning about the physical world as well as the most immediate environment. Adeniyi (1987) takes this idea and builds on it when he says that all students should be taught to look at the world as scientists—those who observe, solve problems, and apply the techniques of discovery and experimentation.

The National Science Teachers Association (NSTA) produced a position paper, "Science-Technology-Society: Science Education for the 1980s" (1982) which said that the goal of science should be to help individuals understand how science, technology, and society impact one another; in effect the goal was to have scientifically literate citizens. The hope was that future voters would have the knowledge and problem-solving skills to deal with societal and environmental problems. In the final analysis, science, technology, and society should be a part of the science curriculum and a key organizer for designing the scope and sequence for the science curriculum in the secondary school (Yager, 1988).

Rutherford and Ahlgren (1988) support the idea that the study of science is for all students and recommend as part of the rethinking process that a common science knowledge base be identified that all students would learn. Along with this common knowledge base is the need to understand concepts and how they relate to each other. They believe that students need to gain an understanding of their world and their role in it.

The architects of Project 2061, previously mentioned, identified key principles for the development and implementation of the K–12 science curriculum for all students. Rutherford and Ahlgren (1988) summarized the Project 2061 report and the 11 key principles are presented below.

1. To identify what the students should know is the first step in building an effective science curriculum

2. To establish for all students a common core of goals designed to meet the scientific needs of a specific student population
3. To express learning goals using concepts that match these goals, otherwise there may be a tendency to redistribute the current science content into new categories
4. To include teaching strategies as the learning outcomes are being identified
5. To represent the full spectrum of the sciences in scope and sequence
6. To integrate mathematics into the science curriculum
7. To include technology in the science curriculum
8. To incorporate other curriculum areas into the science scope and sequence to enrich it and to help students view science in a larger context
9. To include not only facts, laws, principles, and theories, but also to have students view science as a way of thinking and conducting inquiry
10. To relate science to what is happening in our daily lives as well as to other aspects of our human affairs
11. To align science content with the educational criteria that have already been established

These principles can serve as a guide and encourage science educators and curriculum developers to plan and implement a science program that includes a balance between science content, process, and context (Kirkham, 1989). The end product of such a curriculum is scientific knowledge that can be applied to the student's world. For Staver and Small (1990), an ". . . activity based, materials oriented science that is conceptually rich, emphasizes discovery and inquiry through science process skills, relates science and technology to individual needs . . . and provides career awareness experiences, would seem to provide the best foundation for all students . . ." (p. 87). More emphasis, then, needs to be placed on using a thematic approach to foster problem solving, critical thinking, and decision making skills when secondary students are learning about earth, life, and the physical sciences.

OVERVIEW OF THE SCIENCE CURRICULUM GRADES 7 – 12

In spite of all the efforts to involve all students in science courses, science in the secondary school still appears to be geared toward the bright student. Most students take life science, earth science, and physical science at the junior high school level, and biology, chemistry, and physics at the senior high school level. In terms of percentages, most students take a biology course, but fewer take chemistry and very few take physics. Neuschatz and Covalt (1989) report that very few students like physics, which may account for why a low number of students elect to take it.

In grades 7 (life science) and 8 (earth science), the curriculum remains general. The curriculum in life science and earth science is broad, and the degree of hands-on experience varies. It is in these courses that students should have an opportunity to experience the general nature of biology and geology. Also, these courses should focus on those topics of interest to the students. The purpose of junior high school science is to acquaint students with science and interest them in taking more courses in science in high school. However, this has not been the case (McCormack and Yager, 1989). In addition, science at this level should act as a bridge that connects what has been taught at the elementary level with what the students will experience in biology, chemistry, and physics. In the following section, life, earth, and physical science courses will be examined.

Life Science

Students study life science in the seventh grade in most school districts. Another name for such a course is general science, which may be a combination of both life and earth science. In a life science course, themes are studied in conjunction with organisms and their habitats, which include the flow of energy in the biosphere, the basic biological processes of plants and animals, and the human body. When studying the human body, the focus is on its structure, function, and how to maintain it. Students at this age are particularly interested in their bodies and how to make them look as good as possible. In addition, students study about diseases that affect the body, such as AIDS and other diseases.

During the study of living organisms students work in small groups when they conduct laboratory and field investigations. Process skills of observation, inferring, measuring, and predicting are emphasized during their investigations. The laboratory activities provide the students with opportunities to collect data, to make accurate observations, analyze the data, to manipulate laboratory equipment and use it correctly and safely. Laboratory safety is an important dimension of any science course, and junior high school students learn the proper way to carry a microscope to their tables, to wear goggles when working with material that could damage their eyes, to light the Bunsen burner, and so on. Table 14.1 lists many of the key topics and subtopics that junior high students learn in a life science course.

Earth Science

One of the goals of earth science taught at the eighth grade level is to help students become aware about and appreciate the Earth. In addition, students learn about the benefits and applications of historical and physical geology along with the benefits derived from the study of meteorology, oceanography, and astronomy to everyday living. Earth science tends to be multidisciplinary in nature because students learn about several areas of science. By understanding the Earth, for example, students can apply this information as they consider problems related to energy shortages, predicting earthquakes, tracking hurricanes, and managing the planet's resources effectively.

Table 14.1   GENERAL TOPICS FOR SECONDARY SCIENCE CURRICULUM

Grade level	Subject	Topics

7	Life Science	Introduction to life science
		    Ways to investigate the living world
		    Using the tools to investigate
		Exploring the variety of living organisms
		    Plants (nonvascular and vascular with seeds and without)
		    Animals (invertebrates and vertebrates)
		    Protists
		The interaction and distribution of living organisms
		    Ecosystems
		    Balance and preservation
		The living organism
		    The cell
		    Seed plants (uses, structure, functions, and needs)
		    The human body (systems)
		Energy and living organisms
		    Matter, elements, atoms as related to living things
		    Photosynthesis
		    The cycle of matter and energy (photosynthesis, respiration, and decay)
		Continuity of life
		    Reproduction and development
		    Genetics and heredity
		    The influence of the environment on heredity and development
		The nature of life — past and present
		    Change (fossil record, natural selection)
		    Understanding diversity among living things
		The environment
		    Problems, conserving, and preservation
		    Future directions

Earth science focuses on the physical features and the processes that change its surface. The concepts of change and interrelationships are essential when studying about the Earth's crust and how it has been altered over time. A major goal of earth science instruction should be not only to teach facts, principles, and theories, but to have students engage in laboratory investigations. The hands-on experience enables students to understand such concepts as erosion, mountain building, volcanoes, the crystallized shapes of many minerals, and making and using weather-related instruments.

In 1962, the Earth Science Curriculum Project (ESCP) was developed in an attempt to bring together several disciplines — astronomy, geology, meteorology, oceanography, and physical geography — which were often part of an earth science course. This project tried to weave three themes into the curriculum: science as inquiry, comprehension of scale, and prediction. A more general course of study, as described above, can be found in the middle/junior high schools today.

Table 14.2 identifies the major topics taught in an eighth grade earth science course. The topics include those in astronomy, geology, meteorology, and oceanography as well as the topics of change and modification.

Physical Science

The focus of physical science is on the study of matter and energy. Students learn about the properties of matter, atomic structure, compounds and mixtures, chemical reactions, acids and bases, salts, metals, nonmetals and metalloids, carbon compounds, force and energy, work and machines, motion, heat, electricity, and many other topics. One of the major goals of physical science, as with other courses in the secondary science curriculum, is to expand the students' conception of science ". . . to include an understanding of science processes, or the skills scientists use to gather new knowledge (McCormack and Yager, 1989, p. 47).

Table 14.2   GENERAL TOPICS FOR SECONDARY SCIENCE CURRICULUM

Grade level	Subject	Topics
8	Earth Science (study of the Earth)	Introduction
		Defining Earth science
		Scientific method
		Measurement
		Tools
		Map skills
		Reading maps
		Types of maps, e.g., topographic maps
		Map making of Earth's features
		Astronomy
		Location
		Structure of Earth
		Earth's movements
		Seasons
		The Moon and its relationship to Earth
		The Earth and the Sun
		Origin of the solar system
		The Sun, its features, and the energy generated
		The solar system
		Members of the solar system: planets, asteroids, comets
		Exploring space
		The universe
		Observing stars and considering distances
		Types of stars and life expectancy
		Galaxies

Table 14.2   GENERAL TOPICS FOR SECONDARY SCIENCE CURRICULUM *Continued*

Grade level	Subject	Topics
		Geology
		Earth's structure
		The origin of the Earth
		Earth's minerals (identification and
		properties)
		Matter and atoms
		Three types of rocks (the rock cycle)
		Earth's resources (renewable and
		nonrenewable)
		Pollution
		The changing Earth
		Weathering and erosion
		Plate tectonics and continental drift theory
		Volcanoes and earthquakes
		The Earth and time—record in rocks,
		formation of fossils, methods of dating,
		geologic time scale
		Meteorology
		Atmosphere: temperature and air pressure
		Wind and types
		Changing weather—air masses, fronts,
		thunderstorms, tornadoes, hurricanes
		Forecasting weather
		Oceanography
		Earth's fresh water
		Earth's oceans and resources

Physical science was included in the first public high school, which opened in 1821, and it remained a part of the curriculum until about 1900 (Beckner and Cornett, 1972). It was dropped when interest in the subject began to decline. From as early as the turn of the century, students have avoided physical science, with less than 20 percent taking physics 50 years later (Beckner and Cornett, 1972). With this as a backdrop, the Physical Science Study Committee (PSSC) met in 1956 to develop a physical science course that was relevant, included up-to-date information, and integrated the many diverse topics that were a part of this course.

Table 14.3 includes many of the key topics that are taught in a typical physical science course. It is evident that the students are studying more advanced concepts than was true in life and earth science. Since the concepts are more complex, it is recommended that students have opportunities to investigate them in greater depth in a laboratory setting.

In 1985 the Texas Learning Technology Group (TLTG) was formed to develop ways to use technology in the classroom. The TLTG Physical Science course, which utilizes interactive videodisc technology, was developed. As a

Table 14.3   GENERAL TOPICS FOR SECONDARY SCIENCE CURRICULUM

Grade level	Subject	Topics
9	Physical Science	Introduction
		Tools needed
		Investigating physical science
		Exploring matter
		Properties of matter (volume, mass, density)
		Classifying matter (elements, compounds, mixtures, and solutions)
		Building blocks (atoms, bonding)
		Chemical structure of matter
		Chemical reactions (chemical change, equations, chemical energy)
		The chemistry of acids, bases, salts
		Carbon (bonding, types of carbon compounds)
		Carbon in living things
		Mechanical energy
		Work, force, and power
		Motion
		Forms of energy (conversion and conservation)
		Electrical energy
		Currents (conductivity, sources of electricity, voltage)
		Electronics
		Magnetism
		Magnets
		Magnetic field
		Electromagnetism
		Societal issues
		Balancing electrical energy needs against environmental considerations
		Heat energy
		Motion, temperature
		Kinetic theory
		Sound energy
		Waves
		Pitch, intensity
		Application (music)
		Light energy
		Waves
		Color and intensity
		Reflection, refraction
		Spectrum
		Technology and physical science
		Resources (electronic, industrial, energy)
		The environment
		The future directions for physical science
		Development of energy ideas
		Possibilities for the future: Superconducting Super Collider

two-semester course, it promises to increase student achievement, to provide students with a greater conceptual understanding, and to stimulate student interest in science. The TLTG Physical Science course includes the following components: 15 videodisc slides, software on computer diskettes, a teacher resource guide, and a student manual containing summary notes, practice sets, and laboratory activities, along with a technical support guide. This group boasts that the TLTG Physical Science course includes the most current information that most ninth graders in physical science courses would learn, utilizing state of the art equipment.

Science in the high school includes biology, chemistry, and physics, as well as advanced versions of these courses. The content for each of these courses is broad, but taught in greater depth than was the case of the courses at the middle/junior high school level. General biology is taught in the tenth grade and expands on topics that were presented in the seventh grade life science course. Students in their junior year take chemistry if they are preparing to go to college, and some of these students take physics. Each of these courses will be described in detail in the following section.

Biology

Of all the science courses taught in the secondary school, biology remains the most popular, with more students taking this course than others. The field of biology has experienced many changes in the last 25 years. In 1959, about 30 biologists, teachers, and other science educators met and formed the Biological Sciences Curriculum Study (BSCS) group. This group was responsible for developing many modern biology courses. Three versions of the BSCS programs were developed, which included the Blue Version, which focused on the physiological-biochemical aspects; the Green Version, which focused on the environment and had an ecological orientation; and the Yellow Version, which had a classical development with a cellular emphasis.

The biology course described here will be of a general nature, which tends to include the concepts present in all three of the BSCS versions. Students take a general biology course in their sophomore year, and the course is laboratory oriented. The course includes a study of cells, genetics, invertebrates, botany, body systems, plant and animal systems, diseases, and ecology. In some high schools, students can also take honors biology or biology II. The major focus of these courses is a more in-depth study of the topics already mentioned. These students are expected to conduct research as well. If students take honors biology, they can take the advanced placement test and receive college credit if they successfully pass the test. Table 14.4 provides more specifics regarding the scope and sequence of a general biology course.

Chemistry

Students usually take chemistry in their junior year after a year of biology, algebra I, and geometry. Since mathematics is an important part of chemistry, concurrent enrollment in algebra II is often required.

Table 14.4   GENERAL TOPICS FOR SECONDARY SCIENCE CURRICULUM

Grade level	Subject	Topics
10	General Biology	Introduction to the nature of life
		The science of biology
		The scientific method
		Using the microscope
		The nature of life
		Origins of life
		Environmental relationships: change, adaptation, and survival
		The chemical dimension of life
		Cell theory, processes, functions, and structure
		The organization of life (levels)
		The cell
		Osmosis and diffusion
		Active transport and absorption
		Nutrition at the cell level (energy production, photosynthesis)
		Metabolism at the cell level (anabolism, catabolism, and energy transport)
		Cell growth and reproduction (mitosis, meiosis, and fertilization)
		Patterns of heredity
		Principles of heredity (Mendel's law, dominance, and chance)
		The genetic code (genes, chromosomes, sex of offspring, gene action, mutation, aberrations)
		Population genetics (gene pool, sex-linked characteristics, genetically linked diseases and disorders)
		Applying genetics
		Variation among living organisms (geologic timetable, speciation, and benefits of change and adaptation)
		Classifying living things (based on physical and physiological characteristics)
		Microbiology
		Viruses and bacteria
		Diseases related to viruses and bacteria
		Protozoans, fungi, and algae
		Botany: multicellular plants
		Mosses and ferns
		Gymnosperms and angiosperms
		The leaf, roots, and stems, and how they function
		Relationship of water in plants
		Growth, reproduction, and responses in plants
		Invertebrates
		Introduction
		Sponges and coelenterates
		Worms
		Mollusks and echinoderms
		Arthropods
		Insects

Table 14.4   GENERAL TOPICS FOR SECONDARY SCIENCE CURRICULUM *Continued*

Grade level	Subject	Topics
		Vertebrates
		Introduction
		Fishes
		Amphibians
		Reptiles
		Birds
		Mammals
		Studying man
		Historical development
		Systems of the body
		Nutrition, transport, and excretion
		Health (alcohol, narcotics, tobacco)
		Ecology
		Introduction
		Habitat and changes in the environment
		Resources
		Distribution of plants and animals and conservation of species

The curriculum in chemistry has changed little during the past 70 years, and it has been criticized for being so traditional (Beckner and Cornett, 1972). In addition, students in chemistry have to memorize facts and formulas, often without really understanding what they mean. The best known of the chemistry courses was Chemical Education Materials Study (CHEM Study) which focuses on structural chemistry and chemical dynamics.

In a general chemistry course, the following topics are included: basic atomic theory, gas laws, use and application of moles, nomenclature, writing and balancing chemical equations, acid-base theory, and basic laboratory techniques and procedures. In honors chemistry students learn about kinetics, thermodynamics, atomic energy, equilibrium, stoichiometry, electrochemistry, and nuclear and organic chemistry. Along with the advanced study of specific content, students are expected to demonstrate advanced laboratory and research skills. Table 14.5 includes additional topics and subtopics for a high school junior level general chemistry course.

Physics

Students in their senior year of high school usually take physics if they are going to college or if they plan to major in science or mathematics. One of the most famous programs was the Harvard Project Physics course, which was developed in 1962. It differed from the PSSC and the traditional physics course in the following way: it was designed for the educated citizen, and it included

Table 14.5 GENERAL TOPICS FOR SECONDARY SCIENCE CURRICULUM

Grade level	Subject	Topics
11	Chemistry	General skills and concepts
		Individuals and events in the history of chemistry
		Terminology relevant to common scientific laboratory work
		Application of scientific skills and knowledge to daily living
		Safe and proper use of equipment and supplies
		Data collection and techniques
		Experimental laboratory procedures
		Methods of quantification, computation, and measurement
		Principles of classification, sequencing, and inference
		Matter and energy
		Physical and chemical properties
		Atoms and their structure according to the quantum theory
		Molecules and ions
		Understanding the mole to solve problems
		Solid, liquid, and gaseous states of matter
		Phase changes in terms of pressure and temperature
		Chemistry of solutions
		Chemistry of electrolytes and the theory of ionization
		Kinetic theory
		Principles of thermodynamics
		Enthalpy, entrophy, and free energy
		Elements and compounds
		Chemical notation and the properties of elements
		Periodic Table
		Types of chemical compounds and their classification
		Electron configuration
		Chemical bonds (types and characteristics)
		Equations and reactions
		Notation, classification, and balancing chemical equations
		Reaction rate
		Chemical equilibrium
		Acids and bases
		Oxidation-reduction reactions
		Electrochemistry
		Aqueous equilibria
		Organic and nuclear chemistry
		Terminology and classification of organic chemistry
		Properties of organic compounds and their reactions
		Applications of organic chemistry
		Principles of nuclear radioactivity
		Principles of nuclear reactions
		Applications of nuclear chemistry

content that increased in complexity, but the details were presented as a means of creating a sense of what nature is all about.

Although classified as a science course, physics requires students to do extensive mathematical calculations. Hence, algebra I and geometry and possible concurrent enrollment in algebra II are prerequisites. A general course in physics includes the study of motion, forces, work, energy, heat, waves, and electricity. Also offered in some secondary science programs is honors physics or physics II for those students who are interested in taking the advanced placement test and receiving college credit. In advanced physics students concentrate on such complex topics as mechanics, Newton's Laws of Motion, rotation, oscillation-gravitation, electricity, and magnetism.

It is evident from this list of topics that physics is taught as a body of knowledge, facts, figures, and theories as accepted by physicists in the field. Teachers take this information and translate this into a standard presentation that they teach in their physics class (McCormack and Yager, 1989). Table 14.6 lists the many different topics taught in a general senior level physics class.

In the overview of the chapter, the basic science courses in grades 7–12 were presented. From the descriptions, it may seem evident that the content in each of these courses have remained rather constant even though over the years there have been efforts to update them. It was our objective to present the concepts that are generally presented in the various science courses that can be found in the secondary schools today. As discussed earlier in this chapter, Project 2061 is a model that curriculum developers can use to guide them in revising their current science program for grades 7–12.

In the next section several trends and issues regarding science education are presented. It is in this section that information about the future direction of the science curriculum is presented. In this last section of the chapter, other features are presented that curriculum developers should consider as they review the science curriculum in their school district.

TRENDS AND ISSUES IN THE SCIENCE CURRICULUM

One of the trends in science education is to help students appreciate the role of science in their lives. If students value the science they learn, they develop a more positive attitude toward science in general (Hodson, 1988). In Imperial, Missouri, for example, junior high school students help solve some of the problems in their city. Helping to resolve problems was an integral part of their science program. It was hoped that if students recognized the value of what they were learning in their science classes, they would attach more importance to it and would view science learning in a more positive light (Hodson, 1988). Science instruction, regardless of the specific course, should provide opportunities for students to practice what they have learned.

Another way students value the science they learn is by connecting that topic to something relevant to them. There are several "Troika" Programs

Table 14.6   GENERAL TOPICS FOR SECONDARY SCIENCE CURRICULUM

Grade level	Subject	Topics
12	Physics	Relativity
		Of time, mass, energy, velocity
		Particle properties
		Electromagnetic waves
		Quantum theory of light
		X-rays
		Compton effect
		Photons and gravity
		Wave properties of particles
		De Broglie waves
		Waves of probability
		Wave equation
		Velocities
		Particle diffraction
		Uncertainty principles I, II and their application
		Atomic structure
		Rutherford model
		Alpha particle scattering and formula
		Nuclear dimensions
		Atomic spectra
		Bohr atom
		Energy levels and spectra
		Correspondence principle
		Nuclear motion
		Laser
		Quantum mechanics
		Wave function and equation
		Schrodinger's equation
		Tunnels effect
		Harmonic oscillator
		Hydrogen atom: the quantum theory
		Schrodinger's equation
		Quantum numbers
		Zeeman effect
		Electron atoms
		Wave functions
		Periodic Table (atomic number)
		Configuration of electrons
		Molecules
		Bonding
		Vibrational energy levels
		Statistical mechanics
		Distributions
		Maxwell-Botlzmann statistics
		Quantum statistics
		Distribution of electrons and energy
		Dying stars

Table 14.6   GENERAL TOPICS FOR SECONDARY SCIENCE CURRICULUM *Continued*

Grade level	Subject	Topics
	Solid state	
	Different types of solids	
	Bonds	
	Ohm's law	
	Semiconductors	
	Atomic nucleus	
	Neutron	
	Nucleus (shapes and sizes)	
	Models (liquid-drop, shell)	
	Radioactivity	
	Radioactive decay	
	Radiometric dating	
	Nucleus reactions	
	Nuclear fission, fusion	
	Elementary particles	
	Leptons, hadrons	
	Quarks	

sponsored by the National Science Foundation. The Interactive Middle-Grades program is one of the Troika Programs that attempts to make science useful to all students. It addresses the problems of science, technology, and society. The project is housed at Florida State University.

A second trend is to integrate all the sciences in the curriculum. This is not a new idea and has been a goal that many scientists and educators have had for decades. However, progress has been slow in integrating the sciences because scientists tend to protect their area of study. To successfully integrate the sciences in the secondary curriculum, teachers, curriculum specialists, and scientists from all fields need to identify appropriate content and instances where the integration can take place. In effect, a scope and sequence needs to be generated to provide the guide for the integration process. For example, when dealing with the issue of acid rain, several sciences are involved—life, Earth, and chemistry. In addition, acid rain is no longer a domestic political problem, but one that is international in scope. To resolve this issue, it will take the expertise of many scientists, in both the natural and social sciences. In addition, there is overlap in each science course related to such topics as measurement, laboratory safety, handling of equipment, use of formulas, and general laboratory procedures.

Project 2061 is one example of how the sciences have been integrated and the designers of the project feel that the students are benefiting greatly from their experiences. In California as many as 100 high schools and 85 middle schools are integrating their science curriculum using the plan developed by the National Science Teachers Association. If the sciences are integrated, students will be encouraged to view facts, theories, and principles in a larger context beyond an individual science course.

The third trend is "learning by doing," which has been advocated by many science educators for decades. However, few secondary science teachers feel comfortable taking the time away from lecturing because they feel obligated to "cover the book." The current emphases on the discipline, a structured direct lesson design, and teacher evaluation/accountability also inhibit the use of a hands-on investigative approach. Even though secondary teachers know that students should have opportunities to explore and learn through trial and error, they usually resort to a very structured lesson presentation in order to cover the material. The commonly used method of science teaching at the secondary level is to introduce new vocabulary first, have the students read from the text in turn, do study questions, and check for comprehension (Kingsbury, 1990). This method almost ensures shallow, superficial learning that is easily forgotten.

A four-step approach is recommended to ensure that hands-on experiences are provided for all students. The steps include enrichment, discussion, guided reading, and vocabulary development (Reinhartz, 1988). Enrichment provides the relevant experiences and background information which help students relate to the science concept under study. The enrichment step helps students fine-tune, focus on what is being presented, extend what they already know, and build a solid foundation for future experiences. Take, for example, how electricity is produced. Junior high school students are given batteries, bulbs, and wires. They are asked, "What can you do to get the light to come on like it does in a flashlight?" Terms such as circuit, potential and kinetic energy, dry cell, positive and negative charges, conductors, and so on are mentioned, and the teacher models the correct usage. It is during this step that the students have opportunities to respond to materials, exchange ideas, translate thoughts and events into words, sentences, and stories, and to function as problem solvers.

The second step is discussion. As students discuss terms, they begin to zero in and grasp more specifically the meanings of these terms in relation to the concept, electricity. Hands-on experiences provide students with situations in which they create a frame of reference, and the discussion serves to delimit the concept, electricity, from a larger possible field of concepts.

Next the students are ready for the guided reading phase. Since the students have now had some experience with the concept, the text is predictable and will not require an elaborate introduction. Also, the terms are familiar because they have been using them as they interacted with the materials.

The fourth and final step is vocabulary development. In a sense the technical vocabulary and related concepts have been pretaught. By so doing there is a greater chance for success. In this last step, the teacher directs the vocabulary and concept instruction as if it were a review. Traditional content reading skills, such as focusing on the prefixes and suffixes, matching definitions with terms, categorizing concepts, developing a semantic map, playing games, and so on may be used at this time. These activities should prove to be highly successful due to the expanded concepts provided by the sequence of prior steps.

The "learning by doing" approach helps communicate to students the real complexities of the world of science. A hands-on approach encourages more students and teachers to experiment, fail, analyze, redo, and really learn new science concepts.

A fourth trend is to apply Piaget's theories of cognitive development to the teaching and learning of science. Take, for example, the concept of genetics in biology. Students can learn about this topic when they work with fruit flies by using a three-step instructional approach, which includes exploration, conceptual invention, and expansion of the concept. Each step requires students to expand their concept of genetics by engaging in investigations, drawing diagrams, demonstrating the concept, describing the demonstration in writing, discussing the concept, and reading about it. Such an instructional learning cycle is based on Piaget's theory of mental functioning and encourages students to experience the concept of genetics in a variety of ways. For some students, these new experiences may create a state of disequilibrium until the new experience is processed and accommodated into previously learned experiences.

Teachers in the Norman Public Schools in cooperation with the faculty at the University of Oklahoma Science Education Center have written a high school biology program using the three-step instructional approach of exploration, conceptual invention, and expansion. They believe that this approach allows the students to function first at the concrete level and progress to the more formal level of intellectual functioning (Cate and Grzybowski, 1987). From research conducted by Ewing, Campbell, and Brown (1987), the results indicated that students were more positive about biology when they had opportunities to experience and discuss the concept rather than just read or be told about it. In addition, a similar approach has been used in chemistry and physics, and these science courses have shown increases in enrollment of up to 150 percent.

Using technology in the science classroom is certainly a trend that is continuing to gain in importance in secondary classrooms. In fact, the largest number of videodiscs on the market relate to science topics, and it is on the increase (Litchfield, 1990). According to Cushall, Harvey, and Brovey (1989), using videodiscs improves learning as well as participation. The TLTG Physical Science program described in the overview section is one example of this technology, and the developers indicate increased student participation.

Litchfield (1990) recommends using the videodisc technology in all the areas of science, but especially in life, Earth/space, and physical sciences. She says that the use of technology is one way that science instruction can be enriched because it can be used in a variety of ways. For example, it can provide a general overview of the information; it allows resource people to enter your classroom; and it provides in-depth study for students who would like to learn more about the topic. Students have opportunities to practice skills, simulate roles, make models, and gather and analyze data. Take, for example, the "Physical Science Baseball" software program, in which students participate in a competitive baseball game. They learn the basic terms and definitions in physical science as they role play a member of a team. "Volcanoes" is another computer program that uses a gaming strategy that involves up to four players. As a result of playing this game on the computer, students learn how volcanologists study potentially active volcanoes. And "Rendezvous" simulates an actual space flight from liftoff to docking with the space station. The student has to ensure that a minimum amount of fuel is used during liftoff so that the next three stages can be performed. These few examples illustrate the type of material that has been developed in science.

Valuing science, integrating the sciences, doing science, applying the theories of Piaget when teaching science, and using technology in the classroom are features that secondary educators should keep in mind as they begin to design and develop a 7–12 science program. These features help to make the secondary science curriculum timely and meaningful for students entering the twenty-first century.

SUMMARY

Chapter 14 began with an introduction to the state of science education and a brief mention of new projects underway. Also, included was a history of science education beginning with the 1950s. The historical overview highlighted some of the significant developments that have occurred during the last 40 years. The goals for the secondary science curriculum were presented. The goals and content of a science curriculum should take into account how students learn science, the important content to be learned along with appropriate skills, and the constructs of science. In addition, the secondary science curriculum should encourage students to use and apply their science knowledge and investigative skills to new situations.

The next section of the chapter discussed the components of the science curriculum. First, the courses offered in the junior high school were presented including life science, earth science, and physical science. Each course was described along with topics taught. The same format was used for high school science subjects—biology, chemistry, and physics.

The last section described five trends in the science curriculum. Among those discussed were valuing science in our daily lives, integrating the sciences, learning science by doing, using the theories of Piaget when teaching biology and chemistry, and enriching science instruction by using videodiscs and computers in your classroom. In the final analysis, the objective of Chapter 14 was not only to include what is happening in secondary school science classrooms, but to provide a direction for what a secondary science curriculum should include if it is going to prepare students for the next century.

YOUR TURN

14.1 Because of the number of new terms and definitions students learn in each science unit, teachers as well as students are bogged down with memorizing them. It may be helpful to develop a concept matrix for specific content that will be learned so students can see relationships and patterns among and between terms. For example, if the students are studying the topic of biomes in life science or general biology, the following chart helps organize what the students are expected to learn and it helps them interpret the text material better. Develop one for another concept in science.

Name of the Biome	Temperature Ranges	Plant Life	Animal Life	General Climatic Features	Food Sources for Living Organisms	Shelter	Physical Features

14.2 Look at Table 14.7, which analyzes several major reports in mathematics and science. This chart was distributed at the 1989 Conference of the Illinois Mathematics Supervisors Association. With a science text and/or curriculum guide in hand, respond to the following questions.

(a) How does Project 2061 differ from the overall thrust of the text(s) and/or guide(s) you are reviewing?

(b) Are the technological imperatives addressed? What is included specifically in the text/guide you are reviewing?

(c) Is there an emphasis on integrating mathematics or the sciences?

(d) What can you conclude about your text/guide and its relationship to the synthesis as reported by IMSA.

14.3 The issue of scientific illiteracy remains a major concern among science educators. Below are several statements that relate to this issue (*Modified from:* Champagne, A.B. (1989 October). Science. *Educational Leadership, 47,* 2, 85–86). What do you believe is an appropriate level of scientific literacy necessary for citizens to make judgments about social concerns?

Directions: Respond to the following questions. Circle a 1 if you believe the statement is significant and a 5 if the statement is not significant.

	1 Significant	3 Neutral	5 Not Significant
1. Able to state a question that can be investigated using the scientific method	1	3	5
2. Able to explain what occurs in nature in scientific terms (e.g., energy conservation, the food web)	1	3	5
3. Able to sequence the steps to an investigation	1	3	5
4. Able to read a newspaper article featuring a science concept/problem, summarize it, and explain the scientific principle involved	1	3	5
5. Able to read a graph and interpret the results	1	3	5
6. Able to define basic terms (e.g., physical and chemical change, pH, acids and bases)	1	3	5
7. Able to use scientific information when making a decision (e.g., pollution, recycling)	1	3	5

Table 14.7 1989 IMSA LEADERSHIP CONFERENCE

SYNTHESIS—ANALYSIS OF MAJOR REPORTS

Critical Dimensions	Project 2061	Everybody Counts	NCTM Standards	Technology: National imperative	Illinois State Goals	Synthesis
Curriculum "What is taught"	Physical science Biological sciences Humanities topics Historical breakthroughs Mathematical topics	Number sense Symbol sense Function sense Common core for all K–12 Relevant to present/future	Estimation, number, operational and spatial "sense" Relevance and interrelations	Historical breakthroughs Processes of invention, innovation, and experimentation Behavior of adaptive systems and subsystems Technical elements	Concepts, vocabulary, principles, and application to science Computation, percentages, measurement, problem solving, geometry, data, estimation, and prediction in math	Focus on connections between various disciplines Problem solving and real world applications-centered Value of creativity, innovation, and experimentation for adults and learners
Instruction "How it is taught"	Interdisci-plinary/ thematic Scientific inquiry Scientific values Counteract anxieties Extend and time	Student-centered Broad-based math power Natural curiosity Concrete to conceptual Internal construction	Discovery and integration Variety of teaching strategies Student communication Assessment, manipulatives, technology, thinking skills	Integrated Activity-oriented Problem solving Models (as tools)	Inference Application Hands-on use of the tools of mathematics and science	Higher level of use of instructional tools Student-centered classrooms and laboratories All students are capable of hands-on learning
Use of Technology	Relationship between science and technology Principles of technology Technology and society Technological applications	Full use of calculators and computers	Full use of calculators and computers as tools in mathematical problem solving	Integrating role Technology education laboratory	Social and environmental applications Processes, techniques, methods, equipment	Technology extends our ability to change our world with complicated and sometimes unpredictable results

Habits of Mind	Values and attitudes; Skills	Importance of mathematics in today's society	Conceptually oriented; Thinking skills; Differing perspectives	Values and attitudes; Coping; Open-minded; Involvement	Inference from goals; Principles of scientific research; Problem solving	Science is investigating real world problems; Exploring scientific phenomena is an intimate experience with discovery; Connections between disciplines exist and are exciting to explore
Student Behaviors	Effective learning; Use of scientific inquiry	Teams to solve problems; Learning how to learn	Active involvement; Problem situations; Orientation	Active, "hands-on" involvement with technology	Categorizing of learner expectations; Suggested sequencing of capabilities	Children can understand and interact successfully with scientific and mathematical concepts
Global/ Societal Frames of Reference	Need for scientific literacy assessment of current global scene	Rigorous, active science of patterns; "Pump" versus "filter"; Bridge; research/ schools/change/ leadership	Equity; Application; Social goals for education; Change	Economic forces; Integration; Services; Advanced technologies; Productivity/ competition	Concerned with identifying the primary purpose of schooling	Benefits to society will come from raising the level of scientific, mathematical, technological literacy
Assessment	Analysis of analogous systems; Computer simulations; Hypothesis testing	Responsive to future needs	Outcomes; Program expectations; Multiple means	Assessment of outcome or "products"	Goals are accountability driven; Clearly written objectives to possibly assess goal achievement	
Effective Teaching	Collaboration is essential	Teacher as: Consultant; Moderator; Interlocutor	Teacher as: Facilitator; Moderator; Catalyst; Coach	(Not addressed in this document)	(Not directly addressed in this document)	The learner should be in an atmosphere where student initiated questions are more numerous than teacher or curriculum initiated questions; Effective and lasting change occurs at the level of the classroom teacher

Source: Illinois Mathematics and Science Academy, 1500 West Sullivan Rd, Aurora, Ill. 60506-1039 (708-801-6058). Used with permission.

325

	1 Significant	3 Neutral	5 Not Significant
8. Able to cite ways that science has affected society (e.g., elimination of diseases, chemical warfare)	1	3	5
9. Able to explain what the superconducting supercollider technology is	1	3	5
10. Able to cite positives and negatives of scientific discoveries (e.g., benefits to man from experimentation with cryogenetics and use of chemicals)	1	3	5

14.4 With all the technology available to science teachers, it is essential that teachers preview and evaluate computer software and videodiscs that have been produced. Obtain a list of materials that are available in a school district as well as a copy of a computer software evaluation form. The purpose of the evaluation is to determine:

A. Type of software
   —Drill/practice
   —Simulation
   —Game
   —Prescriptive/diagnostic
B. Subject area _____
C. The quality of the presentation
   1. Ease of use
   2. Reliability
   3. Success in motivating and maintaining student interest
   4. Clear instructions
   5. Types of reinforcement
   6. Use of graphics
D. The quality of the content
   1. How accurate
   2. Type of feedback used
   3. Grade level appropriateness
   4. Reading level and use of terms/vocabulary
E. Overall evaluation (general statement about how you feel about the software and its potential use in a science classroom)

REFERENCES

Adeniyi, E.L. (July 1987). Curriculum development and the concept of integration in science. *Science Education, 71,* 4, 523–533.

Ahlgren, A. (1990). Science. *Educational Leadership, 47,* 5, 84.

Ashworth, R.P. (January 1990). Math and science: A nation still at risk. *Principal, 69,* 3, 15–17.

Atkin, J.M. (Spring 1983). The improvement of science teaching. *Daedalus, 112,* 2, 15–17.

Beckner, W. & Cornett, J.D. (1972). *The secondary school curriculum: Content and structure.* Scranton, Pa.: Intext Educational Publishers.

Boyer, E.L. (1985). *High school.* New York: Harper & Row.

Brook, A., Drive, R. & Johnston, K. (1989). Learning processes in science: A classroom perspective. In J.J. Wellington (Ed.). *Skills and processes in science education: A critical analysis.* London: Routledge.

Cate, J.M. and Grzybowski, E.B. (1987). Teaching a biology concept using the learning cycle approach. *The American Biology Teacher, 49,* 2, 50–52.

Champagne, A.B. (October 1989). Science. *Educational Leadership, 47,* 2, 85–86.

Cushall, M.B., Harvey, F.A. & Brovey, A.J. (March 1989). Research on learning from interactive videodiscs: A review of the literature and suggestions for future research activities. Paper presented at the annual meeting of the American Educational Research Association, San Francisco.

Ewing, M.S., Campbell, N.J. & Brown, M.J.M. (1987). Improving student attitudes toward biology by encouraging scientific literacy. *The American Biology Teacher, 49,* 6, 348–350.

Harms, N.C. & Yager, R.E. (1981). *What research says to the science teacher.* Washington, D.C.: National Science Teachers Association.

Hodson, S. (1988). Toward a philosophically more valid science curriculum. *Science Education, 72,* 1, 19–40.

Hurd, D.P. (1988). New directions in science education. In L.L. Motz & G.M. Madrazo, Jr. (Eds.). *Third sourcebook for science supervisors.* Washington, D.C.: National Science Supervisors Association and National Science Teachers Association.

Kingsbury, P. (March 1990). Ways teachers can increase student motivation. *The Texas Science Teacher, 19,* 1, 25–27.

Kirkham, J. (1989). Balance science equilibrium between context, process, content. In J.J. Wellington (Ed.). *Skills and processes in science education: A critical analysis.* London: Routledge.

Kyle, W.C., Jr. (no date cited). Curriculum development projects of the 1960s. In D. Holdzkom and P. B. Lutz (Eds.). *Research within reach: Science education.* Washington, D.C.: National Science Teachers Association.

Litchfield, B.C. (September 1990). Slipping a disk in the classroom: The latest in video technology. *Science and Children, 28,* 1, 16–21.

McCormack, A. & Yager, R. (February 1989). A new taxonomy of science education. *The Science Teacher, 56,* 2, 47–58.

McNeil, J.D. (1990). *Curriculum: A comprehensive introduction* (4th ed.). Glenview, Ill.: Scott Foresman.

National Science Teachers Association. (1982). Science-technology-society: Science education for the 1980s. (NSTA position paper). Washington, D.C.: National Science Teachers Association.

Neuschatz, M. & Covalt, M. (1989). *Physics in the high school.* New York: American Institute of Physics.

Reinhartz, J. (November 1988). A Model for promoting science learning through learning by doing. Paper presented at the annual meeting of Science Teachers Association of Texas, San Antonio, Texas.

Rothmer, R. (1987). NSF urged to boost K–12 effort. *The Scientist, 10,* 7.

Rutherford, F.J. & Ahlgren, A. (1990). *Science for all Americans.* New York: Oxford University Press.

Rutherford, F.J. & Ahlgren, A. (1988). Rethinking the science curriculum. In R.S. Brandt (Ed.). *Content of the curriculum: 1988 ASCD yearbook.* Washington, D.C.: Association of Supervision and Curriculum Development.

The science report card: Elements of risk and recovery. (1988). Princeton, N.J.: National Assessment of Educational Progress at Educational Testing Service, No. 17-S-01.

Stake, R.E. & Easley, J. (1978). *Case studies in science education.* Urbana, Ill.: University of Illinois.

Staver, J.R. & Small, L. (1990). Toward a clearer representation of the crisis in science education. *Journal of Research in Science Teaching, 27,* 1, 79–89.

Weiss, I.R. (1978). Report to the 1977 national survey of science, mathematics and social studies education. Research Triangle Park, N.C.: Center for Education Research and Evaluation.

Wellington, J.J. (1989). Skills and processes in science education: An introduction. In J.J. Wellington (Ed.). *Skills and processes in science education: A critical analysis.* London: Routledge.

Yager, R.E. (1988). Fifty years of science education, 1950–2000. In *Third sourcebook for science supervisors,* 15–22. Edited by L.L. Motz and G.M. Madrazo, Jr. Washington, D.C.: National Science Supervisors Association and National Science Teachers Association.

Chapter
15

Other Subjects of the Secondary Curriculum

*T*he first four chapters in this section have focused on specific content areas — social studies, English language arts, math, and science — the core or required subjects in the secondary curriculum. This chapter will describe the subjects that are usually categorized as electives in the secondary schools. The areas of health and physical education, foreign languages, fine arts, and vocational subjects are offered to students, but few are required. These subjects are included as a part of the secondary curriculum to provide options for students and to allow students to pursue subjects of interest to them. These courses also serve to round out the total curriculum of the secondary school and to provide college preparatory courses as well as vocational choices.

Since this chapter represents several diverse subjects, it is organized somewhat differently from the others. The chapter is designed to explore the nature of each elective subject area. Historical and background information, a general overview of the subject area, and the general trends and issues in the teaching of each subject will be presented. The intent is to provide a general awareness of the value, purpose, and function of each curriculum area rather than a detailed description of the content and methodology for each area.

HEALTH AND PHYSICAL EDUCATION

At no other time in the history of American education have the issues related to health and physical education been more in the news. The media almost daily reports on some aspect of the nation's health risks and the fitness of American youth and the general population. Fitness centers have been one of the fastest growing businesses in the country. Schools have been forced to fully address the nature of health and physical fitness, especially in the secondary school curriculum. This subject area, therefore, includes two different content emphases: health education and physical education.

Health Education

Health education is often considered a separate course from the physical education component. Although relatively new to the secondary curriculum, at least ½ unit in health education is frequently required for graduation in secondary programs. The *Health Activities Project* (HAP) was developed to meet the needs and interests of students in the intermediate and junior high school grades. The program was developed to create a positive attitude toward health by giving the students a sense of control over their bodies and helping them understand the body's potential for improvement (McNeil, 1990). Topics included in the HAP program and other health courses as well include: fitness, interaction, growth and development, responsible decision making, hair, skin, and teeth care, personal grooming, and nutrition and diet.

At the high school level, students focus on their own growth and development as they mature physically. In addition to topics such as personal hygiene and the effects of advertising on self-image, students study the changes that occur in their bodies as a result of developing sexual maturity. Students are also challenged to evaluate their diet and fitness habits and to improve in these areas. Recent topics in the health curriculum include concerns about AIDS, alcohol and drug abuse, stress, and human sexuality. Rather than approaching these subjects from a judgmental view (i.e., "thou shalt not"), students are provided with information and factual data that demonstrate the effect of these concerns on overall human development. General goals of the health education curriculum include:

1. Understanding and development of concepts and skills that foster individual personal health and safety
2. Knowledge of health-related concepts and skills that involve interaction between and among individuals
3. Understanding and development of skills that encompass the wellness or well-being of people
4. Understanding concepts related to health and wellness as a life-long process
5. Development of responsibility for personal fitness, health, safety, and personal hygiene throughout life

In an effective health education program, students realize that good health is not just the absence of disease, but a state of total physical, mental, and social well-being.

The typical content includes the following concepts:

1. *Personal health and fitness related to personal wellness or well-being:* personal responsibility for health; benefits of fitness; role of exercise in overall fitness; aspects of physical fitness; establishing an exercise program; risks of exercises; components of physical fitness — flexibility, strength, and endurance; aerobic and anaerobic exercise; injury risks; proper care of skin, hair, nails, and feet; healthy mouth and teeth; healthy eyes and ears

2. *Knowing self and getting along with others:* factors that influence personal mental health, behavior, and personality; emotions, fears, and phobias; stress and how to manage it; mental disorders; dealing with problems and conflicts; knowing when to ask for help

3. *Nutrition and health, fitness, and wellness:* good nutrition and its importance in everyday diet; eating habits and nutrition; nutrients, food groups, and a balanced diet; vitamins, minerals, water, and fiber in our diet; dieting, weight control, and good health

4. *Alcohol, tobacco, and drugs:* alcohol — a risk to your well-being; the effects of alcohol on the body; the effects of alcohol on prenatal development; the effects of alcohol in combination with other drugs; alcohol — social implications; alcoholism and dependency; tobacco in various forms; effects of smoking on the body; dangers of smokeless tobacco products; drugs as medicine; the body's reaction to drugs — tolerance, dependence, interaction, dosage; consumer protection and drugs; prescription drugs; drug abuse and illegal use of drugs — terms, dangers, and physical and psychological reactions

5. *Maintaining a healthy body system:* the nervous system — structure and function; the skeletal system — structure and function; the muscular system — structure and function; the endocrine system — structure and function; the reproductive system — structure, function, disorders, and diseases; the circulatory and respiratory systems — structures and functions; the digestive system — structure and function

6. *Family and social health:* the healthy family system — structures and functions; marriage, parenthood, and the family cycle — commitment and responsibility; sex education, teenage pregnancy, and why people have children; the first nine months of pregnancy; life cycle and theories of growth and development

7. *Consumer health issues:* factors that influence health care purchases; consumer rights and labeling; health services and health care facilities and agencies; trends in the delivery of health care

8. *Safety and emergency care:* safety behavior — attitudes, risks, and behaviors; characteristics of accidents; making the home a safe living

area; recreational and outdoor safety; providing first aid and emergency care; acting in an emergency—first aid and CPR

9. *Treating, controlling, and preventing diseases:* infections and viral diseases; natural and artificially acquired immunity; communicable diseases—symptoms, treatment, and prevention; noncommunicable diseases and disorders

10. *Health of the environment and the community:* environmental factors that affect health; the effects of air and water pollution; energy and conservation

This list of concepts and the content for each is not intended to be an exhaustive list of the scope and sequence of the secondary health curriculum. It is, however, representative of the topics that are covered in such a course, and the content may be modified based on local needs and issues. Perhaps the dominant issues related to this content area have focused on education concerning Acquired Immune Deficiency Syndrome (**AIDS**). Schools have had to be a part of the nation's efforts to educate students and prevent the spread of the disease. Yarber (1988) recommends the following guidelines to use in developing an **AIDS** curriculum for the schools:

1. Emphasize appropriate health behaviors.
2. Promote risk-avoiding knowledge.
3. Approach the subject and instructional materials objectively and scientifically.
4. Provide complete information regarding prevention.
5. Place instruction within the context of the health curriculum.
6. Focus major instructional efforts toward adolescents.
7. Select quality instructional materials and assure teacher competence.
8. Maximize community support and involvement and defend students' rights to know.

In addition to these recommended guidelines, school faculty and staff should have a thorough knowledge and understanding of the disease so they can adequately address students' concerns or refer the students to someone who can help.

Physical Education

The second content emphasis for this subject area is physical education. According to McNeil (1990), physical education received national attention in the 1960s when President John Kennedy proposed a national standard of physical fitness. This led to annual assessments of physical fitness and the President's fitness awards. However, the emphasis of this period was also on competition, which produced disappointment and humiliation for many students because being good was often not good enough. The physical education curriculum of the secondary school emphasized traditional team sports and often fostered aggression and competitiveness as a prerequisite to sportsmanship (McNeil,

1990). Girls were often overlooked within this framework, with few opportunities to participate.

In recent years, the teaching of physical education has taken new directions based on the curriculum of the secondary schools. The days of the coach throwing a ball out and watching students play are all but gone. The decade of the 1980s, with attention to personal fitness and health through jogging, workouts, and "dancercise," have brought about a new focus for physical educators. Physical education programs are becoming more flexible and are incorporating units that address individual needs and interests and include personal physical development and lifetime recreational sports as well as team sports (Seaton et al., 1985).

In junior high school, physical education is normally required in the seventh and eighth grades and emphasizes movement skills, team sports, physical fitness, and lifetime sports. Physical education at the high school level is required for at least two years and involves physical fitness skills in the beginning, then progresses to lifetime and team sports, along with specialized activities in later grades. Students are often allowed to substitute courses such as drill team, marching band, and athletics for physical education courses.

Goals for the junior high physical education program include having students:

1. Safely and efficiently participate in movement skills included in sports, stunts, and other activities
2. Improve perceptual motor skills
3. Participate with other students in individual, dual, and team sports
4. Develop new and more complex skills needed for success in games and sports
5. Learn and practice behavior that reflects good sportsmanship
6. Participate daily in vigorous activities for periods of increasing duration
7. Assess the level of fitness they attain
8. Obtain knowledge and skills for leisure and lifetime sports activities

These goals are attained through such activities as physical fitness testing, recreational games, conditioning exercises, rehearsal of skilled movements such as tumbling, individual sports such as tennis or badminton, and team sports such as flag football, basketball, or softball.

The goals for the high school physical education curriculum include having students:

1. Participate in a variety of skilled movement activities that require efficient movement and the ability to analyze and correct basic motor skills
2. Practice the introduced activity skills until they become proficient enough to participate in the sport
3. Practice the skills required to maintain a positive working relationship with others, including leadership abilities

4. Become familiar with the rules, etiquette, and safety procedures for a variety of individual, dual, and team sports
5. Develop physical fitness to individual capacity and continue to maintain it while participating in skilled activities
6. Recognize the major elements of physical fitness and acquire the knowledge needed to incorporate these elements into a healthy life-style
7. Participate in a physical fitness program designed to evaluate fitness and develop students' ability to assess individual level of fitness
8. Become aware of the recreational activities offered in the community and those that can be developed within the family
9. Be exposed to a variety of activities that can become a lifetime sport for the individual

To implement these goals in the classroom, students participate in a variety of activities, including fitness testing; skilled movement activities; conditioning (aerobic and anaerobic) exercises; individual, dual, and team sports (e.g., golf, bowling, tennis, basketball, softball); learning history, rules, and etiquette of sports; and recreational sports. Table 15.1 includes a recommended scope and sequence chart for the middle school grades through high school.

In addressing the trends associated with physical education, McNeil (1990) cites the work of the American Alliance for Health, Physical Education, and Recreation, which has recommended five guidelines for the future development of physical education programs. These guidelines include:

1. Break down the large group, mass education techniques currently employed
2. Increase the flexibility of physical education offerings and provide greater course variety and different teaching methods
3. View physical education and sports as more than competitive athletics
4. Increase coeducational classes and include more speciality courses such as self-defense, sailing, and camp counselor training
5. Promote and encourage physical activities that will support the desire to maintain fitness throughout life

These guidelines are designed to meet the needs of the whole person and courses should be designed to introduce students to the potentials of their bodies. To do this, the association suggests four kinds of activities:

1. *Movement education:* where students develop an understanding of the creative and expressive movements of the body
2. *Centering oneself:* where students learn to develop a state of alert calm
3. *Structural patterning:* where students become aware of the unique patterns of movement for each person
4. *Relaxation techniques:* where students learn how to deal with habitual tensions through rhythmic breathing procedures

Table 15.1 SCOPE AND SEQUENCE CHART FOR AN OPTIMAL PHYSICAL EDUCATION PROGRAM

Types of experiences	Grades						
	6	7	8	9	10	11	12
Career Education[a]							
Awareness	R						
Investigation		R	R				
Exploration & Preparation				R	R	E	E
Fitness and Conditioning Activities[b]							
Cardiorespiratory Endurance	R	R	R	R	R	E	E
Muscular Strength, Flexibility, and Power	R	R	R	R	R	E	E
Fitness Testing	R	R	R	R	R	E	E
Gymnastics[c]							
Stunts and Tumbling	R	R	R	R	O	E	E
Apparatus	O	R	R	R	O	E	E
Trampoline	O		O		O	E	E
Floor Exercise	R	R	R	O	R	E	E
Rhythms and Dance							
Ballet	O	O	O	O	O	E	E
Folk and Square Dancing	R	R	O	O		E	E
Marching	O					E	E
Modern Dance			O	O	R	E	E
Modern Jazz			O	O	O	E	E
Social Dancing			R	R		E	E
Tap Dancing	O	O				E	E
Team Sports							
*Basketball	R	O	R	O	O	E	E
*Field Hockey		O	O	R	O	E	E
*Flag Football		R		R		E	E
*Indoor Floor Hockey		O		O	O	E	E
*La Crosse		O		O		E	E
*Soccer	R	O	R	O	R	E	E
Softball	R	O	R	O	O	E	E
*Speedball	O	R	O	O	O	E	E
*Team Handball			O		O	E	E
Volleyball		R		R	O	E	E
Outdoor Adventure Activities[d]							
Backpacking						E	E
Bike Touring					O	E	E
Boating and Water Sports						E	E
Camping	R	R	R		O	E	E
Canoeing						E	E
Casting/Angling			R		O	E	E
Hiking	R	R	R		O	E	E
Hunter Safety		R				E	E
Orienteering	R	R	R			E	E
Rapelling/Rock Climbing						E	E
Recreational Shooting						E	E
Sailing						E	E
Wilderness First Aid	R	R	R		O	E	E

continued

Table 15.1 SCOPE AND SEQUENCE CHART FOR AN OPTIMAL PHYSICAL EDUCATION PROGRAM *Continued*

Types of experiences	Grades						
	6	7	8	9	10	11	12
Aquatics							
Swimming/Personal Safety		O	O	R	R	E	E
Life Saving & Water Safety	R	R	R	O	O	E	E
Diving (Must have ability to swim width of pool)	O		O		O	E	E
Sychronized Swimming		O		O		E	E
Water Games	O		O		O	E	E
Snorkling			O		O	E	E
Scuba Diving (Must have senior life saving)						E	E
Surfing						E	E
Individual and Dual Sports							
Aerial Tennis		O		O		E	E
Archery		O	R	R	O	E	E
Badminton	R	O	O	R	O	E	E
Bicycling	O	O	O	O	O	E	E
Bowling	O		O		O	E	E
Deck Tennis	O	O				E	E
Fencing		O		O		E	E
Golf	O	O	R	R	O	E	E
Handball				O	O	E	E
Horseshoe	O		O			E	E
Personal Self-Defense			O		R	E	E
Racquetball		O	O			E	E
Shuffleboard	O		O			E	E
Skateboarding	O		O		O	E	E
Skating (Ice or Roller)		O		O		E	E
Skiing	O		O			E	E
Table Tennis	O	O	O	O	O	E	E
*Track or Field	R	R	O	O	R	E	E
Tennis	O	R	O	R	O	E	E
*Power and Weight Lifting				O	R	E	E
*Wrestling	R	R	R		R	E	E

R — Required
O — Optional
E — Elective

aWhen the required sequential steps of career education have been properly integrated in the physical education instructional program, the tenth grade student should have determined his/her interests, aptitudes, and abilities related to physical education career opportunities. Additional career preparation experiences needed for translating skills, interests, aptitudes, and abilities into practice can best be met through innovative elective programs during the eleventh and twelfth grades. Elective programs should be designed for self-directed and personally oriented activities frequently taking the student into the career environment. The scope of exploration and preparatory experiental activities is limited only by the student's and/or teacher's creativity and initiative.

bCycling, jogging, tennis, handball, swimming, badminton, and other aerobic activities.

cWeight training, circuit training, and obstacle course.

dOutdoor adventure activities at the middle/junior high school may be organized in two or three-week units. Activities feasible for instructional units are indicated as "required." A new skill is offered each year while previous experiences are further expanded and developed. During the high school years, constraints of time and geographic area limit instruction in the optional areas indicated. Many experiences should be available in the elective program. Four or five activities can be offered during a 12-week period.

*Activities coeducational in instructional unit but non-coeducational for competition.

Note: Concepts of environmental ethics, wildlife management, and conservation should be infused into all outdoor adventure activities.

Source: Texas Education Agency. (1978). *Guidelines for physical education in the secondary schools*. Austin, Tx.: TEA, pp. 32–36.

Future trends in physical education will be in response to four needs:

1. Strength to perform expected tasks of living
2. Aerobic capacity to maintain cardiorespiratory efficiency
3. Flexibility and abdominal strength to avoid debilitating effects of lower back injuries
4. Maintenance of appropriate levels of body fat (McNeil, 1990, p. 329)

To meet these needs, some sports will need to be deleted from the secondary physical education curriculum and some body development activities, such as jogging, bicycling, and swimming, will need to be added.

FOREIGN LANGUAGES

Foreign languages are one of the oldest subject areas in the secondary curriculum. The first secondary schools focused on language instruction, particularly classical languages. The academy included the modern foreign languages as a part of the program of studies. However, since the early beginnings of secondary education in this country, the foreign languages have steadily declined in popularity and are no longer required for graduation in all states. Foreign languages are now considered to be electives within the secondary curriculum.

There have been recent periods when foreign language instruction was considered an essential part of the secondary curriculum. During the 1950s, especially after the launching of Sputnik, there was almost a national panic regarding the advancement of scientific and technological research and this created a need to understand foreign languages. As a result, the study of foreign languages became a requirement in most secondary schools. In addition to the study of languages, the method that was developed was called the aural-oral or the audiolingual method, and it was based on the science of structural or descriptive linguistics, which had been developed as a method of teaching languages during World War II (McNeil, 1990).

During the late 1960s and early 1970s, language instruction declined, and the emphasis on science and mathematics subsided in the secondary schools. Many universities developed an "open door" policy, which allowed any and all students to enter, regardless of their previous coursework in high school. During this time, college entrance requirements were minimal and many universities dropped the foreign language requirement for entrance. McNeil (1990) reports that by 1980, "only 15 percent of high school students were enrolled in foreign language courses [and] . . . only 4 percent of pupils graduating from high school had studied a foreign language for as long as two years" (p. 354).

Following the studies and reform reports of the 1980s, efforts to revive foreign language instruction have gained momentum. Met (1989) notes that the need for foreign language instruction is once again a concern for business and political leaders. One of the reasons for this increased interest involves the marketplace. Jennings (1987) refers to economic competition as the Sputnik of the 1980s. International trade and global economics have made it imperative that American students have a knowledge of other languages if this country is to be competitive economically and survive in the world marketplace. As Met (1989) notes, "Since competitiveness depends, in part, on our ability to communicate effectively about our products, it should come as no surprise that foreign language proficiency is gaining the attention of the business community" (p. 54).

In addition to the economic factors, there are even greater implications for the study of foreign languages. As the world becomes more interdependent, as old barriers to the exchange of ideas as well as trade are torn down, it becomes essential that students learn other languages in order to communicate with those with whom they will share the world. As Met (1989) notes, "The political implications of a linguistically incompetent America are far-reaching and frightening" (p. 55).

In spite of this concern voiced in numerous reports, enrollment in foreign language courses has not, as yet, increased significantly. The other issue concerns which language students should study. Although 86 percent of the secondary schools in this country teach Spanish (the fourth most commonly spoken language in the world), less than 2 percent of the schools offer Mandarin (which is the most common language), or Russian (fifth), or Japanese (tenth) (Met, 1989; *The World Almanac and Book of Facts*, 1989). In examining the current trends in enrollment, Dandonoli, (1987) reports that approximately 58 percent of students taking a foreign language take Spanish, 28 percent take French (twelfth most common), and 8 percent take German (eleventh most common). The issue in the decade ahead will be which foreign language courses should be taught in the secondary schools.

Regardless of the language chosen, there are common goals that each language seeks to develop within the curriculum for junior and senior high school students. These goals of foreign language instruction generally include (American Council on the Teaching of Foreign Languages, 1986; Texas Education Agency, 1989):

1. *Listening:* understanding the main ideas of most speech in a standard dialect; understanding most routine questions, statements, commands; the foundations of everyday conversations on nontechnical subjects
2. *Speaking:* the ability to converse in a clearly participatory fashion; to respond to most routine questions, statements, and commands; to speak intelligibly and use vocabulary sufficient to express oneself simply and to discuss situations relevant to everyday life
3. *Reading:* following successful points of written discourse and understanding parts of texts which are conceptually abstract or unfamiliar; understanding most routine expressions learned orally; understanding nontechnical material on familiar subjects with the aid of references
4. *Writing:* writing routine social correspondence and joining sentences in simple discourse of at least several paragraphs in length on familiar topics; production of essential messages; communication of everyday situations using basic constructions and simple vocabulary
5. *Culture:* knowledge and awareness of the history, customs, and culture of the people who speak the language

6. *Language:* understand generalizations about how a language operates; application of the language learning process to the study of other languages, including English

In accomplishing these goals of the foreign language curriculum, teachers are concerned about teaching techniques, materials, and content. These areas of concern include explicit versus implicit teaching strategies, the use of more interactive student activities, and the use of computer assisted instruction (CAI) and video materials.

In the area of explicit and implicit teaching strategies, the concerns center around the best method to achieve a fit in promoting mastery of a foreign language. Scott (1989) indicates that the explicit method of grammar instruction stresses the importance of "skill-getting" in order for students to be able to organize the linguistic elements of the new language to communicate. According to this view, when language skills have been learned well enough, the new language becomes automatic. Those who support the implicit method of grammar instruction claim that students can learn all they need to know about the grammar of a new language through exposure to comprehensible, meaningful, linguistic examples or models. The acquisition of language skills is informal and subconscious rather than overt and deliberate. In Scott's (1989) study of the two methods, the explicit method showed greater student achievement on written tests over particular targeted grammatical constructions. On oral achievement, there was not a significant difference produced by either method.

Another area of interest to language teachers is the use of more interactive activities to improve student communication skills. In an interactive classroom proficiency is stressed as students engage in speaking, writing, and listening as they communicate in an authentic context (O'Neil, 1990). For example, in role playing in the foreign language classroom, students are presented with real-life situations involving the unexpected, which requires the use of language in order to reach a solution. Students practice, perform, and evaluate the role playing scenario, with the emphasis placed on open-ended rehearsal of numerous possibilities rather than one definite script (Knop, 1988). An additional interactive technique involves the use of conversation practice centers where students would practice initiating, maintaining, and closing a conversation; responding; interrupting; asking for and giving advice; showing annoyance or anger; and even stalling (Kaplan, 1989).

Another area of concern in today's foreign language classroom is the use of computer assisted instruction (CAI) and videotapes. In regard to computer assisted instruction, key factors that influence this process are the teachers' computer backgrounds, the availability of computers, and the software programs available. Cummins (1989a) offers advice on each of these areas and notes that CAI programs can be a valuable tool to the language teacher for drill and practice, and for supporting and reinforcing interactive instruction in the classroom. Curran (1989) describes how computer programs can be used and how the printer can be customized to print foreign language accents and special characters. Cummins (1989b) has also examined the use of video in the language classroom and has found it to be an excellent teaching tool. Videos can be easily stopped to allow teacher explanations or student responses and can be replayed to emphasized major points. The video activities should be tailored to the language level of the students in order to produce the best results.

In describing language instruction for the next decade, McNeil (1990) says that students are being encouraged to participate in the development of new language courses. The content of the foreign languages will be designed to ensure relevant materials and applicability to everyday life. The curriculum will emphasize "basic speaking skills as well as those needed for reading and writing [and] speaking skills will be related to foreign cultural topics that range from dating customs to urban problems" (McNeil, 1990, p. 355). Foreign languages should continue to grow in popularity as many colleges and universities have reinstated the requirement of a foreign language as an entrance requirement.

FINE ARTS

Perhaps of all the curriculum areas, the arts have become the most vulnerable in terms of the public's perception of what is required and what is expendable. Frequently in times of declining budgets, the fine arts programs are the first to be cut. Broudy (1983), however, believes that the schools should emphasize the arts and cultivate aesthetic experiences, not because it is fun to do, but because the arts are necessary for intellectual development. Broudy also advocates the teaching of an awareness of the appearance of things, the examination of the properties of color, sound, texture, and perspective, and the construction of images, sounds, and events that portray aspects of reality in forms of feeling and tone. Dewey (1934) said it best over 50 years ago:

> The arts which today have most vitality for the average person are things he [or she] does not take to be arts: for instance, the movie, jazz music, the comic strip, and, too frequently, newspaper accounts of love nests, murders, and exploits of bandits. For, when what he [or she] knows as art is relegated to the museum and gallery, the unconquerable impulse towards experiences enjoyable in themselves finds such outlet as the daily environment provides (pp. 5–6).

Artistic expression, whether visual, musical, theatrical, or in combined forms, makes the human experience truly unique, and the fine arts are an important part of the secondary curriculum.

The fine arts are typically represented by three content areas, which include music, art, and theatre. This section will examine each of these areas in terms of their scope and sequence and some possible trends and issues associated with each.

Music

Music is a part of daily living and would seem a natural part of the school curriculum. That is not the case, however, for as Beckner and Cornett (1972) note, ". . . because its presence in the background of our activities is so pervasive, the tendency to hear without listening becomes a formidable barrier to true music appreciation and understanding" (p. 339). There is also difficulty in the fact that for most students, music has either been in the form of popular music or has been performance oriented, such as playing in a rock group or band. They have not been accustomed to studying music and exploring its patterns, deeper meanings, and implications. However, the music program of the secondary schools should seek to meet the musical needs of students by providing listening, performing, creating, and evaluating activities (Beckner and Cornett, 1972).

As it is implemented in the secondary school, the music content area has several major subareas. In the middle and junior high school, the music curriculum is often expressed as general music. Students receive an overview of musical notation, rhythm, beat, instrumentation, and the history of music accompanied by representative pieces from the historical period. Table 15.2 represents a typical scope and sequence for the junior high school general music course.

In addition to general music, students can also begin to take band and choir during the middle and junior high school years and continue these courses in high school. In pursuing a specialized area, students develop specialized performance training in each area and work to become musically proficient. Tables 15.3 and 15.4 provide the typical scope and sequence, with general learning goals, for both band and choir.

Art

Art education has often focused on the mechanics of the process by stressing precise execution of object drawings. Gradually, the dimension of aesthetics orientation was added, and in today's curriculum students are led to ". . . an awareness of their visual experience and to development of their capacity to communicate personal understandings through aesthetic form" (Barkan, 1955, pp. v–vi). As stated by the National Art Education Association (1986), the purpose of art education is to help students learn "to develop, express, and evaluate ideas; to produce, read, and interpret visual images in an increasingly visually oriented world; to recognize and understand the artistic achievements and expectations of civilized societies" (p. 3). Art education, therefore, is designed not only to develop artistic skills in students, but to help all students "identify and solve problems more effectively through manipulation of visual, as well as verbal and numeric symbols . . . and to increase the possibility of communicating with visual images and thus make positive contributions to society" (National Art Education Association, 1986, p. 3).

To accomplish these objectives, art is offered on an exploratory basis in the

Table 15.2   SCOPE AND SEQUENCE FOR GRADE 6–8 GENERAL MUSIC

Objective	6	7	8
1. Identify pitch names of the great staff (treble/bass clefs)	I	T	T
2. Perform rhythmic and melodic notation	I	T	T
3. Identify/interpret musical symbols and terms	I	T	T
4. Discuss/exhibit use of key signature and time signature	I	T	T
5. Identify/sing/play musical and harmonic intervals	I	T	T
6. Define/demonstrate dynamic markings (pp-p-mp-mf-f-ff)	I	T	T
7. Demonstrate ability to sing in tune	I	T	T
8. Demonstrate correct posture and breathing	I	T	T
9. Produce a pleasant singing tone	I	T	T
10. Exhibit use of proper diction	I	T	T
11. Exhibit flexibility and growth of vocal range and dynamics	I	T	T
12. Demonstrate ability to follow a conductor	I	T	T
13. Demonstrate use of solfege syllables and Kodaly hand-signs in music reading	I	T	T
14. Discuss history and development of modern instruments	I	T	T
15. Identify and categorize instruments by sound and sight	I	T	T
16. Sing a variety of songs from folk and popular sources	I	T	T
17. Listen to and identify a variety of musical styles, cultures, forms, and media	I	T	T
18. Express the mood/meaning of music through body movement, language, symbols, dramatization, dance, art	I	T	T
19. identify/discuss major composers of a variety of musical styles, cultures, forms, and media	I	T	T
20. Listen to/discuss live and recorded musical performances	I	T	T
21. Participate in group, ensemble, or individual vocal or instrumental performance (formal or informal)		I	T
22. Exhibit appropriate audience behavior and attitudes during concerts	I	T	T
23. Discuss attitudes/skills for group membership in musical ensembles		I	T

I = Introduced   T = Taught   R = Reinforced

middle and junior high school. At the high school level, general courses in art I and II are offered, as well as specialized areas such as sculpture, advanced drawing, and two- and three-dimensional design studios. Table 15.5 provides the general goals and objectives for the secondary art curriculum for grades 6–12.

Theatre

This area of the secondary curriculum is truly an elective and is often referred to as drama. The theatre curriculum area receives the greatest attention in the high school, but can make a significant contribution at the middle and junior high school levels as well. As Beckner and Cornett (1972) point out,

> The knowledge, skills, habits, understandings, attitudes, and character traits essential for rich personal living, . . . for effective participation in a vocation, for

Table 15.3 SCOPE AND SEQUENCE FOR SECONDARY CHORAL MUSIC

Objective	6	7	8	9	10	11	12
1. Demonstrate correct posture and breathing	I	T	T	T	T	T	T
2. Produce a good vocal tone	I	T	T	T	T	T	T
3. Exhibit use of proper diction	I	T	T	T	T	T	T
4. Exhibit flexibility and growth of vocal range and dynamics	I	T	T	T	T	T	T
5. Demonstrate ability to match pitch, dynamic level, quality with other voices at unison (blend)	I	T	T	T	T	T	T
6. Demonstrate ability to sing in tune and balance with other sections	I	T	T	T	T	T	T
7. Demonstrate ability to sing in a vocal ensemble (small group, choir)	I	T	T	T	T	T	T
8. Demonstrate ability to follow a conductor	I	T	T	T	T	T	T
9. Identify pitch names of the great staff (treble/bass clefs)	I	T	T	T	T	T	T
10. Discriminate single vocal part from a full score	I	T	T	T	T	T	T
11. Perform rhythmic and melodic notation	I	T	T	T	T	T	T
12. Discuss/exhibit use of key signature and time signature	I	T	T	T	T	T	T
13. Identify musical symbols present in music being rehearsed/performed	I	T	T	T	T	T	T
14. Define/demonstrate dynamic markings (pp-p-mp-mf-f-ff)	I	T	T	T	T	T	T
15. Use musical notation to write dictated (sung/played) melodies	I	T	T	T	T	T	T
16. Accurately sing melodies which are played or sung	I	T	T	T	T	T	T
17. Sing correct pitches/rhythms utilizing solfege or numbers (unison/parts)	I	T	T	T	T	T	T
18. Demonstrate ability to conduct simple choral selections					I	T	T
19. Perform music from a variety of eras, styles, and composers	I	T	T	T	T	T	T
20. Listen to/discuss/evaluate recorded and live choral performances	I	T	T	T	T	T	T
21. Sing in concert with a group, small ensemble, and individually	I	T	T	T	T	T	T
22. Participate in a variety of performance experiences (live concert, TV, radio, video/audio taped, formal, informal, etc.)	I	T	T	T	T	T	T
23. Observe/discuss/explore skills and attitudes related to music careers	I	T	T	T	T	T	T
24. Sing with/follow directions of other conductors, including those from instrumental backgrounds		I	T	T	T	T	T
25. Exhibit appropriate audience behavior and attitudes during concerts	I	T	T	T	T	T	T

I = Introduced T = Taught R = Reinforced

Table 15.4   SCOPE AND SEQUENCE FOR SECONDARY BAND

Objective	6	7	8	9	10	11	12
1. Exhibit appropriate attitudes/attention during rehearsals/performances	I	T	T	T	T	R	R
2. Follow musical/nonmusical directions of conductor	I	T	T	T	T	R	R
3. Perform musical selections from memory (scales, exercises, parts, solos)	I	T	T	T	T	T	T
4. Execute marching drills by memory (as appropriate)				I	T	T	T
5. Keep written account of individual practice times	I	T	T	T	T	T	T
6. Exhibit appropriate behaviors/attitudes as member of a band	I	T	T	T	T	R	R
7. Exhibit leadership skills (as appropriate)					I	T	T
8. Demonstrate marching fundamentals (as appropriate)				I	T	R	R
9. Participate in field and parade marching rehearsals/performances (as appropriate)				I	T	T	T
10. Perform music from a variety of eras, styles, and composers	I	T	T	T	T	T	T
11. Listen to/discuss/evaluate recorded and live musical performances	I	T	T	T	T	T	T
12. Identify pitch names of all clefs (treble, alto, tenor, bass)	I	T	T	T	T	R	R
13. Discriminate single instrumental part from a full score		I	T	T	T	R	R
14. Perform rhythmic and melodic notation	I	T	T	T	T	T	T
15. Discuss/exhibit use of key/time signatures and scales/arpeggios	I	T	T	T	T	T	T
16. Identify musical symbols present in music being rehearsed/performed	I	T	T	T	T	T	T
17. Define/demonstrate dynamic markings (pp-p-mp-mf-f-ff)	I	T	T	T	T	T	T
18. Use musical notation to write dictated (sung/played) melodies	I	T	T	T	T	T	T
19. Play melodic/harmonic intervals in tune	I	T	T	T	T	T	T
20. Demonstrate ability to conduct simple instrumental selections					I	T	T
21. Assemble/disassemble instrument and demonstrate proper care/maintenance	I	T	T	T	R	R	R
22. Demonstrate correct posture, breathing, vibrato, and embouchure	I	T	T	T	R	R	R
23. Demonstrate characteristic tone for the instrument	I	T	T	T	R	R	R
24. Demonstrate correct fingerings on all scales, exercises, and pieces	I	T	T	T	R	R	R
25. Demonstrate correct articulation (slur, tongue) on all selections	I	T	T	T	T	T	T
26. Clap/chant/play/sing rhythmic patterns and melodic exercises	I	T	T	T	R	R	R
27. Play in concert with a group, small ensemble, and individually	I	T	T	T	T	T	T

Table 15.4 SCOPE AND SEQUENCE FOR SECONDARY BAND *Continued*

Objective	6	7	8	9	10	11	12
28. Participate in a variety of performance experiences (live concert, TV, radio, video/audio taped, formal, informal, etc.)	I	T	T	T	T	T	T
29. Observe/discuss/explore skills and attitudes related to music careers	I	T	T	T	T	T	T
30. Play with/follow directions of other conductors		I	T	T	T	T	T
31. Exhibit appropriate audience behavior and attitudes during concerts	I	T	T	T	T	T	T

I = Introduced   T = Taught   R = Reinforced

Table 15.5 SCOPE AND SEQUENCE FOR SECONDARY ART

Objective	6	7	8	9	10	11	12
1. Discriminate between natural and man-made objects	I	T	T	T	R	R	R
2. Utilize the elements of design (line, value, texture, color, space, shape, form)	I	T	T	T	T	R	R
3. Utilize the principles of design (unity, emphasis, balance, variety, movement, rhythm, pattern)	I	T	T	T	T	R	R
4. Demonstrate creative expression through a variety of art media	I	T	T	T	T	R	R
5. Experiment and compose utilizing a variety of techniques (drawing, painting, printmaking, 3-dimensional media, fibre, crafts)	I	T	T	T	T	T	T
6. Develop appreciation of art history and culture Past, present, future trends Aesthetics of various periods	I	T	T	T	T	T	T
7. Critique own artwork		I	T	T	T	T	T
8. Compare/contrast variety of artworks	I	T	T	T	T	R	R
9. Recognize/discuss/emulate styles of known artists		I	T	T	T	R	R
10. Visit/observe practicing artists		I	I	T	T	T	T
11. Discuss/demonstrate skills and attitudes necessary for art career	I	T	T	T	T	R	R
12. Explain difference between copying and truly creative expression		I	T	T			
13. Demonstrate skill in finished works of variety of media					I	T	T	T
14. Develop exhibition skills Explore methods of presentation Exhibit in a show Organize/set up exhibit					I I	T T I	R T T	R T T

I = Introduced   T = Taught   R = Reinforced

satisfying human relationships, and for responsible, contributing citizenship can be encouraged and developed through drama and related activities in ways perhaps impossible otherwise (p. 340).

The theatre curriculum emphasizes expression and skills that are important in everyday communication. Students often, through a role that they perform, have an opportunity to express themselves in ways they would not normally use. Their membership in an ensemble also creates the need for teamwork in order for the performance to be a success. Table 15.6 provides a scope and sequence chart for the general objectives of the theatre arts program in the secondary schools.

In summarizing the state of fine arts education, McNeil (1990) says that there is an effort to help students see the relationships between and among elements of the art form:

> In drama, for example, students deal separately with plot, character, setting, and the role of the director, using the concept of choice as an organizing theme. . . . Always students are taught to see the interconnections among basic components. In brief, the arts . . . curricula are moving toward the creation of art forms (production and performance), the promotion of creative expression, along with discourse about the arts and the students' critiquing of their experience (p. 360).

As Beckner and Cornett (1972) note, "The fine arts share the common purpose of communicating experience — through the most appropriate medium" (p. 342) and serve as the curriculum area where students learn to express themselves in imaginative and creative ways.

OTHER CURRICULUM AREAS

In addition to the traditional academic courses of the secondary school curriculum, other curriculum areas are sometimes included as electives in the secondary school program. These are vocational courses in business, agriculture, and home economics designed to offer students choices in areas they wish to pursue after graduation. Although not all secondary schools offer vocational courses, they are an established part of the secondary school program. Willis (1991) notes that vocational education needs, however, to respond to the challenge of educating the forgotten students who do not attend college, yet need skills for jobs after graduation. Ingram (1965) has described the characteristics of vocational programs which make these programs different from general education. These characteristics include:

1. Education designed to improve the performance or efficiency of an individual in a specific occupation — either in preparation for a position or while employed
2. Education presented in relationship to the actual job requirements of a specific occupation
3. Education of more value to persons pursuing a specific occupation or who will pursue a specific position

Table 15.6 SCOPE AND SEQUENCE FOR SECONDARY THEATRE ARTS

Objective	6	7	8	9	10	11	12
1. Demonstrate spatial/sensory awareness/perception	I	T	T	T	R	R	R
2. Demonstrate use of mental/physical preparatory techniques (concentration, relaxation, breathing, exercise)		I	T	T	R	R	R
3. Demonstrate improved confidence in use of body/voice for creative self-expression	I	T	T	T	R	R	R
4. Identify/demonstrate stage/body positions		I	T	T	R	R	R
5. Demonstrate pantomime/observation skills	I	T	T	T			
6. Demonstrate skills/attitudes related to vocal expression and diction		I	T	T	R	R	R
7. Identify/demonstrate acting skills through a variety of media (dialogue, characterization, puppetry, role playing, children's theatre, dance, musical theatre, radio, television, film)	I	T	T	T	T	T	T
8. Improvise dramatic scenes utilizing structural components (beginning, conflict, resolution, conclusion)	I	T	T	T	R		
9. Apply movement/vocal techniques for interpretation/characterization in improvised and scripted activities	I	T	T	T	T	T	T
10. Compare/contrast performance and production styles/techniques of major historical periods				I	T	T	T
11. Identify skills/attitudes related to theatrical careers				I	T	T	T
12. Analyze/interpret scripts with regard to dramatic type/style, text/subtext				I	T	T	T
13. Analyze/interpret characters using physical and vocal acting techniques				I	T	R	R
14. Perform scenes from plays using styles appropriate to historical period of script				I	T	T	T
15. Identify basic vocabulary related to acting and theatrical production		I	T	T	R	R	R
16. Exhibit skills/attitudes in accepting and applying director suggestions		I	T	T	T	R	R
17. Identify/exhibit skills/attitudes for group/individual participation in a theatrical production	I	T	T	T	T	R	R
18. Identify/demonstrate skills/attitudes related to theatre safety				I	T	R	R
19. Identify/demonstrate skills related to technical theatre (lighting, scenery, costumes, makeup, publicity)		I	T	T	T	T	T
20. Demonstrate skills in organizing and directing theatrical productions					I	T	T
21. Evaluate personal and group dramatic experiences as participant or audience member	I	T	T	T	T	T	T
22. Exhibit skills/attitudes associated with appropriate/courteous audience behavior	I	T	T	T	R	R	R
23. Demonstrate sensitivity to audience response				I	T	T	T

I = Introduced   T = Taught   R = Reinforced

4. Education taught in such a way that the student can apply what is learned as it is taught in a useful and productive way
5. Education which teaches skills and knowledge of a particular occupation in a practical and applicable way

As Ingram (1965) says, "education is vocational when it provides instruction in the 'why' and 'how' to persons engaged in or preparing to enter a specific occupation rather than instruction 'about' things to those who might be interested" (p. 3).

Business Education

Business education refers to all of the courses in business that provide personal skill development as well as consumer economic understanding. Typical business courses include: recordkeeping, keyboarding, typing, accounting, personal business management, personal finance, shorthand, data processing, and office machines. Many of the changes in the business education curriculum reflect the demands made in recent years by those in industry. These changes include skill development in word processing and computer programming.

O'Neil (1989) notes that business education programs have been buffeted by declining enrollments and are struggling to keep up with increasing demands from business and school reformers by updating traditional course offerings and expanding into fields like information and data processing. The impact of technology on the business workplace is being felt in the business curriculum of the secondary school.

Agricultural Education

Agricultural programs represent one of the oldest vocational offerings in secondary curriculum. Originally designed for students preparing for a vocation as farmers, today's programs include a variety of experiences and courses, including agribusiness. Recent changes to this curricular area have not only given it a new name, agriscience, but have totally revised the traditional program in favor of more specialized topic courses that are taken a semester at a time. Figure 15.1 represents the scope and sequence of the new version of agricultural education.

The purposes of the vocational agricultural program in the secondary schools are twofold: to complement and contribute to the broad educational objectives of the public schools and to provide an education for students seeking employment in the field of agriculture (Beckner and Cornett, 1972). Goals of the agricultural education program include:

1. Develop leadership concepts and skills
2. Provide a basic education for students who will later go into an agricultural related business
3. Develop concepts and skills related to successful employment in agricultural related businesses

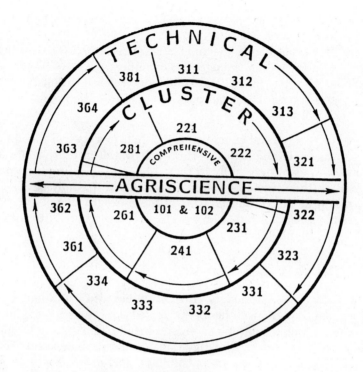

100 SERIES
101 - Intro. to World Agricultural Science & Technology
102 - Applied Agricultural Science and Technology

200 SERIES
221 - Intro. to Agricultural Mechanics
222 - Home Maintenance and Improvement
231 - Animal and Plant Production
261 - Introduction to Horticultural Sciences
281 - Energy and Environmental Technology

300 SERIES
331 - Agribusiness Management and Marketing
312 - Personal Skill and Development in Agriculture
313 - Entrepreneurship in Agriculture
321 - Agricultural Structures Technology
322 - Agricultural Metal Fabrication Technology
323 - Agricultural Power Technology
331 - Diversified Agriculture
332 - Animal Science
333 - Plant and Soil Science

334 - Equine Science
361 - Landscape Design,
        Construction & Maintenance
362 - Horticulture Plant Prod.
363 - Floral Design &
        Interior Landscape Development
364 - Fruit, Nut and Vegetable
        Production

Figure 15.1 Agricultural science and technology (*Source:* Texas Education Agency. (1988), *Basic curriculums for semester courses in agricultural science and technology.* Austin, Tex.: TEA.)

4. Assist with the occupational and vocational guidance of students in high school
5. Provide instruction that will allow students to be successful in post-high school training
6. Develop concepts and skills related to safety and safe working conditions in an agricultural setting
7. Develop concepts and skills related to personal and business management within the agricultural industry
8. Develop specialized knowledge related to soils, plant science, animal science, construction, and the environment—water and energy conservation

The agricultural education program is in a state of flux due to the introduction of new technologies to the agricultural enterprise. Students in this program are adapting rapidly to these changes. In spite of the many reforms that question the value of vocational programs, especially agricultural related curricula, students affirm the value of these programs, not only as a motivation to remain in school, but as a way to prepare students to enter the workforce (Koeninger, 1988).

Home Economics Education

This area of the secondary curriculum has also had a long history as a part of secondary programs. It has been viewed as a professional field that is an applied science which performs a service to society "and its aim has been one of action relating theoretical knowledge to particular problems and situations" (Beckner and Cornett, 1972, p. 380). The basic goal of the home economics education curriculum is to provide instruction that will enable families to improve their quality of life by more effective and efficient use of their resources, both human and material. The content for the home economics area can be divided into major areas that include:

1. Human growth and development and the family
2. Housing and interior design
3. Foods and nutrition, both family and institutional
4. Textiles, clothing, and design
5. Home management and economics

The arrangement of courses varies from program to program and the home economics curriculum, like agriculture, is undergoing changes. A typical scope and sequence chart of the home economics curriculum is provided in Figure 15.2

Vocational home economics education prepares students and adults for the occupation of homemaking and for gainful employment, for example, in service occupations (Willis, 1991). Both occupational home economics education and consumer and homemaking education are relevant in meeting the needs of today's students, who must prepare for a career and for the responsibility of a home and family where responsibilities will be shared. For these reasons, the

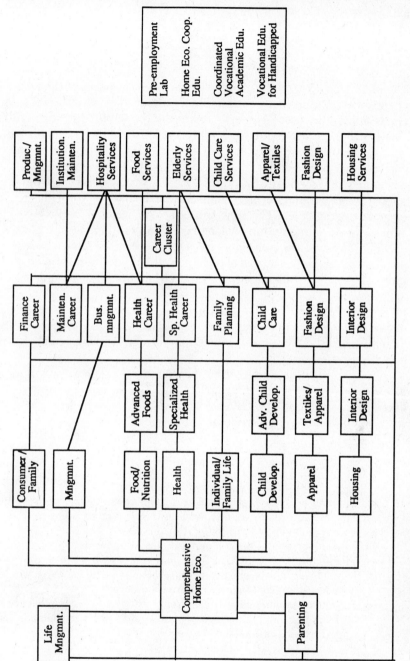

Pre-employment Lab

Home Eco. Coop. Edu.

Coordinated Vocational Academic Edu.

Vocational Edu. for Handicapped

Figure 15.2 Vocational home economics education

351

home economics curriculum is a viable component of today's secondary school curriculum.

SUMMARY

The elective courses described in this chapter are perhaps the most vulnerable of all the courses in the secondary curriculum. They must be responsive to the needs and interests of students, while at the same time responding to the changes that are occurring in society. Not only are these courses vulnerable to changes in students' attitudes, but they are also at risk due to the numerous changes that occur within the world and national communities. Clearly home economics and agricultural education are vastly different from the courses offered 50 years ago. Foreign languages have changed from classical languages to modern languages. The new trend, according to O'Neil (1990), is toward offering less commonly taught languages, such as Japanese, Chinese, and Arabic. The fine arts are vulnerable because they are frequently seen as frills and not basics, yet they are essential to a well rounded educational program and ultimately make students aware of their unique human quality of creative expression.

This chapter focused on the curriculum areas not considered part of academic basics. These subject areas represent a wide range of content areas, including health and physical education, foreign languages, fine arts, and vocational programs.

The chapter discussed each of these areas in a general way and provided a historical perspective for their inclusion in the secondary program. A general overview of goals and objectives was presented for each area and some content areas were described by scope and sequence charts.

YOUR TURN

15.1 Visit a junior or senior high school health classroom. Interview the teacher and the students in this class. Possible questions that you might want to ask include:
   (a) What is the most interesting part of this class?
   (b) Do you feel free to discuss personal health issues with your teacher?
   (c) What is the most important thing that you have learned in this class?
   (d) Do you have friends who use alcohol, tobacco, or drugs? What would you say to them based on what you have learned in here?
   (e) Do you know someone or have a friend who is pregnant? What are some of the problems that this person faces? What would you say to someone your age who wanted to get pregnant?

15.2 Look through the course offerings in languages for a school district. What languages are offered? At what levels? How many years can students take a foreign language if they start in junior high school? What languages are offered in junior high school? Develop a proposal to offer one of the less commonly taught languages in your school.

15.3 Examine the fine arts offerings in a local school district. How many different fine arts courses are offered in the district? Which ones are the most popular (do a three-year enrollment trend for each course)? Interview the instructors for the fine arts courses and ask them how they are able to differentiate between performance and knowledge and appreciation of the art. How much emphasis is placed on being competitive in the art form?

15.4 Of the vocational education courses identified in this chapter, which ones are the most popular in a local school district? Why? Develop a curriculum proposal that would integrate at least two of the academic areas into the vocational areas for presentation to the school board as a new core course for the junior high school.

REFERENCES

American Association of Teachers of French. (1989). The teaching of French: A syllabus of competence. *AATF National Bulletin, 15,* 1–35.

American Association of Teachers of Spanish and Portuguese. (1986). *AATSP provisional program guidelines.* Mississippi State, Miss.: AATSP.

American Council on the Teaching of Foreign Languages (1986). *Proficiency guidelines.* Hastings-on-Hudson, N.Y.: ACTFL.

Barkan, M. (1955). *A foundation for art education.* New York: Ronald.

Beckner, W. & Cornett, J.D. (1972). *The secondary school curriculum: Content and structure.* Scranton, Pa.: Intext Educational Publishers.

Broudy, H.S. (1983). A common curriculum in aesthetics and fine arts. In G. Festermaker and J. Goodlad (Eds.). *Individual differences and the common curriculum. NSSE Yearbook.* Chicago: University of Chicago Press.

Cummins, P.W. (1989a). CAI and the French teacher. *The French Review, 62,* 3, 385–410.

Cummins, P.W. (1989b). Video and the French teacher. *The French Review, 62,* 3, 411–426.

Curran, L. (1989). Appleworks does foreign languages. *The Modern Language Journal, 73,* 1, 66–70.

Dandonoli, P. (October 1987). Report on foreign language in public secondary schools, fall 1985. *Foreign Language Annals, 20,* 5, 457–470.

Dewey, J. (1934). *Art as experience.* New York: Minton, Balch.

Ingram, J.F. (1965). *What makes education vocational.* Washington D.C.: American Vocational Association.

Jennings, J.F. (October 1987). The Sputnik of the eighties. *Phi Delta Kappan, 69,* 2, 104–109.

Kaplan, J.P. (1989). Reviews. *The French Review, 62,* 3, 563–564.

Knop, C.K. (1988). Reviews. *The French Review, 62,* 2, 374–375.

Koeninger, J.G. (November/December 1988). Value added vocational classrooms. *Vocational Education Journal, 63,* 8, 39–41.

McNeil, J.D. (1990). *Curriculum: A comprehensive introduction.* Glenview, Ill.: Scott Foresman.

Met, M. (September 1989). Which foreign languages should students learn? *Educational Leadership, 47,* 1, 54–58.

National Art Education Association. (1986). *Quality art education goals for schools.* Reston, Va.: NAEA.

O'Neil, J. (September 1989). Business education: Implementing technology dominates new agenda. *Curriculum Update. 33,* 7.

O'Neil, J. (January 1990). Foreign languages: As enrollments climb, a new focus on proficiency. *ASCD Curriculum Update, 34,* 1. Reston, Va.: Association for Supervision and Curriculum Development.

Scott, V.M. (1989). An empirical study of explicit and implicit teaching strategies in French. *The Modern Language Journal, 73,* 1, 14–22.

Seaton, D.C. et al. (1985). *Physical education handbook.* Englewood Cliffs, N.J.: Prentice Hall.

Texas Education Agency. (1989). *Framework for languages.* Austin, Tx.: TEA.

Texas Education Agency. (1988). *Basic curriculums for semester courses in agricultural science and technology.* Austin, Tex.: TEA.

Texas Education Agency. (1978). *Guidelines for physical education in the secondary schools.* Austin, Tex.: TEA.

Willis, S. (September 1991). Vocational education: Applied academics, tech-prep programs serve the forgotten half. *ASCD Curriculum Update.* Reston, Va.: Association for Supervision and Curriculum Development.

The world almanac and book of facts. (1989). New York: Pharos Books.

Yarber, W. (May 1988). What makes a good AIDS curriculum? *Educational Digest, 53,* 9, 49–51.

Chapter
16

Epilogue: Future Issues and Curriculum Change

The previous chapters of this book have focused on the foundations of the curriculum development process and the "nuts and bolts" or the mechanics of curriculum planning and development. Curriculum development has been discussed from the vantage point of someone who will teach or implement a curriculum within the instructional context of a district, school, and/or the classroom. This chapter brings closure to the curriculum planning and development process by suggesting future issues related to curriculum development and identifying factors to consider when initiating change in the curriculum.

As discussed earlier in Chapter 4, the social forces that are present in society not only generate issues but work to bring about change as well. As Jarolimek (1981) notes, "The most significant thing that can be said about change in the contemporary world is the *rate* at which it takes place" (p. 295). He continues by saying,

> In the field of education, changes are occurring constantly. Some of these changes are minor, as, for example, when a school decides to lengthen or shorten its school day by fifteen minutes. [However,] when . . . compared with a change calling for school desegregation . . . we see a vast difference (p. 296).

It is clear that in the future, curriculum developers will have to contend not only with the issues of the moment, but they will also have to anticipate the impact of these issues. As Brandt (1988) points out, "the task of deciding what students should learn, and what schools should teach, is never complete" (p. 1).

The curriculum of the future may look very different from the ones presented in this text. O'Neil (1990) notes that educational reforms of the 1990s will significantly impact the character of the school curriculum in favor of a broad fields of study approach. Indeed, as we enter the twenty-first century, the focus of curriculum development may shift from the mere identification of the essential knowledge and skills to a more complex view of what it takes to be an educated citizen on a national or international level (Smith, O'Day, and Cohen, 1990).

FUTURE ISSUES

The curriculum development process of the future may focus on the elimination of needless review and pay closer attention to the needs of secondary students. Ornstein and Hunkins (1988) have identified the following areas which have implications for the development of the secondary curriculum of the future:

1. Basic skills programs—with emphasis on improving basic literacy in reading and writing
2. Materials and media—with textbooks and workbooks revised to make them relevant and the updating of media to make it more relevant to multicultural and multiethnic populations, to include the use of computers, laser discs, and other educational technology
3. Instructional packages and approaches—with the development of kits that are often individualized and self-instructional and contain multisensory and diagnostic materials and programs
4. Guidance and counseling programs—with emphasis on social, psychological, and vocational services for disadvantaged students
5. Tutoring programs—often involving peers and structured around small group and individual assistance in after school or summer programs
6. Auxiliary school personnel—use of aides, paraprofessionals, and volunteers to reduce the teacher-pupil ratio and enhance the instructional capacity of the teacher
7. Parent-linkage programs—with an emphasis on the involvement of parents in the school instructional program as instructional aides, clerks, or supervisors of student activities
8. School organizational patterns—the development of alternative school program structures that include extended school days, flexible scheduling, team teaching, and nongraded programs
9. Community-centered programs—which provide for recreation activities, fine arts activities in theatre and music, and other programs such as health assistance and legal aid

   10. Dropout prevention and vocational programs — with an emphasis on vocational and career education which include work study, on-the-job training, and financial incentives to remain in school

   In addition to these program areas, the curriculum will also need to address the development of higher level thinking skills. Recent concerns over students' lack of problem solving skills may force curriculum developers to restructure each content area. In compiling the results of numerous national studies related to specific content areas, the Association for Supervision and Curriculum Development (O'Neil, 1990) notes that 17 year olds know basic factual information in history or geography, understand simple principles and concepts in science, and can only perform basic mathematical operations such as addition and subtraction. Few, however, can solve multi-step problems using algebraic operations, read and synthesize information from specialized documents, infer relationships or draw conclusions from scientific data, construct a persuasive argument, or interpret historical information or ideas (see Figure 1.1).

   Since adolescents cannot perform multi-step higher level cognitive tasks, curriculum developers have an agenda for planning instruction, for the next several decades. Educators will need to work to develop instructional materials and strategies that will improve the level of intellectual functioning for these students. First on the agenda, curriculum developers will need to scrutinize each content area for redundancy of basic factual information; in addition, each area will need to be examined for ways to improve students' thinking capabilities. Not unlike the early work in the content areas of the 1960s, the curriculum development process of the future will need to focus on ways to help students move beyond the basics and into a more interactive, problem solving mode of learning. This cannot happen unless the curriculum reflects a problem solving focus which is implemented by teachers in the classroom.

   The current flurry of curriculum development activities is not new, however. As alternative ways to improve the curricular program and the instructional capabilities of students are developed, it is helpful to review recurring curriculum issues which are "central to the organization and implementation of the curriculum" (Oliva, 1982, p. 455). The eight curriculum issues identified by Oliva (1982) include:

   1. Scope — the selection of topics to be studied and the specific instructional objectives
   2. Relevance — the congruence of the subject matter and school activities and the social order in which today's youth will spend their adult lives
   3. Balance — attention to each of the problem areas (e.g., neglecting scope at the expense of integration)
   4. Integration — identifying and emphasizing the relationships of subjects to each another
   5. Sequence — the order in which concepts are presented to students
   6. Continuity — an examination of courses by grade level to determine the degree of repetitiveness and levels of complexity

7. Articulation—an examination of concepts by grade level to determine the sequencing and flow from level to level and across boundaries
8. Transferability—the degree to which transfer of learning is or can be promoted within the content

Many of these issues were presented and discussed in Chapters 7 and 8 as factors to consider when building curricular programs. As presented here, these issues need to be considered when assessing the current curriculum and when developing future curriculum. It should be noted that all eight areas are interrelated and a change in one affects the others. As curriculum developers work to integrate more advanced intellectual skills into the curriculum, it is important to keep these eight factors in mind.

The issue of interrelatedness is essential as well when writing curriculum. Without curriculum interrelatedness, the addition of new subjects or topics can result in what Willis (1990) calls "infusion overload" (p. 6). In dealing with the continuing issues associated with the curriculum, especially with the pressure to add more topics to the already full curriculum, educators at some point in the future will have to assert, as Willis (1990) does, that "less is more and more is too much" (p. 6). Willis (1990) continues by saying,

> As the number of topics recommended or mandated to be taught in schools mounts, educators are being asked to "infuse" more and more of them throughout the curriculum —that is, to integrate them into the subjects they already teach, where doing so makes sense (p. 6).

The basic question to address in planning a curriculum of the future becomes one of deciding what should be taught and what should not be taught. Yet in doing so, there is the recognition that in today's society there is a need for students to know more about drugs, nutrition, use of leisure time, technology in the workplace, and health issues related to drugs, pregnancy, and AIDS. The list is endless and the time frame short; the dilemma for curriculum developers in determining what goes and what stays is very real.

Another major concern confronting educational planners is global education. Included in global education is an increased emphasis on world history, geography, politics, and economics, as well as increased attention given to foreign languages, especially nontraditional languages such as Japanese, Russian, and Arabic. Anderson (1991) describes global education as a way to "expand students' understanding of cultural diversity through the cross-cultural study of literature, art, music, dance, religion and social customs" (p. 13).

The rationale for such a curricular component is provided by Tye (1991) when he says that "citizens of today's world, more than ever before, need to learn attitudes and behaviors that recognize and promote interdependence and cooperation" (p. 8). In an ever changing world, curriculum developers will need to take into account the role of global education in the secondary curriculum.

   While Chapter 16 does not provide a comprehensive view into the future, it does provide a sample of the issues and concerns that curriculum developers must address. These issues and concerns best illustrate the dilemmas that confront all curriculum workers. As society changes and as new demands are placed upon the instructional system and personnel, questions such as what should be continued, what should be eliminated, what should receive more attention, what should receive less, and how can we best utilize the resources and materials currently available while developing and implementing new ones continue to confront curriculum developers. The process of curriculum development is *never* static, but ever changing. For this reason, curriculum developers must know how to implement strategies for change within the content areas as one content area or concept replaces another.

CURRICULUM CHANGE

   In addition to dealing with the issues for developing curriculum in the future, educators must also be concerned with bringing about change within the current instructional program of the secondary schools. As Beach and Reinhartz (1989) note, "Change often seems to surround the school environment and . . . when not planned and orderly, may seem chaotic . . ." (p. 272). In curriculum development it is important to keep the change from seeming chaotic and to instill a sense of orderliness. The purpose of change in curriculum development is to make a difference in the ability of the secondary students to perform successfully. As Ornstein and Hunkins (1988) observe, "simply put, curriculum activity is change activity" (p. 229). Curriculum change, however, may not be an easy task to accomplish. Zais (1976) describes the situation by saying,

> Curriculum improvement and curriculum change, as well as curriculum revision, are generally synonyms in the literature. However, . . . curriculum change involve[s a] transformation of the entire curriculum scheme, including design, goals, content, learning activities, scope, etc. (p. 19).

Curriculum change, then, involves a change in values and beliefs. As Taba (1962) confirms, "To change a curriculum means, in a way, to change an institution" (p. 454). It is not surprising, therefore, that curriculum change is often very difficult to accomplish because of the requisite change in values on the part of a large number of people. As Zais (1976) cautions, it is rare that "widespread, significant, and lasting curriculum change" occurs because "attempts to change the curriculum are almost always vehemently resisted" (p. 19).

   To help curriculum developers be more effective in dealing with the change process, Gorton (1987) suggests the following questions to guide the process.

   1. What activities or actions are needed in order to produce the desired change?

2. What resources (i.e., personnel, facilities, materials, equipment) are needed to produce the change?
3. What kinds of problems, reactions, or resistance can be expected to be generated as a result of the implementation of the change?
4. What is the best sequence of activities and the best use of resources to maximize acceptance of the change?
5. What is the best possible time line for implementation of the change?
6. What kinds of decisions are required to implement the change and what kind of follow-up will be provided to monitor the success of the change?

In addition to these questions Ornstein and Hunkins (1988) provide a set of five guidelines derived from research that also can assist in successfully implementing change:

1. Curricular change should reflect what has been shown to work and not work rather than what is popular
2. Curricular innovations often require a change in the organization of the instructional program (i.e., the use of facilities, the assignment of students and teachers, etc.)
3. Curricular change must be considered feasible and manageable for the average teacher
4. Curricular change is more effective if it is the result of grass roots efforts to address problems and conditions of the school rather than the result of a bureaucratic mandate
5. Curricular change should be based on sound and rational ideas that address specific instructional problems, rather than an attempt to just do something rather than nothing

Clearly, implementing changes in the curriculum can be a difficult process because of the natural resistance on the part of the people affected by the changes. When implementing change, specific needs of faculty and students must be addressed, and it takes careful planning, because the development of trust at all levels is essential. Jenkins (1949) recognizes that change will only occur when the driving forces that push for change overcome the restraining forces that oppose change. To bring about a change in forces, there can be (1) a reduction in those who oppose change (transfer personnel to other buildings); (2) an increase in the number of those who favor change (hire additional faculty with the desire to change); or (3) a redirection of the forces (through training or incentives which provide the prerequisite skills for teachers to feel successful in implementing the change). To become permanent, the change must be stabilized by having teachers who favor the new curriculum outnumber those who oppose any change.

If it is not apparent by now, it should be clear that change is inevitable. It is a part of life just as it is a part of the curriculum development process. Change occurs despite resistance to it; in fact, the resistance itself often produces change. It should also be noted that change is neither good nor bad; "it is the value judgement placed on it that determines its goodness or badness" (Zais, 1976, p. 19).

If change is neither good nor bad, and difficult to achieve although inevitable, why should curriculum developers be concerned? What does a change in the curriculum accomplish? Gorton (1987) responds by saying,

> (1) Although the status quo is not necessarily bad, there is usually room for improvement; (2) while all change does not necessarily lead to improvement, improvement is not likely to occur without change; (3) unless we attempt change, we are not likely to know whether a proposed innovation is better than the status quo; and (4) participation in the change process can result in a greater understanding and appreciation of the desirable features of the status quo and . . . a better understanding and appreciation of, and skill in, the change process itself (p. 136).

Throughout the history of the secondary school, changes in the curriculum have been implemented. Change is at the heart of the educational process. And if education is to improve and schools continuously assess the effectiveness of their instructional programs, change must be a part of the improvement efforts. Perhaps Tyler (1949) has provided the best summary when he says that curriculum development

> is a continuous process and . . . as materials and procedures are developed, they are tried out, their results appraised, their inadequacies identified, [and] suggested improvements indicated; there is replanning, redevelopment and then reappraisal; and in this kind of continuing cycle . . . the curriculum and instructional program [are] improved (p. 123).

Curriculum development involves change as the result of a continuous process of determining learning expectations, implementing the planned curriculum, and evaluating the results.

As a culminating activity for this chapter, it is your turn to try your hand in determining the curriculum priorities for the future. In the activity (Beach, 1973) that follows, you will have the opportunity to identify the priorities for the long-range planning of the secondary curriculum. In this exercise, you are to rate the following list of curriculum priorities on a scale of 1, 3, and 5, with 1 being the lowest rating and 5 being the highest rating. You can have no more than six items rated as a "5" and no more than six items rated "1." Compare your list of the most important priorities with others in your school or in your class.

CURRICULUM PRIORITIES

_____ 1. DEVELOP SOPHISTICATION IN WORKING WITH COMMUNITY
      a. Increase parental involvement in schools
      b. Allow parents within a given neighborhood or community to select from a range of educational philosophies

     c. Build a closer relationship between home, school, and community

_____ 2. **DEVELOP PROGRAMS ORIENTED TO OCCUPATION SELECTION AND PREPARATION**
   a. More emphasis on terminal education "other than college"
   b. Development of programs that include career education within entire school curriculum

_____ 3. **DEVELOPMENT OF SKILLS FOR CONTINUED LEARNING**
   a. Integration of intellectual skills (problem solving, creative thinking, evaluation) into entire curriculum
   b. Develop programs that help learner receive and adjust to new information

_____ 4. **DEVELOP WELL-PLANNED, WELL-EXECUTED, WELL-EVALUATED PROGRAMS THAT RECEIVE FULL FINANCIAL SUPPORT FOR 20–30 YEARS**

_____ 5. **COMMITMENT TO THE QUEST "WHAT *SHOULD* PUPILS OBTAIN FROM SCHOOLS?" NOT HOW TO DO BETTER WHAT HAS ALWAYS BEEN DONE**

_____ 6. **CONTINUOUS FOCUS ON SCHOOL SUBJECTS (READING, LANGUAGE ARTS, MATH, SCIENCE, SOCIAL STUDIES)**
   a. Development of subject areas by cleaning out current "deadwood"
   b. More affective domain introduced into subject areas
   c. Greater use of subject matter specialists

_____ 7. **DEVELOPMENT OF WAYS TO UNITE EDUCATIONAL RESEARCH AND SCHOLARSHIP WITH PRACTICE**
   a. Systems approach to curriculum planning and evaluation
   b. Situational performance competencies in curriculum improvement field

_____ 8. **BETTER READING ACHIEVEMENT AT ALL GRADES FOR ALL LEARNERS**

_____ 9. **REVISION OF ALL CURRICULAR PROGRAMS**
   a. Develop ways of making curriculum responsive to changes in society
   b. Develop ways of making curriculum responsive to input from teachers, students, parents, and the public
   c. Reduction of emphasis on acquisition of fixed skills and facts

_____ 10. **DEVELOPING HUMAN SKILLS**
   a. Try alternative ways of teaching human qualities that lead to a "satisfying life"
   b. More emphasis on affective or emotional growth, human relations, and interpersonal process skills for staff and students
   c. Explicit attention to nonverbal modes of thought and action
   d. Development of ways to encourage students to study themselves
   e. Help students cope with change as a way of life
   f. Help students with attitude and value clarification and the development of appropriate personal values

_____ 11. **BUILDING CURRICULUM FOR CERTAIN GROUPS BASED ON CREATIVE ARTS AND GREATER INCLUSION OF CREATIVE ARTS IN SCHOOL CURRICULUM**

_____ 12. **IMPROVEMENT OF THE SCIENCE CURRICULUM**
   a. More emphasis on ecology and environment
   b. Better programs for nonscience-oriented students
   c. More emphasis on space exploration and technology

_____ 13. DEVELOPMENT OF PROGRAMS FOR SPECIAL GROUPS
   a. Non-English speaking, unusually talented, disadvantaged, nonmotivated, or at-risk programs
   b. Establishment of pupil development centers for remedial, renewal, or enrichment
_____ 14. A WIDER RANGE OF CURRICULAR OFFERINGS
   a. Courses more in tune with community or world
   b. Courses dealing with current topics or problems (drugs, pollution, mental health, pregnancy, AIDS)
   c. Use of learning situations outside school walls
   d. Expansion of alternative forms of education
_____ 15. IMPROVEMENT OF THE MATH CURRICULUM
   a. More emphasis on math as a language
   b. Better programs for developing math literacy for all students
_____ 16. IMPROVEMENT OF THE SOCIAL STUDIES CURRICULUM
   a. Less provincially and more internationally oriented
   b. Integration of ethnic studies into entire curriculum
   c. Preparation of students for cultural pluralism
   d. More concern for responsible citizenship in students
   e. More emphasis on consumer education
_____ 17 DEVELOPMENT OF PROGRAMS TO HELP INDIVIDUAL LEARNERS ACHIEVE OPTIMAL POTENTIALS
   a. Individualizing instruction and giving recognition to unique achievements of learner
   b. Build curriculum upon strengths of learners rather than their weaknesses
   c. Effect a balance between serving the needs of individuals and the needs of society
   d. Creation of an array of learning resources that students can use with minimal or no adult guidance
   e. Increase toward "ungradedness" in all levels of schooling; multi-aged grouping
_____ 18. DEVELOPMENT OF EFFECTIVE IN-SERVICE EDUCATION FOR PROFESSIONAL PERSONNEL
_____ 19. BUILD CURRICULAR PROGRAMS ON CHARACTERISTICS OF TEACHERS
   a. Realize that characteristics of teachers are the most significant learning experiences of students
   b. Differentiated staffing and changes in teacher certification
_____ 20. DEVELOP MODES OF EVALUATION, ACCOUNTABILITY, AND RESEARCH PROCEDURES RELATED TO HUMAN QUALITIES
   a. Determining the impact of school on learners and teachers
   b. More dynamic, "closer-to-what-we-really-value" modes of evaluation

REFERENCES

Anderson, L.F. (1991). A rationale for global education. In K.A. Tye (Ed.), _Global education: From thought to Action._ Alexandria, Va.: Association for Supervision and Curriculum Development.

Beach, D.M. (1973). Identifying priorities for the long-range planning of the public school curriculum. Unpublished doctoral dissertation. Nashville: George Peabody College.

Beach, D.M. & Reinhartz, J. (1989). *Supervision: Focus on instruction.* New York: Harper & Row.

Brandt, R.S. (1988). Introduction: What should schools teach: In R.S. Brandt (Ed.), *Content of the curriculum.* Alexandria, Va.: Association for Supervision and Curriculum Development.

Gorton, R.A. (1987). *School leadership and administration.* Dubuque, Iowa: Brown.

Jarolimek, J. (1981). *The schools in contemporary society.* New York: Macmillan.

Jenkins, D.H. (May 1949). Social engineering in educational change: An outline of method. *Progressive Education, 26,* 7, 193–197.

Oliva, P. (1982). *Developing the curriculum.* Glenview, Ill.: Scott Foresman.

O'Neil, J. (September 1990). New curriculum agenda emerges for '90s. *ASCD Curriculum Update, 34,* 1 & 8.

Ornstein, A.C. & Hunkins, F.P. (1988). *Curriculum foundations, principles and issues.* Englewood Cliffs, N.J.: Prentice Hall.

Smith, M.S., O'Day, J. & Cohen, D.K. (Winter 1990). National curriculum American style. *American Educator, 14,* 4, 10–17 & 40–43.

Taba, H. (1962). *Curriculum development: Theory and practice.* New York: Harcourt Brace Jovanovich.

Tye, K.A. (1991). Introduction: The world at a crossroads. In K.A. Tye (Ed.), *Global education: From thought to action.* Alexandria, Va.. Association for Supervision and Curriculum Development.

Tyler, R.W. (1949). *Basic principles of curriculum and instruction.* Chicago: University of Chicago Press.

Willis, S. (February 1990). The inclusive curriculum, *ASCD Update, 32,* 2, 1, 6, & 8.

Zais, R.S. (1976). *Curriculum principles and foundations.* New York: Harper & Row.

Author Index

Subject Index

44   68